ROUTLEDGE LIBRARY EDITIONS:
CULTURAL STUDIES

Volume 2

DYNAMICS OF CULTURE

DYNAMICS OF CULTURE

J. ZVI NAMENWIRTH AND
ROBERT PHILIP WEBER

Routledge
Taylor & Francis Group

LONDON AND NEW YORK

First published in 1987 by Allen & Unwin, Inc.

This edition first published in 2017
by Routledge
2 Park Square, Milton Park, Abingdon, Oxon OX14 4RN

and by Routledge
711 Third Avenue, New York, NY 10017

Routledge is an imprint of the Taylor & Francis Group, an informa business

© 1987 Allen & Unwin, Inc.

British Library Cataloguing in Publication Data
A catalogue record for this book is available from the British Library

ISBN: 978-1-138-69145-2 (Set)
ISBN: 978-1-315-45997-4 (Set) (ebk)
ISBN: 978-1-138-69946-5 (Volume 2) (hbk)
ISBN: 978-1-138-69948-9 (Volume 2) (pbk)
ISBN: 978-1-315-51217-4 (Volume 2) (ebk)

Publisher's Note
The publisher has gone to great lengths to ensure the quality of this reprint but points out that some imperfections in the original copies may be apparent.

Disclaimer
The publisher has made every effort to trace copyright holders and would welcome correspondence from those they have been unable to trace.

DYNAMICS OF CULTURE

J. Zvi Namenwirth

Robert Philip Weber

Boston
Allen & Unwin
London   Sydney   Wellington

Allen & Unwin, Inc.
8 Winchester Place, Winchester, MA 01890, USA

The U.S. Company of
Unwin Hyman, Ltd
P.O. Box 18, Park Lane, Hemel Hempstead, Herts HP2 4TE, UK
40 Museum Street, London WC1A 1LU, UK
37/39 Queen Elizabeth Street, London SE1 2QB, UK

Allen & Unwin Australia Pty Ltd
8 Napier Street, North Sydney, NSW 2060, Australia

Allen & Unwin (New Zealand) Ltd, in association with
Port Nicholson Press Ltd
Private Bag, Wellington, New Zealand

Library of Congress Cataloging-in-Publication Data

Namenwirth, J. Zvi, 1931–
　Dynamics of culture.

　Bibliography: p.
　Includes index.
　1. Culture.　2. Content analysis (Communication)
I. Weber, Robert Philip.　II. Title.
HM101.N29　1986　　　306　　　86-28753
ISBN 0–04–497037–4

British Library Cataloguing in Publication Data

Namenwirth, J. Zvi
　Dynamics of culture.
　1. Culture　2. Ethnology
　I. Title　II. Weber, Robert Philip.
　306　　　GN357
ISBN 0–04–497037–4

Printed and bound in Great Britain by
Biddles Ltd, Guildford and King's Lynn

To Our Sons
Aron B. Namenwirth
Derek Saxon Weber

Also, to Cynthia Moenen from Dr. M.

Contents

3
Theoretical and Methodological Issues

4
A Concluding Assessment

Acknowledgments

Our work has been aided by numerous individuals and institutions. They are acknowledged at the beginning of each essay. If we omitted anyone, it was only through our negligence.

Chapter 3 is a revision of Namenwirth (1973); Chapter 4 is a revision of Weber (1982). Chapter 5 incorporates material published in Weber (1981). A longer version of Chapter 6 was originally published in Spanish (Weber and Namenwirth, 1985). Chapter 8 was originally published as Weber (1983a).

Weber's work has been generously supported by ZUMA, the Center for Surveys, Methods, and Analysis, Mannheim, FRG. Special thanks to Hans-Dieter Klingemann and Peter Philip Mohler, and to the Executive Directors of ZUMA who at various times made Guest Professorships possible, including Max Kaase, Karl Ulrich Mayer, Manfred Kuechler, and most recently, Hartmut Esser.

Thanks to Philip J. Stone for graciously supplying the General Inquirer programs and to the staff of the University of Connecticut Computer Center for its assistance. Weber thanks the Harvard University Computing Center for providing computer resources.

We are also indebted to Philip J. Stone for an incisive critique of an earlier draft of the manuscript. Although we did not always agree with the anonymous reviewers, we thank them for their comments and suggestions. We also appreciate the enthusiasm and efforts of Lisa Freeman-Miller, our editor at Allen & Unwin.

Ray Blanchette did the figures. We appreciate his efforts.

Finally, we gratefully acknowledge and remember the late Harold D. Laswell for his unfailing support in the initial phases; our work is in part an extension of his pioneering ideas.

1

A Theoretical and Methodological Framework

1

Culture and
Culture Dynamics[1]

THE STUDY OF CULTURE

Classical social theorists—Spencer, Durkheim, Marx, Weber, Pareto, Parsons, and Sorokin, for example—asked questions concerning social and cultural change such as

- Is the form of change linear, curvilinear, or cyclical?
- Is change continuous and evolutionary, or discontinuous and perhaps revolutionary?
- Is culture merely a reflection of political economy or the major determinant of social interaction?

We are convinced that contemporary social scientists can address these questions using modern quantitative techniques. What are these methods, and what answers do they provide?

To answer the classical questions, we study the dynamics of culture by analyzing the content of a variety of texts: party platforms in American presidential campaigns 1844–1964 (Chapters 3 and 6), the speeches given at the opening of each session of the British parliament 1689–1972 (Chap-

[1]We thank Barry Glassner, Elizabeth Long, Eliezer B. Namenwirth, Karl Erik Rosengren, Robert H. Ross, Susan Spiggle, Philip J. Stone, and Robert R. Weaver for helpful comments and suggestions. The errors that remain are ours.

J. Zvi Namenwirth and Robert Philip Weber jointly wrote this chapter.

ters 4 and 5), and the presidential addresses of three scientific associations[2] in three decades of this century (Chapter 7). Our content analysis techniques (Weber, 1983a, 1984a, 1985a; Kelly and Stone, 1975; Stone *et al.*, 1966) produce quantitative indicators of textual content that we then directly and indirectly relate to social, political, and economic indicators. In our view, content analysis is an important tool for generating reliable and valid indicators of culture content over long periods of time such as two or three centuries. In comparison, reliable quantitative economic, political, and social indicators seldom exist for similar time periods.

Our methods frequently reveal aspects of cultural change not easily detected by interpretive or qualitative techniques. As a result, and because of the long time periods spanned by our data, the theories that seem most plausible to us are often drawn from "grand" theories rather than from more narrow or "middle range" theories that currently predominate in contemporary social science. Also, sociological theories in the classical tradition were often monocausal: Of all possible causes, only one could be the true one. However, because of methodological, substantive, and theoretical innovations, most contemporary sociological theories are multicausal and often conditional. Ours are no different. In short, we find that the dynamics of culture have multiple causes and consequences, and may depend on specific historical circumstances.

What, then, are our answers to the classical questions of cultural change? We find that the long-term dynamics of cultural change are partly cyclical[3] and partly discontinuous. We also find instances where culture and other realms causally interact with each other, where culture change intervenes between economic and political change, and where cultural change appears to constrain political change.

Specifically, we find in America (Chapter 3) and in Great Britain since 1795 (Chapter 4) long-term changes in concern with broad political issues that constitute 150-year sequences or cycles. We interpret these broad political themes using a variant of the Bales–Parsons functional paradigm[4]

---

[2]These are the American Association for the Advancement of Science, the American Chemical Society, and the American Economics Association.

[3]As is often observed, mystics see cycles everywhere. Also, cycles often emerge in quantitative analyses from the summation of random events (Slutzky, 1937). Nevertheless, adequate cyclical theories must provide explanations for changes in cycle length, amplitude, and phase sequence (Weber, in press). We believe that Chapters 3–5 and other work (Namenwirth and Bibbee, 1976; Weber, 1983b; Powers, 1980, 1981; Powers and Hanneman, 1983) constitute a serious attempt in this direction. Besides, our thematic cycles are related to political and economic changes. Therefore, our cycles are most unlikely to represent either mystical apparitions or statistical artifacts.

[4]In the works cited in the text, Parsons argued that social systems had to solve four fundamental problems, what he called Adaptation, Goal attainment, Integration, and Latency. This sequence is also known as the AGIL scheme. To make their meaning clearer, we have returned to Bales's Instrumental/Expressive distinction. With Bales, we refer to Instrumental rather than Goal attainment problems and to Expressive rather than Latency problems. More detailed treatments are given in Chapters 3 and 4.

(Parsons *et al.*, 1953; Parsons and Bales, 1953; Parsons and Smelser, 1956; cf. Bales, 1950, 1953; Bales and Strodtbeck, 1953), which posits that societies must solve four problems: Expressive, Adaptive, Instrumental, and Integrative. These correspond to the following questions: "What does it mean to be American or British" (Expressive)? "How shall we organize the social institutions required to achieve the good society"[5] (Adaptive)? "How shall we produce the material and social goods required for the good society" (Instrumental)? and "How shall we achieve social and economic justice" (Integrative)? Moreover, changing concern with these questions is related to party realignments in both America (Burnham, 1976) and Great Britain (Chapter 4). The driving forces behind these changes are the succession of citizen cohorts (cf. Beck, 1974) and the dynamics of culturally determined societal problem solving.

Weber (Chapter 4) also finds a discontinuity in the dynamics of thematic concerns in Great Britain. Specifically, in the period 1689–1795 (the Mercantilist period) there is a long cycle of themes whose length is half the length of the long cycle after 1795 (the Capitalist period). Also, the sequence of themes differs between these periods. This discontinuity results from changes in political economy between these epochs—in particular, the replacement of state-directed control by the marketplace in the economic factors of land, labor, and capital (Polanyi, 1957).

We also observed a second, shorter thematic cycle in America (Chapter 3) and post-1795 Britain (Chapter 5) that is related to long-term expansions and contractions of the economy noted by Wallerstein (1980), Gordon *et al.* (1982), and others. Weber (Chapter 5; 1983b) argues that this thematic cycle reflects a debate concerning economic performance generally, and specifically concerning the need to restructure the economy whenever long-term performance declines. It is our belief that this periodic restructuring constitutes the adaptation of the world system to changing internal and external conditions, thereby maintaining the long-term vitality and viability of capitalism.

Of course, not all culture changes occur over the long run. Chapter 6 examines the relationship between short-run changes in economic performance in America, concern by the major political parties with selected political issues, and changes in voter support for the major parties. We find that concern with selected political issues intervenes between economic performance and election outcome: Each party appeals to the electorate using issues selected to cast economic performance in terms most favorable to itself.

Culture indicators are also useful for analyzing the dynamics of smaller collectivities such as business firms, voluntary associations, and professional groups. Namenwirth (Chapter 7) analyzes presidential addresses of three

[5]As discussed later, the Adaptive theme in Britain concerns responses to threats from other countries. This difference may reflect the geopolitical differences between Britain and America in the nineteenth century.

American scientific associations in three selected decades. He finds that thematic concerns vary among associations, over time, or both. Also, some thematic concerns vary in opposition to societal concerns. Specifically, when scientific associations stress internal problems, a prosperous America is preoccupied with matters at or beyond its boundaries. Conversely, when America is preoccupied with internal, economic difficulties, scientific associations stress the relationship between themselves and the larger society wherein they operate. Thus, quantitative culture indicators are an important tool for investigating the dynamics of culture, including the relations among society, its subunits, and their respective cultures.

In short, assessing culture dynamics using quantitative measures of textual content is an important research tradition. Its importance lies first in the fact that texts and therefore culture indicators exist for much longer periods than do political and economic indicators. Second and more important are the theoretical and substantive conclusions about the dynamics of culture that result from culture indicators research. While our answers are certainly provisional—replication, triangulation, and evaluation by others are clearly required—they nevertheless demonstrate that modern quantitative methods are not fundamentally opposed or inimical to the issues raised by Durkheim, Marx, Weber, and the other founders of social science. A fortiori, without these methods, the complex, multidetermined dynamics of culture systems cannot be factually disentangled, and theories that explain the causes and consequences of culture change can be neither adequately formulated nor tested.

Before addressing the culture concept in detail, we continue these introductory remarks with a short digression on the nature of this book and our intentions.

We are presenting the results of a long-term research project, parts of which were published before.[6] Here we conduct a dialogue with ourselves: Our theoretical and methodological chapters are extended commentaries on the lessons learned, problems solved, and difficulties remaining in our research. This volume is consequently both a summary of our past and present efforts and a platform for future research. We believe the analysis of culture dynamics using quantitative culture indicators will grow in importance during the coming years, and this collection of selected essays in one place must aid the evaluation of our procedures and findings.

Given our small and biased sample of documents, we have intentionally pushed our theorizing far beyond our data. Some colleagues will be uncomfortable with this gap between theory and data. However, our strategy is

[6]Chapter 3 was originally published as Namenwirth (1973). Chapter 4 is a revision of Weber (1982); Chapter 5 incorporates material published in Weber (1981). A longer version of Chapter 6 was originally published in Spanish (Weber and Namenwirth, 1985). Chapter 8 was originally published as Weber (1983a).

based on the premise that large claims are easier for ourselves and others to falsify. Indeed, certain aspects of Namenwirth's explanation of 150-year culture cycles (Namenwirth, 1973; Chapter 3; Namenwirth and Bibbee, 1976) are explicitly falsified, while others are confirmed by Weber's findings presented in Chapters 4 and 5. Also, we have no doubt that future research will both confirm and falsify arguments and results presented in this volume. This is as it should be.

This book presents a series of related essays; many were drafted independently. Consequently, some differences in assumptions and theory existed. We have now resolved most, but not all differences between us. Therefore, the reader may observe some differences in conceptualization and explanation among chapters by the same author and between chapters by different authors. We thought it better to note them at the outset. Sometimes they are only implicit; in Chapter 10, however, a few specific controversies are made explicit as we explain our divergent assumptions. We chose to share our debate with the hope of involving colleagues in difficult but important issues.

The concepts of "culture dynamics" and "culture indicators" were only implicit at the outset, but have since been explicated in our theoretical reflections and methodological innovations and explorations, not to mention our more substantive investigations. We hope that this codification of our methods, assumptions, and theories will stimulate others to consider critical revisions and to engage in the exploration of culture dynamics and their interactions with social and personal transformations. As is often the case in social science research, we have only just begun to address these issues; there remain fascinating topics for future inquiry and widening understanding.

Since the culture concept is central to our work, the remainder of this chapter discusses our definition and use of this concept, how our views of culture indicators differ from others, and several theoretical and conceptual problems inherent in the analysis of culture systems and their dynamics.

WHAT IS CULTURE?

Students of culture divide on three main issues:

- Does culture consist of abstract systems of ideas or of behavior? Does culture include material artifacts?
- Is culture real, or is it a convenient fiction indistinguishable from the sum of individual ideas or individual behavior?
- Does cultural change cause change in society and other systems, or does cultural change result from change in these same systems?

Our positions on these issues constitute the basic themes of this book. Here we briefly summarize our answers.

We believe that culture consists of systems of ideas rather than behavior or material artifacts. To be sure, ideas are imperfectly manifested in the dynamics of action systems such as society, polity, economy, organizations (e.g., Deal and Kennedy, 1982; Schein, 1985), and in the behavior of individuals. Still, for us a fundamental premise is the ontological distinction between ideas and action.

If culture consists of ideas, then in answer to the second question we take a realist rather than nominalist position (cf. Berger and Luckman, 1966). Specifically, we believe that culture is a system that has structure, has an identity, and maintains boundaries. The dynamics of culture, moreover, cannot be reduced to the dynamics of subcultures and the ideas of individuals, such as opinions, beliefs, attitudes, and the like. For reasons elaborated below, we believe that cultural dynamics are the dynamics of culture as a whole and that both culture as a system and cultural dynamics exist apart from the cultures of its constituent elements.

Although we are realists, we do not assume the position of cultural determinism, which holds that changes in culture determine changes in other realms. Instead, the results of our research indicate that not only are there many dynamics of culture, but each of these stands in a different relationship with action systems such as society or economy. As noted earlier, the relationship between culture and action systems must be a matter of empirical investigation rather than theoretical assumption. Indeed, the results presented in the five substantive chapters of Part 2 elaborate this point.

Having stated our general position on these major issues, we now provide more detailed answers to the questions, What is culture? and, What are culture indicators?

Culture is a design for living (Kluckhohn, 1951; Kluckhohn and Kelly, 1945).[7] Just as with a design for a house or a garden, culture has only a programmatic and conceptual existence. For instance, in the design for a house and its garden, the symbols on the plans are scratches and are hardly made of mortar, stone, or plant materials. Hence, the media of the plans (or design) and the "reality" it intends are of different sorts. Besides, there are dimensional differences: The plans are sequentially arranged in two-dimensional arrays; the dwelling and its garden are at least three-dimensional, but are also changing in time, growing, decaying, and transforming through the

---

[7]As noted below, culture as a design has no designer but emerges from, and interacts with, society. We could define culture as conceptions of the good life and society, but those terms do not equally stress the opposition between design or plan and its realization, or between culture and society. It is this opposition that a telling definition must stress.

seasons. Yet one would be hard put to maintain that the garden is more real than its design. Indeed, Platonists would argue the opposite.[8]

Within this definition we take the metaphor of design quite seriously because it points at many substantive and formal features of culture that are often overlooked and that stress the difference between culture and society. This difference is quite similar to the difference between musical composition, resulting in a score, and its performance.[9] Until the discovery of musical notation, this distinction was hard to "visualize" and even harder to examine.[10] Notational systems for culture as a composition of (or design for) interaction remain very incomplete. For some institutional areas we now have written constitutions replacing oral traditions. Where those come to exist, the difference between design and its actualization becomes immediately obvious. As in music, the same composition allows for a great variety of performances. In many institutional areas, the designs exist only in oral traditions or in very partial notations. Yet, the distinction can be indicated[11] even if not measured now.

At times, the design has a designer, an author, composer, or architect. However, what about communally built or reproduced artifacts? Because there is no individual designer, does it follow that the folk tale, myth, or "primitive" dwelling has no design? Of course, it does; but here, as with all of culture, the designer is not just unknown: there is no one or more individual designers. These collective designs and their component parts evolve, become, and in themselves are rarely the outcome of other designs, conscious constructions, or experimental interventions. For instance, language may well be a design for speech, but no one designer, or even concert of designers, can produce a new everyday language from scratch.

Documents produced by collectivities are often preoccupied with designs, discrepancies between designs and perceived reality, and attempts

---

[8]The claims of conceptual art wherein the conception of the art work does, but the art work itself often does not, exist, illustrate the vagaries of the argument. Is the conception more or less real than the nonexisting art work?

[9]This is obviously analogous to the well-known distinction between language and speech.

[10]As anyone who wishes to perform medieval music from a bare and primitive notation of a *cantus firmus* speedily comes to recognize, this notation is itself subject to long-term development and refinement.

[11]Measurement is a form of direct assessment in standard units such as inches, degrees centigrade, or dollars. Indication is always indirect, since it measures the manifestation of a latent thing or process. Further, standard units are missing in the measurement of the manifestation(s). Clearly, unconscious content and processes are indicated rather than measured. Karl Erik Rosengren (personal communication) suggests that there are natural and created measures. In addition, some created measures are so widespread and have been used for so long that they are taken to be natural ones. Dollars might be an example of the latter. We agree that many created measures are believed to be natural ones. However, we deny the existence of natural measures. All measures are a matter of convention and hence a matter of culture.

to resolve problems that prevent the actualization of these designs. Although no collectivity ever fully carries out any of these designs, the articulation of the plan reaffirms the shared culture and collective identity.

But of course there are many plans rather than a single one. Culture is a storehouse of templates, designs, and plans. Adages such as "a stitch in time saves nine" and "haste makes waste" remind us that culture consists in part of contradictory rather than complementary elements. Moreover, among various sets of plans some are more central to one culture than another. Also, the centrality of one or another set of plans is not a constant but may change over time. Belief in the virtues of active political intervention will constitute a central nexus of a culture at one time, while opposite beliefs may do so at earlier or later points. Our methods detect such changes in culture's themes and issues. Thus, we are convinced that quantitative content analysis is an important tool for identifying cultural themes and issues that themselves implicitly address cultural designs. We elaborate below.

CULTURE VERSUS SOCIAL INDICATORS

Parsons (1951; Parsons and Shills, 1951) and MacIver (1942; MacIver and Page, 1949), following Alfred Weber (1951), made analytical distinctions between culture and society, but denied a factual distinction. Under the influence of behaviorist traditions, they presumed that individual behaviors or purposeful actions constituted the ultimate factual realities. Both society and culture were merely different abstractions of the same observable behaviors. If this is so, then the relationships between society and culture must be analytic rather than causal, but these authors did not make this necessary inference. Instead, they argued for the causal priority of cultural over social systems. We disagree on both scores. First, we argue for a factual (rather than analytic) distinction between cultural and social orders. They constitute different realities and consequently different indirect observables. Second, we again insist that questions of causal priority between the two orders are not a matter of theoretical argument, but of empirical inquiry alone. These positions also determine our stands on several current controversies in culture indicator research.

Social systems are **interaction** systems. The actors are at times persons but are more often collectivities. Social indicators (Bauer, 1966; Land and Spillerman, 1975; Carley, 1981; Wilcox, 1972) therefore, gauge the state of these interactions[12] and their collective outcomes. Some selected examples

[12]Interactions are just that, **inter**actions **among** actors (or social parties) and not **by** them. Sociology proper studies interactions and their structure and transformations to provide causal explanations.

are marriage, birth, death, and divorce **rates**. These rates characterize features of the society as a whole and tell us nothing about any particular family or its individual members. Similar observations can be made about crime rates, incarceration rates, or other rates as social indicators. Even though predominant, rates are only a class of social indicators.[13]

Economic indicators gauge the performance of the economic subsystem of the entire society (or its parts); they gauge the performance of its productive and distributive functions. Familiar examples are inflation and unemployment rates. The distinction between social and economic indicators is not universal but is itself a function of economic and social development. In a pre-money and predominantly barter economy, economists would be hard pressed to define and collect purely economic indicators. Also, the differentiation between economy and society is nowhere complete, and, consequently, neither is the differentiation of economic and other social indicators.[14]

Culture indicators (cf. Melischek *et al.*, 1984),[15] then, gauge the state of a culture, allowing for a quantitative comparison of changes in that state over time or differences in states among cultures or parts thereof. Thus, Weber's (1984a, p. 302) definition: Culture indicators are "time series which describe changing states of a cultural system—for example, moral values or political ideology—while social indicators are time series which describe changing states of a social system, e.g. changes in infant mortality rates or crime statistics." However, our position on this score is not widely shared.[16] Different conceptions of culture[17] and society are the cause of the resulting disagreements. For example, Peterson (1979; Peterson and Hughes, 1984), Horowitz (1981), Rosengren (1984), Martin (1984), and many others identify culture indicators in whole or in part with so-called

[13]Other indicators include total numbers, such as population; size figures, such as GNP; and measures standardized for population, such as density. Social accounting methods use dollars as the standard units.

[14]Therefore, the question remains whether in capitalist countries indicators of the severity and duration of industrial strikes are indicators of economic performance or rather of power struggles and political performance.

[15]The concept of culture indicator is of recent vintage but the practices and purposes the concept implies are not. Indeed, efforts to guage the state of culture and to calibrate measures of its changes have a long history. As demonstrated by Vico (1968), Montesquieu (1949), the Scottish moralists (Schneider, 1967), Enlightenment thinkers and their critics (Gay, 1966–1969, 1973), and many other luminaries of the eighteenth century, the birth of systematic social science coincided with the effort to more precisely describe and register change in social and cultural orders.

[16]For example, Firestone (1972) and Stone (1972) both discuss analyzing the content of texts as a means of generating **social** indicators.

[17]There is an immense literature on the culture concept. Discussions by Durkheim (1974; 1954), Kroeber and Kluckhahn (1952), Kroeber and Parsons (1958), Radcliffe-Brown (1952), Wuthnow *et al.* (1984), helped us to clarify our understanding. Clearly, we use the culture concept in its broad anthropological sense rather than in its restricted and common sense of high culture.

cultural statistics that measure culture production and consumption. *Culture production* refers to statistics indicating the quantity of plays, movies, books, dance, music, and other art forms produced within a society. We believe that these indicators measure social and economic products and not culture content, which for us is the *sine qua non* of culture indicators. Since they measure social interaction rather than culture content, measures of culture consumption based on leisure time activities are also social rather than culture processes. Finally, the cultural statistics definition of culture indicators derives from a more restricted conception of culture. It equates culture with high art or with the popular arts.

The construction and use (both practical and theoretical) of culture indicators is itself associated with social and cultural development. The very existence of culture indicators already suggests a certain level of cultural development; it presumes, for instance, a critical self-monitoring of cultural achievements. However, most societies and cultures in history do not have the wherewithal—including information, needs, or inclinations—required for this purpose; only a fraction of human societies do. Therefore, the presence and character of culture indicators are themselves determined by the culture that they measure and the society wherein they operate. To maintain the distinction between indicators of culture and indicators of society (and parts thereof), we prefer the term *culture* indicator rather than the more commonly used *cultural* indicator because all indicators are part of culture.

METHODOLOGICAL COLLECTIVISM VERSUS INDIVIDUALISM

Since culture is a property of the collectivity, it seems to us that methods to assess the dynamics of culture should acknowledge this basic fact. Our factual and theoretical investigations therefore often support and use the procedures of methodological collectivism (Namenwirth *et al.*, 1981; Weber, 1984a; cf. Mandelbaum, 1955; Lukes, 1968; Macdonald and Pettit, 1981, pp. 106ff.; Sproule-Jones, 1984).

Usually, we strongly doubt that knowledge of the state of individuals or society can provide reliable indicators of the state of culture. This is so because individuals are always incompletely socialized (Wrong, 1976): Deviance is the norm rather than the exception (Cohen, 1974). Also, societies are always incompletely enculturated and the close fit between culture and society is a functionalist myth. To functionalists, all tensions and conflicts represent temporary aberrations and sick disturbances of a prevailing harmony or equilibrium. This vision of the relations between culture and society is certainly not ours. Instead, we insist that the incompleteness of both socialization and enculturation has important implications for culture indicator research, which we elaborate later in this chapter.

Survey research, including culture indicator research, is a predominant method in social science. This is especially true in efforts to produce national value profiles or inventories (Rokeach, 1973, 1974, 1979) and to assess value change over the past few decades (Inglehart, 1977, 1984; Yankelovich, 1981). To make inferences about the state of culture, all these studies sum the responses of individuals. Our critique of this and similar procedures is twofold. First, we believe that the concept of "personal values" is a contradiction in terms. Values are collective properties of culture, and individuals have only differing attachments, opinions, and attitudes toward value ideas. These attachments and orientations are psychological properties rather than cultural ones: They are not values in and by themselves. Second, survey research of this kind usually confuses modal personality characteristics with features of culture: this results from its democratic bias, counting each individual as an equal witness. Individuals are unequally informed about their culture and society, and their orientations do not count equally in some, or even all, societies. Therefore, if we sample from all adults in a society and ask them their opinions about their culture to estimate that society's culture, we only average informed and uninformed opinions. If we ask the sample more specific questions about their individual orientations, we still weigh these orientations as equally informed and of equal importance. However, in the creation, maintenance, reproduction, and transformation of culture, individuals are of unequal importance. Other collective actors, such as churches, universities, or governments, are also important in the culture arena but are systematically excluded from survey research. Consequently, traditional survey research of individuals cannot produce unbiased culture or social indicators (Namenwirth et al., 1981; Weber, 1984a). This is hardly the case for content analysis of documents produced by such collective actors.

Content analysis is a set of procedures for making inferences from texts (Weber, 1983a, 1984b, 1985a; Rosengren, 1981; Krippendorff, 1980; Ogilvie et al., 1980; Kelly and Stone, 1975; Stone et al., 1966; Gerbner et al., 1969; Holsti, 1969). We discuss these procedures in detail elsewhere in this chapter and book.[18] Our immediate concern is with texts. We note that content analysis per se does not imply methodological collectivism; rather, it is the choice of documents to be analyzed that does so. After all, many researchers have applied content-analytic techniques to texts produced by individuals. However, in all of our research, we have deliberately chosen texts that are the outputs of collective processes—for example, party

---

[18]Various aspects of content classification are taken up in Chapter 2. Chapter 8 addresses the use of measurement models in content analysis. Chapter 9 discusses ideography, i.e., the description and explanation of idea systems by content analysis.

platforms in presidential campaigns, the speeches of the British monarch,[19] and the presidential addresses of selected American scientific associations.

Our choices presume that one can make inferences about the dynamics of collective processes by analyzing the outputs. Compared with survey research, these and similar documents already weight the data by inequalities in power and privilege among both individual and collective actors. And while some will argue that as indicators these texts are deficient because they represent primarily the views of the elites and ignore the views of the lower orders, it is a working assumption of our studies that stratification weights the relative import of ideas and other features of cultures in the same manner as it weights the contributions of various social divisions. Existing forms of stratification determine a goodly part of the collective processes that produce public documents. Consequently the analysis of those documents is more likely to generate valid culture indicators than does the summing of individual responses in national sample surveys.

CULTURE ELEMENTS AND THEIR STRUCTURE

Culture as a design for living is a conceptual or idea system. We observed in texts that concepts (content categories) cluster in bundles that we refer to as themes (equivalently, issues or problems). Similar themes were found in different types of documents and in different time periods since 1689.[20] Having investigated only a few and a biased set of cultures and their documents, we are yet unable to guarantee that these culture themes have a universal existence. However, our research strongly suggests some of their formal features:

- Themes—for instance, Expressive and Instrumental themes (Chapters 3 and 4)—come in polar pairs.
- In one document the presence (or attention) to one theme excludes to that extent the attention to the opposite theme.[21]

---

[19]The Queen's Speech is delivered at the opening of each parliamentary session and is similar to the American "State of the Union" address. The dominant parliamentary coalition uses the speech to respond both to national concerns and to the concerns of various interest groups vying for power and influence. The issues discussed reflect the domestic and foreign policy concerns of the elites, if not the nation, while policy recommendations show the current government's strategy for solving these problems. Thus these speeches reflect the outcome of collective processes rather than the views of a single person.

[20]We elaborate the nature of themes in Chapters 2, 8, and 9. They figure prominently in the substantive analyses presented in the second part of the book.

[21]It therefore follows that when the attention to one theme rises, the attention to the opposite theme must decline.

- Each pole itself is only an ideal type or limiting case that is useful for theoretical exposition; however, these themes rarely, if ever, appear in their extreme, ideal typical form.
- No existing document ever presents just one set of polar themes. In fact, each document can be characterized by its profile across many sets of polar culture themes.

These four points summarize a conception that informs our methodologies. These methodologies, in turn, allow for a quantitative description of culture differences and changes using culture indicators that are now under development.

In our view, each document contains the implicit answer(s) to one or more problems or dilemmas. The exact number of these problems remains yet unknown. In fact, most of the time, these dilemmas are inferred from the prose by the investigator and may remain consciously unknown to its producer or consumer. Each dilemma has two opposing and limiting answers that typify the dilemma but that rarely occur in this extreme form in the actual prose of the documents. These idealized responses we refer to equivalently as *orientations*, *poles*, or *themes*.

Furthermore, we have observed similar dilemmas in diverse texts. For example, in many documents, the question "From where come our enemies?" poses a serious dilemma because one answer, "from within," excludes both logically and strategically the alternative, "from outside." Even if insiders and outsiders combine at the same time, there is still the question of which of the two camps is in charge. The dilemma has a strategic component because threats from the inside require different responses to those from the outside. At any rate, many documents display a persistent concern with the survival of the system and a preoccupation with internal or external enemies who will threaten this survival.

This Survival Dilemma, then, is posed by the question "What is the likely location of potential enemies, threats, or disturbances to the social system?" To this question, the two limiting answers exist. In one extreme case it is argued that each threat to the survival of a social order must result from a grave disturbance within the system, if not at its center. The disturbance will threaten the core, its identity, its continuity, and therefore its very existence. We named this orientation *Parochial*. The opposite orientation holds that all critical disturbances must arise at the boundaries with other social worlds, whether small or large, and that the outcomes of cross-boundary exchanges will determine the fate of the nation, the tribe, or the family. We named this orientation *Cosmopolitan*. In brief, events or actors threaten the survival of the collectivity at hand. Therefore, when events occur, documents produced by collectivities may ask, "Does it threaten us, and if so, where: at the center or at the periphery?"[22]

---

[22]This and other often-observed dilemmas are discussed at length in Chapter 9.

As the Survival Dilemma illustrates, culture problems are ordered in sets of polar themes. Each document, or set of documents, is situated in a multidimensional conceptual or meaning space, each dimension of which consists of a polar opposition, or dilemma.[23] Each document can be represented by a set of numbers, each member indicating the location of the document on each dimension. These numbers range from large positive ones to zero, to large negative ones,[24] with extreme values indicating great preoccupation with one of the poles of the dilemma and zero indicating no concern with the dilemma. How do we measure change in culture content? Distance measures in this multidimensional meaning space suggest the differences between cultures or subcultures that the texts represent. The greater the distances, the greater the dissimilarities between sets of documents.

There remain a few related questions. First, is the discussed ordering of culture themes and the location of a culture (or subculture) unique to each culture, or is the discussed meaning space universal, applying to the ordering of all cultures? Second, if the historicist position that there exists no universal meaning space be true, what will follow? In that case, comparisons among cultures using culture indicators is impossible. Then, it is also unclear what it means to speak of the location of a culture or of changes in that location in history. In fact, how can anyone describe change in the absence of an invariant coordinate system?[25] The third question concerns the process of deciding for or against the existence of a universal meaning space. Can it be based on facts, or does it result from theoretical presuppositions, or both? At present, we don't know. Certainly, whether culture as a whole is structured is a difficult problem. A culture has an identity and boundaries; these imply global structure. Now, however, we are able to show only that the components of culture such as dilemmas, themes, and issues discussed throughout this volume themselves have structure. To the extent that culture is structured, our efforts are an attempt to decipher the "deep structure" of culture from its surface manifestations.

THE RELATIVE ATTENTION PARADIGM

Thus far we have stressed the design aspects of culture to underline its dynamic features. While designs may constitute a central feature of culture,

[23]Our conceptualization is analogous to that of factor analysis. However, we have inferred dilemmas using methods other than factor analysis (Chapters 3–5).

[24]The units of measurement vary across sets of documents; for comparison they can be scaled to standardized scores with a mean of zero and a standard deviation of one.

[25]Of course, one could argue that culture-specific systems of meaning could be described by a "metacoordinate system," but this is not only unparsimonious, it just moves the universal system up one level of abstraction.

there is more to culture than that. It certainly includes Tylor's (1924, p. 1) references to knowledge, belief, arts, morals, law, and custom. Thus Weber (1984a, p. 313) argued that in literate societies, culture, including its dynamic plans and designs, is partly located in libraries, museums, and other repositories, but not in interactions.[26] Culture also constitutes the collective memory of past designs that continue to operate on present-day culture itself and subsequently on society. Culture processes also entail learning from the collective experience and then using the lessons learned in later circumstances perceived to be analogous to earlier ones. These lessons are stored in culture that functions as long-term collective memory. Thus, Alker *et al.* (1980) point out that these historical lessons become precedents for later decisions.

The idea of memory is first a human metaphor, but it is also a computer metaphor that we find suggestive. We believe that culture is ordered or structured because of programs that sort, file, retrieve, and interpret past experience for application to current and future operations on the physical, biological, and social environments. These programs are part of culture too, but now we can only infer their existence while analyzing their outputs, leaving their specification for future research.

If culture does contain programs that operate on meaning, where are these programs run or processed? We believe that they are processed within and by action systems. Thus we stated earlier that culture constrains and defines the problems that societies must solve, but the actual solution occurs at the intersection of ideas and action.

Within the broad category of culture indicators our work has focused on the changing concerns or attention of the collectivities that produced the texts we have analyzed. Underlying our work are a set of assumptions that together with some of the results reported here and elsewhere constitute a framework or paradigm for culture indicators research and theories of culture dynamics. Because the analysis of collective attention is a central feature of our approach, we refer to the following set of assumptions and findings as the relative attention paradigm (cf. Csikszentmihalyi and Rochberg-Halton, 1981, Ch. 1). Specifically, we assume

- Collectivities such as society pursue short-term and long-term goals.
- These goals are part of culture; they are periodically reassessed and modified (Namenwirth, 1973; Chapter 3; Weber, 1982; Chapter 4).
- Culture functions as short- and long-term memory; it is the repository of accumulated learning and knowledge.
- Some knowledge and learning pertain to problems encountered in the pursuit of goals.

---

[26]In nonliterate cultures, culture is maintained and passed intergenerationally through oral communications. In these cultures, designs are less differentiated from their manifestations.

- Knowledge about recurring events is stored in structures of varying sizes, internal complexity, and abstractness, including scripts (Schank and Abelson, 1977; Schank, 1982), themes, dilemmas, precedents (Alker *et al.*, 1980), ideologies, and other idea and knowledge systems.
- Collectivities have limited amounts of energy that can be devoted to problem solving in the pursuit of goals.
- Collective attention is an active process that directs and focuses energy toward particular problems.
- Attention is generally zero-sum: attention devoted to one problem requires that less attention be devoted to other problems.
- Text-encoded concerns reflect the attention of the collectivity.
- Collective perception is not determined by the intrinsic nature of events, but rather by culture dynamics (Chapter 4).
- Therefore, specific dilemmas or themes invoked by collectivities to interpret events reflect the state of culture rather than the state of the social or physical environment.

Designs for society and its long-term memory—in short, culture—are collectively produced, stored, retrieved, transformed, and applied. This conception of culture, some would argue, becomes dangerously collectivist and akin to the dismissed notion of collective mind. Allport (1924) observed that individuals have minds and are therefore capable of thought, forethought, introspection, and other mental functions. Collectivities are not superpersons with minds of their own and it is silly to argue otherwise. When Allport most successfully dismissed the concept of group-mind, the more circumspect culture concept increasingly replaced it. Perhaps social scientists cannot do without a group-mind concept to describe and understand the dynamics of collective phenomena and processes. When we use the culture concept, it sounds more innocuous and more acceptable. In fact, social groups as groups do collect information, order and catalogue it, store and retrieve it, and implicitly or explicitly create institutions for these tasks. Is it so silly to think of these functions as group mental operations?

SPECIFIC PROBLEMS IN CULTURE ANALYSIS

Having considered culture indicators and our basic assumptions at length, we return to culture and the culture concept to address five major theoretical and methodological points (cf. Namenwirth, 1984):

- The relationship between culture and society is only partially congruent.

- The internal order of cultural systems is often contradictory rather than consistent.
- The relationship between the nation-state and the national culture is of recent origin and is by no means perfect.
- The differentiation of societies and cultures implies difficult sampling issues.
- The boundaries of culture systems are often fuzzy and ill defined.

Rather than precluding empirical culture indicator research, these problems require investigators to proceed with care and caution. Where possible, investigators must formulate methods and research strategies to minimize whatever threats to validity arise from these difficulties.

Cultures Are Not Societies

The already discussed incompleteness of enculturation implies gaps and conflicts between culture and society rather than a close fit and harmony. If culture is a design for collective living and living arrangements, we should not be surprised by the absence of a close fit. As with the design for a garden, culture exists in a different medium from society. It exists in concepts for patterns of interaction and not in the fabrics of interaction themselves. Inherently, the realization of one medium into another is always only partial. In the specific case of sociation, this is also true for some additional reasons: its material history, its very fabrics and their limits of malleability, human imperfections, economic scarcity, and the sovereignty of the laws of nature. Besides, all designs are normative structures, and normative laws (in contrast to natural laws) are never without deviations. In fact, they are frequently broken, their realization is hardly automatic, and deviance seems a necessary part of social life. Culture as a design is in large part prophetic and therefore critical of the status quo. It is a design of the good society and thus not necessarily of the prevailing one. Part of each culture has therefore either utopian or reactionary elements (Mannheim, 1936) (or both at once) and so most cultures exist in opposition to the established social order. It is thus most hazardous to infer culture from existing or reported social arrangements. Because of these oppositions, culture indicators diverge from social indicators by definition as much as by fact.[27]

---

[27]Social critique, therefore, comes in two kinds. The first mode critiques established patterns of sociation in prevailing cultural expectations and mandates. The second and more fundamental mode critiques these mandates themselves in terms of another and perhaps transcending culture system. The latter mode is culture critique per se, and probably better named by that term to distinguish it from social criticism.

The Contradictions within Culture

Not only does culture frequently conflict with actual social arrangements, but its own internal order is frequently contradictory.[28] The unity of a culture system does not resemble the unity of a logical thesis but rather a musical composition with major and minor themes and the dialectics of counterpoint. The characterization of any culture, therefore, can never be monothematic. Benedict (1961) notwithstanding, cultures are neither Dionysian nor Apollonian. Instead, culture contains a wide variety of conflicting designs, dilemmas, and issues. The designs implemented and the dilemmas and themes explicitly addressed by culture participants reflect, as Nietsche (1968) taught, extreme and countervailing tendencies coexisting in a shifting balance. Our own research offers many illustrations of this point.

Namenwirth's research (Chapter 3) summarizes these countervailing and shifting tendencies. For example, now and then society is preoccupied with Expressive themes. When attention to Expressive issues declines, attention to Instrumental issues increases. Or when Expressive themes are ascending, Instrumental themes are descending, and vice versa. Yet neither theme is ever completely absent. In fact, in American culture, both are always abundantly present, but to shifting degrees. Weber found similar dynamics in British Speeches from the Throne (Chapter 4). Besides, the same applies to many other culture themes. So, shifting yet contradictory unity is a central characteristic of the structure of culture and its dynamics. This kind of tension in culture, therefore, is not the exception; it is the rule. Hence, the assessment of the extent of tension and contradiction must constitute a central objective of culture indicator research.

One of the causes of cultural contradictions and diversity is culture diffusion and other sources of culture change. In diffusion, isolated elements of foreign cultures are imported and borrowed, leading to syncretic structures. This is so because older elements are rarely completely discarded in the process but are rather reinterpreted in the light of newer themes. As an illustration, consider the transformation of religious symbols and rituals from, for instance, Jewish Passover to Christian Evening Meal, from Jewish transcendentalism to Christian- and Greek-influenced fatherhood of the divinity. In the latter case, strict monotheism is modified into a pantheon of the trinity, the mysteries of Maria devotion, and the veneration of saints, martyrs, and lesser creatures. The resulting contradictions are overcome by making their acceptance a matter and test of true faith. Paradoxically, this test elevates cultural contradictions to a sign of cultural superiority. At any rate, these contradictions characterize dominant cultures

---

[28]These contradictions greatly help the cultural justification of "aberrant" parts of the social status quo. Considering these contradictions, what is truly aberrant?

to a varying degree and should not be confused with divergences between them and subcultures.

The notion of "contradictory" or "contradiction" in culture presumes that the logic of culture resembles the logic of diction or syllogisms (cf. Archer, 1985),[29] and this is certainly a mistake. For instance, Peterson (1979) raises questions concerning the primacy of the four factors of culture, that is, values, norms, beliefs, and symbols. But his question itself is in error, for it presumes that if one of the factors is known, then the others can be known by logical derivation. The remaining debate would merely concern the determination of the first factor. However, it is our contention that the principle of culture organization is not syllogistic logic. Even Levi-Strauss's (1966, 1969, 1979) principles of association are too cerebral by far. Instead, the logic of culture must resemble the logic of Freud's (1950a, 1950b; Freud and Oppenheim, 1958) interpretation of dreams, Jung's (1969) archetypes, metaphor (cf. Dallmayr, 1984, pp. 148ff.; Lakoff and Johnson, 1980), and poetic imagination. The well of all culture is mythic, and the logic of myth, whatever that may be, is the logic of culture. To use a human metaphor, this logic is a left-brain rather than a right-brain phenomenon.

To summarize, the wells of cultures are fairy tales of sorts that suggest poetic truths about the nature of things and relationships (Bettelheim, 1976). Take, for example, the story of the prince who must kiss the deeply slumbering maiden, thus bringing forth her sexual self so that they will live happily ever after. Therefore, it takes a man for a woman to become alive, proving her dependency forever. In the late 1950s, a counter myth scandalized the rounds of Amsterdam when it was said that in March maidens walked the streets, nonchalantly slinging silken magic ladders on their left shoulders, to climb into the bedrooms of virgin boys and provide them with practical instruction in the facts of life. The scandal was not in the graphic details, but in the inversion of the dependency relationships between the sexes that transformed metaphorically and not logically designs, values, norms, beliefs, and expressive symbols that are deeply rooted and not of trivial consequence.

It follows that we believe that culture has structure. However, since the better part of culture and its organization is made of unconscious material that can be inferred only indirectly, the logic of this structure is only partly known and knowable. With Pareto (1935), we are convinced that rational and cerebral constructions, including our own, are but the tip of an iceberg: They unwittingly must hide as much as they reveal. But we disagree with

[29]In most work the syllogism is more implied than explicit. Bell (1978, pp. 14ff.), for example, argues that contradictions arise because society, polity, and economy have conflicting norms. The essence of this conflict in Bell's usage is logic rather than myth.

this author and others that culture is and can be subjected to rational manipulation, deceit, or fraud by ruling classes, or any conscious agent.[30] No doubt, not just Pareto but all the classics, such as Marx (1964; Marx and Engels, 1930), Weber (1963), and Durkheim (1954; 1974)[31] struggled with the very same problems. Whether actors were individuals or collectivities such as social classes, our sociological forefathers overestimated by far the influence that intentional acts have on culture dynamics. To the contrary, our substantive results show that many dynamics of culture either operate over such long periods of time or entail such fundamental shifts in the terms used to interpret the world (i.e., from Mercantilist to Capitalist culture) that they are unlikely to result from intentional acts designed to bring about the observed changes—if these acts could indeed exercise such power.

National Cultures

National cultures are features of national societies, and not all human societies are thus organized. In fact, national cultures are the accomplishment of the developing nation-state. In social and political evolution, this is a very recent phenomenon associated with the process of nation-building and the extension of citizenship (Bendix, 1964; Lipset and Rokkan, 1967; Rokkan *et al.*, 1969; Torsvik, 1981). Such "universal" inclusion in the dominant culture by all mature males also existed in small tribal societies of hunters and gatherers, fishers, and nomadic herdsmen, but was often lost during the evolution to horticulture and agriculture (Lenski and Lenski, 1982). With the development of slavery and other forms of extreme stratification, most human beings were defined as subhuman; chattel without voice, political or otherwise; and uncultured. Culture was thought to exist only at court among the rulers and their officials (i.e., clerics), including the clergy or priesthood.[32] With capitalism or industrialization and associated social transformations, stratification became mitigated, and

---

[30]We also disagree with Pareto that these "myths" are simple derivations of psychological residuals or tendencies. They are the constituent part of culture and its elements. We note in passing that Powers (1980, 1981) argues that the psychological reductionist interpretation of Pareto's theory is wrong, and that in fact Pareto was much more wholistic and sociological.

[31]Durkheim (1954, p. 444) denied that culture or any part thereof was unconscious; it was all pure French logic. Admittedly, the distinction between culture and society remained unclear to him.

[32]Thus far our research has included only documents from advanced agricultural and industrial societies. Our methods, however, do not preclude similar culture indicator research from very different societies such as herding, maritime, or advanced horticultural societies with many surviving records. It is only a lack of resources that has precluded our investigation of such records from the republics of Athens, Genoa, Venice, or the Seven Provinces, the kingdoms of Judea and ancient Israel, or the empires of Rome, the Tigris and Euphrates valley, Egypt, and China. Also, in these societies, elite cultures may stand in for national cultures.

23

citizenship extended. Also, however, new forms of social and economic differentiation came about, leading to the proliferation of subcultures (cf. Gordon *et al.*, 1982). Thus, functional differentiation produces a variety of different institutional subcultures such as domestic culture, various work and professional cultures, leisure cultures, and political cultures. Stratification further complicates and crisscrosses this institutional specialization by differentiating high-, middle-, and low-brow cultures and perhaps the culture of poverty. Ethnic, race, age, and gender differentiation are other sources of stratification, producing variant subcultures in many advanced industrial societies. Regional differentiation between city and country or between center and periphery are further examples of this process. Because of these facts, one wonders whether a dominant national culture ever existed or could survive in a pluralistic society.[33]

Pluralism, however, suggests not only that modern societies possess a variety of subcultures, but also that these subcultures are all of equal worth, consequence, and power or centrality. Obviously, the latter is not so. Subcultures are stratified from better to worse as are the strata that reproduce them.[34] These strata and cultures are perceived to be inherently unequal.[35] Apart from strata, the various social institutions are not of equal social centrality and their degree of centrality varies over time and from society to society. The same holds for the various institutional subcultures. Hence the national culture is the dominant subculture, and the determination of the degree of dominance is itself a culture-induced variable. At any rate, numerical considerations regarding the sizes of strata or institutional personnel are rarely of importance, and national cultures are usually carried and maintained by small elites.

Sampling Problems

The gauging of national cultures raises unresolved sampling problems. The question, What institutional realms or strata in the society are dominant and therefore carry the culture? produces the first problem. The second sampling question concerns the medium or media of the national culture: Where is it located? In literate societies, the printed medium is an important but not exclusive source. Some argue that mass electronic media are now dominant. Gerbner (1969) introduced the term *cultural indicator* with that medium in mind. Our own research extends the Lasswellian tradition of the

---

[33]National culture might be an ideological concept rather than an existing fact. The Romantic movement inspired the idea, suggesting that true culture was not made at court, but nurtured by the folk. Since the French revolution, national culture was thus a clarion call for nationalism and national independence, first in Europe and now everywhere on our globe (Smith, 1981).

[34]Accordingly, people speak of high-; middle-; and low-brow cultures in some societies.

[35]Admittedly, the gauging of centrality and consequent dominance is no easy matter.

World Attention Survey (Lasswell, 1941), which compared the attention devoted by newspapers to various topics in various countries.

Under Lasswell's guidance, we first chose political documents and in particular the party platforms of the two major American parties (Namenwirth and Lasswell, 1970; Namenwirth, 1973; Chapters 3 and 6). British Speeches from the Throne were later added (Weber, 1981, 1982; Chapters 4 and 5). This was done with the understanding that such documents would articulate not only the dominant political culture but the national culture as well. At that time, we justified our selection as follows (Namenwirth and Lasswell, 1970, pp. 6–7; Namenwirth, 1973, pp. 651–652):

1. The two-party system in the United States is competitive in most states of the Union—that is, the parties compete in one electoral market for the sympathies of various interests. The planks therefore contain the platform committee's best guesses about policies that will maximize the party's appeal to the electorate, and, to survive, parties must guess their voters' preferences correctly more often than not. Consequently, the content of party platforms is especially suitable for the study of concerns of the entire society.

2. Party platforms not only reflect predominant issues, but they also create or modify orientations by their presentation and the ensuing public disputes during election campaigns.

3. Because parties and party platforms are features of many other societies, their examination allows for cross-national comparisons.

Since then we have also investigated articulations of scientific culture or cultures (Chapter 7) to examine similarities and dissimilarities between a possible national and a specialized culture. The dissimilarities can be of different kinds. First, subcultural change may be out of phase with changes in the dominant culture—descending from upper-status groups, such as the court, to intermediary- and lower-status groups—or they may be ascending from, for instance, teenagers to more powerful age groups. Second, whether in or out of phase, the magnitude of change may differ between subcultures and dominant ones. Third, it is possible that national and subcultures have neither themes nor patterns of themes in common, or that the commonality is only partial.

Finally, comparative analysis of national culture and scientific subculture in America (Chapter 7) suggests an altogether different and structural dissimilarity: Culture themes that are central to the dominant culture are peripheral to specialized subcultures. Alternatively, national culture and specialized subcultures may be out of phase. As argued in Chapter 7, in American party platforms, British Speeches from the Throne, and other political sources, Parochial themes usually prevail when the economy is seriously depressed, while Cosmopolitan themes appear preponderant when economic growth is at its long-term peak. In American science speeches, these generalizations do not hold: they seem reversed. Specifically, when the economy contracts, party platforms and speeches from the throne—or society-wide articulations—become Parochial, concerning themselves more than otherwise with the problems at the center of, and therefore central to, society. In contrast, the sciences in bad times, and perhaps all specialized institutions of society, maximize their Cosmopolitan concerns, stressing problems arising at the periphery. For institutions, these are problems of interaction with other institutions and society as such. This interpretation strongly suggests an inversion of cultural or social dynamics: Issues that appear as central to society become peripheral to its institutions and vice versa.

More precisely, when the economy is at a 50-year low, the national culture concerns itself predominantly with issues central to society and especially its economy: The national culture is Parochial. At those times, the sciences (and perhaps other societal institutions) concern themselves with issues of society at large and the relationships between the institution and society: They are Cosmopolitan. In contrast, when the economy is at a 50-year high, the national culture concerns itself with other societies and cultures: It is Cosmopolitan. Yet the sciences concern themselves in such times with issues of the sciences, their organization, and membership: They are Parochial. Therefore, national culture and subcultures are out of phase because they relate differently to common social system characteristics.

These results show that questions concerning the existence of national culture and the relationships between national cultures and specialized subcultures are in part matters of definition and in part sampling issues, but are also to a large extent problems of factual inquiry. More importantly, our methods for assessing the dynamics of culture through quantitative culture indicators proved adequate to the task: these methods do reveal differences in the dynamics of national and institutional cultures.

Boundaries and Identities

The relationship between dominant culture and subculture is but one example of questions concerning the boundaries among cultures and their identities—two sides of the same coin. After all, boundaries determine what does or does not belong to one or another culture at different times and therefore also delimit their identities. Change over time of a culture does not exclude the maintenance of the "same" identity. French culture differed from British culture for a long period although both have changed rather drastically during the last millennium.

What needs to be distinguished here is change **within** the system from change **of** the system (Namenwirth and Bibbee, 1976). The operationalization of this distinction—no easy matter—requires the separate determination of culture elements such as themes and the structure (or pattern) of attention devoted to these themes. In short, change affects the elements, transformation affects their pattern (Piaget, 1970; Hernes, 1976). Consequently, culture indicators must show both the elements and their structure to determine a culture's identity and boundaries. No doubt, this is a difficult task. Nevertheless, the following brief summary of results presented elsewhere in this volume shows that content-analytic culture indicators are useful tools for operationalizing changes within and of the system.

In America (Chapter 3) and Great Britain (Chapter 4), society is sometimes preoccupied with the identity of the social system. Issues of system identity are manifest in what we call Expressive themes, whose central focus is the question: What is or is not American (or British)? In America this debate was the major preoccupation of the Civil War period. In Great Britain after 1795, the debate addressed the relationship between England and Scotland and England and Wales, but most centrally the "Irish Question." In America and in Britain after 1795, fluctuations in societal concern with identity issues constitute change within the system. In Great Britain before 1795, the Expressive theme also address the question "What is or is not British?" but here the specifics differ from those of the later period. The Expressive question of the early period concerns church–state relations, especially Protestant succession. As elaborated in Chapter 4, there is in the 1790s a transformation of the system so that what is perceived to be problematic about the identity of Britain changes. This change constitutes change of the system.

CONCLUDING REMARKS

For studying the long-term dynamics of culture, quantitative indicators based on text are important tools. As noted, they often reveal aspects of culture change not easily detected by other methods. A key element in the content analysis process is the classification of text by computer. In the following chapter we explain how content analysis is used to classify the content of documents, and discuss the resolution of several difficult problems in text analysis.

2

Classification and Interpretation in Content Analysis: The Lasswell Value Dictionary

Culture indicator research based on content analysis requires investigators to pose and answer the following three questions:

- What text or other media should be classified?
- In the process of classification, how many and what kind of categories should be used?
- Should categories be mutually exclusive?

The answers to these and related questions interact with all phases of inquiry, including research design, data collection, data analysis, interpretation, and explanation. In fact, the introduction of computer-assisted content analysis led to a reexamination of categories. Using the computer to code large amounts of text quickly, investigators could easily categorize the same texts using different category schemes, producing several descriptions or interpretations of the same textual reality. This multitude of interpretations confronted investigators with the question, Whose category scheme, or dictionary,[1] should be used? Iker (1974; Iker and Harway, 1969), Cleveland *et al.* (1974), McTavish and Pirro (1984), and Krippendorff (1980, p. 126) argued for the use of categories inherent in the

[1]A content analysis dictionary consists of the definitions of various categories together with the actual assignment of words or other semantic units to categories. It is more like a thesaurus than a dictionary, but the latter term has become traditional among content analysts.

J. Zvi Namenwirth and Robert Philip Weber jointly wrote this chapter.

language of the messages' producers. In contrast, we and others (Stone *et al.*, 1966; Dunphy *et al.*, 1974) insisted that interpretation must use the observers' categories. The latter authors engaged in a further debate concerning the proper relationship between theory and categories and the selection of the most adequate theory. Before we discuss these concrete issues, let us first place them in a more theoretical context.

INTERPRETATION AND CLASSIFICATION

We note in Chapter 9 that meaning is a collective phenomenon. We define meaning as shared understandings. In our view, the phrase *private meaning* entails a logical contradiction. Individuals may attribute significance to their inner lives or to the external world, but unless that significance is shared, it is not meaningful in our sense of the term. Interpretation answers the question, What does it mean?[2] Explanation answers the question, What are its causes (Chapter 9)? Although in practice the two questions interact, the analytical distinction is crucial, since we hold that interpretation is in principle a prerequisite of explanation.

What is the **process** of interpretation? In our view, interpretation consists of the translation of one set of meanings into another (Winch, 1970; Turner, 1980; Edelson, 1975; Macdonald and Pettit, 1981). Content analysis entails several different levels of interpretation, each with its own problems and choices. For example, our content analysis dictionary is an interpretation of the meaning of words, phrases, and idioms in terms of our category scheme. We use the dictionary to classify text and then use the

---

[2]Interpretation raises questions about the meaning of language. This meaning is strictly linguistic and not metaphysical. Consider the following question:

What is the meaning of life?

Here, the concept of meaning has at least two distinct meanings, a linguistic and a metaphysical one. For the semanticist the question is

What is the meaning of the word *life*?

A good dictionary should contain most of the answers but these answers would certainly not satisfy a philosopher worth his or her salt. For the philosopher the earlier question means

If life makes any sense at all, what is its final purpose?

Clearly, no dictionary or other linguistic analysis can ever hope to answer this metaphysical query, and the confusion arises from a semantic trick of all language: The sense of a word (a sentence, or other language unit) is never the same as the sense of the "things" thus worded (Whitehead and Russell, 1910–1913; Bateson, 1972, 1979). The same applies to the verb *understood*, so revered in phenomenological practice especially in its German rendition of *verstehen*. Understanding a sentence or two is hardly the same as understanding what its speaker is really about. The term *really* betrays the metaphysical nature of the latter concern.

PROCEDURES

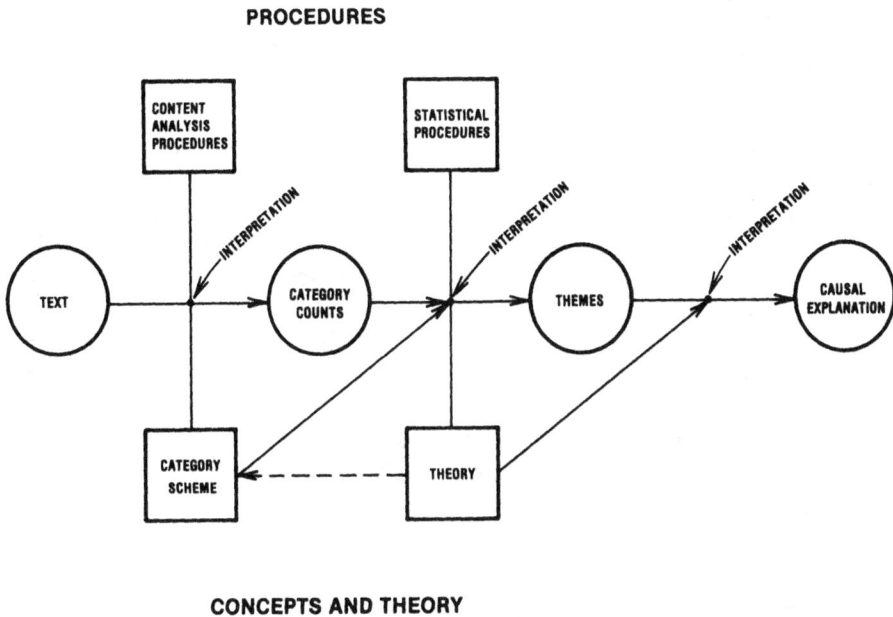

CONCEPTS AND THEORY

FIGURE 2.1. **The Process of Content Analysis.**

results of this classification to identify and interpret larger chunks of meaning in texts, such as themes, issues or dilemmas.

At the same time, interpretation entails the translation of language protocols from one language into another—for instance, from the dream or myth protocols of one culture and language into the interpretative protocols of psychoanalytic, anthropological, or theoretical languages. Content analysis, and certainly computer-aided content analysis, their dictionaries, and other coding rules formalize some aspects of the process of interpretation.

In content analysis there are at least three major interpretive moments. In fact, one of the main advantages of content analysis is that it brings these interpretive moments out into the open rather than obscuring them, as do many quantitative and qualitative social science procedures of inquiry. As shown by Figure 2.1, the content of texts analyzed through our various procedures is interpreted using concepts and theories. Content analysis dictionaries consist of a set of categories usually derived from one or more theories. Our dictionary, the Lasswell Value Dictionary (LVD), contains more than 60 mutually exclusive categories[3] based on Lasswell and Kaplan's (1963) concepts and theoretical frame of reference. The classification or

---

[3]The appendix to this chapter discusses the category scheme. Weber (1983a, 1984b, 1985a, Chapter 8) considers problems in dictionary construction.

mapping by computer of the text into the dictionary concepts constitutes the first of three interpretations. Category counts, expressed as the percentage of words in each document in each category, are further analyzed using statistical procedures such as factor analysis. The output of the statistical procedures is then interpreted using one or more sociological theories and the concepts that define the dictionary. This second interpretation identifies several dilemmas, issues, or problems discussed in the texts. Elsewhere we elaborate the fact that the theory used to interpret the dilemmas is usually not the theory that informed the category scheme (Chapter 8)—hence the broken line in Figure 2.1 between "category scheme" and "theory." Chapter 9 discusses at length the interpretation of themes and then goes on to note that the investigator(s) causally interprets variation in concern with these themes using various theories of culture dynamics. In contrast with the second, descriptive interpretation, this third, causal interpretation is the main goal of culture indicator research.

Interpretation is part of human inquiry, including scientific inquiry. Concepts, even a full-fledged specialized language, play a critical role in all of science. However, the translation of common language observations into mathematical formulations is so routine and so much taken for granted that the natural sciences more easily overlook the interpretative moment than is the case in humanist or social science practice. Besides, there is an additional complication that requires our attention.

Some of the objects of social science inquiry are observers themselves, that is, humans who think, count, explain, and use language for the interpretation of their own actions and those of others. In many of the natural and life sciences, either the objects of inquiry do not interpret or else the objects' interpretations are of no concern.[4] In our research, the interpretations of objects that are therefore really subjects are of great and central interest, especially if they are collective rather individual actors. Yet the speech and interpretations of collective actors have no privileged position. They constitute but data or protocols for our own subsequent interpretation and explanation. Our detractors will reject this position as rank positivism, a most pernicious and fatal disease! But what is positivism (cf. Bryant, 1985)?

Comte (1976) believed in three successively more adequate forms and modes of knowledge: theology, metaphysics, and science. And in his time, the 1840s, science would replace all previous and therefore outdated knowledge systems. It would even provide the foundation for the new religion. We have no such illusions today. These three systems nevertheless

---

[4]Medicine presents an interesting mixed case because the patient's or object's interpretation may be itself diseased, requiring material intervention in the form of cure through a process of interactive interpretations, or if "healthy," they may point at purely somatic disorders. What is natural or social science here?

raise distinct questions and adhere to different methodologies. In fact, metaphysical positions predicate all other forms of knowledge, including science. We therefore agree with Kant (1952) and the neo-Kantians (Becker, 1967; Holzhey, 1984) who disagreed or rejected this positivist position with the recognition of qualitatively distinct and irreducible modes of knowing and knowledge.[5] On this basis, Max Weber (1946, 1951) argued that factual knowledge could not provide the reasons for value judgments of any kind. Alas, many detractors reject both Comte and Weber as equally positivistic. If that is so, the term has little substantive meaning left.

The opponents of positivism often equate the doctrine with a method—that is, the belief that only the positive scientific method is adequate for the solution of true theoretical and factual problems. They reject that doctrine and so will any enlightened thinker. Yet what is the scientific method?[6] There is no such thing. Instead, there are many (Kaplan, 1964).

More often, the opponents of so-called positivism equate the scientific method with quantification. In their view, the analysis of meaning and the interpretation of human actions require qualitative analysis only. They argue that mathematics is an unsuitable language for interpretation. Yet this position makes the following errors:

- Qualitative analysis plays an important role in many natural sciences.
- The distinction between qualitative and quantitative procedures is itself not as qualitative as argued.
- There exist many qualitative systems of mathematics.
- Neither mathematics nor linguistics is a factual science and neither are their methods.
- The quantification of former qualitative distinctions always requires the introduction of new qualitative demarcations; quantification and qualification are always dialectically related (Ackoff, 1953).
- In both rational and factual analyses, advances often depend on new quantifications and therefore new qualifications. It is shortsighted to

[5]Yet we also disagree with Kant's individualistic position.

[6]Two doctrines that push the scientific method position to the extreme are behaviorism and instinctualism. Watson (1925), Skinner (1971), Lorenz (1966), and Tinbergen (1951) all deny the relevance of meaning, speech, and language for the explanation of human phenomena. Both doctrines either deny or belittle the existence of the inner person. They adhere to a naive methodological realism (Kaufmann, 1958) that denies existence to all that is not immediately observable. Clearly, many factual existences are only observable in their manifestations—not just psychological, social, or cultural entities, but many properties of the physical and organic worlds as well. True, outside the universes of primitive humans, no one can observe an entire society or culture—that is why investigators rely on social and culture indicators—but so what? Who has physically observed one or more instincts? That is why we clearly and emphatically reject these two doctrines with their naive epistemologies.

deny the utility of quantitative descriptions for interpretation and explanation on purely metaphysical grounds. The proof is in the pudding.

In sum, by any definition there is no warrant for the charge of positivism. It merely reflects a distaste for, and incomprehension of, mathematics and rational analysis (cf. Sylvan and Glassner, 1985).

Controversies Regarding Proper Instruments of Interpretation

In the formalization of linguistic interpretation, there exists a long-standing dispute over the selection of proper categories. This methodological debate, or Methoden Streit (Rickert, 1926; Menger, 1963; Herbst, 1965; Weber, 1977), has raged since the turn of the century among economists, sociologists, anthropologists, psychologists, historians, philosophers, and even jurists. Subjectivists such as phenomenologists maintain that the investigator can understand behavior, including speech and language, only in the subject's own terms and meanings, or so-called subjective meaning.[7] Therefore, subjectivists insist that meanings be assessed only in the speaker's own terms and explicit or implied categories. Thus, the validity of the observer's interpretation must derive from his or her interaction with the individual subject or respondent. In contrast, objectivists maintain that interpretation must be in the observers' terms. The subjects' terms can never validate the observers' terms and resulting interpretations. Hence, in the validation of interpretation only the investigators' own meanings are the object of investigation.

Subjectivists are usually nominalists. They hold that collectivities such as societies or formal organizations are sometimes useful fictions but are otherwise reifications that, apart from their constituent individual members, have no existence, features, or properties. Hence, irrespective of how one assesses and validates the meanings of individuals, micro- or individual understandings and their dynamics explain macrostructures and their dynamics.

Taking a realist and observationalist or externalist position,[8] our goal is to assess the meaning in documents produced by collective actors. Because particular texts have not one but a multitude of meanings, there is no reason to assume a priori that individuals comprising the collective, either in their role as senders or receivers of the communication, are aware of all the

[7]Phenomenologists deny the existence of objective meaning as mere reification, while we consider *subjective meaning* a contradiction in terms. Further, they do not make a distinction between speech and language and therefore do not note that language is a normative rather than a behavioral system.

[8]We reject strong claims of objectivity based on a single, correct interpretation.

various meanings in the text. Our goal is not the assessment of the "true" or correct meaning, but rather the decoding of the text in ways that are relevant for our theories. As Slater (1966) points out, it is the salience of an interpretation for a particular theory rather than the truth of an interpretation that is the appropriate criterion for choosing among competing interpretations.

It is useful to consider the subjectivist/objectivist controversy juxtaposed to the methodological individualist/collectivist controversy discussed in Chapter 1. As noted, we hold a realist rather than nominalist position: Properties of collective actors and their dynamics cannot be reduced to the sum of their individual constituents and their behavior. Subjectivist methodology, symbolic interactionism, phenomenology, hermeneutics, and ethnomethodology, to cite specific doctrines, leads to the summing of the meanings of individuals, a method we explicitly rejected in Chapter 1. Applied to collective documents, these methods cause serious problems. For example, since we cannot query the producers of 200-year-old documents, how shall we assess their meanings (even if we grant that querying individuals is useful)?

There is yet another set of problems that we have alluded to but not yet explained. Our enterprise consists of making inferences about the nature and dynamics of issues, themes, dilemmas, and similar meaning units in documents produced by collective actors. These inferences require the use of methods entailing several classifications of meaning that vary in complexity. The content analysis dictionary provides one of the most elementary levels of classification. The classification of text also uses larger and more complex meaning units, such as issues, themes, and dilemmas. We note in Chapter 9 that these larger meaning units are important because they bear in complex ways on the collective perception of the social and physical environments, and on choices among various possible courses of action. Yet whose explanation of choices is to be utilized?

The answer to the previous question is of the essence. Is it Everyperson in the role of problem-solver or is it the "scientific" observer of the scene? The former case argues that Everyperson has a folk theory of choice and consequently, that the dictionary should reflect first, Everyperson's category system of meaning, and second, his or her classification of language in this category system. In the latter case, all observers (or investigators) have their own theories of meaning dynamics and, by implication, their own category systems and classifications. Also, the investigator's dictionary need not—probably could not—match those of our multitudinous problem-solvers to be valid. For practical and theoretical reasons, the Lasswell Value Dictionary does not pretend to duplicate Everyperson's folk theory of choice.

Furthermore, it remains impractical to rely on a folk theory of choice because there is not one; there are all too many. Besides, Everyperson is a fictional creature. Either one must create as many dictionaries as there are problem-solvers of different folk-theoretical inclinations, or one must choose among the extant folk theories. In that case, the observer's theory becomes again the critical criterion. The theoretical considerations are equally simple. Folk theories, including folk theories of choice, are more often wrong than right. One might wish to study wrong theories for various reasons: because of their folkloristic interest, for their ethnographic detail, as an adjunct to social history, or as a sociology of knowledge inquiry into the social conditions of error and bad ideas. Yet these investigations will teach us precious little about the true dynamics of problem solving and culture generally.[9]

CATEGORY SCHEMES

Confronted with the impracticality of subjectivist methods in content analysis, some investigators (Iker, 1974; Iker and Harway, 1969; Cleveland et al., 1974; McTavish and Pirro, 1984; Krippendorff, 1980, p. 126) try to salvage the intent of subjectivist methods, using, however, objectivist techniques. Recognizing that it is unlikely that people when queried can formulate their folk theories of choice—after all, they are only dimly aware of the categorical bases of their argument—these investigators advocate an inferential approach that at times has been quite prevalent in automated content analysis.[10] Its defenders see special merit in the fact that the dictionary makers do not **impose** the resulting category system; it emerges from the speaker's own speech patterns.

Specifically, these investigators claim to induce Everyperson's categories from the covariations of her or his use of words. The basis of this inductive process is the assumption that words that appear together mean the same thing and therefore belong in the same category. For instance, when speaking about "father," Everyman might use only endearing words refer-ring to "good," "friendly," "sweet" father but never mentions nasty qualities or mother in any shape or form. Conversely, when speaking at other times (or in other documents) he has nothing but nasty things to say about mother, never mentioning father while using any terms of endear-ment. Obviously, this thinker discerns categorical distinctions between sweet Dad and nasty Mom.

---

[9]Our Value Dictionary cannot be based on observing how untutored judges will group words, that is, what content categories they will create and how they will classify the dictionary entries into their own categories. If the judges' dictionary would match our own, then we can only conclude with the melancholy observation that Lasswell's Value theory is as un-enlightened as Everyperson's.

[10]See Weber (1985a, pp. 37–38; Chapter 8) for further discussion.

While it is true that such opposing covariances in word usage may suggest contrasting attitudinal predispositions, let us not confuse attudinal predispositions with either latent or manifest categories of meaning. In fact, categories of meaning must exist in the investigator's mind before he or she can even interpret patterns of covariation in word usage.[11] Moreover, this inferred and dubiously named category system[12] is probably unique to a particular subject (or folk theorist). It would therefore not allow for comparisons among a community of language users and thus would be useless for the description and comprehension of, for instance, Everywoman, who happens to concern herself with "good mothers" and "good sisters," never mentioning fathers or daddies, good, bad, indifferent, or otherwise. In short, the pitfalls of the ethnomethodological premises of this approach underlie the limitations if not impossibilities of atheoretical and conceptless content analysis.

If this sort of inductive approach will not do, what then? Early attempts to justify particular category schemes asserted that investigators must have a theory as a foundation for their dictionary and its categories[13] (Stone *et al.*, 1966; Namenwirth and Weber, 1974). Some dictionaries operationalized a narrow theory, such as McClelland's ideas concerning the role of achievement orientation (Stone *et al.*, 1966, pp. 194ff.), while others operationalized broad theoretical or conceptual schemes, such as that advanced by Lasswell and Kaplan (1963). However, the claim that classification schemes were grounded in theory turned out to be first, weakly supported in practice, and second, reducible to much weaker claims concerning the operationalization of variables at a low level of abstraction. We take up each of these issues in turn.

Stone and his collaborators (1966) chose to combine categories derived from several theoretical frames of reference into one fairly comprehensive category scheme.[14] But in practice, the **relationships** among the variables suggested by a particular theory were seldom, if ever, found relevant to

[11]Osgood (Osgood *et al.*, 1957, 1975) makes the same error. Unless the names of "objects" have the same linguistic meaning to all his subjects, their evaluation of the object's attributes remains indeterminate. Therefore, Osgood does not measure the variable linguistic meaning of the same object among different subjects but the variable attitudes of different subjects toward shared meanings of a variety of symbols. His term, *measurement of meaning*, is a misnomer.

[12]As noted in Chapter 8, the dispute between those advocating inferred and those advocating assumed categories turns on a terminological misunderstanding. *Inferred categories* consist of words with different meanings that covary empirically, while *assumed categories* consist of words with similar connotations that may or may not covary empirically. We use the term *category* to refer to assumed categories unless otherwise noted.

[13]Stone *et al.* (1966, p. 134, emphasis in the original) claim: "A content analysis category consists of several **language signs** (words, idioms, phrases, and so on) that together represent a variable in the investigator's theory."

[14]We have argued elsewhere (Namenwirth and Weber, 1974) that dictionaries must be theoretically based in the strong sense of theory. However, we now reject that view for the one developed in this chapter.

interpretation and explanation. The theory that had originally suggested the categories thus became irrelevant to the explanation of the content-analytic data. In short, variables and concepts were never reintegrated into the original theoretical framework (cf. the discussion of Figure 2.1).

Furthermore, the original framework sometimes proved inadequate for the analysis of particular texts, and ad hoc categories[15] were added to the classification scheme. Used only for a particular set of texts, these categories reduced the generality of results based on them.

Weber (1983a; Chapter 8) soon noted a paradox of sorts: Investigators analyzing data using the Lasswell Value Dictionary never interpreted and explained their results using Lasswell's theory, while investigators analyzing text using the Harvard Dictionary seldom, if ever, explained their results using the Parsonian, Balesian, and Freudian theory on which that dictionary is predicated. Ironically, investigators found that text classified with the Lasswell Dictionary could be interpreted using Bales's and Parsons's (Bales, 1950, 1953; Bales and Strodtbeck, 1953; Parsons *et al.*, 1953; Parsons and Bales, 1953; Parsons and Smelser, 1956) theories (Chapters 3 and 5; Namenwirth, 1973; Weber, 1982) and neo-Marxian and Schumpetarian ideas (Chapters 3 and 4; Namenwirth, 1973; Weber, 1981, 1984b). In practice, therefore, no relationship exists between the theory that informed the category scheme of a general dictionary and the theory used to interpret and explain the content-analytic findings.

If theory in its strong sense cannot justify categories, what then? Investigators face three main choices:

- categories derived experimentally from individuals,
- categories inferred from the texts to be analyzed, and
- categories chosen by the investigator on utilitarian or pragmatic grounds.

For reasons already given, we reject the first two options. Instead, we opt for pragmatic categories assumed by the investigator. There are several reasons for our choice. First, we believe that inquiry is best served by defining a range of categories that appear to capture a diverse set of meanings. Second, there is factual evidence that research outcomes do not depend on the category scheme used (Namenwirth and Bibbee, 1975, p. 61; cf. Weber, 1985a, 1983a; Chapters 2 and 8). Third, to the extent that this is so, standardizing categories will lead to the accumulation of research results based on equivalent dictionaries. This accumulation is necessary for the advancement of culture indicator research.[16]

---

[15]We describe ad hoc categories for the LVD later in this chapter.

[16]Nor would we insist that the LVD become **the** standard measuring instrument. To us, any well-constructed broad category scheme is equally pleasing. The central issue is the standardization of indicators.

Irrespective of what particular set of categories inform the dictionary, investigators must confront several problems that affect category construction. For instance, both hostile and friendly critics sometimes attack the construction of a particular category as being either too narrow, broad, vague, or fuzzy[17] for their taste. Categories represent variables. Thus, the construction of categories is not different from the operationalization of any variable. As Kaplan (1964, pp. 62–71) notes, concepts vary in their degree of openness. Some concepts have fuzzy edges; it is occasionally difficult to determine the boundaries of the concept. Other concepts are vague because the theory in which they are embedded is also vague. As the theory develops and researchers apply it to a wider range of situations, the meaning of the concept clarifies.

In the operationalization of concepts through category construction, similar issues exist. In the concluding sections of this chapter, we note insights gained from several studies using the LVD that suggest enhancements, or at least changes, in our category scheme, and hence changes in the concepts available for model and theory construction. Here we focus on the interaction between language and categories and on the openness of category definitions.

Language often constrains category definitions.[18] For example, to construct a category indicating concern with self-references, one might have separate categories for first-person-singular and -plural pronouns. The few first-person pronouns in English obviously constrain the number of entries in the category. Nevertheless, while the use of any particular first-person pronoun might be ambiguous, especially taken out of its larger context, the meaning of such categories is not generally disputed. For instance, first-person-singular pronouns indicate individual self-reference, while first-person-plural pronouns indicate group self-reference. Thus, both the number of entries that might be classified as indicators of self-reference and the relative openness of these categories are limited by language itself.

Critics often argue that the inclusion of borderline cases shows that a content category definition is vague, and therefore invalid. However, as Searle (1969, p. 8) argues, the judgment that a particular case does or does not fit the concept requires an understanding of the concept itself. Otherwise, the critic could not judge at all. Thus these debates often turn not on the definition itself, but rather on the inclusion of borderline cases. At best, these discussions address real limitations and errors in category construction

[17]Following fuzzy logic (Zadeh, 1965, 1971, 1972; McCawley, 1981, pp. 360ff.; Negoita, 1985) one might attempt to assign to each entry the probability (between 0 and 1) that it belonged in a particular category. As noted elsewhere in this chapter, it is not entirely clear how one goes about reliably determining these weights. If one could do so, then fuzzy classification techniques (Kandel, 1982) might be useful.

[18]In Chapter 9, Namenwirth briefly discusses the interaction between conceptualizations and perceptions that constitute another form of constraint.

that require correction; at worst, they represent nitpicking by critics intent on rejecting content analysis methods and the validity of their results.

Ambiguities, and hence disagreements among judges, arise when many

TABLE 2.1
Enlightenment Gains Entries, Lasswell Value Dictionary

Nouns	Modifiers	Verbs		
anecdote	announce#1	account#5	disclose#2	record#3
announcement	articulate#1	acquaint	display#2	relate#2
bulletin	articulate#2	address#1	distinguish#2	related#2
clue	civilize#1	air#4	educate	remind
comprehension	classify#1	analyze	enlighten#2	reveal#1
deliberation	detect#1	announce#2	enunciate	said#1
detection	disclose#1	answer#1	evaluate	say#1
diagnosis	enlighten#1	appraise	evidence#2	school#2
dialogue	expressive	ascertain	experience#2	see
direction#2	instructive	ascribe	explain	sense#6
disclosure		attest	express	shout#1
display#1		break#3	eye#2	show#1
dissemination		bring#2	eye#4	solve
evaluation		bring#3	eye#5	speak#1
expression#1		bring#4	fathom#2	spot#2
expression#2		bring#6	gauge#2	state#3
hunch		broke#4	hand#8	study#1
illustration		calculate#2	hear#1	summarize
instruction		case#2	hear#2	talk#1
interview#1		civilize#2	hit#3	taught
investigation		clarify	identify	teach#1
measure		classify#2	illustrate	telegraph#2
new#2		comment#2	indicate	tell#1
testimony		communicate#1	inform#1	tell#2
vigilence		compile	inspect	testify
warn#1		comprehend	instruct	told#1
		compute	interpret	trace#2
		conceive	interview#2	train#2
		confer	label#2	understand#1
		contact#2	mention#1	understood
		converse	monitor	verify
		convince#1	orient#2	view#3
		convinced#2	ponder	voice#2
		counsel#2	predict	warn#2
		dawn#3	prove#1	watch#1
		define	publish	watch#5
		depict	rate#2	wise#5
		detect#2	read#1	witness#2
		differentiate	read#2	work#3
		dig#2	reason#3	write#2
		direct#1	recognize	written#1

synonyms, connotations, and shades of meaning exist. Consider the task of constructing a category indicating concern with the gain or granting of information, knowledge, or wisdom, a category we call ENLIGHTENMENT GAINS.[19] Table 2.1 presents a list of the entries in ENLIGHTENMENT GAINS.

While categories such as SELF are quite precise,[20] we agree with Kaplan's (1964) caution against spurious precision. Some words and word-senses[21] clearly belong in ENLIGHTENMENT GAINS, while others indicate the category less strongly. Sense numbers indicating that the word is either a homograph or is part of an idiom follow some entries. The sense numbers are not immediately useful [Kelly and Stone (1975) provide details], but a detailed discussion here will take us too far afield. Words such as *ascertain*, *express*, and *reveal*, clearly belong to the category, but what about *civilize*? The inclusion of this word perhaps reveals our own Western prejudices and maybe it really belongs in some POWER subcategory.

Usually, we have little trouble deciding between primary and secondary examples of a category, but it would be excessive to assign weights indicating how strongly the entry represents the category. How would the weights be determined? One suggested answer to this problem is to calculate the weights using multivariate statistics such as factor analysis or multidimensional scaling. But this approach is fraught with difficulties. The weights might vary from context to context, thus requiring an explanation for the **variation** in weights, let alone the **magnitude** of the weights themselves. Such a venture would, we think, lead to spurious precision. It is better to live with moderate imprecision and to resolve these problems in successive approximations, as research results accumulate about the consequences of imprecision.

Thus, imprecision in category construction is inherent in content analysis. It comes with the territory, so to speak. Rather than ignore its presence, we suggest vigilance and caution. More important, we believe that content analysis will thrive and mature to the extent that researchers empirically investigate these difficulties and use their results to improve the instrumentation.

Having considered a number of problems in dictionary construction, we will now briefly describe the Lasswell Value Dictionary.

[19]As noted, category names are capitalized throughout. A full discussion of the Lasswell category schemes is presented in the appendix to this chapter.

[20]As noted, SELF contains references to first-person pronouns, of which there are few. Compared with other categories—for example, references to the gain of wisdom and understanding (ENLIGHTENMENT GAINS)—the entries in SELF are much more constrained, unambiguous, and therefore precise. Even when the exact reference of "I" is unclear from the context, it should be quite obvious that attention is focused on SELF rather than first-person-plural pronouns, a category we call SELVES.

[21]The dictionaries and software in our latest studies distinguish among the various senses of homographs. See Kelly and Stone (1975), Weber (1985a, 1984b, 1983a; Chapter 8).

THE LVD BASIC CATEGORIES

When the Lasswell Value Dictionary was first implemented in the late 1960s (Lasswell and Namenwirth, 1968), it was conceived as a category scheme that would operationalize Lasswell's understanding of concepts important for political analysis (Lasswell and Kaplan, 1963). It was hoped that the resulting empirical analyses would illuminate Lasswell's view of political dynamics.

More recently, as noted previously in this chapter, theoretical justifications for category construction have become less important given "Weber's Paradox," namely, that the theories used to construct various content analysis dictionaries have not been useful in the interpretation of results based on those categories. Instead, we believe that general dictionaries consist of many commonsense categories of meaning. Consequently, we are not overly concerned with our category definitions' being valid in the sense that they exactly match Lasswell's definition of the category. Instead, we rely on face validity in this regard. We are much more concerned about the validity of the assignment of particular words and idioms to categories, a topic we address just below and in the appendix to this chapter. Here we give a brief overview of Lasswell's eight main categories. We present the full dictionary architecture in the appendix.

Lasswell (Lasswell and Kaplan, 1963) asserts that there are two broad classes of values: deference and welfare. "Deference values are those that consist of being taken into consideration [in interaction between actors]" (pp. 55–56), while "welfare values [are] those whose possession to a certain degree is a necessary condition for the maintenance of the physical activity of the person" (p. 55).[22] Each of these two broad classes contains four subsidiary categories. The four deference values are POWER, RECTITUDE, RESPECT, and AFFECTION, and the four welfare values are WEALTH, WELL-BEING, ENLIGHTENMENT, and SKILL. For example, POWER contains such words as *conflict*, *subversion*, *empower*, and *engage*; AFFECTION includes *human*, *tender*, *widow*, and *sexual*; and SKILL includes *inept*, *career*, *plumber*, and *artistic*.

As noted, the appendix to this chapter elaborates these eight along with other LVD categories. At this point the question arises, why eight classes of values rather than seven or nine, and why this rather than some other classification? This grouping is in essence both a convenient mode of arranging commonsense experience and an economic way of synthesizing specialized social science information. Also, the institutions of society itself

---

[22]Henceforth, all unattributed page numbers in this chapter and its appendix refer to Lasswell and Kaplan (1963).

seem differentiated along such classificatory distinctions.[23] In short, the eightfold classification seems useful.

SOURCES OF ERROR AND THEIR RESOLUTION

Using these and other category definitions, we classified the entries of the dictionary. Not surprisingly, disagreements did occur and they stemmed from two sources: ambiguities of the definitions, and ambiguities of the entries. Let us first consider the limitation of category definitions.

The usual procedure when coders disagree is to estimate the extent of their disagreement (measure of reliability) and to accept or reject the coding because of some level thereof. Here, we did not follow this practice because we felt that agreement should be perfect once the rules of procedure were known. Consequently, wherever disagreement occurred the coders were asked to resolve their disputes by commonly accepted standards. By keeping a running account of these disputes we hoped that we could translate implicit practices into explicit rules. Such rules would constitute a more definite set of definitions for our categories. Although disputes were always resolved, the decision rules frequently remained implicit or ad hoc. No doubt, considerations of power rather than enlightenment were often a final arbiter—that is, the investigator's prejudices made the difference.[24] Consequently, we know the rules of classification primarily as they are explicitly contained in the actual groupings of entries in our dictionary. Therefore, the definitions of the categories only partly represent the actual grouping of entries. Nonetheless, the procedures of classification were not completely arbitrary. Implicit rules are still rules and besides, this type of disagreement among coders seldom occurred. Far more frequent were disagreements about the meaning of entries.

The ambiguity in the meaning of words needs but little illustration. Take the word *kind*. What kind of word is that? In one sense it refers to a class of objects, while in another it describes or evokes a benevolent disposition. An even (but not uneven) better example is the word *just*. Perhaps it denotes a concern with RECTITUDE ETHICS, but more frequently it means "just something else," "if it did not just happen." What will resolve these riddles? We used three different approaches: disambiguation routines, elimination by frequency, and classification in the category UNDEFINED.

---

[23]Lasswell and Kaplan (1963, pp. 72, 86, 99) provide a summary argument in their Tables I, II, and III.

[24]In retrospect, our procedures were not the best. As Krippendorff (1980, p. 132) points out, researchers should calculate the reliability **before** disagreements are adjudicated so that the minimal reliability is known. See Weber (1985a, pp. 16–24) for further discussion.

High-frequency words—that is, words occurring at least 200 times in 250,000 words of text[25]—were disambiguated. Kelly and Stone (1975) detail these procedures. Medium-frequency words—those occurring between 10 and 200 times in 250,000 words of text—were also disambiguated, but in this case, the disambiguation was restricted to the most frequently, rather than all, occurring senses. Finally, we made no special effort to include words that occurred with less frequency than 10 in 250,000. Since most of these kinds of words were not included in the dictionary, by implication they were also of no concern if they had more than one meaning per word.

At times, disambiguation routines cannot discriminate between the implications of the various word senses of one or another entry. Therefore, these entries were classified in the category UNDEFINED.[26]

Although the difficulties of entry classification are many, let's not exaggerate them. After all, not all ambiguities pertain to the categorical distinctions that are operationalized by this particular dictionary. Often, shades of meaning (and even large slices) do not have differential implications for the category scheme at hand and therefore cannot affect culture assessments (Weber, 1985a, Ch. 4). This is but another way of saying that the everyday dictionary used by Everyperson is not identical with the present one. These two dictionaries differ to the extent that they are predicated on different theories about meaning and the organizing principles of material, social, and psychic realities. Lasswell's conceptual discourse has a range of meanings that is more restricted that the discourse of everyday language. Therefore, the range of pertinent meanings of dictionary entries is narrower by far.

Our diligence notwithstanding, misclassifications do occur. Yet our research procedures limit the importance of even these mistakes. If the purpose of our research were to estimate the absolute magnitude[27] of, for instance, POWER CONFLICT in a document, misclassification could lead to serious misestimation. Our purpose, however, is always comparative; we want to know how much more one document is concerned with a category than some other document (or group of documents). Unless the entry is systematically misclassified in one document and not in another, the misclassification will not affect our conclusions. Furthermore, statistical procedures provide a safeguard, for these will estimate such errors (if they are

---

[25]Kelly and Stone (1975) provide the criteria for high-, medium-, and low-frequency words.

[26]Note that this category also includes words with only one dictionary meaning where the implications of these meanings still vary from context to context. Entries include such words as *smooth*, *raw*, *bilateral*, and *left*.

[27]In this context, the word *absolute* is misleading. After all, measurement is comparative; we compare an observed value with a standard, and the absoluteness of the standard is in all cases arbitrary. However this may be, at this time there are no standards in terms of which it could be decided that a document is either high or low on a specific measurement.

random). Whether they are random is hard to prove, but it is an assumption of the present mode of inquiry that experience to date well supports.[28]

When classifying an entry, the investigator really answers the question, Does the entry generally have a certain attribute (or set of interrelated attributes)? There are two answers to this question. Yes, the entry does, and it is therefore thus classified; or no, and therefore the investigator does not classify the entry under this heading. This formulation points at two complications. First, having one attribute does not logically exclude the possession of another. Second, not all entries need have the same attribute to the same extent (i.e., there are variations in intensity). Double (or multiple) classification of entries resolves the first problem (but creates others). However, the gain in semantic precision does not outweigh the loss in logical distinctness and exclusivity.[29] Above all, logical exclusiveness is a precarious precondition of all classification for subsequent multivariate statistical analysis.[30] Therefore, if we could classify an entry under more than one category or subcategory, then we classified it in the category that seemed most appropriate, most of the time, for most of the texts. There was one exception to this rule. We double-classified entries in any of the subcategories under one of the eight main Lasswell value categories. This double classification provided us with a convenient summary measure of the major value concerns. However, to preserve statistical independence, we analyzed either only the summary category or only the subcategories, but not both. As for intensity, although it is true that not all category entries will have the same pertinence to the category, we chose nonetheless a dichotomous rather than a weighted classification scheme.[31] Given the nature of the category scheme and variations in meanings of individual entries from context to context, any other solution would have created only spurious precision. Under these circumstances, weighting each entry in the same category equally is probably the more defensible approach.

The insistence on a general dictionary appropriate for a wide range of analyses has aggravated the problem of entry classification. Appropriateness and precision would increase if we had created categories with a very

[28]If classification errors are not random, then the question should be whether the systematic error component is correlated with any of the independent variables, thereby biasing the results. We have not empirically examined this question, but the fact that several sets of findings replicate across measuring instruments and research designs implies that systematic error is not a large problem.

[29]For an opposite conclusion, see Stone *et al.* (1966, pp. 183–186); Dunphy *et al.* (1974).

[30]Logical exclusiveness is especially necessary for all kinds of scale analysis using correlational techniques. If entries are classified in more than one category, definitional as well as empirical reasons can cause covariation. However, the investigator will never know which part of any correlation is produced by either fact or logical configuration.

[31]The Stanford Political Dictionary uses a different approach. See Stone *et al.* (1966, pp. 189, 208).

specific content in mind and could classify entries accordingly. Yet the improved quality of the instrument is futile because results of the inquiry depend on the ad hoc dictionary. The use of ad hoc dictionaries that differ from investigation to investigation prevents comparison and accumulation of knowledge. Hence, scientific progress proves impossible.[32] On the other hand, not all categories are equally pertinent for all kinds of documents nor do all entries have the same value implications. To resolve these dilemmas, our dictionaries allow for ad hoc categories for special problem areas. However, in practice we found that these ad hoc categories had little substantive importance.

In past research, ad hoc categories largely classified groups of actors. Specifically, for the analysis of party platforms Namenwirth (1973; Namenwirth and Lasswell, 1970; Namenwirth and Bibbee, 1976; Weber and Namenwirth, 1985; Chapters 3 and 6) created five additional categories: U.S. STATES, SUPERNATIONAL STATES, DEMOCRATIC, REPUBLICAN, and AMERICA. The first category contains references to any of the American states. SUPERNATIONAL STATES includes entries describing supernational political institutions. The concept DEMOCRATIC connotes all references to the Democratic party and similarly, the concept REPUBLICAN connotes references to the Republican party.[33] Finally, the category AMERICA contains all references to the United States itself as an actor and political party. Ad hoc categories for different projects follow a similar logic.

To date, our claims for the validity of the Lasswell Value Dictionary are based on consistency of rule application. The meaning of dictionary categories is defined by the explication of rules that differentiate categories and subcategories. These rules specify the attributes of words that belong to each category. Conversely, inspecting all words belonging to a particular category will confirm or disconfirm whether they have specified criteria in common. Therefore, words that violate the rule must be reclassified.

Finally, Lasswell's conceptualization of the value process dictates the rules themselves. Face validation of this kind, however, is not the only approach. What about validation with an external criterion? We have found

---

[32]An anonymous reviewer suggested that comparability of results rests on the categories of analysis, such as the Parsonian AGIL scheme used in Chapters 3 and 5, rather than the categories of coding discussed here. This comment confuses the first and second interpretive moments depicted in Figure 2.1. If the categories of analysis and the categories of coding both varied, how would one know the extent to which variation of the former resulted from variation of the latter? By holding constant the categories of coding, one tries to ensure that variation in categories of analysis reflects substantive results rather than methodological artifacts. Chapter 10 addresses a similar issue, the relationship between categories of coding and themes in text.

[33]To maintain a distinction between *Democratic* as an attribute of the Democratic Party and the word *democratic* as a more generic political philosophy.

patterns of results suggesting that our category scheme and the assignment of words to it have hypothesis validity (Brinberg and McGrath, 1982); that is, our empirical results and their interpretations are consistent with various hypotheses based on theory. We will elaborate.

The fact that the major categories of the LVD are divided into sub-categories produced the not-unexpected result that subcategory counts are impressively correlated with one another, but far less consistently so with counts of other categories, thus indicating convergent and discriminant validity (Campbell and Fiske, 1959; Alwin, 1974; Althauser, 1974; Campbell and O'Connell, 1982). For instance, various content analyses of different types of documents revealed repeatedly that if a document shows great concern with WEALTH TRANSACTIONS (e.g., buying, selling, renting, or loaning), then such documents also show great concern with the role names of various WEALTH PARTICIPANTS and other WEALTH categories. This finding of convergent and discriminant validity holds true for all eight major value categories except for POWER, and this anomaly requires further discussion.

POWER subcategory counts rarely correlate with counts of the total category POWER. Indeed, these subcategories split into two clusters whose members correlate positively with one another and negatively with the members of the other cluster. Indicative of the two clusters are, on the one hand, the categories POWER AUTHORITATIVE and POWER AUTHORITATIVE PARTICIPANT and, on the other hand, the categories POWER CONFLICT and POWER COOPERATION. In other words, if there exists a large concern with the authoritative functions of the state then there is limited concern with conflict and cooperation among various groups of citizens and their social and political organizations, and vice versa.

These findings suggest that the concept of power requires reconceptualization: In cultural conceptions of society there exist really two contrasting power processes. Provisionally, we might speak of Power A and Power B; but in fact there is already an ample literature suggesting more illuminating terms (Parsons, 1969, pp. 352–404). In the first case, power is a facility of society as an actor and is required to execute society's projects. Conceptually it is the political equivalent of the economic gross national product. In the second case, we deal with a distributive phenomenon inherently linked with inequality, where the increase in power of one societal group—for instance, a class—necessarily leads to the decrease in power in another. In short, here power is zero-sum (cf. Thurow, 1980). It is within the more conventional power concept that power is a facility of conflicting persons or groups within society to move others about (van Doorn, 1962). But whatever the contrast between these two types of power, the point here is to show that empirical analysis can provide criteria for the examination of the validity of our constructs and identify desirable future changes in dictionary architecture.

CONCLUDING REMARKS

This chapter examined the little-understood process of linguistic interpretation and the role of dictionary-based content analysis therein. This conception of interpretation and its formalization and operationalization remain controversial. Therefore, we found it necessary to extensively document and justify our conception and procedures by contrasting them to contending positions.

We maintain that linguistic meaning is an objective and collective phenomenon, part of language and culture rather than individual speech and behavior. Further, we assert that interpretation is a necessary part of all forms of knowing, and that it is part of public procedures rather than private whim or intuition. In sum, this chapter begins to formalize the process of interpretation; the use of dictionaries in computer-aided content analysis is a prime example thereof. Accordingly, we described the Lasswell Value Dictionary, which constitutes the basis of interpretation for the descriptive and explanatory studies of Part 2 of this volume. While the present chapter centers on principles, the following appendix contains specifics in great detail.

APPENDIX: THE STRUCTURE OF THE LASSWELL VALUE DICTIONARY

As noted, we take Lasswell's scheme as a set of commonsense categories of meaning that proved useful in actual research. Table 2.2 summarizes the architecture of the dictionary. Beside the eight basic value categories (WEALTH, POWER, RESPECT, RECTITUDE, SKILL, ENLIGHTENMENT, AFFECTION, and WELL-BEING), the dictionary scheme distinguishes between substantive goals and the elements and attributes of the process of distributing values—that is, personal evaluation and social allocation. The latter elements and attributes are transactions. The classification of content maintains these distinctions. Concerns with particular values are classified under particular substantive goals. The classification scheme also distinguishes several kinds of value transactions:

- What kind of actors participate in the process? The dictionary distinguishes between various classes of PARTICIPANTS.
- Does the actor gain or lose in the exchange? To answer this question the dictionary distinguishes between various GAINS and LOSSES.
- Is the value under consideration pursued for its intrinsic worth (i.e., as an ultimate end), or is it pursued to be exchanged in a more encompassing value process (i.e., as a means)? Lasswell and Kaplan (1963)

TABLE 2.2.
Classification of the Value Dictionary

I. Category	*Substantive values*	*Value transactions*
1. Power	Other Authoritative Power Cooperation Solidarity Conflict Doctrine	Arenas Gains Losses Ends General Participants Authoritative Participants
2. Rectitude	Ethics Religious	Gains Losses Ends
3. Respect	Other	Gains Losses
4. Affection	Other	Gains Losses Participant
5. Wealth	Other	Transaction Participants
6. Well-being	Physical Psychological	Gains Losses Participants
7. Enlightenment	Other	Gains Losses Ends Participants
8. Skill	Aesthetics Other	Participants

II. General value transaction indicators

1. Transaction Gains
2. Transaction Losses
3. Transaction
4. Means
5. Ends
6. Arenas
7. Participants
8. Nations
9. Self
10. Audience
11. Others
12. Selves

III. Anomie

1. Anomie

TABLE 2.2. (cont.)

IV. Sentiments

---

1. Positive Affect
2. Negative Affect
3. Not
4. Sure
5. If

V. Space–time

---

1. Space–Time

VI. Residual categories

---

1. Undefinable
2. Undefined
3. N-Type Words

---

define the intrinsic values as scope values, and the others as base values; however, to make this distinction the dictionary differentiates between ENDS and MEANS value indicators.

- What is the situation and/or environment of the process? Where possible the dictionary distinguishes among various ARENAS.

At times it is possible to determine the specific substantive goal of a particular transaction. This is the case, for instance, with the entry *admire*, which is classified as RESPECT GAINS. Inspection of the meaning of a word usually cannot determine the substantive goals of a transaction. In that case we can determine only the general transaction component of a given entry, and ask whether it indicates an actor, loss, gain, or whatever. A good example of such entries are the personal pronouns. The dictionary distinguishes among various classes of actors: for example, SELF, AUDIENCE, and OTHERS (first-, second-, and third-person pronouns, respectively). Such indicators of value-unspecific transactions are called *general value transaction indicators*.

The scheme of the LVD is logically incomplete; there are not the same number of subcategories for each of the major categories. This asymmetry results from the confrontation between Lasswell's theory and the actual rules of language usage. These two are by no means coterminous. It is perfectly feasible, and at times even useful, to introduce concepts such as SKILL LOSSES, but this is not to say that there are many words in present-day language that would show such a transaction. In fact, there are not.[34] The scheme of the dictionary, therefore, meets the facts of language rather than the abstract mandates of Lasswell's theory. With this overview in mind, we now offer more specific definitions of the dictionary categories.

Deference Values

There are four deference values (p. 55; see note 22). POWER "is a special case of the exercise of influence, it is the process of affecting policies of others with the help of (actual or threatened) severe deprivations for non-conformity with the policies intended" (p. 76). Having defined power as a relational process, power as a value pertains to this process as a desired good, RECTITUDE "comprises the moral values . . . virtue, goodness, righteousness, and so on" (p. 56). RESPECT "is the value of status, honor, recognition, prestige" (p. 56). AFFECTION comprises "the values of love and friendship" (p. 133).

Within the POWER category, the dictionary distinguishes between five substantive subcategories and six transaction subcategories. The category AUTHORITATIVE POWER includes entries indicating a concern with or description and invocation of formal power, "the expected and legitimate possession of power" (p. 133) (*govern, decree, statute, authorize*). Entries of the category COOPERATION denote "the integration of diversified perspectives" (p. 30) (*colleague, consent, mediation, overtures*). Usage of this category therefore shows a concern with the use of power and group action for the coordination of individual pursuits. The category CONFLICT contains entries that describe and denote the collision among actions and actors in the pursuit of power, whereby the use or threat of violence (both physical and psychological) is often a final arbiter among contending parties (*discord, oppose, deadlock, patrol*). The category DOCTRINE contains the names of various recognized systems of thought describing "basic expectations and demands concerning power relations and practices in the society" (p. 117) (*democracy, socialism, totalitarianism, laissez-faire*). The category POWER OTHER is a residual category that contains all entries indicating a concern with power but not defined by any of the other POWER subcategories[35] (*concession, conformity, response, diplomatic*).

Among the transaction subcategories, the category ARENAS contains the names of political places and environments except for the names of nation-

---

[34] An interesting question asks why certain categories are well represented by entries in the English language while entries for other categories are missing (cf. Whorf, 1956). Questions of this kind raise important issues for the sociologies of language and knowledge and also have implications for the foundations of culture analysis itself.

[35] Similar residual categories have also been used for other subcategories to secure logical exclusivity.

states (*Africa, realm, territory, nonaligned*). Entries in the category POWER GAINS denote transactions in the power process resulting in an increase in power (*appoint, assert, defend, take*). Conversely, entries in the category POWER LOSSES denote deprivations in this process (*block, restrict, resign, suppress*). The subcategory POWER ENDS is composed of entries showing a concern with the intrinsic values or goals in the power process (*ambition, leadership, persuade, prevail*). The category POWER AUTHORITATIVE PARTICIPANTS consists of a list of individual and collective actors in the power process, each being able to make or enforce authoritative decisions (*administrator, agency, governor, senate*). The category POWER PARTICIPANTS includes all actors in the power process not defined as either POWER AUTHORITATIVE PARTICIPANTS, ARENAS, or NATIONS[36] (*actor, candidate, faction, volunteer*).

Finally all entries defined in any of the above subcategories are also classified under a summary category, POWER TOTAL.[37]

Among the RECTITUDE subcategories there are two substantive categories and three transaction categories. The category ETHICS includes all those rectitude values that invoke in the final analysis the social order and its demands as a justifying ground (*conscience, sincerity, trust, wicked*). Conversely, the category RELIGIOUS includes all those entries that invoke either transcendental, mystical, or supernatural grounds (*awe, church, holy, soul*). Among the possible transactions concerning rectitude, the dictionary distinguishes among RECTITUDE GAINS (*pardon, reparation, forgive, worship*), LOSSES (*convict, sin, denounce, implicate*), and ENDS (*almighty, forgiveness, virtue, ought*). The meaning of these concepts follows from previous definitions.

In regard to RESPECT, the dictionary distinguishes between two transaction categories, RESPECT GAINS (*congratulation, admire, complement, honor*) and LOSSES (*admission, insinuation, shame, ridicule*), and a residual category, RESPECT OTHER. The latter contains all entries denoting respect concerns not otherwise defined and in so doing describes largely a concern with substantive respect values (*maturity, unworthy, vulgar, noble*).

The dictionary categorized AFFECTION entries into three transaction subcategories: GAINS (*caress, engage, love, sympathize*), LOSSES (*alienation, divorce, impersonal, alone*), and PARTICIPANTS. AFFECTION PARTICIPANTS contains the names of recognizable roles in the pursuit of this value (*brother, kin, humanity, mistress*). The remaining entries that suggest concern with substantive affection concerns are grouped into the residual category AFFECTION OTHER (*amicable, ardor, nest, tender*).

---

[36]Where the category NATIONS includes the names of all the nations in the world not otherwise classified.

[37]Similar summary categories were created for each of the other seven minor categories. The rationale of this procedure and the ensuing problems of double classification were discussed before.

Welfare Values

There are four welfare categories. WEALTH is defined as "income [or] services of goods and persons accruing to the person in any way whatever" (p. 55). This category includes all references to production resources and the accumulation or exchange of goods and services. All references to "the health and safety of the organism" (p. 55) belong to the category WELL-BEING.

ENLIGHTENMENT denotes a concern with "knowledge, insight and information concerning personal and cultural relations" (p. 55). Therefore, all entries denoting and describing academic matters and the processes that generate and communicate information, thought, and understanding belong to this category. SKILL is "proficiency in any practice whatever, whether in arts or crafts, trade or profession" (p. 55). Entries thus classified exemplify a concern with the mastery of the physical environment and the skills and tools used to that purpose.

The WEALTH category contains three subcategories. WEALTH PARTICIPANTS contains the generic names of the trades and professions involved in the wealth process (*banker, corporation, employee, profiteer*). References to the pursuit of wealth constitute the category WEALTH TRANSACTIONS (*auction, buy, loan, repaid*). Finally, all remaining references to this concept constitute the residual category WEALTH OTHER. Again, most of its entries denote substantive concerns (*agriculture, corn, oil, tariff*).

Within the WELL-BEING category, the dictionary distinguishes among two substantive subcategories and three transaction subcategories. PHYSICAL WELL-BEING contains the references to physical health and the issues of life and death (*blood, clinic, nutrition, wounds*). PSYCHOLOGICAL WELL-BEING, on the other hand, contains references to happiness and other preferred or avoided psychic states (*anxiety, excitement, sad, unhappiness*). Among the possible WELL-BEING transactions, WELL-BEING GAINS (*amuse, comfort, heal, clothe*), LOSSES (*depression, infirmity, low-income, wound*), and PARTICIPANTS (*alcoholic, counselor, dentist, victim*) were selected as defining categories.

ENLIGHTENMENT consists of four transaction subcategories and one residual and largely substantive subcategory. The former include GAINS (*detection, define, see, trace*), LOSSES (*deception, forget, misunderstand, perplex*), PARTICIPANTS (*advisors, faculty, media, spokesman*), and ENDS. The ENDS subcategory contains entries denoting the pursuit of intrinsic enlightenment ideas (*ask, observer, reflect, think*).

The SKILL category has one transaction subcategory, SKILL PARTICIPANTS. It contains the generic names of actors specialized in the pursuit, production, and transmission of skill values (*artist, inventor, manager, technician*). AESTHETICS is a special substantive subcategory containing references to a special proficiency: the pursuit of beauty and cultural creativity as a mode of mastering the physical and natural environment (*architecture, music, graceful, poetic*). Finally, the category SKILL OTHER contains all entries showing concern with skill not otherwise defined (*failure, labor, compose, unattractive*).

As in the case of the four deference values, the entries in each of the four welfare categories are also placed in a TOTAL category, such as WEALTH TOTAL.

Remaining Categories

There are 12 general transaction indicators, most of which were defined before. Of the three types of transaction categories, TRANSACTION GAINS includes all entries denoting an exchange whereby the actor of the transaction will gain in the process. However, the entries do not reveal the specifics of the exchange (*acquisition, inducement, grant, reward*). Conversely, for TRANSACTION LOSSES, the actor will lose (*accident, fall, hinder, upset*). Finally, the category TRANSACTION is a residual category. Its entries do not suggest either gain or loss but merely the process of exchange (*sort, throw, transmit, wipe*).

There are six categories of actors. The category NATIONS includes the names of all nation-states. The category SELF includes the first-person-singular pronouns; AUDIENCE, the second-person-singular and -plural pronouns; OTHERS, the third-person-singular and -plural pronouns; SELVES, the first-person-plural pronouns.[38] The category PARTICIPANTS, finally, is a residual category containing the generic names of all actors not otherwise defined (*client, women, men, nobody*).

The dictionary contains one unusual category: ANOMIE. This category usually shows a negation of value preference; people consider one value as good or as bad as any other. Frequent usage of this category therefore indicates a loss, or at least a lack of, value preference.[39]

The categories so far discussed allow inferences to be made about substantive preferences and about concerns with various parts of transactions. But what about different and changing feelings toward such preferences and concerns? To assess these feelings, the dictionary includes five categories of sentiment. POSITIVE AFFECT is a list of entries denoting positive feelings, acceptance, appreciation, and emotional support (*favorable, thank, warm,* and *welcome*). Conversely, the category NEGATIVE AFFECT includes entries denoting negative feelings and emotional rejection (*cry, awful, pernicious,* and *disgust*). The category NOT includes entries that show the

---

[38]These pronoun categories were adapted from the General Inquirer (Stone *et al.*, 1966, pp. 144, 176–177).

[39]ANOMIE contains words such as *anarchy, disillusion,* and *dishearten*. Thus far, this category has been of little use. Actual documents rarely contain words that fit this concept. There are relatively few words in the category to begin with. In addition, we suspect that collective actors seldom acknowledge the possibility of anomie since their continued existence depends in part on the continuity of culture. Culture, as we noted in the first two chapters, entails preference.

denial of one sort or another (*no, neither, nothing,* and *deny*). SURE indicates a feeling of sureness, certainty, and firmness (*fact, particular, unmistakable,* and *very*), whereas the category IF includes entries denoting feelings of uncertainty, doubt, and vagueness (*chance, doubt, perhaps, seem*).

The three last sentiment categories make it possible to extend the range of inquiry into the feeling tone of communications beyond mere acceptance and rejection.[40] Therefore, the classification of an entry in one or another value category (rather than sentiment category) has no affective implications whatever; the entry does not by itself suggest acceptance of the value category because it is thus classified. This explains why, for instance, both the entries *poverty* and *wealth* are classified as WEALTH OTHER and the entries *death* and *health* are classified as WELL-BEING PHYSICAL.

Time and place are important dimensions of all human actions (valuation not excluded) (Catton, 1966). To preserve this information, the dictionary contains a general SPACE-TIME category[41] (*long-range, next, north,* and *toward*).

Finally the dictionary includes three residual categories. The category N-TYPE WORDS contains entries with no semantic meaning. Most of the entries in this category are high-frequency words with little meaning if taken individually. Examples are *a, about, am, an, and, as,* and *at*. The category UNDEFINABLE includes entries that have no value implications or that have value meanings that the present category scheme cannot define (*prohibitive, quaint, unreal,* and *cling*). The category UNDEFINED includes words with value implications that vary from context to context and that, despite disambiguation routines, present procedures cannot assess reliably (*order, maximum, molecular,* and *visual*).

[40]These three categories were adapted from Stone *et al.* (1966, pp. 175–176, 180).

[41]Were the dictionary to be revised, we would probably divide this category in two separate categories, one for space and one for time. Such a division would increase the precision and semantic validity of subsequent text classification.

2

Studies in
Culture Dynamics

3

The Wheels of Time and the Interdependence of Culture Change in America[1]

Most studies of culture are purely descriptive. They reveal a never-ending fascination with far and distant places, while in ethnographic hands even the near and commonplace becomes exotic. The present study's concerns are of a different kind. They are causal and functional so that descriptions are but a means to further ends. Therefore, this study asks, what are the causes and consequences of culture change for thought and action? And, in the course of these changes, what is its form? Is there progress, decay, or, as the ancients thought, merely fluctuations? These are questions not about the matching of actions to ageless ideals, but about fluctuations in society's concern with these ideals themselves. Consequently, this study asks, do collective conceptions of the good society progress, becoming ever more civilized, or do they decline? Whether progressing or declining, the additional questions arise, Why and to what effect?

In examining these questions, this inquiry arrives at the conclusion that

[1]The research of this chapter was funded by a National Science Foundation grant to the Yale Political Data Program and by a contract from ARPA, Behavioral Sciences, monitored by the Office of Naval Research. This essay reports on a larger endeavor once directed by Harold D. Lasswell. Donald R. Ploch suggested the sine curve detrending; Hayward Alker, Jr. and Albert K. Cohen reviewed and added to the substantive interpretations. Mary Frank Gaston, Kathleen Bayes, John R. Hall, Robert H. Randolph, Earl D. Sacerdoti, Susan Johnson, and Holly Swanson offered assistance in computations and other research procedures. Namenwirth (1973) published an earlier version of this contribution. For more recent references to the K-cycle, see Chapter 5.

J. Zvi Namenwirth wrote this chapter.

the history of culture change in America is neither progressive nor regressive, but cyclical. Accordingly, the study tries to demonstrate the plausibility of this assertion. During the investigation, it was observed that the various content categories demonstrated two cycles rather than one. Each cycle is of a distinctive length; the longer cycles are usually about 152 years and the shorter cycles usually about 48 years long. These two cycles occur frequently in the same content category, one superimposed on the other. Furthermore, cycles in one content category are systematically related to those in others because they do not peak and bottom out at once but in a determined and interpretable sequence of time. This sequence is depicted in the wheel of time.[2] In fact, there are two wheels: The long-term wheel summarizes the time sequence of peaks in the longer cycles; the short-term wheel summarizes that sequence in the shorter cycles. As noted, each cycle depicts the waxing and waning preoccupations with a particular culture concern. This chapter attempts to interpret at length the meaning of both wheels, discussing how the increase in some culture concerns always precedes an increase in others. Finally, it concludes with a discussion of possible causes and consequences of findings and interpretations.

Concerning the longer cycles, a society-wide problem-solving mechanism produces the observed sequence of peaking concerns. This mechanism first articulates the founding ideas of the society. Subsequently, it disputes the political infrastructure and constitutional arrangements. Next, it confronts questions of a preferred economic infrastructure. Finally, it questions the unequal distribution of society's resources with arguments about a new dispensation. At that point, the same sequence starts all over again.

Concerning the shorter cycles, a 50-year contraction and expansion in the economy produces the sequence of peaking concerns in the shorter cycles. When the economy bottoms out, content articulations are Parochial. When the economy expands, articulations in platforms turn liberal. During the height of the boom period, these documents are preoccupied with Cosmopolitan concerns. Finally, during the downturn of the economy, they become increasingly conservative in their orientations. At that point, the economy again enters a depressed phase and political articulations return to very Parochial preoccupations.

In conclusion, two very distinct types of dynamics seem to produce the two kinds of cycles: More ideational dynamics create the longer-term

---

[2]The year that a content category peaks is marked on the rim of the wheel. Categories that peak in the same year are therefore placed at the same point. Categories that peak together within a few years "behave" similarly and constitute a theme. Categories that locate on the opposite side of the rim dip when the former peak. They "behave" in an opposite manner and constitute the polar-opposite theme of an underlying issue. The sequence of peaking concerns in all variables follows around the rim of the wheel in clock fashion. The details are further explored below and in Chapter 9.

problem-solving cycle, and material dynamics cause the shorter-term political orientations cycle.

ASSESSMENT OF CULTURAL PREOCCUPATIONS

To assess changes in priorities over time, American Republican and Democratic party platforms from 1844 through 1964[3] were content-analyzed using procedures described by Stone and associates (1966). The use of content analysis is predicated on two assumptions. First, the differential occurrence of a content category is an indication of the differential preoccupation with the concern classified by that category; and second, the relative concern thus measured is an appropriate measure of its relative priority in the total scheme of each and all documents. The content analysis, then, produces a profile of frequency changes concerning 73 categories.[4] What are these categories? Since not all categories are of equal importance, the pertinent categories will be discussed in greater detail in the report of the findings. This and the following paragraphs offer only a more general overview. About 95% of the words that occur in party platforms were entered in a dictionary, and these words were defined by one or more of the 73 categories.

Using both this instrument and computers, the full text of the platforms was matched with the dictionary (or word classifications), and this matching produced the noted frequency profiles. Even if agreeing that these frequencies may show changing preferences in party platforms, the reader may well question the relevance of such data. Why bother with party platforms?[5]

The choice of party platforms to assess magnitude and direction of culture change in American society seems justified for the following reasons (Namenwirth and Lasswell, 1970):

- The two-party system in the United States is competitive in most states of the Union—that is, the parties compete in one electoral market for the sympathies of various interests. The planks therefore contain the platform committee's best guesses about policies that will maximize the party's appeal to the electorate, and, to survive, parties must guess

---

[3]In 1844, 1848, and 1852, there were no Republican platforms since the Republican party did not exist before 1856. For the first three campaigns, the research used the Whig platforms because the Whigs are in many respects the precursors of the Republican party.

[4]See Chapter 2 for a discussion of all categories. Thirty-one categories were eliminated from the analysis because of low frequencies or poor distribution.

[5]Chapter 6 gives additional reasons. Benson (1961) and Klingberg (1952) studied party platforms for reasons other than the assessment of culture changes.

their voters' preferences correctly more often than not. Consequently, the content of party platforms is especially suitable for the study of concerns of the entire society.

- Party platforms not only reflect predominant issues, but they also create or modify orientations by their presentation and the ensuing public disputes during election campaigns.
- Because parties and party platforms are features of many other societies, their examination allows for cross-national comparisons.

DATA AND CYCLES

Basic data of this investigation are as follows: For each Democratic and Republican platform and for each campaign from 1844 to 1964 (31 campaigns), there are 73 observations, with one observation for each content category (or variable). Each observation is the frequency of that category in the particular platform. This frequency is then expressed as a percentage of words in that category of all words in the document, since this manipulation controls for the fact that campaign documents are of varying lengths. A plot of the 31 observations for the category WEALTH TOTAL[6] (a summary measure of all wealth subcategories) over the years 1844–1964 indicates that the concern with wealth varies a good deal from campaign to campaign. Figures 3.1 and 3.2 illustrate this point.

These same figures show that usually the concern with WEALTH is low in the 1840s and 1850s; it increases over the next 80 years, to decrease again after 1932. This longer-term cyclical tendency is estimated by a sine curve (the dotted line in Figures 3.1 and 3.2). As will be noted, the actual observations do not lie on the dotted line (i.e., the sine curve estimates but does not perfectly fit the observations); the actual observations are often rather removed therefrom. If we plot the deviations from the dotted line (residuals) over time (Figure 3.3, which represents these deviations for the Democratic platform), then we note a secondary cyclical trend that has a more limited swing (or amplitude) and a shorter time span. This secondary cycle is also described by a sine curve that varies about the first one, and these secondary curves are represented by the drawn line in Figures 3.1 and 3.2. In conclusion, two cyclical trends seem to describe, if not operate on, changing concern with WEALTH in American platforms. Also, similar cycles tend to operate in most other categories as well.

Plots of the data revealed provisional outlines of a curve in each

---

[6]Category names are capitalized throughout. Chapter 2 describes the architecture of the content category scheme and provides definitions for all these categories. To aid the reader, most definitions in this chapter appear again in footnotes.

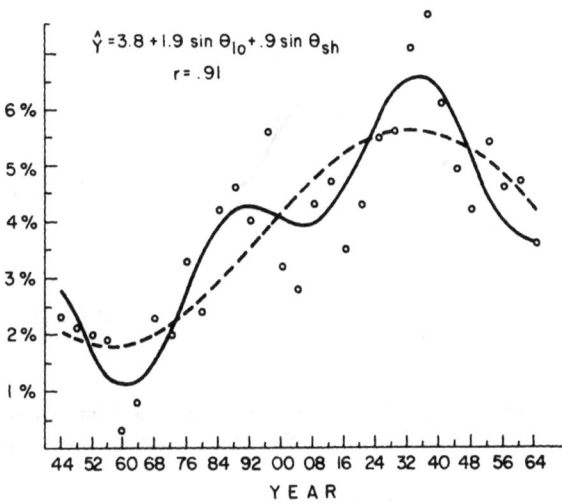

FIGURE 3.1. **Two Superimposed Sine Curves Fitting Percent Concern with References to** WEALTH **in Democratic Party Platforms 1844–1964.**

category and, therefore, the amplitude, wavelength, and year of maximum (or minimum) of each of these curves. These first estimates were subsequently tested and adjusted by an iterative computer program. The technical details are reported elsewhere (Namenwirth and Weber, 1979; Chapter 4), and here it suffices to note that a particular sine curve is considered an acceptable estimate of the underlying cyclical trend if it correlates with the data at $r = .45$ or better. This conservative decision rule is not completely arbitrary since it provided a unique solution only here.

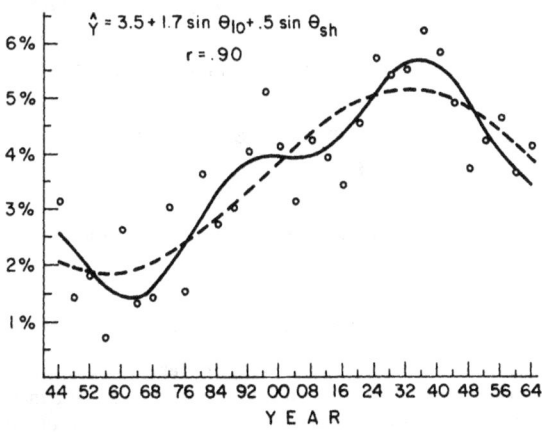

FIGURE 3.2. **Two Superimposed Sine Curves Fitting Percent Concern with References to** WEALTH **in Republican Platforms 1844–1964.**

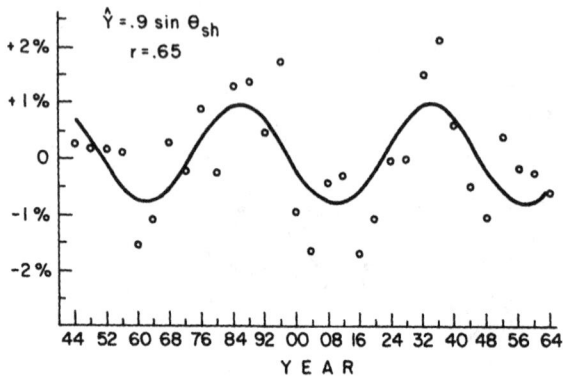

FIGURE 3.3. **Short-Term Sine Curve Fitting Deviations from Long-Term Cycle Describing References to** WEALTH **in Democratic Party Platforms 1844–1964.**

In a similar manner, if a shorter-term cycle correlated .40 with the data, this showed the existence of a secondary curve.[7] Of the 42 categories, about 80% displayed some type of cycle. The particulars are presented in Table 3.1.

To state that sine curves approximate a good part of change is not just to say that these changes display fluctuations, but that they display fluctuations of a particular kind.[8] First, they fluctuate around an average level of concern that is constant over time. Second, the magnitude of these fluctuations (or amplitude) is also constant over time. Third, the time span of each wavelength is constant as well. For the primary curve, the data, therefore, suggest static equilibrium. For the secondary curve, the findings suggest a moving equilibrium, since the curve varies about an average level that itself is subject to constant change—that is, the primary curve.

In this manner, one can conceive of all concerns and their changes as consisting of longer-term curves, shorter-term curves, and detrended fluctuations. These three component parts have their own causes and dynamics. In the remainder of this chapter, I will discuss the fit, interdependent structure and meaning, and explanation of the various curves for long- and short-term changes.

[7]Considering the different margins of measurement error, it seemed appropriate to lower the cutoff point for the shorter-term cycle.

[8]In more precise terms:

$$y = a + b \sin \theta_{\text{long}} + c \sin \theta_{\text{short}} + e$$

whereby y is the level of concern at each campaign and for each particular platform and category; a is a constant assessing the average level of concern for that category during all campaigns; b is a constant assessing the amplitude of the fluctuations of the longer-term curve; θ is a simple function of time—that is, $(\pi t/C)$ where t is time (year of platform) and C is number of years in the cycle; c is a constant assessing the amplitude of the fluctuations of the shorter-term sine curves; θ_{short} is the same as θ_{long}; and e is an error term that can be considered detrended, so that its fluctuations are random about time.

TABLE 3.1
Number of Categories with and without Longer- and Shorter-Term Sine Curves in Democratic and Republican Platforms

	Democratic	Republican
Both curves (superimposed)	16	16
Longer-term curves only	14	9
Shorter-term curves only	4	8
Neither curve	8	9
Total	42	42

THE FIT OF LONG-TERM CYCLES

Table 3.2 presents all of the content categories that fit a longer-term sine curve and four characteristics of each curve: (1) the party—Democratic or Republican; (2) wavelength (or time span) in number of years; (3) the peak, or year when the curve is at its maximum; (4) r^2, a measure of goodness of fit. The table shows that in the long run, concern with the category OTHERS in the Republican platform, for instance, is at its height in the year 1808, and that this will again be the case in the year 2040 (in other words, 1808 + 232). The longer-term cycle explains about 64% of the variance in references to the category. In other words, the curve fairly well describes the varying usage of this concept over time, since the variance explained would equal 100% if it were to describe the variation perfectly, and 0% if it were not to describe this variation at all. Even so, there was no party platform in 1808, and the statement about the platform in 2040 is only a projection into the future. The estimation of longer-term change in concerns is therefore often based on extrapolation.

In the Republican platforms, about three-fifths of the content categories, and more than seven-tenths of the categories in the Democratic platforms, were estimated by the longer-term sine curve. Approximately one-fourth of the categories did not fit a longer-term sine curve in either the Democratic or Republican party platforms; the details are given in Table 3.3. One point, however, needs to be stressed. Of the 55 cycles, 23 curves occur similarly in all or most aspects in both Democratic and Republican platforms. This form of replication in nearly 84% of all cases certainly increases confidence that these cycles are not just a methodological artifact.

Unfortunately, the 55 longer-term sine curves do not all have the same wavelength, and this complicates their interpretation. Although the modal wavelength is 152 years, the shortest cycle runs 104 years, while the longest lasts 232 years—or more than twice as long. Table 3.4 presents the specifics.

TABLE 3.2
Selected Characteristics of 55 Longer-Term Sine Curves

Content category and party*	Peak	Wavelength (in years)	r^2
1. *Others*	1808	232	0.64
2. Undefined	1816	184	0.46
3. Rectitude Ends	1820	232	0.37
4. *Rectitude Ends*	1860	168	0.43
5. *Respect Gains*	1864	168	0.46
6. Rectitude Total	1864	152	0.40
7. Affection Total	1864	152	0.30
8. *Respect Total*	1868	152	0.49
9. *Rectitude Total*	1868	136	0.45
10. *Affection Total*	1872	120	0.38
11. Respect Total	1872	152	0.21
12. Respect Gains	1880	136	0.32
13. Power Authoritative Participant	1880	184	0.28
14. Power Participant	1884	136	0.22
15. Power Authoritative	1888	168	0.35
16. *Power Authoritative Participant*	1896	152	0.18
17. Positive Affect	1924	152	0.62
18. *Wealth Participant*	1928	136	0.58
19. *Skill Total*	1928	184	0.53
20. Wealth Transaction	1928	184	0.34
21. *Nations*	1928	184	0.24
22. *Wealth Total*	1932	152	0.73
23. *Wealth Other*	1932	152	0.73
24. Wealth Other	1932	152	0.69
25. Wealth Total	1932	152	0.69
26. *Skill Other*	1932	184	0.51
27. Wealth Participant	1932	136	0.46
28. *Wealth Transaction*	1936	152	0.32
29. *Transaction Gains*	1940	184	0.54
30. Skill Total	1944	152	0.67
31. Selves	1944	168	0.65
32. *Selves*	1944	184	0.30
33. Skill Other	1948	152	0.69
34. *Well-being Total*	1948	136	0.34
35. Transaction	1948	168	0.26
36. *Transaction*	1948	184	0.25
37. Well-being Total	1952	136	0.68
38. *Well-being Physical*	1952	152	0.32
39. Well-being Physical	1956	152	0.74
40. *Means*	1956	168	0.70
41. Transaction Gains	1956	184	0.65
42. Means	1956	168	0.46
43. Power Conflict	1960	104	0.23
44. Ends	1964	168	0.85
45. *Ends*	1964	200	0.71

TABLE 3.2. (cont.)

Content category and party*	Peak	Wavelength (in years)	r^2
46. Power Gains	1968	232	0.48
47. Well-being Participant	1968	168	0.42
48. Well-being Losses	1968	152	0.34
49. Enlightenment Total	1972	152	0.28
50. *Power Cooperation*	1972	152	0.21
51. *Power Conflict*	1976	152	0.34
52. Power Cooperation	1988	152	0.45
53. Power Doctrine	1988	184	0.25
54. *Power Gains*	1996	216	0.36
55. *Power Doctrine*	2008	232	0.41

*Republican Party Platform categories italicized.

The interpretation assumed that the true wavelengths of all of these sine curves is 152 years and that their estimated deviations are because of measurement error. Although bold, this assumption is more parsimonious than the assumption that the wavelengths of the cycles vary from category to category. Therefore, we standardized the wavelength of all categories to 152 years and transformed the peak estimates accordingly.[9] In most cases,

TABLE 3.3
Frequency of Content Categories with and without Longer-Term Cyclical Change by Party

Republican platform categories	Democratic platform categories		
	With cyclical change	Without cyclical change	N
With cyclical change	23	2	25
Without cyclical change	7	10	17
N	30	12	42

[9]Peaks were measured in number of years removed from 1932; the transformed peak equals the original peak times 152 divided by the original wavelength. In this formula, the year 1932 was chosen since many curves peak at that year; most of these curves have a wavelength of 152 years; 1932 is the median year of peaks ordered chronologically.

TABLE 3.4
**Distribution of Longer-Term Sine
Curves by Wavelength**

Wavelength	N
104 years	1
120 years	1
136 years	7
152 years	20
168 years	9
184 years	11
200 years	1
232 years	5

this transformation does not greatly affect the original peak estimates; nevertheless, it makes the following interpretation only approximate.

THE STRUCTURAL INTERDEPENDENCE OF LONG-TERM CULTURE CHANGE

Figure 3.4, a circle, presents the long wheel of time and the internal relationships among the longer-term sine curves. The relationships among these content categories are depicted graphically by plotting the location of the year of maximal concern (peak) on the rim of the circle in the figure. Its circumference represents a 152-year period, or one complete cycle. Each labeled point on this circumference represents the year(s) where concern with a particular category reaches its maximum value. Although not shown on the figure, concern with this category reaches a minimum during the year represented by the point on the circle directly across from the labeled point (or a half-cycle later). Thus, the rim of the "wheel" portrays a 152-year sequence of rising and falling concern with various content categories. Also, categories that rise and fall together will locate close together on the rim of the wheel: they constitute a theme or issue. Conversely, the categories that locate diagonally across from the former constitute the opposite theme or issue. Finally, the two opposite themes will define an underlying dimension or dilemma.

In that fashion, a category that peaks before another precedes it in a clockwise manner. Additionally, the peaks of Democratic platform categories and cycles appear on the outside of the rim, while such peaks of Republican platform categories appear on the inside. Accordingly, to the right of the top of the wheel—that is, the year 1932—one finds sine curves

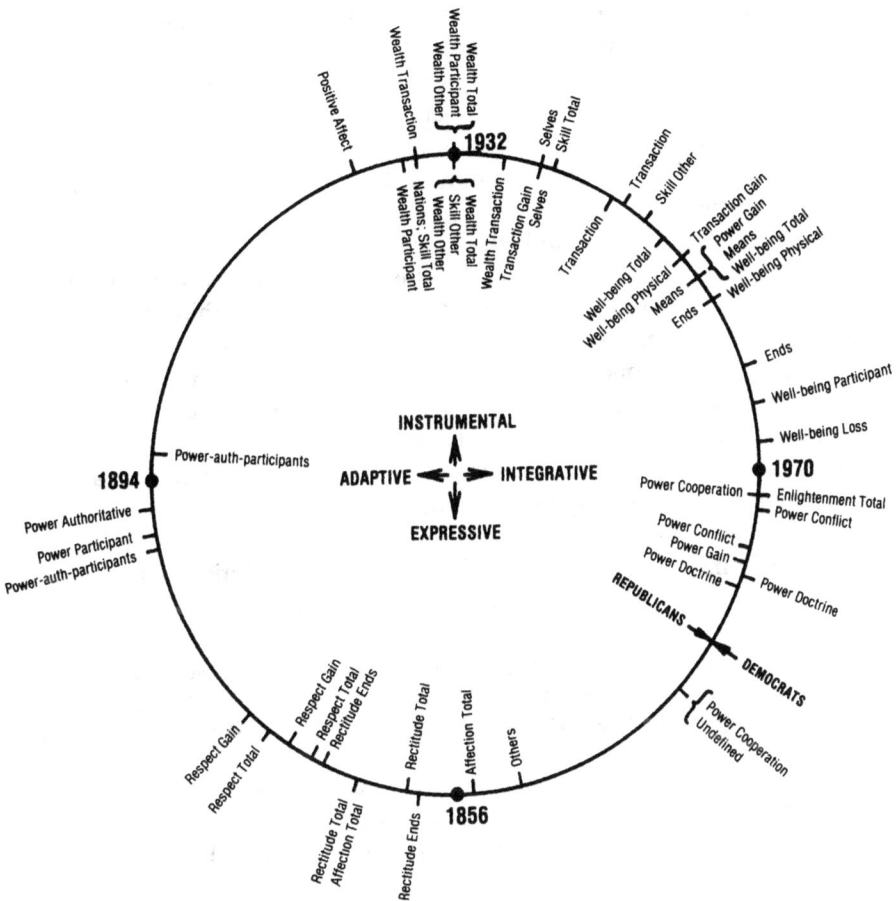

FIGURE 3.4. The Internal Structure of Long-Term Value Changes (Cycle lengths set at 152 years, variable origins).

that peak in later years; to the left one finds the curves that peaked in previous years.[10]

Visual inspection reveals that the entire circle represents a 152-year sequence of peaking and dropping concerns with a variety of indicators.[11] For instance, while long-term concern with the category WEALTH peaks

[10]As Weber (in press) notes, this presentation of the processional structure of culture change abstracts from other features of the discovered cycles. For instance, it does not present the variable magnitudes (or swings). Since a cycle's amplitude is a function of the category's mean (or equilibrium state), and since the latter is a function first of English word usage, the cultural implications of varying amplitudes across different content categories remain yet unknown.

[11]Factor analysis produced a very similar sequence and two factors that explain 98% of the variance among longer-term curves.

around 1932, long-term concern with the categories AFFECTION, RESPECT, and RECTITUDE peak half a cycle earlier or later (76 years); in other words, where concern with WEALTH is at its peak, preoccupation with AFFECTION and RESPECT is at a low.[12] Also, an increasing concern with wealth over time leads to a fixed decrease in concern with RESPECT, and vice versa. An understanding of these dynamics requires a description of the sequence of peaking concerns around the wheel of time.

Around 1856, concern with the categories OTHERS, AFFECTION TOTAL, RECTITUDE TOTAL, RESPECT TOTAL, and several of their subcategories is at a maximum. The category OTHERS contains all references to the third-person-plural pronoun (*they, their, theirs, themselves*). In party platforms, such references often stand for a concern with the "other" party, but more often with people in general, and their wishes and qualities. A frequent usage of this category invokes a distinction between leadership and the masses, the "they" and all those without a name, and it therefore indicates an elitist orientation to social reality and the political order.

The category AFFECTION contains references to love and friendship, and in party platforms, such references often show an association between devotion to family life and loyal patriotism. For instance:

Resolved that, with our Republican Fathers [AFFECTION PARTICIPANT], we hold it to be a self-evident truth, that all men are endowed with the inalienable right to life, liberty, and the pursuit of happiness. [Porter and Johnson, 1961, p. 27]

In party platforms, the category RESPECT includes the words *honor, equality*, and *inequality*. The category RECTITUDE contains recurrent words, such as *ought* and *must*, that suggest a call for natural duty and principles. To illustrate:

We recognize the equality [RESPECT OTHERS] of all men before the law and hold that it is the duty [ENDS] of the government in its dealings with the people to mete out equal and exact justice [RECTITUDE ETHICS] to all, whatever nativity, race, color or persuasion, religion [RECTITUDE RELIGIOUS] or politics. [Porter and Johnson, 1961, p. 41]

Slavery was the preponderant issue in these years. Policy preferences on this score divided the parties and changed over time—the Democrats

---

[12]WEALTH TRANSACTION contains references to the pursuit of wealth; WEALTH PARTICIPANTS includes the generic names of trades and professions; WEALTH OTHER, a residual category, contains all of the remaining references to wealth; and WEALTH TOTAL is a summary category. AFFECTION TOTAL is a summary category that contains all references to love and friendship. RESPECT GAINS contains references that denote the conferral of respect (e.g., the verbs *admire, appreciate*, and *honor*). RECTITUDE ENDS contains references indicating that the sentence expresses concern with ethical matters, whatever the substance of this concern. The words *ought, must, principle*, and *virtue* are examples. RECTITUDE TOTAL is a summary category, including all references to moral values, such as virtue or goodness.

favored the extension of slavery into the territories, and the Republicans opposed it. However, our findings pertain to similarities, not differences, between the two parties, and the mutual concern with RECTITUDE shows that whatever the substantive policy differences, there was a great and similar concern with the justification of policy preferences. Also, at that time the terms of justification were largely rectitudinous.

In the 1890s, concern with RECTITUDE, RESPECT, and AFFECTION declined, while concern with POWER AUTHORITATIVE PARTICIPANT and POWER AUTHORITATIVE was at a peak.[13] These categories contain many words, but most frequent are references to the federal government and the Constitution. At first sight, it seems as if over the past 37 years the political issues remained the same, that is, the relationship between the states and the federal government. However, the justification of policy preferences changed in this time span from ethical to legal grounds, from substantive to formal justice, from traditional to legal. To illustrate:

> During all these years the Democratic party has resisted the tendency of selfish interest to the centralization of governmental [POWER AUTHORITATIVE] power established by the founders of this republic of republics. Under its guidance and teachings the great principle of local self-government has found its best expression in the maintenance of the right of the states and in its assertion of the necessity of limiting the general government [POWER AUTHORITATIVE PARTICIPANT] to the exercise of the power granted by the constitution [POWER AUTHORITATIVE] of the United States. [Porter and Johnson, 1961, p. 97]

On further inquiry, one notes that the central issue is no longer the relationship between federal and state government, but the role of the federal government in the creation and maintenance of the economic infrastructure of an industrial society. The parties are in conflict about this role concerning tariffs, transportation, politics (domestic and international, e.g., a canal through the isthmus), homesteading, banking and monetary policy, antitrust legislation, immigration, and taxation. Yet the essential conclusion remains the same. Divergent policy preferences may appear from party to party and from campaign to campaign, but the justification of the divergent preferences is in very similar legalistic constructs.

By 1932, the role of the federal government is much less disputed. The party program does not elaborate on justification, but simply states its preferences in economic policy. The peaking concern with WEALTH and its subcategories suggest this finding. Thus, one reads in the Democratic platform:

[13] POWER AUTHORITATIVE PARTICIPANT includes all references to governmental actors in the power process. POWER AUTHORITATIVE includes entries that suggest a concern with, or a description and invocation of, formal and legitimate power.

We favor the maintenance of national credit [WEALTH OTHER] by a federal budget [WEALTH OTHER] annually balanced on the basis of accurate executive estimates within revenues [WEALTH OTHER], raised by a system of taxation [WEALTH OTHER], levied on the principle of ability to pay [WEALTH TRANSACTION]. We advocate a sound currency [WEALTH OTHER] to be preserved at all hazards and an international monetary [WEALTH OTHER] conference called on the invitation of our government to consider the rehabilitation of silver [WEALTH OTHER] and related questions. [Porter and Johnson, 1961, p. 331]

And the Republican platform states:

Generally in economic [WEALTH OTHER] matters we pledge the Republican party: 1. To maintain unimpaired the national credit [WEALTH OTHER]. 2. To defend and preserve a sound currency [WEALTH OTHER]. 3. To stand steadfastly by the principle of a balanced budget [WEALTH OTHER]. [Porter and Johnson 1961, p. 350]

First, there is a near-total absence of justification of policy preferences. Second, a preoccupation with the material and technological (SKILL) well-being of the nation is a characteristic for the platforms at this time. This is further confirmed by the frequent references to the category SELVES.[14] In party platforms, the use of we, us, ourselves, and so forth often reveals a denial of status differentiation, either within the party or within the nation.

Typical for platforms in the 1950s and 1960s is an orientation toward the future rather than the past. This is revealed by maximum preoccupation with the category TRANSACTION.[15]

We shall [TRANSACTION] insist [TRANSACTION] on businesslike and efficient administration of all foreign aid....We shall [TRANSACTION] erect [TRANSACTION] our foreign policy on the basis of friendly firmness....We shall [TRANSACTION] pursue [TRANSACTION] a consistent foreign policy....We shall [TRANSACTION] protect the future. [Porter and Johnson, 1961, p. 453]

Frequent references to MEANS and ENDS with such words as plan, strategy, future, project, and development point in the same direction. In this framework, there is also maximum concern with health and WELL-BEING in general.[16]

Projecting the findings, which originated in the late 1960s, into the future, the major concerns of the 1970s should be again of a different order. Since the 1930s, society was the object of concern; in the 1970s, we predicted, the major preoccupation should be with conflicting groups and individuals. Frequent words in the subcategory POWER COOPERATION are

[14]SELVES contains all first-person-plural pronouns.

[15]TRANSACTION contains references to transactions without specifying the specific value substance.

[16]MEANS contain references showing that values pursued are considered Instrumental. ENDS contains words denoting that concerns pursued are intrinsic rather than instrumental. WELL-BEING PHYSICAL contains references to physical health and issues of life and death. WELL-BEING TOTAL is a summary category denoting the health and safety of the organism.

agreement, coalition, compromise, cooperative, organization, solidarity, and *unity*; and, in the subcategory POWER CONFLICT, *agitation, anarchy, breakdown, disagreement, disunity, fight, hostility, rebellion, resistance,* and *revolution.*[17] It seemed that problems of the distribution of power and other social resources will be the major issue at that time.[18]

THE STRUCTURE OF LONG-TERM CULTURE CHANGE

Thus far, we have merely described the nature of concerns around the wheel of time while noting that first, there is some preoccupation with all of the selected issues at all times, and second, that relative concern with various issues rises and falls in a definite sequence, indicating an underlying structure of change. In other words, there appears a unitary order to long-term culture change, and the question is: What is the meaning of this order?

Contrasting and comparing the various preoccupations, we observed already a maximum concern with ethical and moral principles in the 1860s. These concerns seem typical issues for a more traditional community. In the 1890s, however, the concerns differ, indicating a preoccupation with the allocation of resources and more generally with the problems of power centralization. In the 1930s, there occurred a maximum of attention to questions of economy, industry, and technology, and therefore with the problems of instrumentation. In contrast, in the 1970s, there arises a great involvement with the distribution (rather than concentration) of power.

The order of culture change has some further intriguing qualities. From about 1837 through 1913, justification seemed the major issue, or, in Weberian terms, it seemed centered on an "ethic of ultimate ends" (Weber, 1946, p. 120). From 1913 through 1989, in contrast, concerns appear more instrumental. It is as if the goals of society and organized politics are seen as already given and the choice is one of efficient means. Again, in Weberian terms, issues in that period seem centered on an "ethic of responsibility."

Furthermore, during the phase of justification, the concern is first substantive and raises matters of justice, honor, and loyalty. Subsequently, the terms of justification become more formal and legalistic rather than substantive. In the Instrumental phase, finally, the choice of politics is first collectivist, dealing with problems of the nation and especially its economy.

---

[17]POWER COOPERATION denotes the integration of diversified operations or diversified perspectives. POWER CONFLICT contains entries that describe and denote the collision among actions and actors in the pursuit of power, wherein the use or threat of violence is often the final arbiter among contending parties.

[18]These predictions appear now quite accurate.

But after the 1950s, a change occurred and articulations became more distributive—*participatory* seems the word—dealing with problems of citizens and particular groups of citizens rather than with problems of the entire nation.

The meaning of these particular sequences could be seen as merely a rhetorical reflection of the major political and moral issues of the day. No one needs to be reminded that the concerns of the traditional community coincided with the Civil War, while the issues of authority peak during the Victorian age. Wealth and industry are preoccupations that go together with the Great Depression, and the projected concentration on problems of the distribution of power seems related to the revolt of the deprived, be they black, young, or otherwise forgotten. But why did the young revolt then? Why was there a Victorian age, a Civil War, a Great Depression? Or are these historical accidents, without either internal necessity or external contingency? Were this the case, then random events would produce a highly ordered sequence of interrelated culture changes. The latter proposition is contrary to reason, and a more systematic understanding is in order.

One contested explanation goes thus: The temporal sequence of events—the Civil War, Victorian industry and its authoritarianism, the Great Depression, and a seemingly anarchist revolt by marginal strata—is not fortuitous; it is itself the cultural reflection of universal changes in society and social organization, such as the coming of industrialization and the processes of modernization. As it is often argued, this universal process involves in most if not all societies the violent overthrow of a feudally organized community, the following centralization of governmental powers, the penetration of these powers in the management of economic affairs to rectify imbalances in free market systems of exchange, and finally, the growth of disadvantaged groups that are passed by or even produced by these very same processes. Again, the discovered cycles are but epiphenomena reflecting the modernization of social organization. Even if this particular sequence of changing social organization were both universal and true, which is at any rate a disputed proposition, there would remain further objections (Huntington, 1966). For instance, the disintegration of the feudal community, the concentration of political powers, and the transformation of free market economies are surely processes of unequal duration, and this does not fit the rather equal periodization of the four sectors in the wheel of time. Theoretical objections may weigh even more, since the process of modernization is evolutionary, while the culture process seems cyclical. Consequently, there can be no simple and linear relationship between the suggested social structural sequence and the interdependent structure of culture cycles.

My understanding begins from a different interpretation of the meaning of the wheel of time and its internal structure of culture change. This interpretation is derived from the formulations of Parsons *et al.*, (1953) on problem solving. Bales (1950) and Bales and Strodtbeck (1953) argue that group problem solving involves the solution of four distinct functional problems and therefore involves four distinct phases. Bales thus discerns *Expressive, Adaptive, Instrumental,* and *Integrative* problems. This terminology seems most useful for an interpretation of the rising and falling concerns as indicated by the wheel of time. In party platforms, the expression of community concerns, RECTITUDE, AFFECTION, and RESPECT in the late 1850s indicates, in this view, a preoccupation with Expressive problems and therefore with the emotional reunification of society, its component parts, and its myths. The concern with the federal government and federal authority in the 1890s constitutes a preoccupation with Adaptive problems and goal selection. The devotion to economic remedies during the Depression is a particular example of concentration on Instrumental problems. Finally, the contemporary stress on the distribution of power and the instant amelioration of substantive injustice denotes a demand for integration. Scheme 3.1 recapitulates the previous interpretations.

If these interpretations of the deep structure of culture changes are correct,[19] two further questions arise. First, what causes these changes to become structured in this manner, and second, what causes this particular phase sequence?

SCHEME 3.1
Fourfold Classification of Outstanding Culture Preoccupations in the Long-Term Wheel of Time

	Justificatory (ethics of ultimate ends)	Substantive (ethics of responsibility)
Task (external)	1894	1932
	Adaptive problems	Instrumental problems
	Power Authoritative Participant	Wealth Total
	Power Authoritative	Skill Total
Social emotional (internal)	1856	1970
	Expressive problems	Integrative problems
	Rectitude Total	Power Conflict
	Respect Total	Power Cooperation
	Affection Total	Well-being

[19]This book generally interprets the cooccurrences of content categories in terms of themes or orientations as a first step in a causal explanation of alternating themes. Chapters 1, 8, and 9 provide the details.

A CAUSAL THEORY OF LONG-TERM CYCLICAL CULTURE CHANGES

Freely interpreted, Parsons and Bales state that (1) any social system is forever faced with four functional problems, (2) the solution of these four problems is a necessary prerequisite to the survival of the system, and (3) all social systems try to survive—they try to maintain their boundaries and identities so that energy will be expended to solve these functional problems. However, in the process of solution, some problems take precedence over others in a determined sequence or phase movement. The sequencing of phases, in turn, depends on dynamics inherent in social problem solving. To illuminate the point, let us consider the sequence of phases in greater detail.

The Expressive Phase

For a problem to be solved, problems and problem-solvers need to be identified and confirmed. The Expressive phase concentrates on such cultural issues of identity by raising questions about the nature of social reality, including the definition of society as a collective actor or participant. This, however, is not a civil and academic debate about ontological controversies; it is a passionate and emotional engagement more reminiscent of the struggles of Jacob wrestling with the angel. Thus, questions predominate regarding current cultural conceptions of the nature, identity, and boundaries of society, while in more concrete terms the disputes rage about who and what is or is not American, and what are and should be America's most general characteristics and purposes. Accordingly, the Expressive phase defines and disputes what we are and what we want to be, and, hence, the most basic articulations of culture about the social system.

The Adaptive Phase

Once Expressive problems are fully articulated, it becomes possible and necessary to think about the proper organization of the collectivity for the attainment of its goals. This requires the translation of a rather vague consensus into concrete political priorities and concomitant formulation for the design and transformation of political institutions and constitutions to improve the authority structure, the decision-making apparatus, the executive machinery, and all that is needed to move the collectivity to the resolution of its public problems.

The Instrumental Phase

Neither basic solidarity nor political organization—and certainly not their design—is sufficient by itself for the solution of public problems. At least in thought, even the partial attainment of these ends create new problems of material means, man-made instrumentations, and engineering facilities. During the Instrumental phase, the potentialities of new political structures create new culture concerns. Questions arise about new adaptive possibilities and new solutions for outstanding and especially economic problems. This concentration explains the stress on economic designs for production and accomplishment in this phase.

The Integrative Phase

One would expect that the problem-solvers are now attuned to attain their original goals, solve their critical problems, and thus enjoy the fruits of the joint efforts. This is rarely the case, however, and chagrin or conflict are more likely results. Perhaps once attained, goals always fall short of original expectations, and the game is no longer worth the candle. Also, each phase unintentionally creates other problems. For instance, a search for more effective political organization of the nation in the pursuit of its goals disrupts the consensual unity by creating inequalities. The same is true of the differentiation of labor that follows the pursuit of economic efficiency. The problem-solving sequence is therefore likely to produce solutions that in society enhance structural inequalities so that the benefits of the problem solution flow unequally to different strata in the population. This must create growing disparity, real or perceived, between privileged and deprived groups and classes. To maintain the existing social institutions and arrangements within the existing moral framework, mounting pressures and counterpressures will arise for the redistribution of material and immaterial goods in the hope of resolving or undoing these pressing inequities. This process explains why collective thought turns to issues of and designs for integration.

The Expressive Phase Returns

In the efforts to solve the basic problems of the system previously confirmed in the Expressive phase, the political, economic, and social orders are drastically transformed and therefore conflict with the founding conceptions and preferences. The nation as problem-solver is therefore confronted with the task of restoring a sense of common collectivity that transcends conflicting interest grupings. Concerning meanings, there is at the same time a modification or even a radical transformation of basic understandings and expectations. With this rebirth of the system, new problems are raised, new sights are set, and the problem-solving sequence begins anew.[20]

[20]Parsons *et al.* (1953, pp. 187–188) deny the necessity of only one particular phase movement.

The various functional requirements impose specialized tasks and energy expenditures. For instance, Adaptive problems require responses different from those required by social emotional problems, and, in dealing with the external Adaptive problem, the collectivity must neglect the internal social emotional demands. This neglect creates a deficiency, actually a disequilibrium, that, given the principle of boundary maintenance, fuels the recurrent cyclical process.

Applying this theoretical explanation to empirical findings, one implicitly stretches the meaning of *problem solving*. In Bales' small groups, there are concrete individuals attempting to resolve specific issues that arise in a limited time span. In society at large, even in the political process per se, issues and actors are far more diffuse, efforts are often implicit rather than deliberate, and the time span for problem solving is far more extended. According to the present findings and their interpretation, it would take society 152 years to solve its four functional problems. Whether one can speak of problem solving in this regard is surely a matter of dispute. Also, why would it take 152 rather than any other number of years?

Generational succession provides one answer to the last question. For most people, major preoccupations do not change much during the life cycle. Their preoccupations and interpretations tend to become fixed during young adulthood, and therefore, contemporaries often resemble one another in modal attitudes that differentiate one generation from the next. This is the case because peers are moved by similarly critical matters, concerns, and issues of the day that leave deep marks for the rest of the generation's days. Also, once a generation that is thus marked comes of age, peer preoccupations enter the body politic. With death or political retirement, the generation's preoccupations are removed from the societal arena some 40 years after they were entered. Although it is true that recruits are continuously entered into the arena—a phenomenon that is itself an explanation of the continuous nature of culture transformation—it takes four entire and consecutive generations to traverse the complete problem-solving sequence (Marias and Rintala, 1968; Mannheim, 1952). This generational succession might therefore well delineate the succession of alternating preoccupations presented by the long-term wheel of time. Other explanations, however, may prove more convincing, considering extant disputes about the true and variable duration of various and, at times, contemporaneous generations.

THE FIT OF THE SHORT-TERM CULTURE CYCLES

Table 3.5 presents all of the categories that fit a shorter-term sine curve. According to this table, Republican concern with the category WELL-BEING TOTAL tended to be at its height in 1908, as it did in 1868 and 1948. The

TABLE 3.5
Selected Characteristics of 44 Shorter-Term Sine Curves

Content category and party*	Peak	Wavelength (in years)	r^2	Total variance explained
1. *Well-being Total*	1908	40	.26	.17
2. *Arena*	1908	68	.22	—
3. *Respect Total*	1908	36	.19	.10
4. Respect Total	1910	32	.22	.18
5. *Others*	1912	68	.23	.08
6. Enlightenment Total	1916	52	.21	.15
7. Power Gains	1916	44	.20	.11
8. Ends	1916	32	.17	.03
9. Undefined	1920	80	.30	.16
10. *Power Authoritative Participant*	1920	32	.23	.19
11. *Undefinable*	1920	32	.20	—
12. *Power Ends*	1926	32	.30	—
13. *Power Gains*	1926	32	.17	.13
14. Well-being Participant	1928	32	.25	.14
15. ·Wealth Transaction	1928	48	.17	.13
16. Power Participant	1928	48	.12	.09
17. *Power Arena*	1932	40	.24	—
18. Wealth Other	1934	48	.43	.13
19. Wealth Total	1934	48	.43	.13
20. *Rectitude Total*	1934	68	.35	.19
21. *Wealth Total*	1936	48	.26	.07
22. *Wealth Other*	1936	48	.24	.06
23. *Wealth Transaction*	1936	48	.20	.15
24. *Power Cooperation*	1936	64	.18	.15
25. Power Conflict	1938	36	.25	.19
26. Power Cooperation	1940	40	.33	.18
27. *Power Other*	1940	64	.30	—
28. Wealth Participant	1940	48	.21	.11
29. Rectitude Ends	1942	48	.24	.15
30. *Undefined*	1944	20	.21	—
31. *Transaction*	1944	44	.17	.13
32. *Selves*	1946	48	.27	.19
33. Affection Total	1946	52	.23	.16
34. Positive Affect	1946	44	.17	.06
35. Power Ends	1948	64	.23	—
36. *Positive Affect*	1950	60	.24	—
37. Power Doctrine	1952	60	.21	.16
38. *Enlightenment Total*	1954	60	.27	—
39. Rectitude Ethics	1956	80	.23	—
40. *Skill Total*	1960	64	.28	.13
41. Nations	1960	56	.22	—
42. *Ends*	1964	80	.30	.09
43. *Skill Other*	1968	72	.26	.13
44. *Nations*	1970	68	.35	.27

*Republican party platform categories are italicized.
†Where blank, curve fitted to raw data.

TABLE 3.6
Frequency of Content Categories with and without Shorter-Term Cyclical Change by Party

	Democratic platform categories		
Republican platform categories	With cyclical change	Without cyclical change	N
With cyclical change	12	12	24
Without cyclical change	8	10	18
N	20	22	42

shorter-term sine curve explains 26% of the residual variance in the category over time. The shorter-term cycle is therefore only a tendency in the data that often explains but a limited part of the total amount of culture change. Also, the estimation of the cycles is based in part on extrapolation.

Table 3.6 shows that 10 categories did not fit a shorter-term sine curve in either Republican or Democratic platforms. Of the 2 times 42 variables, slightly more than half (44) fitted this type of sine curve. Of these 44 categories,[21] 12 (or 54%) occurred in the platforms of both parties. This level of replication may raise some doubt about the true form of culture changes at this level of analysis. Yet the assertion that shorter-term culture changes are in fact cyclical remains very plausible.

According to Table 3.7, the modal wavelength of the shorter-term sine curves is 48 years. Dispersion about the mode, however, is hardly normal, which makes it unlikely that this dispersion was produced by measurement error. This means that each category, or group of categories, varies according to its own cycle with a unique wavelength for each group of categories—an equally unlikely proposition. To resolve this dilemma, the researchers tried grouping the sine curves in three categories with wavelengths of 36, 48, and 64 years, but this did not enhance later interpretation. At this point, rather than rejecting the findings of shorter-term cyclical changes as untrue, the original estimates, attributing the dispersion about the mean to an unknown source of error, were retained and interpreted.

As was done with the longer-term cycles, the wavelengths of the shorter-term cycles were set at the modal length of 48 years and the peaks were transformed accordingly. Here the wavelength of the transformed sine curve is considerably less than the period under observation, and therefore, each point on the circle represents a set of peaks that are 48 years apart.

---

[21]Of these variables, 33 were fitted to the residuals of longer-term cycles, and 11 to the original data.

TABLE 3.7
Distribution of Shorter-Term Sine Curves by Wavelength

Wavelength	N
20 years	1
32 years	6
36 years	2
40 years	3
44 years	3
48 years	10
52 years	3
56 years	1
60 years	3
64 years	4
68 years	4
72 years	1
80 years	3

For instance, the top of the circle in Figure 3.5 represents the years 1844, 1932, and 1980.

THE STRUCTURE OF SHORT-TERM CULTURE CYCLES

Figure 3.5, a circle, presents the short wheel of time and the internal relationships among the shorter-term sine curves. Again, on the rim of the wheel we see the categories that display such curves according to the years when each cycle peaked. Therefore, a category that peaks before another precedes it in a clockwise manner.[22] Also, the peaks of Democratic platform categories and cycles appear on the outside of the rim while such peaks of Republican platform categories appear on the inside. This presentation will facilitate a comparison between Democratic and Republican cultural preoccupations.

Although approximate, some meaningful organization appears in the sequence of peaking shorter-term concerns. What is this sequence?

At the bottom of the circle, there appears a peak in concern with the economic affairs and the WEALTH of the nation. Shortly after the years 1844, 1932, and 1980, references to WEALTH TOTAL and WEALTH subcategories are preponderant in both parties. In comparison with other years along the

[22]Again, this presentation summarizes some critical features of the various cyclical findings and their sequential ordering while dismissing others.

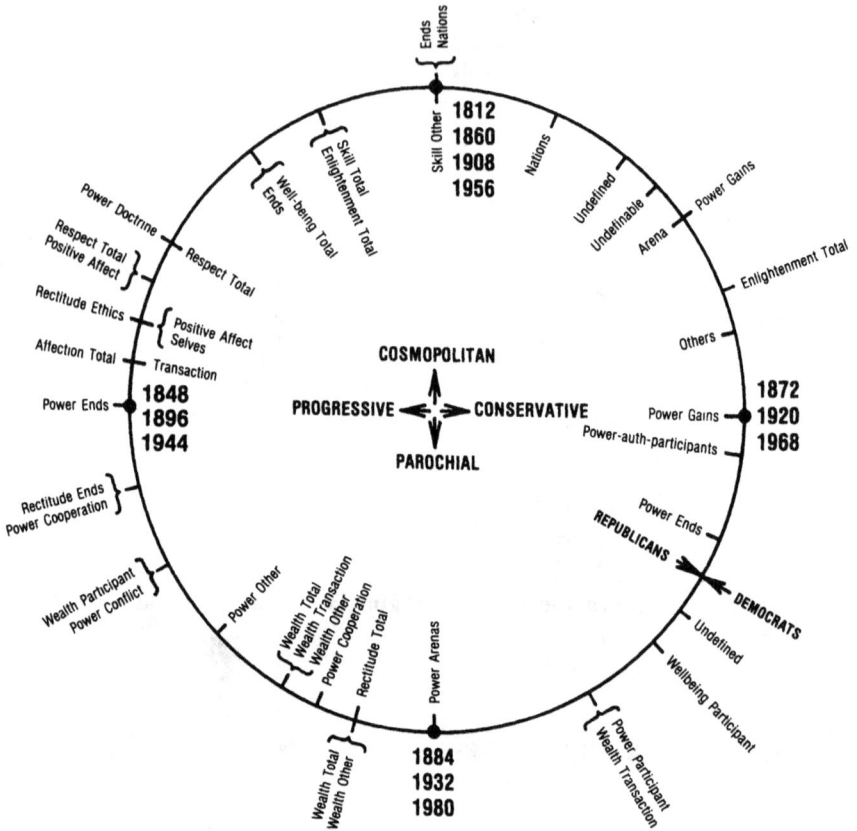

FIGURE 3.5. **The Internal Structure of Short-Term Value Changes (Cycle lengths set to 48 years, variable origins).**

circle, there is in these years a clearly outstanding concern with the economic performance of the nation.

Moving to the left of the circle (or from 1884 to 1896, and from 1932 to 1944), there appear in the platforms of both parties a decreasing concern with economic matters and an equally increasing concern with political strife. For instance, the category POWER CONFLICT includes words such as *adversary, anarchy, conflict, disagreement, disunity, opposition,* and *revolutionary.* These are the words that are more frequently used during these periods. This is similar to the category POWER COOPERATION, including the words *compromise, cooperative, integration, together,* and *unity.* Concerns with conflict and cooperation, therefore, increase and decrease during the same time periods; they are concomitant concerns. In party platforms, then, it seems that if domestic conflict is noted, cooperation and unity are advocated to overcome dissension; or disputes and conflicts of interest are seen while it is argued that strife is likely, inevitable, or even desirable. To illustrate:

> Millions of workers just now seeking to organize POWER COOPERATION| are blocked |POWER CONFLICT| by federally organized authorized "right-to-work" laws, unreasonable limitations on the right to picket, and other hampering legislative and administrative provisions.... We will repeal the authorization for [these] laws, limitations on the right to strike |POWER CONFLICT|, to picket peacefully and to tell the public the facts of a labor dispute |POWER CONFLICT|. [Porter and Johnson, 1961, p. 584]

At times the categories POWER CONFLICT and COOPERATION occur together because of joint concerns with foreign enemies and alliances. In either case, however, this combined concern seems a reflection of changing levels of strife or perceived strife, be it in the domestic or international order. This interpretation is supported by the apparent salience of the categories TRANSACTION, RECTITUDE, RESPECT, and POWER DOCTRINE.[23] In short, not only is strife increasing, but there also appears a timely and associated interest in the formulation and justification of political innovation, intervention, and programmatic politics in general.

Frequent references to the category TRANSACTION are often triggered by innocuous words, such as *will* and *shall*. In party platforms, this happens when the party suggests new policies or measures, as in the phrase, "We [the party] shall or will do this." Note in the above quotation, for instance, "We will [TRANSACTION] repeal the authorization for [these] laws." The category POWER DOCTRINE includes the names of organized political doctrines, such as *democracy* and *communism*. When suggesting political or military innovations, the party seeks to justify its stance in doctrinal terms. For instance:

> Our objective, however, is not the right to coexist in armed camps on the same planet with totalitarian |POWER DOCTRINE| ideologies |POWER DOCTRINE|; it is the creation of an enduring peace in which the universal values of human dignity, truth and justice under law are finally secured for all men everywhere on earth.... The new Democratic administration will recast our military capacity in order to provide forces and weapons of a diversity, balance, and mobility sufficient in quantity and quality to deter both limited and general aggressions.

Within this quotation from the Democratic platform (Porter and Johnson, 1961, p. 584) one notes the invocation of doctrine, justifying military and political innovations to contain or resolve military conflict. At the same time, these innovations are also justified in highly abstract ethical terms, such as *right, peace*, and *justice* (the category RECTITUDE ETHICS), and RESPECT, denoted here by the word *dignity*. Furthermore, frequent references to the

---

[23]RECTITUDE ETHICS contains references to words that invoke, in the final analysis, the social order and its dynamics as the justifying ground.

categories POSITIVE AFFECT and AFFECTION TOTAL signal a tendency in these times to appeal to, or invoke, unity. Finally, there appears at the same time in the Republican platforms a peaking concern with the category SELVES, which includes the personal pronouns *we, us, ours,* and *ourselves.* As was noted before, the use of these pronouns most often suggests a denial of status differences and, in platform rhetoric, a denial of such differences between party leaders and followers, or between partisans and the citizenry. Such pronouns suggest to the public a concert of purpose and will in society. In summary, we find in the "9 o'clock" position of our circle (and during the times there represented), a preponderant concern with political strife, programmatic means, and justifications to alleviate these tensions.

Moving to the top of the circle, there appears in both parties an increasing concern with the category ENDS; values, whatever their substance, are considered and invoked for their intrinsic merits. The category contains a great many words, but the most frequent are *accomplish, attain, choice, development, future, outlook, plan, scheme, strategy,* and *value.* The use of these words suggests leisurely deliberation about future goals. Whereas some 12 years before, concerns appeared conflict-ridden and somewhat impetuously directed toward urgent goals and immediate political intervention, now the concern is more philosophical, stressing long-range strategies and planning. In the Republican party platforms, this mode of political thought is in line with an increasing concern with technology, industry, and training, and education (SKILL OTHER and SKILL TOTAL). In both platforms there appears a maximum concern with the world at large as exemplified by peaking references to the category NATIONS. Finally, at the end of this sector in our circle, Republican party platforms become most preoccupied with the categories UNDEFINED and UNDEFINABLE. A usage of the category UNDEFINABLE, and therefore of words with no value implications, indicates that platforms tend to become more descriptive and less value-laden and political. Similarly an increasing concern with the category UNDEFINED suggests a greater use of words with ambiguous meanings. In conclusion, Republican platforms of these times not only become less value-laden, but also, if concerned with valuational matters, they become more ambiguous and tentative than in other times.

To summarize, around the years 1860, 1908, and 1956, platform rhetoric is philosophical in tone, concerned with long-range problems and programs, international in orientation, and perhaps preoccupied with the future of industry and education. Finally, Republican platforms either avoid controversies or deal with such issues in a rather ambiguous manner.

Moving to the "3 o'clock" position of the circle, another shift occurs in predominant articulations. In both platforms, there is a maximum of concern with the category POWER GAINS, and therefore with such words as *appease, follow, obey, restore, safeguard,* and *strengthen.* Also, much concern appears with the federal government and other governmental agencies (POWER AUTHORITATIVE PARTICIPANT). In combination, concern with these categories shows a conservative preoccupation with authoritative restoration of former structures.

THE STRUCTURE OF SHORT-TERM CULTURE CHANGE

Contrasting and comparing the various preoccupations, we note already an outstanding concern with the economic performance of society at the bottom of the circle. To the left, this concern is replaced by worries about political and economic inequities and exploration of more radical innovations. Following this phase, there comes a preoccupation with long-range planning and world affairs. The circle ends with a conservative preoccupation with restoration.[24]

Contrasting the left with the right side of the circle, the polarity is rather obvious: It is the Progressive vs. Conservative opposition, so that great concern with political intervention, strife, and inequities excludes concerns with restoration, and vice versa. The bottom vs. top contrast seems less obvious at first sight, but no doubt represents a Parochial vs. Cosmopolitan polarity, or isolationism vs. interventionism.[25] When concern with WEALTH is at a peak, there is little concern with the world, and long-range planning or the concern with wealth is associated with a "fortress America" stance. Similarly concern with the world precludes wide interest in domestic economic performance. The bottom of the circle, then, represents a restrictive and exclusive concern with one political issue: the state of the economy. A reading of the pertinent documents suggests, also, that this concern is extremely partisan and domestic in scope. In contrast, the opposite of this axis represents articulations that strike one as far more sophisticated, open-ended rather than restricted, diffused along a wider spectrum of issues, politically detached, and, in attention span, world-wide.

Scheme 3.2 will further clarify the conceptual interpretation of the empirical findings. The diagonal polarities have been discussed; the row and column contrasts will further characterize the structure of short-term culture change. The consensus vs. conflict contrast are representations of two opposing theories of morality. In the consensus view, man is essentially evil and all good stems from human associations under the guidance of the wisdom of the past and of all culture. Therefore, it is only by the preser-

---

[24]As is a standard procedure, the analysis attempts to interpret cooccurring content categories in more common and recurring themes and polarities of themes revealing underlying culture issues. These interpretative efforts always aid later generalized causal analysis. Chapters 1, 8, and 9 discuss these procedures and similar findings in greater detail.

[25]Schlesinger (1939) discusses periodic alterations along the Conservative vs. Progressive continuum; Klingberg (1952) discusses the Parochial vs. Cosmopolitan contrast. While using a very different methodology, Klingberg's periodization of 50-year cycles is strikingly similar to my own.

SCHEME 3.2
Fourfold Classification of Outstanding Culture Preoccupations in the Short-Term Wheel Of Time

Theories of worth	Theories of morality	
	Consensus	Conflict
Particularistic	1872, 1920, 1968 *CONSERVATIVE* Power Authoritative Participant Power Gains	1884, 1932, 1980 *PAROCHIAL* Wealth
Universalistic	1860, 1908, 1956 *COSMOPOLITAN* Skill Nations Ends Undefined Undefinable	1848, 1896, 1944 *PROGRESSIVE* Power Conflict Power Cooperation Transaction Rectitude Respect Power Doctrine Selves

vation of the essence of culture, and consensus in particular, that anarchic forces can be controlled and the moral order preserved. In the conflict view, man is essentially good and all evil is produced by faulty protrusions in the forms of human association. Therefore, permanent strife and conflict are necessary for the attainment of an elusive moral order (Lenski, 1966, pp. 22–27). The particularistic and universalistic contrasts represent two opposing theories of worth. In the universalistic view, criteria of worth reside in essences and mechanisms that exist separately from the objects of evaluation, be they actions, performance, persons, or groups. For instance, the criteria of utility, truth, and grace are extrinsic and objectively manifested by self-regulatory mechanisms of the market, debate, and appreciation. In the particularistic view, the criteria of worth are intrinsic, unique while lacking objective existence: They are inseparable from the essences of the object under evaluation (Gouldner, 1970, pp. 61–65).

In this interpretation, the more familiar contrasts of political philosophy (the diagonal polarities) can be seen as the varying and combined expressions of seemingly more abstruse theories of the nature of worth. Also, these philosophies and theories define the underlying structure of shorter-term culture change.[26] Finally, the various understandings are subject to

[26]Hence the Parochial orientation is a combination of particularistic and conflicting preoccupations; the Progressive orientation is a combination of conflicting and universalistic concerns; the Cosmopolitan orientation is a combination of universalistic and consensual attitudes; and finally, the Conservative orientation is a combination of consensual and particularistic predilections. The rim of the wheel could be seen as representing a continuously changing preferential sequence, rather than as qualitatively distinct phases.

systematic, continuous, and cyclical change over time. In this manner, the succession of four phases can be identified as particularistic (peaking in 1866, 1914, and 1962); consensual (peaking in 1830, 1878, 1926, and again in 1974; conflicting (peaking in 1842, 1890, 1938, and again in 1986); universalistic (peaking in 1854, 1902, 1950, and again in 1998); consensual (peaking in 1866, 1914, 1962); and particularistic (peaking in 1830, 1878, 1926, and again in 1974).

Before being carried away by the closure of this interpretation, some caveats must forewarn the reader. First, the actual level of concerns in party platforms is determined to a far larger part by longer-term rather than shorter-term cycles; the short-term cycles describe only a small part of the campaign-to-campaign fluctuations. Therefore, the interpretations pertain only to tendencies that operate beyond longer-term trends. Second, long- and short-term trends are often opposed and rarely coincide. For instance, the 1970s should have been characterized by a concern with integration and therefore should have revealed and a good deal of attention to political strife, at least according to the longer-term cycle. In actuality, the violence in American ghettos all across the land and the rising discontent among other forgotten minorities, such as women or the young, illustrate the point. The short-term wheel of time, concomitantly, suggests Conservative preoccupations with a suppression of political conflict. In this manner, long- and short-term mechanisms may pull or push articulations in opposite directions. Third, considering the extent of data manipulation, the findings and interpretations of the short-term wheel of time must remain approximate.

AN EXPLANATION OF SHORTER-TERM CYCLICAL CHANGES

The reader will have noted that the early 1890s and the years around 1932 represent periods of sustained depression and business contraction in the American and world economies. Besides, 25 to 30 years earlier or later were periods of sustained economic growth (Mitchell, 1927, pp. 226–230; Fellner, 1956, pp. 43–54; Burns and Mitchell, 1946, pp. 429–435; Gordon, 1961). In short, there appears a rather striking fit between the short-term wheel of time and a particular economic cycle. What is the latter cycle?

Economists distinguish among various cyclical fluctuations in business activity: seasonal fluctuations, the business cycle, the long wave, and the secular trend. The long wave, even though disputed by some economists, is said to vary, extending and contracting over a period of 50 to 60 years. This is the so-called Kondratieff (1926) or K-cycle. How does the latter process relate to culture articulations?

During long-wave economic deterioration, the nation turns inward, gradually relinquishing international ventures and then obligations, becoming more and more inward in its orientations. The shifting orientations are first Conservative, probably stressing discipline, the tightening of belts, and the necessity of temporary unemployment and charity to overcome the economic decline. Usually, this goes together with growing indifference, if not hostility, toward foreign claims and conditions as the outside world is seen as competitive and fickle, a cause of troubles, and an object of scapegoating. At the height of the economic calamity the nation becomes neither Progressive nor Conservative; rather, its culture turns Parochial. However, with the slowly passing depression (or severe recession), the mood will change from Parochial to Progressive. Increasingly, belt-tightening and charity will be seen as palliatives. A growing demand will arise for a change in collective arrangements and structural intervention.

Whether cause or effect, the ensuing structural change seems to work, since prosperity returns. With increasing surplus, attention turns again to the world scene and articulations become more Cosmopolitan, at first in a Progressive vein. Progressive intervention works at home; therefore it needs to be exported in the fulfillment of America's ethos and liberal designs. At any rate, money is there in growing abundance. However, once the growth turns its peak and contraction sets in, the Cosmopolitan impulse turns from Progressive to Conservative, from national mission to national interest, from, for instance, Marshall Plan to Green Berets. One may well speculate that with the Vietnam War and the Nixon doctrine, the Parochial phase was on the rise again.

The relationship between long-wave economic contraction and expansion on the one hand, and a shift in basic understandings regarding morality and criteria of worth on the other, are equally systematic. Briefly, the shift from conflict to consensus and vice versa starts at the beginnings of the period of sustained debacle and prosperity, while the shift from particularistic to universalistic orientations or vice versa) begins at the onsets of sustained growth (or contraction).[27]

CONCLUSIONS

A content analysis of American party platforms produced results that seem to fit a variety of trends in a great many different content categories. Besides a longer-term trend of about 152 years, one can often discern shorter-term trends of about 48 years. The latter represent variations in concerns beyond longer-term trend variations. In combination, the short- and long-term cycles describe (or explain) a good part of the variation in concerns, as illustrated in Table 3.8.

----

[27]Pareto (1935, paragraph 2,387) provides a general discussion of the relationship between economic cycles and political, if not philosophical, thought.

Two wheels of time summarize the internal structure of both types of cycles. Sequentially, the varying concerns of the long wheel of time are explained in terms of four fundamental functional problems of any society as articulated by its culture. Accordingly and in collective thought, the solution of one problem always takes precedence over the solution of the next one, until all four problems—Adaptive, Instrumental, Integrative, and Expressive—have been articulated to the fullest and the progression starts anew.

The sequential articulations of the short wheel of time—Parochial, Progressive, Cosmopolitan, and Conservative—are most likely produced by dynamics that differ from the long-term functional mechanisms, and the K-cycle periodic contraction and expansion of the national and international economy seems, for the moment, the most plausible explanation.

Long- and short-term dynamics are not equally important in the determination of culture change. On the average, longer-term cycles describe about three times as much of the variance in these changes as do shorter-term cycles. The larger part of changing articulations in platforms is therefore attributed to the dynamics of social problem solving rather than to social structural changes. Yet, the theory is not purely functional, since I think economic mechanisms are operating beyond and above the functional dynamics.

TABLE 3.8
Percent Variance Explained by Two Superimposed Cycles in Some Selected Variables*

	Longer term trend	Shorter term trend	Both
1. Ends	85	17	88
2. Wealth Total	69	43	82
3. *Skill Total*	53	28	66
4. *Rectitude Total*	45	35	64
5. Power Cooperation	45	33	61
6. Respect Total	49	19	59
7. *Well-being Total*	34	26	51
8. *Nations*	24	35	51
9. *Power Gains*	36	17	49
10. *Selves*	30	27	49
11. Affection Total	30	23	46
12. Power Conflict	23	25	46
13. Power Authoritative Participant	18	23	37

*Power Total and Enlightenment Total did not display both trends. Apart from the six remaining major content categories, seven subcategories were included because they are important in the interpretation of either longer- or shorter-term trends. Republican party platform categories are italicized.

The exposition assumes that the time span and magnitude of culture change are constant for all times. This seems an unwarranted assumption. Indeed, if the K-cycle explains the short-term wheel of time, then the sine curve may well be too constrictive a model of change. Even though the K-cycle is a recurrent and rhythmically alternating cycle, the magnitude and wavelength of these cycles seem to vary in history. If this is the case for the cause, so it must be for the consequences, and thus the sequences of political philosophies must be of varying duration. One would like to believe that changes in duration and amplitude are themselves a simple function of time and are therefore gradual and continuous, but the world of culture transformations may not submit itself so readily to this persistent search for elegance and order.

Quantitative procedures, such as content analysis and curve fitting, suggest to the uninitiated reader an exactness and precision that is far greater than the results of more customary procedures of historical analysis. This practitioner is under no such illusions: Time and again the reader was forewarned about the approximate nature of estimates and the speculative character of later interpretations and explanations. In 1973, Namenwirth wrote that the correctness of these estimates could not be established in one experiment, and judgments on that score would have to await future examinations of different historical sources, using different procedures of analysis. Even at that juncture, his judgment was probably over cautious considering the duplication of his cyclical findings from Democratic to Republican platforms. In the intervening years, Weber (Chapters 4 and 5) found similar cycles at least during the industrial area in British political history, while Weber and Namenwirth (Chapter 6), analyzing the residuals from the present cycles, found them related in determined and at times familiar fashions to economic and political events. If the residuals are true (or accurately estimated), so certainly must be these culture cycles themselves. Finally, within in a few years enough elections will have passed to test the cycles in platforms from 1968 onward. Anticipating that the facticity of these cycles will be reconfirmed and therefore established, further debates will certainly still address their interpretation, causation, and consequences.

4

The Long-Term Dynamics of Cultural Problem Solving[1]

Certain cultural sequences are an essential part of the process by which social systems such as societies adapt to their cultural, social, and physical environments. This is the main conclusion to be drawn from Namenwirth's analysis of party platforms in American presidential campaigns from 1844 to 1964, presented in Chapter 3. Utilizing a computer-based method of content analysis (Stone *et al.*, 1966), Namenwirth inferred changing issues or priorities from changes in the thematic content of these documents. He found that attention devoted to particular themes or issues rose and fell in a cyclical fashion. In fact, two independent thematic cycles were observed: 152 years and 48 years in length. Namenwirth interprets the longer cycle to reflect culturally determined societal problem solving; the shorter cycle, economic problem solving. The American short thematic cycle is related to the Kondratieff economic cycle. A similar cycle was found in Great Britain (Weber, 1981); it is discussed in the next chapter. This chapter addresses only the longer cycle.

Namenwirth's results (Chapter 3) are summarized as follows: the 152-year thematic cycle (hereafter L-cycle) is interpreted as a variation of the Bales–Parsons (Bales, 1950, 1953; Bales and Strodtbeck, 1953; Parsons *et al.*, 1953; Parsons and Bales, 1953; Parsons and Smelser, 1956; cf. Hayes,

[1]The research reported here was supported in part by a National Science Foundation Dissertation Research Grant, GS-42403. This chapter is a major revision of Weber (1982).

Robert Philip Weber wrote this chapter.

1980) four-function (AGIL) scheme: Adaptive, Instrumental, Integrative,[2] and Expressive. Concern with each of these themes reflects a debate about a particular issue or question, such as "What does it mean to be American" (Expressive)? "How shall we organize the social institutions required to achieve the good society"[3] (Adaptive)? "How shall we produce the material and social goods required for the good society" (Instrumental)? "How shall we achieve social and economic justice" (Integrative)?

Preoccupation with each of these issues coincides with a particular period in American history. The Expressive theme coincides with the Civil War. The others coincide, respectively, with the Victorian authoritarianism of the 1890s, the Great Depression of the 1930s, and the struggle for civil rights by blacks, women, the young, and others during the late 1960s. Namenwirth asserts that this thematic sequence constitutes a series of problems whose resolution is a necessary but not sufficient condition for the adaptation of society to its social and political environment.

Namenwirth argues that there is a logical order to the sequence of issues of themes. First, during the Expressive phase the collectivity's goals and identity are addressed and the boundaries of the system defined (e.g., what is, or is not, "American"). The Adaptive phase then focuses on the organization of social institutions necessary to attain goals identified in the Expressive phase. Next, during the Instrumental phase attention is focused on the economic and material resources required to achieve these goals. Subsequently, the Integrative phase addresses social and economic dis-locations incurred during the previous phases. Finally, the L-cycle begins again with attention focused on the identity of the system transformed during the previous steps of this progression.

Burnham (1976) observed that this problem-solving sequence is related to fundamental shifts in support within the American electorate for political parties.[4] For example, the "critical" or "realigning" elections of 1896 and 1932 occur at the point of maximal concern with the Adaptive and Instrumental problems, respectively. This correspondence suggests that in democratic societies the prevailing coalition of voters greatly influences the solution of each problem. However, with limited resources and neglected problems that eventually demand attention, each issue is solved only temporarily, and reoccurs 152 years later.

Namenwirth hypothesizes that generational change is the causal

---

[2]Namenwirth uses the terms *Instrumental* and *Expressive* instead of Parsons's terms *Goal Attainment* and *Latency*, respectively.

[3]As discussed later, the Adaptive theme in Britain concerns responses to threats from other countries. This difference may reflect the geopolitical differences between Britain and America in the nineteenth century.

[4]The literature on American realignments is huge. Burnham (1970) and Sundquist (1983) are classics. For a recent, comprehensive examination of realignments in America, see Clubb *et al.* (1980). Chubb (1978, p. 145) states that "critical realignments are not regular periodic occurrences in an ongoing cycle"; the evidence presented below suggests otherwise.

mechanism underlying the progression of issues. Each generation of slightly less than 40 years emphasizes one problem. Later in this chapter both critical elections and the L-cycle are related to population replacement, or cohort succession.

Before turning to the questions that motivate this chapter, a brief theoretical discussion is required to define just a few basic terms and to clarify the ensuing arguments and their supporting empirical evidence.

As noted in Chapter 1, we adopt a dualist position that assumes culture and society are ontologically distinct systems. Specifically, culture is a system of abstract ideas; society is an action system. Furthermore, both Namenwirth (Chapter 3; cf. Namenwirth and Bibbee, 1976) and this chapter argue that the 150-year thematic sequence is a problem-solving sequence. Consequently, one central question addresses the location of this problem-solving: Does culture solve problems, or does society, or does their interaction? The parsimonious answers would be that problem solving is strictly either a societal or cultural process, but this seems overly simplistic. Instead, this chapter adopts another dualist position: Although culture determines the way in which social and cultural reality is interpreted (a theme elaborated later in this chapter) society—the action system—allocates, organizes, and applies the various cultural, social, economic, political, and other resources required to solve the four problems that constitute the 150-year cycle.

Are these problems, however, really "solved?" In one sense the answer is clearly no. As noted above, the four L-cycle problems are certainly not solved forever; they repeat. Also, the explanation of the L-cycle assumes that resources are directed toward solving each of these problems in turn, and that fluctuations in the attention devoted to each problem reflect fluctuations in the tension generated by each problem through cycles of resource mobilization and redirection. But for now the critical question of how perception, resources, and tension are **empirically** related remains largely unanswered and is left for future research. Consequently, the central part of this chapter addresses the empirical evidence supporting the contention that over long periods of time there are cycles in the attention devoted by societies to their cultural, social, and physical environments. While the processes that underlie attention are partly a matter of action, the **content** of attention is a matter of ideas and is therefore part of culture rather than of society.

EMPIRICAL QUESTIONS

Namenwirth's cyclical model of culture change raises several empirical questions: (1) Do thematic cycles exist in any other cultures? (2) If so, do they occur in the expected sequence (E–A–P–I)? (3) Is the length of the cycle(s) consistent with the generational hypothesis? (4) Does the cycle actually repeat itself? Namenwirth analyzed platforms spanning 120 years, and the hypothesis of a 152-year cycle therefore remains unproven. (5) What is the relationship between collective perceptions of historical events and the intrinsic nature of those events? And, (6) what is the relationship between the L-cycle and electoral realignments in nineteenth- and twentieth-century Britain?

To answer these questions, I content-analyzed British "Speeches from the Throne," 1689–1972. These speeches are delivered at the opening of each British parliamentary session.[5] The Queen's speech is delivered at the opening of each parliamentary session (Hansard, 1812; 1804–) and is similar to the American "State of the Union" address. The dominant parliamentary coalition uses the speech to respond to both national concerns and the concerns of various interest groups vying for power and influence. The issues discussed reflect the domestic and foreign policy concerns of the elites, if not the nation as a whole, while policy recommendations indicate the current government's strategy for solving these problems (cf. Herman, 1974).

The following section outlines the content-analytic and curve-fitting techniques applied to these British documents. The results are then presented and interpreted. The principal findings are that long-term change in political issues or themes is in part cyclical and in part discontinuous.[6] Specifically, variation in thematic concerns differs substantially from the period 1689–1795 (the Mercantilist period) to 1795–1972 (the Capitalist period). The lengths of the L-cycles in the British Mercantilist and Capitalist periods are 72 and 148 years, respectively. In the Mercantilist period the thematic progression is interpreted as Integrative, Instrumental,[7] Expressive, Adaptive; while in the Capitalist period it is Adaptive, Instrumental, Integrative, Expressive. Therefore, some aspects of Namenwirth's cyclical hypothesis are only partially confirmed.[8]

This chapter also presents evidence indicating a substantial relationship between the Capitalist L-cycle and party realignments. The following argument is then developed: Coalition realignment is the process by which society's attention and resources are refocused on changing L-cycle prob-

---

[5]The speeches analyzed are listed in Weber (1978, Appendix A). They are printed in Hansard (1812; 1804–).

[6]Initial attempts at analyzing the data in the span 1689–1972 were unsuccessful. Visual analysis of data plots suggested a discontinuity in the 1790s. This discontinuity was not anticipated, but was later shown to correspond to "the Great Transformation" (Polanyi, 1957).

[7]In Weber (1978, 1982) this theme was called "Productive" instead. The distinction being made was not subsequently useful, and for this reason and for the sake of consistency with the usage in Chapter 3 and elsewhere, this chapter returns to the original term.

[8]The American Adaptive phase is primarily concerned with social institutions required for adaptive problem solving, while British Adaptive themes focus on international relations, a difference in emphasis that may reflect America's geostrategic isolation.

lems. In the Mercantilist period these coalitions are comprised of upper-class factions and their supporters. In the Capitalist period the coalitions are comprised of party alignments among the enfranchised. Moreover, population replacement, or cohort succession, is the underlying mechanism of both coalition realignments and the L-cycle.

CONTENT ANALYSIS AND ESTIMATION PROCEDURES

The words of the speeches are classified by computer into many fewer content categories, which are defined by the Lasswell Value Dictionary (hereafter LVD), discussed in detail in Chapter 2. Specific categories and subcategories are defined below as required. The computer reports the percentage of words in each of the 283 documents for each content category.[9]

Namenwirth (1973) inferred themes by fitting sine curves to the data for each category.[10] The fitted sine curve is an estimate of the wavelength and the year(s) of maximal or peak concern for a content category. Themes are inferred from content categories that rise and fall together, i.e., have similar wavelengths and peak together.

For the British data, however, unequal time intervals occur between speeches, and many documents are relatively short.[11] To compensate for these problems, two alternative data transformations or "filters" are used: a 9-year moving average, and the aggregation of speeches occurring within each 4-year interval.[12] Both filters are applied to the raw data in order to

[9]Actually, word senses are counted because the computer system is able to distinguish among the various senses of most words with more than one sense or homographs (Kelly and Stone, 1975). In conjunction with the LVD, the computer program (Stone's General Inquirer System) indicates the suffixes identified and the sense number assigned to each homograph. The General Inquirer was modified slightly to handle British spelling and suffixes. Almost 97% of the 225,000 words were classified by this procedure.

[10]Technical details are reported in Namenwirth and Weber (1979). See Figures 3.1–3.3 in this volume for illustrations of this procedure.

[11]The intervals between the British speeches vary from 3 months to 3 years. The speeches vary between 180 and 1,000 words in length.

[12]For each content category, a moving average transformation was calculated so that each new value

$$Y_t = 1/m(Y_t + Y_{t+1} + Y_{t+2} + \cdots + Y_{t+m})$$

where Y_t is the new value and m is the length of the filter. A series of original length N yields a new series $N - m + 1$ in length. The alternative filter consists of aggregating the total word counts and category counts for all speeches within each 4-year interval. The percentage of words in each category is then recomputed. The moving average filter weights each speech equally; the aggregation filter weights according to the length of each document. Applying each filter separately, estimating sine curves for each series, and comparing the results across each filtered series guards against artifacts resulting from the induction of cycles by moving average transformations, a phenomenon known as the "Slutzky effect" (Slutzky, 1937).

assess the effect, if any, of transformations on the estimate of wavelength and inflection points of the sine curves. The results are unlikely to be artifacts when the estimated sine curves replicate across filters. Moreover, in this instance, when the population of speeches is analyzed and classical inferential statistics are inappropriate, replication across transformations provides a decision rule for distinguishing real curves from artifacts.

After removing a linear trend where present, an iterative nonlinear curve-fitting procedure was used to fit sine curves to the data. Estimates of the wavelength and year of maximal concern with each category (inflection points) were obtained. The rest of this section presents some of the details and discusses several technical issues. The uninterested reader may skip to the beginning of the next section.

After removing what linear trend exists through ordinary least squares (OLS) regression, initial estimates of the wavelength of the curve and the location of a peak relative to the beginning of the series must be provided. These initial estimates are derived either from visual inspection of plots of the residuals from the OLS regression or on the basis of prior hypotheses—e.g., that the wavelength is 150 years. In the first step the program determines whether a change in wavelength by some predetermined amount will increase or decrease the fit between the data and the estimated sine curve. If it will not, then the peak is shifted by a predetermined amount to see whether the fit can be improved. This process continues until neither a change in wavelength nor a change in peak will further improve the fit of the sine curve to the data. In the next step the amount of the shift is reduced by a quarter and the process repeated. In the final step the predetermined shift is again reduced by a quarter and the process repeated. The stability of the solution is assessed by seeing whether the program will converge to the same final estimates from different initial estimates of peak and/or wavelength.

Spectral decomposition (Granger, 1964; Jenkins and Watts, 1968; Bloomfield, 1976; Mayer and Arney, 1974; Gottman, 1981) was not used because a time-series seven times the length of the longest hypothesized cycle is required (Granger, 1964, p. 17). Thus 1,050 years of data (7×150) would be required. Fitting sine curves to the data presumes that the underlying process is deterministic rather than stochastic. In fact, these data can be analyzed with either method (both are used in Chapter 5) but different answers result. In the case of sine curves, the results indicate long-term dynamics that are not stochastic. One can also fit second- or third-order autoregressive models to the data. These suggest that the observed dynamics over time result from previous values of the variable plus random shocks. However, textual evidence strongly suggests, and the theoretical arguments presented support the contention, that long-term deterministic cycles in changing thematic concerns exist in these texts. Thus we prefer the deterministic to the stochastic model. Note too that the residuals analyzed in Chapter 6 represent stochastic rather than deterministic variation.

THE LONG CYCLE, 1689–1795

The cyclical model specifies a long sine curve with variable points (years) of inflection, or peaks.

For the data transformed by the 9-year moving average filter, Table 4.1 presents the estimated wavelength, the estimated year of peak concern, the standardized year of peak concern (explained below), the percent residual variation explained after removing the linear trend where present, and the percent total variance explained by the fitted sine curve. (In the interest of brevity, the estimates for the 4-year aggregation data are not presented here.[13])

The fitted sine curves on average account for 38% of the variance after removing a linear trend (where present), and 28% of the total variance (correlations of .62 and .53, respectively). The best-fitting sine curve (for the category SELF) accounts for 73% of the residual and 64% of the total variance; these correspond to correlations of .80 and .85, respectively. The worst-fitting curve that replicated across data filters (AFFECTION TOTAL) accounts for 10% of the residual and 9% of the total variance (correlations of .32 and .30, respectively). In this period the sine curves fit about as well as those for the British Capitalist data (see below), but not as well as the American data (Chapter 3), possibly because the British documents are generally shorter, thereby producing less-reliable estimates of category variation, or because there are more errors in the British dictionary.

The median wavelength is about 72 years. The most parsimonious and hence desirable assumption is that change in value concerns proceeds at one wavelength rather than at a different wavelength for different value or content categories. Therefore, the estimated wavelengths and peaks, or points of maximal concern, were standarized to the median wavelength and median peak year.[14]

---

[13]Of the 69 categories in the dictionary, 21 were eliminated because of low variance, 17 either did not replicate across filters or did manifest a long sine curve. Categories were eliminated when the estimates of the peak year using both filters were not within an eight of a cycle of each other. The curve-fitting results for the data aggregated within 4-year intervals are reported in Weber (1978).

[14]The estimated curves were standardized to a wavelength of 52 years according to

$$\text{standard peak} = (\text{original peak} \times \text{median wavelength})/\text{observed wavelength}$$

where "original peak" is the distance of the estimated peak in years from the median peak, the median wavelength is the median for all categories retained in the analysis, and the observed wavelength is the estimated wavelength of the curve to be standardized.

TABLE 4.1
**Curve-fitting Results for Long Cycle, 1689–1795, 9-Year Moving
Average Transformation**

Content category	Wavelength in years	Peak year	Standardized peak	Residual variance explained*	Total variance explained*
Power Authoritative					
Participants	63	1742	1744	37	33
Power Arena	69	1738	1738	56	23
Power Authoritative	74	1728	1728	21	17
Power Cooperation	75	1739	1739	56	51
Power Losses	69	1720	1717	25	20
Power Other	51	1732	1734	50	21
Power Participants	55	1722	1720	50	47
Power Ends	92	1697	1704	39	34
Power Total	71	1733	1733	54	32
Rectitude Ends	67	1744	1778	33	26
Rectitude Ethics	75	1753	1752	28	28
Rectitude Religious	76	1722	1723	44	32
Rectitude Total	64	1711	1709	14	12
Respect Total	73	1758	1758	60	45
Skill Total	67	1738	1739	40	32
Wealth Other	80	1702	1704	22	20
Wealth Participants	92	1695	1712	38	30
Wealth Transaction	72	1714	1714	31	26
Wealth Total	72	1707	1707	46	46
Affection Total	49	1717	1712	10	9
Well-being Physical	64	1698	1694	48	44
Enlightenment Total	110	1697	1707	29	16
Not	70	1698	1697	47	15
Sure	69	1727	1729	53	18
Undefinable	57	1742	1746	46	34
Audience	80	1695	1698	22	19
Nations	53	1745	1751	61	58
Participants	68	1729	1729	21	14
Ends	76	1726	1726	30	23
Self	74	1688	1689	73	64
Time–Space	51	1732	1734	20	18

*In percent.

Relationships among content categories are depicted graphically by plotting the location of the year of maximal concern (peak) on the rim of a circle (Figure 4.1). The circumference of the circle represents a 72-year period, or one whole L-cycle. Each labeled point on the circumference of the circle represents the year(s) in which concern with a particular category reached its maximum value. Although not indicated on the figure, concern with this same category reaches a minimum during the year represented by the point on the circle directly across from the labeled point (or a half-cycle

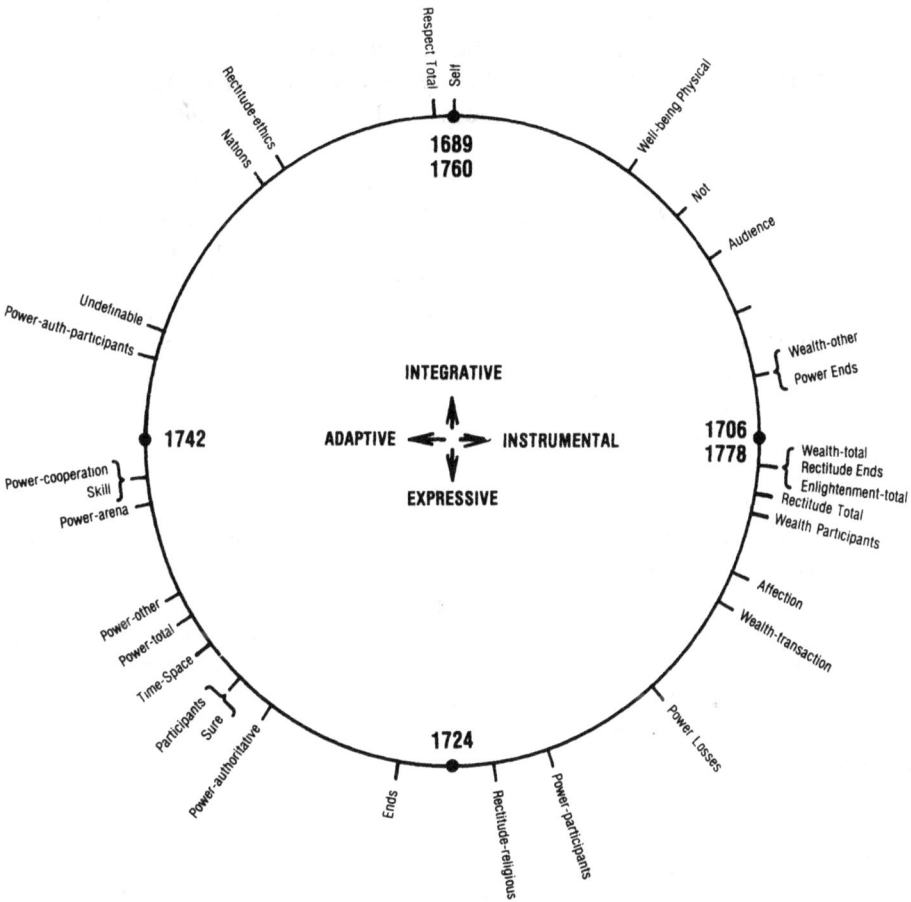

FIGURE 4.1. **Internal Structure of the Long Cycle in Britain 1689–1795 (Cycle lengths set to 72 years, variable origins).**

later). Thus the rim of the "wheel" portrays a 72-year sequence of rising and falling concern with various content categories. Also, I interpret those categories that rise and fall together, as indicated by their proximity on the wheel, as constituting a theme or issue.

More specifically, at the bottom of the circle (1724), there is maximal concern with authoritative or legitimate power (POWER AUTHORITATIVE), the loss of power (POWER LOSSES), nonauthoritative (not necessarily illegitimate) participants in the power arena (POWER PARTICIPANTS), and other social actors (PARTICIPANTS). Maximal concern with religious matters (RECTITUDE RELIGIOUS), ultimate ends or goals (ENDS), and certainty (SURE) are also found during this period. The substance of these concerns is the legitimacy and nature of the state, the Crown, and the church—in short, the identity of England.

Moving clockwise to the left side of the circle, about 1742 there is maximal concern with POWER generally (OTHER and TOTAL), government officials (AUTHORITATIVE PARTICIPANTS), other countries (NATIONS), continents, and regions (ARENAS), and treaties and alliances (POWER COOPERATION), and with SKILL. The documents of this period focus on England's pursuit of power in international relations.

At the top of the circle, in 1760 and 1689, there is maximal concern with physical survival (WELL-BEING PHYSICAL), first-person-singular pronouns (SELF), ethics (RECTITUDE ETHICS), respect generally (RESPECT TOTAL), and negation (NOT). Speeches of this period often state "law and order" themes related to conflicts between the King and his subjects. It is important to note that when there is maximal concern with the categories at top of the circle there is minimal concern with the categories that peak at the bottom of the circle—i.e., when there is maximal concern with church and state (on the bottom) there is minimal concern with "law and order" (on the top), and vice versa.

On the right side of the circle (1706 and 1778) there is maximal concern with problems related to wealth generally (WEALTH OTHER), economic transactions (WEALTH TRANSACTIONS), and persons or collectivities involved in economic processes (WEALTH PARTICIPANTS). There is also maximal concern with AFFECTION, with power and rectitude as goals rather than as means (POWER and RECTITUDE ENDS), with knowledge and wisdom (ENLIGHTENMENT TOTAL), and with second-person pronouns (AUDIENCE)—e.g., *you* and *your*. Speeches from these periods express a concern with economic problems and their practical resolution.

As in the vertical dimension, when there is maximal concern with foreign affairs (the left side) there is at the same time minimal concern with economic issues (the right side) and vice versa.

This progression of issues is interpreted as a four-phase problem-solving cycle: Integrative, Instrumental, Expressive, and Adaptive. The Integrative problem involves the coordination and cooperation among social classes and institutions, and corresponds to conflicts between King and subjects. The Instrumental problem corresponds to periods of economic adversity. The preeminent Expressive question of this period concerns church–state relations, especially Protestant succession. Last, the Adaptive problem corresponds to the War of the Austrian Succession. These interpretations are summarized in Table 4.2.[15]

---

[15]As noted in Chapter 5, there are some differences between American party platforms (Chapter 3) and British speeches in the relationship between categories and themes. For example, while WEALTH categories indicate the Instrumental theme in both sets of documents, POWER AUTHORITATIVE PARTICIPANTS and POWER COOPERATION reflect the same theme in British speeches but not in American platforms. In addition, there are some differences between the Mercantilist and Capitalist periods in the relationship between categories and themes. These results indicate that there are no fixed relationships between categories and themes. In addition, these results also indicate that different documents discuss the **same** issues in **different** terms. See Chapters 9 and 10 for further consideration of this matter.

TABLE 4.2
The Interpretation of Long-Cycle Themes in Great Britain, 1689–1795

Adaptive theme: War of Austrian Succession (1742)	Integrative theme: "Law and order" issues (1688, 1760)	Expressive theme: Church–state conflict (1724)	Instrumental theme: Economic problems (1706, 1778)
Power Arena	Rectitude Ethics	Rectitude Religious	Wealth Participants
Power Cooperation	Respect Total	Power Losses	Wealth Other
Power Authoritative Participants	Well-being Physical	Power Participant	Wealth Transaction
Power Other	Not	Power Authoritative	Wealth Total
Power Total	Self	Sure	Rectitude Ends
Skill Total		Ends	Rectitude Total
Time–Space		Participants	Power Ends
Undefinable			Enlightenment Total
Nations			Affection
			Audience

As noted, I argue that variation in concern with themes in texts causes the observed covariation among sets of content categories. The rest of this section examines portions of texts selected to show that the appropriate themes do exist in these texts and that at some level of abstraction, these themes do repeat from one occurrence of the cycle to the next.

Following the ascension of William and Mary to the throne, there is maximal concern with Integrative matters articulated in terms of "law and order" themes, which are illustrated by this brief excerpt from the address in 1690:

> It is sufficiently known how earnestly [RECTITUDE ETHICS] I have endeavored to extinguish, or at least compose, all differences amongst my subjects, and to that end, how often have I recommended an Act of Indemnity to the last Parliament; but since that part of it [Act of Indemnity][16] which related to the preventing of private suits, is already enacted, and because debates of that nature must take up more of your time than can now be spared from the dispatch of those other things which are absolutely necessary for our common safety [WELL-BEING], I intend to send you an Act of Grace, with exceptions of some few persons only, but such as may be sufficient to show my great dislike of their crimes [RECTITUDE ETHICS]; and, at the same time, my readiness to extend protection to all my other subjects, who will thereby see that they [my other subjects] can recommend themselves to me by no other methods, than what the law prescribes, which shall always be the only rules of my government.

Irrespective of any problem-solving cycle, and skeptical may argue that following a revolution the relation between the Crown and subjects would naturally be a matter of concern. However, advancing one full cycle provides textual evidence of the cyclical nature of thematic concerns. Relations between the Crown and subjects is clearly an issue in the speech of December 1757:

> I have had such ample experience of the loyalty and good affections of my faithful subjects towards me, my family, and government, in all circumstances, that I am confident [WELL-BEING] they [good affections] are not to be shaken. But I cannot avoid taking notice of that spirit of disorder, which has shewn itself amongst the common people, in some parts of the Kingdom. Let me recommend it to you, to do your part in discouraging and suppressing such abuses [RESPECT], and for maintaining the law, and lawful authority.

In 1706 there is maximal concern with WEALTH categories. Concern with economic problems is illustrated by this portion of the address of November 1709:

---

[16]Pronouns used for stylistic purposes obscure value references in text, thereby reducing the accuracy of text classification. The referents of pronouns and ambiguous phrases were inserted in the text and all inserts were placed within brackets for identification.

I think it proper to take notice to you, that the great dearth and scarcity |WEALTH| under which our neighbors abroad have suffered this year, begins to affect us in some measure at home, by the temptation of profit |WEALTH| in carrying out too much of our corn |WEALTH|, while it [corn |WEALTH|] bears so high a price |WEALTH| in foreign parts. This occasions many complaints from the poor |WEALTH|, for whose sake I earnestly recommend |POWER ENDS| to you, to take this growing evil into your consideration, having not neglected anything on my part, towards the remedy of it [the high price |WEALTH| of corn |WEALTH|], that the law would allow.

Some 72 years later there is again maximal concern with wealth-related problems, exemplified by this excerpt from the speech of January 1774:

Among the objects which . . . will come under your consideration, none can better deserve your attention than the state of the gold |WEALTH| coin |WEALTH|, which I must recommend to you in a more particular matter, as well on account of its [the state of gold |WEALTH| coin |WEALTH|] very high importance, as of peculiar advantage which the present time affords for executing, with success, such measures as you may find it expedient to adopt with respect to this great national concern.

The next period manifests great concern with Expressive matters, specifically the nature of the state in general and the King and Protestant succession in particular. Unlike the Integrative phase, which dealt with the King and His subjects, in this period it is Crown–church relations which are problematic.

In 1721 a growing crisis in the financing of government resulted in a loss of confidence in the government (Williams, 1962, pp. 176–178, 186; Plumb, 1963, pp. 25–28). By the following year major steps had been taken, under the leadership of Sir Robert Walpole, to shore up the shaky system of taxation and government finance. In that year, 1722, a plot against the government was revealed, discrediting Walpole's opposition. Much of the speech of October 1722 is taken up with the announcement of the plot, government actions to secure home and hearth, and the following reaffirmation of the system, which represents Expressive concerns:

Having thus in general laid before you the state of the present conspiracy, I must leave to you consideration what is proper, and necessary to be done, for the quiet and safety of the Kingdom. I cannot but believe the hopes |ENDS| and expectations |ENDS| of our enemies are very ill-grounded, in flattering themselves that the late discontents, occasioned by private losses and misfortunes, however industriously and maliciously formented, or turned into disaffection and a spirit of rebellion. Had I, since my accession to the throne, ever attempted |ENDS| any innovation in our established religion |RECTITUDE RELIGIOUS|; had I in any one instance, invaded the liberty or property of my subjects, I should less wonder at any endeavors to alienate the affections of my people, and draw them [my people] into measures that can end in nothing but their [my people's] own destruction.

Although the problems of this period stem from Britain's financial and economic disarray, the issues are cast fundamentally in Expressive terms. Society must be maintained against all threatening forces, both external and internal. The boundaries of culture are defended by reaffirmation of faith in the system of church and state and the constitutional relationship between King and Parliament.

During the Adaptive phase the focus is on power in the international arena. Compared with the previous Expressive phase, what is remarkable about speeches in this period is the rational manner in which the world is described and policy justified, as illustrated by these excerpts from the address of December 1743:

> Since your last meeting [POWER COOPERATION], I have, pursuant to your advice, and in consequence of your support, exerted my endeavors for the preservation of the House [POWER AUTHORITATIVE PARTICIPANTS] of Austria, and the maintenance of the balance and liberties of Europe [POWER ARENAS]. . . . In this conjucture, it is a great satisfaction to me, to acquaint you, that I have been joined [POWER COOPERATION] by a body of troops [POWER AUTHORITATIVE PARTICIPANTS] of my good friends and allies [POWER COOPERATION] the States General. In further prosecution of these measures, the definitive treaty [POWER COOPERATION] between me, the Queen [POWER AUTHORITATIVE PARTICIPANTS] of Hungary, and the King [POWER AUTHORITATIVE PARTICIPANTS] of Sardinia, has been happily concluded, which shall be laid before you.

Taken together, the preceding excerpts provide textual evidence that themes identified quantitatively are not artifacts of the content classification and/or statistical estimation procedures, but represent a textual reality of their own.

THE LONG CYCLE, 1795–1972

Sine curves were also estimated for the post-1795 data. The median wavelength is 148 years. This is virtually identical to the 152-year length of the American long cycle reported in the previous chapter. For the data transformed by 9-year moving averages, Table 4.3 presents the estimated wavelength, year of peak concern, the standardized peak year, the percent residual variance explained after removing a linear trend (where present), and the percent total variance explained.[17]

The fitted sine curves on average account for 35% of the variance after removing a linear trend (where present) and 25% of the total variance (correlations of .59 and .50, respectively). The best-fitting sine curve (the category ENDS) accounts for 77% of the residual and 70% of the total

---

[17]Of the 69 categories in the dictionary, 20 were eliminated because of low variance. Six categories did not replicate across filters.

TABLE 4.3
Curve-Fitting Results for Long Cycle, 1795–1972, 9-Year Moving Average Transformation

Content category	Wavelength in years	Peak year	Standardized peak	Residual variance explained*	Total variance explained*
Power Authoritative Participants	196	1783	1798	35	7
Power Arena	80	1902	1951	29	24
Power Authoritative	156	1873	1872	32	30
Power Conflict	146	1793	1792	32	30
Power Cooperation	166	1793	1799	7	3
Power Ends	128	1846	1846	9	5
Power Gains	168	1798	1803	58	30
Power Participants	183	1874	1868	70	70
Power Total	200	1779	1796	38	9
Rectitude Ends	144	1894	1895	38	35
Rectitude Ethics	156	1888	1886	25	15
Rectitude Gains	162	1883	1880	49	45
Rectitude Religious	96	1835	1830	29	11
Rectitude Total	174	1883	1877	39	25
Respect Gains	120	1898	1911	11	9
Respect Other	100	1907	1937	25	15
Respect Total	105	1905	1930	27	18
Skill Total	166	1954	1942	11	3
Wealth Other	136	1815	1812	32	15
Wealth Participants	128	1846	1846	41	41
Wealth Transaction	140	1815	1813	23	17
Wealth Total	126	1825	1819	31	16
Well-being Losses	150	1860	1860	20	17
Well-being Physical	147	1811	1812	37	16
Well-being Total	125	1829	1826	42	31
Enlightenment Other	134	1885	1889	53	53
Enlightenment Total	178	1882	1876	67	43
If	154	1882	1881	48	32
Sure	144	1934	1936	47	29
Undefined	120	1885	1895	29	8
Undefinable	140	1883	1885	25	12
Arenas	164	1795	1800	45	42
Audience	161	1873	1871	65	39
Means	148	1814	1814	49	40
Nations	146	1894	1895	26	26
Others	186	1800	1809	6	3
Participants	140	1918	1922	6	3
Ends	181	1905	1930	77	70
Self	121	1839	1838	26	20
Selves	160	1790	1794	55	47
Time–Space	168	1885	1882	45	44
Transaction	137	1854	1855	11	4
Transaction Gains	173	1798	1805	54	34

*In percent.

variance (correlations of .88 and .84, respectively). The worst-fitting curves that replicated across filters (OTHERS, PARTICIPANTS) accounts for 6% of the residual and 3% of the total variance (correlations of .25 and .17, respectively). As noted earlier, these curves fit about as well as those for the British Mercantilist data.

The standardized estimates of the year of maximal concern with each category are plotted on the rim of a circle whose circumference represents a 148-year period, or one whole cycle (Figure 4.2). Two aspects of this "wheel" require comment. First, the spacing of the peaks suggests that the durations of the phases may not be equal. Second, some clusters are more

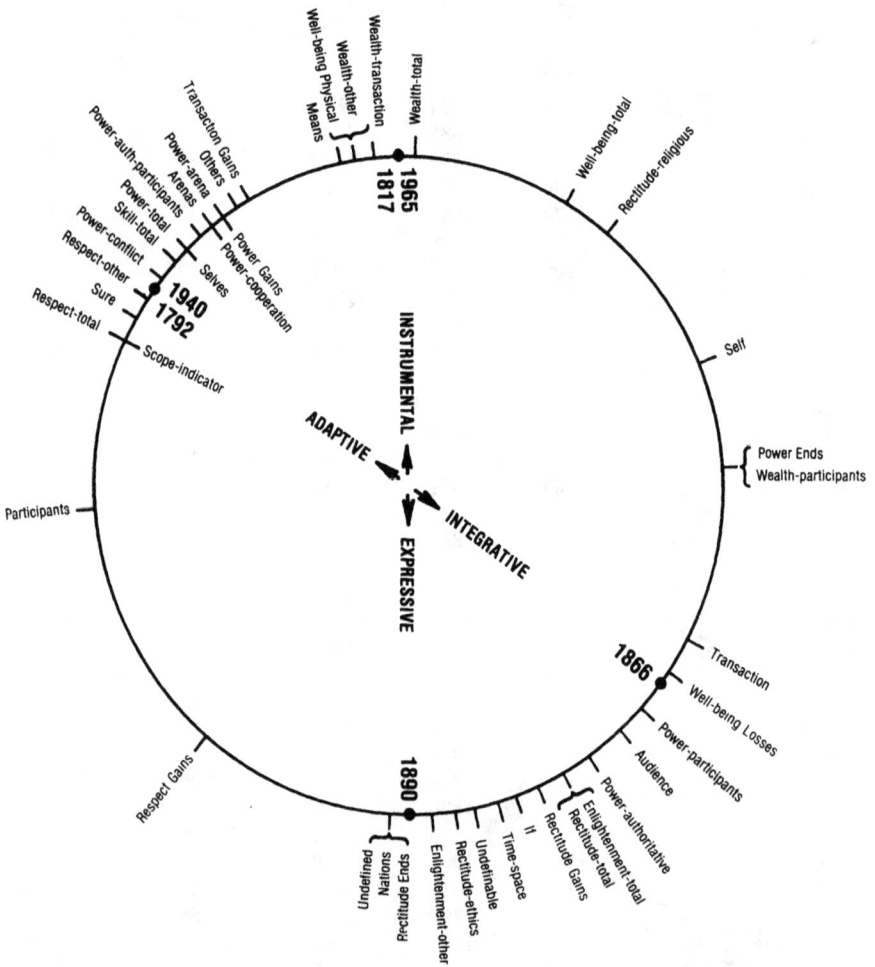

FIGURE 4.2. **Internal Structure of the Long Cycle in Britain 1795–1972 (Cycle lengths set to 148 years, variable origins).**

clearly defined than others, which may indicate that the classification scheme of the Lasswell Dictionary is more sensitive to some themes (e.g., the Adaptive) than others (cf. Chapters 2, 9, and 10).

At the top left sector of the circle (1792 and 1940), there is a maximum attention devoted to POWER, including CONFLICT and COOPERATION in the international ARENA. There is also substantial concern with various officials (POWER AUTHORITATIVE PARTICIPANTS), the granting of power (GAINS), ultimate ends (ENDS) rather than means, RESPECT, and with proficiency and competence (SKILL). The cognitive orientation tends to be "we–they," as indicated by SELVES and OTHERS. The central concerns of the 1790s and 1940s are the war with France and the war with Germany, respectively.

Another group of categories is centered about 1817 (and 1965), including WEALTH and economic TRANSACTIONS, physical well-being (WELL-BEING PHYSICAL), and means exchanged for ultimate ends (MEANS) rather than concern with the ends themselves. Economic adversity is the principal issue in these times.

During the years about 1866 (bottom right sector of the circle) there is substantial concern with the loss of well-being (WELL-BEING LOSSES), authoritative power (POWER AUTHORITATIVE), and nonauthoritative (not necessarily illegitimate) participants in the struggle for power (POWER PARTICIPANTS). There is also a preoccupation with knowledge (ENLIGHTENMENT) and with value TRANSACTIONS. The predominate issues of this period include the vote for the working and middle classes.

During the Victorian period (bottom of the circle), in the 1890s, there is peak concern with ethics (RECTITUDE ETHICS), with goodness and virtue for their own sake (RECTITUDE ENDS), and with increasing virtue (RECTITUDE GAINS) and respect (GAINS). The issues of the day are approached with uncertainty (IF), and debated in general rather than highly specific terms, which is indicated by the high occurrence of words with ambiguous value implications (UNDEFINED and UNDEFINABLE). Finally, there is maximal concern with the names of countries (NATIONS). Retrievals from text indicate the frequent occurrence of the words *Ireland* and *Irish*.

These groups of categories are interpreted as another four–phase sequence: Adaptive, Instrumental, Integrative, and Expressive. The war with France in the 1790s and the Second World War correspond to the Adaptive problem. Concern with the economic well-being of the nation is the hallmark of the Instrumental problem. The Integrative problem addresses the relationship among social classes and includes the extension of the franchise to the urban working class. The Expressive problem corresponds to the Irish Home Rule debate. These interpretations are summarized in Table 4.4.

How do the texts represent these various themes? Around 1792 the central issues are the war on the Continent and its implications at home. Foreign diplomacy is oriented toward the recruitment and support of allies

TABLE 4.4
The Interpretation of Long-Cycle Themes in Great Britain, 1795–1972

Adaptive theme: War with France, First World War (1792, 1940)	*Instrumental theme:* Economic problems (1817, 1965)	*Expressive theme:* Irish Home Rule (1890)	*Integrative theme:* Problems of the working classes (1866)
Power Authoritative Participants	Wealth Other	Rectitude Ethics	Power Authoritative
Power Arena	Wealth Transaction	Rectitude Ends	Power Participants
Power Cooperation	Wealth Total	Rectitude Gains	Well-being Losses
Power Conflict	Well-being Physical	Rectitude Total	Enlightenment Total
Power Gains	Well-being Total	Respect Gains	Wealth Participants
Power Total	Rectitude Religious	Enlightenment Other	Rectitude Total
Respect Other	Transaction Gains	Undefined	Transaction
Respect Total	Means	Undefinable	Audience
Skill Total	Self	If	
Ends		Time–Space	
Sure		Nations	
Participants			
Arenas			
Selves			
Others			

106

against the French. This excerpt from the speech of January 1794 is typical:

> We [SELVES] are engaged [POWER OTHER] in a contest on the issue of which depends the maintenance [POWER OTHER] of our [SELVES] constitution, law, and religion, and the security of all civil society. You must have observed, with satisfaction, the advantages which have been obtained by the armies of the allied [POWER COOPERATION] powers [POWER OTHER] and the change which has taken place in the general situation of Europe since the commencement of the war [POWER CONFLICT] The United Provinces have been protected from invasion [POWER CONFLICT]. The Austrian Netherlands have been recovered and maintained [POWER OTHER].

These same issues predominate some 148 years later during the war with Germany, as illustrated in this portion of the November 1942 address:

> The brilliant victory [POWER CONFLICT] in the Western Desert and the great operation forestalling the attack of our [SELVES] enemy [POWER CONFLICT] upon the French territory in Northern Africa, are notable steps toward final victory [POWER CONFLICT]. My forces [POWER OTHER] by sea, land and air continue [ENDS] to meet with courage and devotion the call which the extension of the war [POWER CONFLICT] has made upon their [my forces [POWER OTHER]] resources.

Instrumental themes focus on wealth-related problems. The well-being of the state and of individuals is tied to economic productivity and growth. The address of January 1817 emphasizes the conditions necessary for economic stability and recovery:

> I regret to be under the necessity of informing you, that there has been a deficiency in the produce [WEALTH] of the revenue [WEALTH] in the last year. But I trust that it [the deficiency in revenue [WEALTH]] is to be ascribed to a temporary cause. And I have the consolation to believe, that you will find it practicable to provide for the public service of the year, without making any addition to the burthen of the people, and without adopting any measures injurious to that system by which the public credit [WEALTH] of the country has been hitherto sustained.

Wealth-related problems predominate 148 years later, as illustrated by this portion of the 1964 address:

> At home my Government's first concern will be to maintain the strength of sterling [WEALTH] by dealing with the short-term balance of payments [WEALTH] difficulties and by initiating the longer-term structural changes in our economy [WEALTH] which will ensure purposeful expansion, rising exports [WEALTH] and a healthy balance of payments [WEALTH].

About 1866 the text indicates two Integrative issues. The first is the extension of the franchise and reform of parliamentary constituencies. The second is the amendment of laws related to commerce and industry, including ameliorative legislation to improve the lot of the working classes. The reforms of the 1860s are taken up in greater detail below in the context of electoral realignments. This section from the address of 1866 exemplifies Integrative concerns:

> I have directed that information should be procured in reference to the rights of voting in the election of members to serve in Parliament for counties, cities, and boroughs. When that information is complete, the attention of Parliament will be called to the result thus obtained, with a view to such improvements in the laws [POWER AUTHORITATIVE] which regulate the rights of voting in the election of Members to the House of Commons as may tend to strengthen our free institutions, and conduce to the public welfare.

Concern with Expressive matters peaks in 1890. A central theme of this period involves the relationship among England, Scotland, and Wales, and especially the relationship between England and Ireland (e.g., see Heyck, 1974). The fundamental question is "Who are we?" or "What does it mean to be British?" In this period, Home Rule for Ireland is the subject of a virtually perennial debate, as illustrated by this portion of the address of 1886:

> I have seen with deep sorrow the renewal, since I last addressed [ENLIGHTENMENT] you, of the attempt to excite the people of Ireland [NATIONS] to hostility against the legislative union between that country and Great Britain. I am resolutely opposed to any disturbance of the fundamental law, and in resisting it [any disturbance of the fundamental law] I am convinced [ENLIGHTENMENT] that I shall be heartily supported by my Parliament and my people.

The primary question concerns the boundaries of the nation-state and the relationship among the parts, not so much in a class sense, as in the preceding phase, but in a territorial sense.[18] England is forced to confront and eventually compromise with Irish nationalism, an alteration that changes the answer to the question "Who are we?" This question is analogous to issues confronting America during its Civil War. After the debate on the identity of British culture, the problem-solving sequence begins again with the next Adaptive phase, which in Great Britain corresponds to the Second World War.

SOCIAL CHANGE AND COLLECTIVE PERCEPTIONS

To insist that sequences of themes repeat themselves is to assert that since 1795 the language used to describe the world repeats itself every 148

---

[18]This is not to imply that there is no social basis for territorial disputes, but whatever its basis, conflict is articulated in territorial rather than in social terms.

years or so. A related implication is that disparate historical events separated by one-and-a-half centuries are interpreted in similar terms. For example, the cyclical culture model equates British perception of the war with France in the 1790s with British perception of the war with Germany in the 1940s. One might argue that the speeches of the 1790s and 1940s are similar because they respond to similar circumstances—namely, war—and that the recurrence of issue concerns merely reflects the recurrence of external events. The following evidence suggests a different conclusion.

The First World War occurs about an eighth of a cycle after 1890, the point of maximal concern with Expressive problems. In contrast to both the 1790s and the early 1940s, the cyclical culture model suggests that during World War I there would be less concern with indicators of Adaptive issues (POWER categories), and greater concern with indicators of Expressive themes (e.g., RECTITUDE). It is instructive to compare the excerpts presented above as examples of Adaptive themes with this portion of the February 1916 speech:

> The spirit of my allies and of my people, who are united in this conflict by ever strengthening ties of sympathy and understanding, remains steadfast in the resolve to secure reparation for the victims of unprovoked and unjustifiable outrages and effectual safeguards for all nations againat the aggression of a power which mistakes force for right and expediency for honor. With a proud and grateful confidence I look to the courage, tenacity, and resources of my navy and army, on whom we depend worthily to perform our part in the attainment of this goal.

The long culture cycle defines the terms of other debates as well. As documented earlier in this chapter, the financial crisis of 1721–1722 is addressed primarily in Expressive terms. The speech of 1722 discusses the identity of English culture in terms of Protestant succession, papal plots, and the loyalty of King and subjects. However, during the Instrumental phase a quarter of a cycle earlier, in 1706, economic problems are discussed in economic terms, such as the high price and scarcity of corn in Britain and on the Continent.

These examples indicate that it is not the objective situation that determines the way in which the world is understood. Instead, the evidence suggests that in the long run L-cycle dynamics partly determine the themes by which history is interpreted.

Even if these culture cycles do reflect long-term patterns in the **perception** of political issues and events, are they merely epiphenomena causally unrelated to power and action processes? Or are these thematic cycles an integral part of long-term contests for power and position, contests whose outcomes determine the political fortunes of classes, institutions, and individuals? The following analysis of the L-cycle and party realignments in nineteenth- and twentieth-century Britain provides evidence supporting the latter conclusion.

PARTY REALIGNMENTS AND THE LONG CYCLE

As defined by V. O. Key (1955, p. 4), realigning or "critical" elections are those in which "the depth and intensity of electoral involvement are high, in which more or less profound readjustments occur in the relations of power within the community, and in which new and durable electoral groupings are formed." Operationally, analysts of critical elections use "sudden increases in voter turnout" and "long-lasting shifts among voters in support for parties" as the indicators of critical elections (e.g., Key, 1955; Burnham, 1970). These indicators of critical elections work well for the analysis of modern mass-party systems, but are less easily applied to the British Victorian era. During the nineteenth century, the most important readjustments of power in British electoral system were the extensions of the franchise in 1832, 1867, and again in 1885 (see Cornford, 1963, 1970; Dunbabin, 1969; Hanham, 1968). It is debatable whether the three Reform Acts and the elections that followed are "critical" elections in the modern American sense of the term. However, these dates denote key changes among the contestants for power and legitimacy within the British electoral system.

The exact points of realignment in twentieth-century Britain are also the subject of an ongoing debate. Nevertheless, there is general agreement (Butler and Stokes, 1974; Crewe et al., 1977; Miller, 1971) that the significant realignments of this period are the decline of the Liberals in 1909–1924, the Labour victory in 1945, and the decline of two-party politics in the 1964 and subsequent elections.

As indicated by Table 4.5, there is a moderate but not perfect relationship between the phases of the British Capitalist L-cycle and critical elections. Proceeding chronologically, there is no significant electoral event that corresponds to maximal concern with Instrumental problems in 1817, neither is there a correspondence between the Reforms of 1832 and the decline of the Liberals 1910–1924 and L-cycle phases. The remaining four critical elections correspond quite well to L-cycle phases: the Reform of 1867 to the Integrative phase of 1867, the Reforms of 1885 to the Expressive phase of 1890, the 1945 Labour victory to the 1940 Adaptive phase, and the decline of Labour–Conservative voting beginning in 1964 to the Instrumental phase of 1964.

The relationship between critical elections and L-cycle phases can be substantially improved by considering a long cycle with equally spaced phases. As noted, the asymmetrical clustering of content categories in the British Capitalist period suggests either that the four phases are not of equal

TABLE 4.5
Electoral Realignments and the Long-Cycle Phases in Great Britain since 1800

Electoral realignment	Date	Estimated long-cycle phases		Theoretical long-cycle phases	
		L-cycle phase	*Date*	*L-cycle phase*	*Date*
	—	Instrumental	1817	—	—
Reforms of 1830–1832	1832	—	—	Instrumental	1832
Reforms of 1867	1867	Integrative	1867	Integrative	1869
Reforms of 1885	1885	Expressive	1890	—	—
Decline of Liberals	1924/1910–1924*	—	—	Expressive	1906
Victory of Labour	1945	Adaptive	1940	Adaptive	1943
Decline of two-party vote?	1964–1974	Instrumental	1964	Instrumental	1980

*Estimated L-cycle phase/theoretical L-cycle phase.

duration or that the phases are actually of equal duration but the content classification scheme yields better indicators of some themes than others. Explanations of the long cycle and critical elections that stress cohort succession will be discussed below. Here it suffices to note that such explanations assume that the rate of change of population replacement is a constant. Consequently, the duration of each L-cycle phase and the interval between critical elections should also be a constant.

Assuming that each phase is 37 years long (a quarter of the 148-year cycle), and that the transformation from Mercantilism to Capitalism occurs in 1795, Table 4.5 also presents the relationship between this theoretical or idealized cycle and critical elections. Also, there is some doubt as to whether the Reforms of 1885 constituted a realignment. Specifically, the Representation of the People Act, 1884, and the Redistribution of Seats Act, 1885, created structural changes in the organization of the constituencies and extended the franchise (Hanham, 1968, esp. pp. 25–26, 35). However, voting patterns suggest that realignment did not occur until the election of 1906 (Cornford, 1963, Graph 5-1, p. 114; Cornford, 1970, p. 53; Dunbabin, 1966, p. 92). Consequently, if a critical realignment does not occur in 1885, then the relationship between the L-cycle phases and realignments is stronger than Table 4.5 suggests. Thus, except for the most recent electoral changes, there is an excellent fit between the theoretical long cycle and critical elections. These findings do replicate in broad detail the relationship in America between critical realignments and problem-solving phases. However, these results are highly suggestive rather than conclusive; additional research remains necessary.

EXPLANATIONS OF THE LONG CYCLE

The explanation of the long cycle is based in part on the conceptualization of culture and society as open cybernetic systems.[19] Viewed as a cybernetic system, a society monitors its current state relative to its culturally determined goals, which in the long run are identified during the Expressive phase.

Open systems are partly characterized by the fact that they process inputs and produce outputs. With respect to culture, information in the sense of facts or raw data[20] is converted by culture systems and their

---

[19] Applications of system theory to the social sciences include Buckley (1967), Deutsch (1966), Geyer and van der Zouwen (1986), Kuhn (1974), von Bertalanffy (1968), and Weinburg (1975).

[20] Since language and other sign systems are used to convey even raw data, culture immediately constrains, shapes, and interprets the collective experience. Thus, except at the limit, experience and information do not exist apart from their interpretation by and within culture.

dynamics into meaning or shared understanding. Information from within and without is thus organized and given meaning partly on the basis of the dynamics of culture.[21] Hence, adaptive problem-solving by societies is always constrained by cultural processes. This is why the perception of historical events is in large measure determined by the long cycle.

Explanation of the L-cycle requires consideration of two related but analytically distinct problems: changes **within** and changes **of** the system (Parsons, 1969; Namenwirth and Bibbee, 1976). Changes **within** the system are alterations that do not transform the fundamental nature (parameters) of culture. For instance, the long cycle is a continuous change within the British Mercantilist and Capitalist culture systems, respectively. In each British epoch the four L-cycle themes represent problems whose resolution is a necessary but not sufficient condition for adaptation to changing social, cultural, and physical environments.

Given the four phases, it may be asked why there is not equal concern with all problems at all times. Namenwirth argues in Chapter 3 that there is a logic of problem solving stating that goal attainment must proceed in phases or subtasks and in a special order. However, in light of the observed transformation of phase sequence, problem solving in terms of a single inherent sequence or logic cannot serve as a general explanation of the long cycle.

The Bales–Parsons–Namenwirth model suggests an alternative explanation. Phase movement is an efficient problem-solving process. Except at some theoretical limit, societies have but a finite supply of those resources necessary for adaptive problem solving. Although some resources will always be devoted to each problem, devoting more than average resources to one problem at a time is more effective and efficient than equal allocations. Irrespective of the particular phase sequence, the likelihood that a social system will survive is increased by efficient and effective utilization of social, cultural, and material resources.

In addition, phase movement in group problem solving as proposed by Bales is a dynamic equilibrium model. Attention devoted to one problem leads to increased tension over neglected problems. Tension is reduced by shifting attention and resources to neglected issues, and party realignments are an essential component of this process. In Western democracies long-term coalitions are determined by party realignments among the electorate, as with the New Deal realignment of the 1930s. The new coalition rises to power by articulating issues that the old coalition did not address and that are strongly felt by the electorate. However, party realignments are not universal features of social organization, and therefore, a more general

---

[21]This is similar to Buckley's (1967) argument, except he analyzes individuals in statuses and roles. Meaning, which refers to shared understanding, is a property of collectivities rather than of individuals. Therefore, in the present analysis, the units that constitute the system are collectivities: groups, organizations, and institutions.

conceptualization of resource allocation is required. I will return to this issue shortly.

Changes **of** the system transform social organization and culture. In Great Britain, the transformation from Mercantilism to Capitalism occurs when the market replaces the state as the primary mode of allocation of land, labor, and capital (Polanyi, 1957). There is also a concomitant change to a less hierarchically structured society.

Culture is also transformed. During the Mercantilist period the boundaries of the cultural system are discussed in terms of Protestant succession and papal plots. During the more secular Capitalist period cultural identity is discussed in territorial terms—i.e., the relationships between England and Wales, England and Scotland, and especially England and Ireland. In a similar fashion the Integrative conflicts concern King and subjects in the Mercantilist epoch and concern the middle- and working-class franchise in the Capitalist epoch.

Another change of the system is the jump in wavelength from 72 to 148 years. The explanation of wavelength is disputed. As originally stated, Namenwirth's generational argument is falsified by the data presented here. He suggests that a change in the wavelength is caused by a change in the length of a political generation. The length of a political generation, moreover, is constrained by the life span and by the age of entrance into the political community (Namenwirth and Bibbee, 1976, p. 154). Namenwirth also believes alterations in wavelength to be gradual rather than sudden (Namenwirth and Bibbee, 1976, p. 158). However, the wavelength of the British L-cycle quickly doubles, and there is little evidence indicating drastic increases during the 1790s in either life span or in the age required for membership in the political community.

An alternative explanation subsumes Namenwirth's generational argument while addressing two key aspects of wavelength: an explanation for the sudden change in wavelength between the Mercantilist and Capitalist epochs, and an explanation for wavelength within these epochs. Specifically, wavelength is determined **within** epochs by the rate of population replacement. Population replacement refers to the turnover of the membership in pertinent decision-making institutions. Within these institutions, the process of coalition formation, dissolution, and reformation is crucial to problem-solving dynamics.

Coalitions are inherent in social organization (Simmel, 1950, pp. 87–180). Party realignments represent a special case in which the composition of the coalition depends upon the structure of the political institutions. For example, in Eastern European single-party systems the analogy to party realignments is coalition formation among high party members, and/or within the Politburo.[22] Similarly, during the British Mercantilist period,

[22]Bunce (1981; cf. Roeder, 1985) provides substantial evidence indicating that elite succession is related to policy innovation in democratic and communist societies.

coalitions among members of Parliament and factions of the aristocracy are analogous to party realignments during the Capitalist period.

The change in wavelength **between** epochs is caused by the change in society's long-term decision-making mechanism that is part of the transformation from Mercantilist to Capitalist political economy. According to Polanyi (1957), 1795 marks the triumph of the market over the state as the allocation mechanism for capital, land, and labor. The logic of the marketplace is one factor in the replacement of monarchy, aristocracy, and their Parliament by universal adult suffrage and representative government. Although the principle of universal suffrage is implied by the ascendancy of the market in 1795, it nevertheless takes twelve decades to fully establish universal suffrage in law. As noted, extending the franchise and reforming government are the leitmotifs of nineteenth- and early twentieth-century British political history.

Within epochs, Namenwirth's generational hypothesis requires elaboration. In the Capitalist period, party realignments are the central mechanism by which one coalition of voters brings a new major problem to the fore. What, then, is the relationship among population replacement, realignments, and the L-cycle? Analyzing realignments in America, Beck (1974) asserts that the progression of cohorts from birth to death is the underlying mechanism of party realignments. He argues, as does Namenwirth, that the individual's political views remain almost constant after adolescence.[23] Beck then divides the population into three groups whose proportions are always changing: (1) the realignment generation, (2) children of the realignment generation, and (3) their offspring, whom he calls the "children of normal politics." The latter group is socialized during periods lacking deep political divisions and therefore has the weakest partisan attachments. Realignments occur both when there is substantial political strife and when, through population replacement, a significant proportion of the electorate has weak attachments to old alignments.

The key question is the cause of "substantial political strife." Beck argues that societal conflict results from random shocks such as wars, depressions, and so forth. Conflict will lead to realignment only when through population replacement the electorate is "ripe for realignment." The difficulty with this argument is that it does not address the nature of social conflict that arises from these random shocks. Therefore, the argument cannot account for the issues and cleavages of the resulting realignment.

Phase movement, however, provides an explanation for the source and content of (in Beck's terms) societal conflict. The social conflict that accompanies realignments reflects societal tension resulting from long-

---

[23]Using panel data and postwar election surveys, Markus (1983) provides strong evidence for the stability of party identification after adolescence. His model shows that as each cohort aged, aggregate partisanship remained almost constant.

neglected societal problems. Communications about these broad issues and conflicts, as indicated by the L-cycle, directs attention toward neglected problems and is one factor in defining the lines of conflict and emerging coalitions.

If the population replacement hypothesis is true, a specific relationship should exist between the turnover of Members of Parliament and the length of the Mercantilist L-cycle. The average tenure for MPs should be about a quarter of a cycle, or 18 years. Further research is also necessary to test the hypothesized relationship between the L-cycle in the Mercantilist period and shifting coalitions in Parliament.

CONCLUSION

The data presented here suggest that the long-term dynamics of social and cultural systems are in part cyclical and in part discontinuous: they are cyclical within epochs and discontinuous between them. This view of historical change stands in marked contrast to theories of linear evolution or progressive development. Within epochs, themes or political issues repeat themselves in essentially the same form, implying that the L-cycle is the result of a deterministic, collective process, rather than the summation of rational, voluntaristic, individual short-term decisions. In this view, there exist some long-term dynamics of social and culture change that remain beyond direct rational control and intervention.

Based on the definition of culture as an abstract system of ideas and on the assumption of cultural realism, this chapter has argued for culture determinism. Yet it must be emphasized that the L-cycle is only one of many culture dynamics. These other culture dynamics have different relationships to other systems. Two examples are pertinent. First, the following chapter argues that culture in part responds to economic change and is also a vital part of the process by which long-term economic problems are solved, either by a structural reorganization of Capitalist political economy, or by adjustment of trade, manufacturing, and inventories in a Mercantilist political economy. Second, Chapter 6 argues that culture is an intervening variable in the (partial) determination of election-to-election changes in voter support for the two major parties. Specifically, certain themes in party platforms intervene between changes in economic performance and election outcome. These themes provide alternative interpretations of economic performance; in effect the electorate is asked to choose between them.

There are many culture dynamics. Consequently, those who insist on monocausal theories or who insist that there can only be one kind of relationship between culture and other systems (culture as cause, culture as consequence) ignore the richness of culture change partly documented in this volume.

5

Culture and Economy in the Western World System[1]

Do you know those charts, where the movement of prices, discount rates, etc. . . . during the year is plotted? To analyze the phenomenon of crisis, I have attempted several times to compute the formulas of those irregular curves (I think that is possible if sufficient reliable material can be made available) in order to determine mathematically the main laws governing the crisis.[2]

MARX TO ENGELS,
May 1873

Economic setbacks in Western industrialized nations since the early 1970s have caused renewed interest in a 50-year economic cycle known as the "long wave" or "Kondratieff cycle."[3] In recent times the low points of the Kondratieff cycle (hereafter K-cycle) correspond to the Great Depression of the 1930s and to earlier depressions in the 1890s and approximately 1850.

[1]This chapter incorporates material published in Weber (1981). Most recently, the writing and research was supported in part by a Fulbright Fellowship and Guest Professorship in the Unit of Mass Communications in the Department of Political Science, University of Gothenburg, Gothenburg, Sweden, March to June, 1986. Earlier, the research reported here was supported by National Science Foundation Dissertation Research Grant, GS-42403. The comments of John Coakley and Ib Damgaard Petersen on Weber (1981) were especially helpful in making revisions. Thanks to Joshua S. Goldstein for making his data available.
[2]Quoted by Barraclough (1974).
[3]The Kondratieff cycle was named after its "discoverer," the late Russian economist N. D. Kondratieff (1926, 1935). Tinbergen (1983) traces the discovery of the economic long wave to two Dutch researchers, van Gelderen and de Wolff. Van Duijn (1979) traces the discovery of the long wave economic cycle as far back as an article appearing in 1847 (Clarke).

Robert Philip Weber wrote this chapter.

The cause of the K-cycle is disputed.[4] For example, Forrester (1976; 1977) argues that the K-cycle is an endogenous cycle caused by the interaction between the capital goods and consumer durable goods sectors of the economy. An explanation with a wider following is based on the work of Schumpeter (1939) on entrepreneurs and technological innovation and on the work of Dean (1950), Levitt (1965), Vernon (1966), and others on product life-cycle theory. Van Duijn (1977, 1979, 1983), Mensch (1979), Mandel (1975, 1980) and others (cf. Freeman, 1983; Kleinknecht, 1981) argue that each upswing represents the widespread exploitation of a new cluster of technological innovations. When the market becomes saturated, that is, when these innovations become widely diffused and less profitable, the economy declines until a new set of innovations is adopted and profitability restored.

In a related line of argument, neo-Marxists equate the K-cycle with so-called crises in capitalist political economy. For example, Gordon's (1978) explanation of the K-cycle also emphasizes profits. He argues that a crisis is caused by a structural impediment to the process of capital accumulation. Each crisis is then resolved by a structural reorganization of the political economy, which restores profitability and promotes capital accumulation. Wright (1978, Ch. 3) has proposed a similar explanation of crises, but without explicitly linking crises to the K-cycle.

Goldstein (1985, 1986a, 1986b; cf. Thompson and Zuk, 1982; Väy-rynen, 1983) demonstrates a relationship between the K-cycle and wars involving "great powers," but whether war is a cause or consequence of the K-cycle remains undetermined. Reasonable arguments exist for both positions. The position maintaining that war is a cause of economic fluctuations holds that the economy expands because of expenditures by the state on war material and personnel. However, the costs of the war soon prove excessive and in the ensuing peace the economy declines as revenue and profits decline in the absence of large state expenditures. People then forget the expense and adverse consequences of the last war, and the state is free to increase expenditures once again for military preparations.

The alternative argument holds that economic expansion causes the focus of the country to shift to external rather than internal issues. Having more funds available for military matters, and buoyed up by confidence inspired by 20 or more years of relatively sustained economic growth, military involvements become much more likely at the end of the upswing than elsewhere during the economic cycle.

Both these arguments are compatible with innovation theory. In the first instance, rising military expenditures are used to foster technological innovation. In the second instance, technological innovation is adapted to military purposes, creating the perception that a country's military is well

---

[4] As noted below, the very existence of the Kondratieff cycle, or long wave, is disputed by Neoclassical economists.

prepared to engage in war. This perception reinforces the sense of strength and well-being mentioned earlier that results from a long period of sustained economic growth.

Goldstein (1985, 1986b), Wallerstein (1980), Metz (1984), and others argue that K-cycles can be found prior to the advent of industrial capitalism in the 1790s and early decades of the nineteenth century. Goldstein, for example, finds K-cycles beginning in 1495. This assertion raises some critically important theoretical and empirical issues. With respect to theory, if K-cycles are a consequence of capitalist political economy, then the contention that K-cycles exist for many centuries requires either the assumption that capitalism existed relatively unchanged in some critical aspects over the same time span, or the assumption that some cause unrelated to the essential nature of capitalism is responsible for this 50-year economic fluctuation. The first position represents my understanding of Wallerstein (1980); for reasons developed later in this chapter I believe this position to be incorrect. The second position is Goldstein's. His results are theoretically attractive exactly because they attribute the K-cycle to war, which may be a more universal process than are the structures and processes of industrial capitalism. Although not definitive, empirical evidence presented later in this chapter suggests that at least for Great Britain in the period 1689–1790, Goldstein's dating of K-cycles is incorrect, thus casting doubt on the validity of his argument.

If K-cycles as such do exist prior to the 1790s, then this fact casts doubt on innovation theories, which require a certain level of scientific and technological achievement as a base to begin with, and which require a capitalism relatively unfettered by the remnants of traditional society. Evidence presented below and in the preceding chapter suggests otherwise. Specifically, in Britain between 1689 and 1790 capitalism existed in the form of mercantilism. During this period the dynamics of culture, economy, and polity differed substantially from the dynamics of post-1790 Britain. I will return to these issues later.

While considerable attention has been given to the technological and material aspects of K-cycles, little attention has been given to the relationship between culture[5] and long-term economic fluctuations. An exception is Namenwirth's analysis of changing themes or issues in American party platforms in presidential campaigns 1844–1964. As described in Chapter 3, Namenwirth found two long-term thematic cycles, 152 and 48 years in length. Namenwirth interprets the longer cycle to reflect political and cultural problem-solving, and the shorter cycle to reflect economic problem-solving.

---

[5] *Culture* refers to abstract systems of ideas, while *society* refers to the system of social interaction. *Attention* refers to the process of selective perception. While there are action processes underlying attention, the content of attention is in the realm of culture. See Chapters 4 and 1 for further discussion.

120 Studies in Culture Dynamics

More specifically, Namenwirth interprets the themes of the 152-year cycle as a variation of the Bales–Parsons (Parsons and Bales, 1953; Parsons *et al.*, 1953; Bales, 1950; 1953; Bales and Strodtbeck, 1953) four-function (AGIL) paradigm: Adaptive, Instrumental,[6] Integrative, and Expressive. Specifically, Namenwirth finds that every 30 to 40 years attention shifts to a new major issue, represented by such questions as "How shall we meet challenges from other states in the international community?" or "How shall we produce the material and social goods required for the good society?" or "How shall we achieve social and economic justice?" or "What does it mean to be American?"

The second, 48-year thematic cycle consists of four issues or phases, each related to a particular phase of the K-cycle. At the lowest point in the economic cycle, wealth is the single overriding issue. Because attention focuses almost exclusively on the internal problem of economic performance, Namenwirth labels this theme the Parochial phase. As the economy begins to expand, attention shifts to social reform; hence this is called the Progressive theme. At the peak of the economic expansion a mood of great optimism exists and attention shifts to the external international arena. Namenwirth calls this phase the Cosmopolitan theme. As the economy begins to decline, traditional values are resurrected, and restraint becomes the fiscal watchword of the times. Namenwirth labels this the Conservative theme. Finally, as the economy reaches the bottom of its decline, the thematic cycle begins again with the next Parochial theme.

PRESENT PROBLEM

To test Namenwirth's cyclical model, I content-analyzed British Speeches from the Throne 1689–1972, which were briefly described at the beginning of the previous chapter.[7] This chapter is a partial report of the research results and addresses the shorter thematic cycle in both the British Mercantilist and Capitalist periods.[8]

[6]Following Bales, Namenwirth uses the terms *Instrumental* and *Expressive* instead of Parsons's terms *Goal Attainment* and *Latency*, respectively. Similar cycles were observed in British Speeches from the Throne, 1689–1972 (Chapter 4). In the Mercantilist (1689–1795) period, the wavelength of the long cycle is 72 years and the thematic sequence interpreted as Adaptive, Integrative, Instrumental, and Expressive. In the Capitalist period, (1795–1972) the wavelength is 152 years and the thematic sequence interpreted as Adaptive, Instrumental, Integrative, and Expressive.

[7]See Chapter 4 for a justification of using the Queen's speech and for methodological details not repeated in this chapter for the sake of brevity.

[8]Weber (1981) addressed only the Capitalist period. In addition, the arguments presented here differ in many respects from my earlier work on culture and economic cycles (Weber, 1978, 1981, 1983b).

Using content-analytic and other data, this chapter argues that in response to changes in economic performance, systematic changes occur in the interpretations of economic and social reality that are offered by elites to justify policy. In the period before 1795, such justifications largely address the means by which Mercantilist economic theory sought to achieve the twin goals of power and plenty (Viner, 1969)—namely, foreign trade, processing of raw materials, manufacturing for export, and the employment of large numbers of the poor in these endeavors. In Capitalist political economy these justifications are an integral part of the process by which the need for innovation and entrepreneurial activity is communicated within the world system during periods of economic depression, and by which capital is reallocated to innovative sectors of the economy from those sectors that are no longer profitable. Finally, in the post-1795 period, these legitimations, and therefore culture, are also an integral part of one process by which core states in the world system go to war and eventually make peace.

More specifically, empirical results presented in this chapter show that the dynamics of culture differ between the British Mercantilist[9] period, 1689–1795, and the British Capitalist period, 1795–1972. In the Mercantilist period, there is a relationship between the 32-year thematic cycle and economic fluctuations. The cause of the 32-year economic cycle, whose existence is implied by the content analysis results, is unclear, but here is a hypotheses: The 32-year economic cycle may be caused by the interactions among investment, trade manufacturing, and inventories, and thus may be similar to the much shorter (3- to 5-year) business or inventory cycle observed in contemporary America. I will return to this issue below.

In the Capitalist period, there is a strong relationship between the Kondratieff (50-year) economic cycle and a 50-year thematic cycle in British and American political texts. Although the wavelengths differ, these two thematic cycles are interpreted as the sequence Parochial, Progressive, Cosmopolitan, Conservative. Further, the wavelength during the British Capitalist period and the phase sequences in both periods replicate Namenwirth's findings for America, reported in Chapter 3.

The following section outlines the content-analytic and statistical estimation techniques applied to the British speeches. The content analysis results are then presented and interpreted.

THE SHORT CULTURE CYCLE, 1689–1790

Using computer-aided content analysis (Stone *et al.*, 1966; Kelly and Stone, 1975; Weber, 1985a), the words of the British speeches were

---

[9]See note 6 in Chapter 4 for comments on the discontinuity between the Mercantilist and Capitalist periods.

classified into content categories defined by the Lasswell Value Dictionary (Lasswell and Namenwirth, 1968; Chapter 2). After assigning word senses to the categories of the dictionary, the computer reports the percentage of words in each category in each document.[10]

As discussed in the previous two chapters, Namenwirth inferred themes by fitting sine curves to the data for each category.[11] The fitted sine curve is an estimate of the wavelength and the year(s) of maximal or peak concern with a content category. Themes are inferred from content categories that rise and fall together—that is, have similar wavelengths and peak together.

For the British data, however, there are unequal time intervals between speeches, and many documents are relatively short.[12] To resolve these problems, two data transformations or filters are each separately applied to the raw data: a 9-year moving average, and the aggregation of speeches occurring within each 4-year interval.[13] Sine curves are then estimated separately for each transformed series and the results compared to assess the effect, if any, of the transformations on the estimates of wavelength and inflection points (year of peak concern) of the sine curves. The results are unlikely to be artifacts when the estimated sine curves replicate across transformations. Moreover, in this instance, when the population of speeches is analyzed and classical inferential statistics are inappropriate, replication across filters provides a decision rule for distinguishing real curves from artifacts.

After removing a linear trend[14] (where present) and, in most cases, the 72-year L-cycle (Chapter 4), a second sinusoidal fluctuation was found in many residuals.[15] The median goodness-of-fit is only moderate. On average,

[10]The current LVD (Namenwirth and Weber, 1974; Chapter 2) classifies text more precisely than did earlier versions of the dictionary. Greater accuracy is achieved by incorporating rules for distinguishing among the various senses of words with more than one meaning, or homographs (Kelly and Stone, 1975). See Chapter 2 and Weber (1985a) for details.

[11]Additional details of the stepwise detrending are reported in Chapter 4.

[12]The intervals between speeches vary from 3 months to 3 years. They also vary between 180 and 1,000 words in length. By comparison, the length of American party platforms varied between 350 and 16,000 words (Namenwirth and Lasswell, 1970).

[13]See note 12 in Chapter 4 for details.

[14]Weber (1978) interprets the linear trend to reflect modernization, so that concern with religious matters declines while concern with economic matters increases. These linear trends are approximations to what are probably logistic of S-shaped curves. Also, changes in slope between Mercantilist and Capitalist Britain reflect the change from community to society or any of the related, similar distinctions. For example, the rate of secularization was higher during the Capitalist than the Mercantilist period.

[15]The short cycle is estimated using data transformed by both 9-year moving average and 4-year aggregation filters. There are, however a number of difficulties: First, the short cycle is typically estimated after variation accounted for by the linear trend and a longer cycle (Chapter 4) have been removed; therefore, it can account for only relatively little of the total variation in concern with various categories. Second, the short document length combines with

the shorter sine curves account for about 20% of the total variance in each content category. Nevertheless, for many categories the estimation results are consistent across the two data filters.[16]

As noted in the previous two chapters, the most parsimonious assumption is that change in concern with these categories proceeds at one rate or wavelength, rather than at a different wavelength for different categories. As before (Chapters 3 and 4), the estimated wavelengths and peaks, or points of maximal concern, were standardized to the median wavelength and median peak year[17] for 24 categories. Table 5.1 presents the estimated wavelengths, year of peak concern, standardized peak, the percentage of residual and total variance accounted for, and the correlation between the estimated curve and the residualized data.[18]

The fitted sine curves on average account for 36% of the variance after removing a linear trend and a long sine wave (where present), and 21% of the total variance (correlations of .60 and .49, respectively). The best-fitting sine curve (for the category MEANS)[19] accounts for 68% of the residual and 54% of the total variance. These correspond to correlations of .82 and .73, respectively. The worst-fitting curve that replicated across data filters (SELVES) accounts for 15% of the residual and 3% of the total variance (correlations of .39 and .17, respectively). In this period the sine curves fit a little bit better than those for the British Capitalist data[20] (see below).

---

the first problem so that in any particular speech there may be relatively few words associated with these themes in the Mercantilist period. Another difficulty stems from the fact that variation attributable to the short cycle represents concern over and above what would be expected (or predicted) on the basis of the linear trend and long cycle. Consequently, it becomes difficult to relate retrievals from text to this "excess" level of concern. Nevertheless, retrievals from text presented below strongly support the existence of this shorter culture cycle in the Mercantilist period.

[16]The ad hoc decision rule adopted here is that the peak year of concern for data transformed by the 9-year moving average filter must be within a quarter of a cycle, or 8 years, of the estimated peak year for the 4-year aggregation data.

[17]The estimated curves were standardized to a wavelength of 32 years according to

$$\text{standard peak} = (\text{original peak} \times \text{median wavelength})/\text{observed wavelength}$$

where "original peak" is the distance of the estimated peak in years from the median peak, the median wavelength is the median for all categories retained in the analysis, and where the observed wavelength is the estimated wavelength of the curve to be standardized.

[18]Of the 69 content categories in the LVD, 20 were eliminated from the present investigation because of low variance. Of the remaining 49, 19 did not manifest any cycle whose wavelength was near 32 years. Of the remaining 30, 6 manifested short cycles that did not replicate across filters, and these were also eliminated from further consideration. The data for the 4-year aggregations are omitted in the interest of conserving space.

[19]Category names are capitalized throughout. See Chapter 2 for detailed definitions.

[20]The difference is about 10%–12% of the variance. One cannot tell whether there is any substantive import to this fact, or whether it reflects the mathematical fact that higher-frequency sine curves (shorter wavelengths) tend to account for more of the variance than do lower-frequency (longer) curves.

TABLE 5.1
Curve-Fitting Results for Short Cycle, 1689–1795, 9-Year Moving Average Transformation

Content category	Wavelength in years	Peak year	Standardized peak	Residual variance explained*	Total variance explained*
Power Authoritative Participants	35	1707	1704	32	18
Power Authoritative	20	1708	1703	40	25
Power Cooperation	25	1708	1706	31	13
Power Losses	31	1708	1708	27	16
Power Participants	28	1718	1718	53	24
Power Ends	42	1733	1729	24	13
Rectitude Ethics	24	1704	1700	60	43
Rectitude Religious	37	1716	1716	42	17
Respect Total	40	1689	1689	19	6
Skill Total	25	1702	1698	55	26
Wealth Other	30	1695	1694	44	31
Wealth Transaction	33	1720	1720	48	27
Wealth Total	31	1693	1693	33	33
Well-being Total	42	1685	1692	30	22
Enlightenment Gains	46	1692	1699	37	34
Undefinable	32	1707	1707	65	26
Audience	30	1721	1722	11	7
Means	42	1716	1716	68	54
Ends	30	1709	1709	22	12
Participants	26	1715	1715	12	8
Self	30	1717	1717	44	10
Selves	28	1711	1710	15	3
Time–Space	31	1698	1699	24	17
Transaction	41	1724	1722	26	24

*In percent.

As in earlier chapters, the standardized peaks are plotted on a circle whose rim represents the 32-year sequence of peak concern with various content categories (Figure 5.1). Each labeled point on the circumference of the circle represents the year(s) in which concern with a particular category reached its maximum value. Although not indicated on the figure, concern with this same category reaches a minimum during the year represented by the point on the circle directly across from the labeled point (or a half-cycle later). Thus the rim of the "wheel" portrays a 32-year sequence of rising and falling concern with various content categories. Also, I interpret those categories that rise and fall together, as indicated by their proximity on the wheel, as constituting a theme or issue.

Although the wavelength is 32 rather than 48 years as in America (Chapter 3) or 52 years as in the British Capitalist period (discussed later in

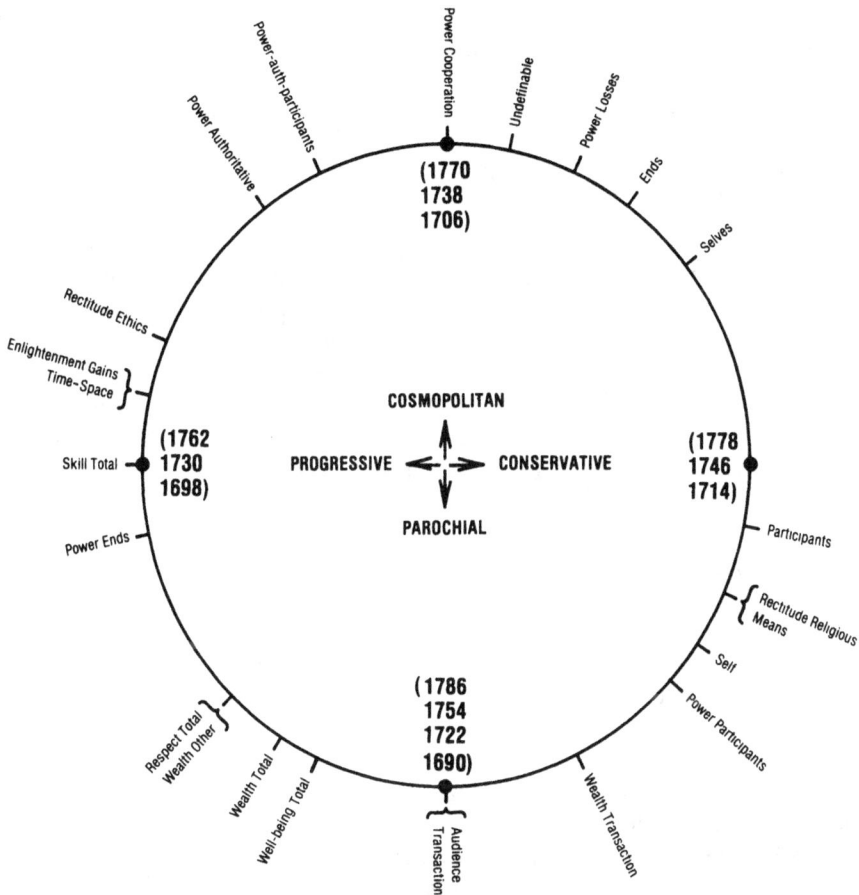

FIGURE 5.1. **Internal Structure of the Short Cycle in Britain 1689–1795 (Cycle lengths set to 32 years, variable origins).**

this chapter), clusters of categories along the rim of this circle are also interpreted as the thematic sequence Parochial, Progressive, Cosmopolitan, and Conservative. More specifically, as Figure 5.1 indicates, about the year 1722 there is maximal concern with economic matters (the WEALTH categories), WELL-BEING, and RESPECT. There is also maximal concern with general value transactions (those in which the substance of the exchange, or whether it is a gain or a loss is unclear from the context or varies widely). One pronoun category, AUDIENCE, peaks in this quadrant. This category contains references to second-person pronominal forms—*you* and *yours*, for example. As shown below, a reading of the text confirms that economic issues are the predominant concern in this period. These issues, moreover, are presented in a style similar to that in the British Capitalist and American parochial periods, but with differences that reflect Mercantilist rather than Capitalist theories of political economy.

Moving clockwise a quarter of a cycle, we find maximal concern with power valued as an end rather than as a mean (POWER ENDS), gains in knowledge (ENLIGHTENMENT GAINS), references to time and space, ethical considerations (RECTITUDE ETHICS), and SKILL. Taken together, these categories suggest Progressive themes.

At the top of the circle there is concern with several POWER subcategories: LOSSES, COOPERATION, AUTHORITATIVE PARTICIPANTS, and AUTHORITATIVE power. There is also concerns with ENDS rather than means, SELVES ("we"), and words whose meaning in terms of the LVD category scheme cannot be specified from one context to another (UNDEFINABLE). During this period, the text reflects concern with foreign affairs in a self-assured, positive tone. Taken together, text and categories indicate concern with Cosmopolitan themes.

Last, in the 3 o'clock position there is high concern with religious matters (RECTITUDE RELIGIOUS), participants in the POWER ARENA, MEANS rather than ends, and the pronoun category SELF ("I"). This cluster of categories is interpreted as the return to traditional moral and economic values that characterizes the Conservative theme. The preceding interpretation is summarized in Table 5.2.

As noted earlier, I assume that covariation among sets of content categories reflects themes in the texts whose words have in part been classified in those categories. The rest of this section presents selected portions of texts, indicating that appropriate themes do exist in these texts, and that at some level of abstraction, these themes do generally repeat from one instance of the cycle to the next. A caveat: Compared with other instances later in this and in previous chapters, reading the text in support of the interpreted four-theme sequence is somewhat less rewarding. While examples of each theme are frequently found in the appropriate years, these themes do not always clearly replicate from one cycle to the next. Taken together, however, the following excerpts do support the preceding interpretation of a four-theme culture cycle.

The speech of 1721 is largely devoted to domestic and foreign wealth-related matters typical of the Parochial theme, as this excerpt illustrates:

> In this situation of affairs, we should be extremely wanting [TRANSACTION] to ourselves, if we neglect to improve the favourable opportunity, which this general tranquillity gives us, of extending [TRANSACTION] our commerce [WEALTH] upon which the riches [WEALTH] and grandeur [RESPECT] of this nation chiefly depend. It is very obvious, that nothing would conduce to the obtaining so public a good, than to make the exportation [WEALTH] and the importation [WEALTH] of the commodities [WEALTH] used in the manufacturing of them [commodities[21] [WEALTH]], as may be

---

[21]Pronouns used for stylistic purposes obscure value references in text, thus reducing the accuracy of text classification. Therefore, the referents of all pronouns and ambiguous phrases were inserted in the text, and all inserts placed within brackets for identification.

TABLE 5.2
Content-analytic Indicators of Short Cycle Themes in Great Britain, 1689–1795

Parochial (1690, 1722, 1754, 1786)	Progressive (1698, 1730, 1762)	Cosmopolitan (1706, 1738, 1770)	Conservative (1714, 1746, 1778)
Wealth Transaction	Enlightenment Gain	Power Cooperation	Rectitude Religious
Wealth Other	Skill Total	Power Authoritative Participants	Means
Wealth Total	Rectitude Ethics	Power Losses	Participants
Well-being Total	Power Ends	Power Authoritative	Power Participants
Transaction	Time–Space	Ends	Self
Audience		Selves	
Respect Total		Undefinable	

practicable and easy as may be. By this means, the balance of trade [WEALTH] may be preserved in our favour, our navigation increased, and great numbers of our poor employed....

I have ordered estimates [WEALTH] to be prepared for the service of the ensuing year, and likewise an account of the debt [WEALTH] of the Navy, to be laid before you. You cannot but be sensible of the ill consequences that arise from such a large debt [WEALTH] remaining [TRANSACTION] unprovided for, and that as long as the Navy and victual bills [WEALTH] are at a very high discount, they do not only affect all other public credit [WEALTH] of the current service. It is therefore very much wished that you could find a method of discharging [TRANSACTIONS] this part of the national debt [WEALTH] which, of all others, is the most heavy and burthensome, and by that means have it in your power to ease your country of some part of the taxes [WEALTH], which from an absolute necessity, they [your country] have been obliged to pay.

In addition to the predominant concern with economic matters, this excerpt is also noteworthy for its clear statement of many of the basic tenets of Mercantilist theory: specifically, the increase in public good (i.e., wealth) that accrues from processing imported goods and exporting finished products and the employment of poor labor in this process (Furniss, 1957).

Although there is concern with wealth-related matters a whole cycle ahead and behind, the clearest repetition of the Parochial theme occurs two cycles beyond the previous example in the address of 1784. This address was given shortly after the conclusion of the wars with France, Spain, and the newly independent American states:

I have ordered the estimates [WEALTH] for the current year to be laid before you; and I trust to your zeal and affection to make such provisions for their [the estimates [WEALTH] farther supply, and for the application of sums [WEALTH] granted in the last Parliament, as may appear to be necessary. I sincerely lament every addition to the burthern of my people, but they [my people] will, I am persuaded, feel the necessity, after a long and expensive [WEALTH] war, of effectually providing for the maintenance of the national faith and our public credit [WEALTH], so essential to the power and prosperity [WEALTH] of the state...

The alarming progress of frauds in the revenue [WEALTH] accompanied by in so many instances with violence [WELL-BEING], will not fail on every account to excite [WELL-BEING] your attention. I must, at the same time, recommend to your most serious consideration, to frame such commercial [WEALTH] regulations as may appear immediately necessary in the present moment. The affairs of the East India Company [WEALTH] form an object of deliberation deeply connected with the general interests of the country.

While in 1722 the government is faced with general economic problems and a lack of faith in economic institutions in general, and the consequences of fraudulent stock manipulations in the South Seas charter company, in this later period it is again the general economic condition that is the object of concern together with the affairs of another trading company (from which the government derives a portion of its revenue). Thus in both periods wealth is the central concern.

With growing economic prosperity, these texts manifest a tone of optimism. By way of comparison, texts from the American and British Capitalist Progressive periods frequently address social welfare legislation in the spirit of liberalism. Although the details reflect Mercantilist society and culture, similar ameliorative concerns appear during the Mercantilist Progressive period, as illustrated by the following extract from the 1728 address:

> I think [ENLIGHTENMENT] myself obliged [RECTITUDE ETHICS] to recommend [POWER ENDS] to you a consideration [ENLIGHTENMENT] of the grestest importance, and I should look upon it as a great happiness, if, at the beginning of my reign, I could see the foundation laid of so great and necessary a work [SKILL] as the increase and encouragement of our seamen [SKILL] in general, that they [seamen [SKILL]] may be invited, rather than compelled by force and violence, to enter into the service of their [seamen's [SKILL]] country, as often as occasion shall require [POWER ENDS] it [to enter into the service of their country].
>
> This leads me to mention [ENLIGHTENMENT] to you the case of Greenwich Hospital, that care may be taken, by some addition to that fund, to render comfortable and effectual [SKILL] that charitable provision for the support and maintenance of our seamen [SKILL], worn out and become decrepit by age and infirmities in the service of their [seamen's [SKILL]] country.

The clearest replication of this theme occurs a whole cycle before, in the address of November 1699:

> The increase of the poor is become a burthen to the Kingdom, and their [the poor's] loose and idle life, does in some measure contribute to that depravation of manners [RECTITUDE ETHICS], which is complained of, I fear with too much reason [ENLIGHTENMENT]. Whether the ground of this evil be from defects in the laws already made [SKILL], or in the execution of them [the laws], deserves [RECTITUDE ETHICS] your consideration [ENLIGHTENMENT].
>
> As it is an indispensible duty [RECTITUDE ETHICS], that the poor, who are not able to help themselves should be maintained; so I cannot but think [ENLIGHTENMENT] it extremely desirable, that such [poor] as are able and willing, should not want employment, and such [poor] as are obstinate and unwilling, should be compelled to labour [SKILL].

During the Cosmopolitan phase there is maximal concern with several POWER categories. Attention is optimistically focused on international affairs. The self-interests of Britain are advanced with a tone of strength, yet there is concern with treaties and international accommodation. Attention is directed toward the European arena, as in the December 1706 address:

> I hope [MEANS] we [SELVES] are all met [POWER COOPERATION] together [POWER COOPERATION] at this time with hearts truely thankful to almighty God, for the glorious successes [MEANS], with which He [God] has blessed our [SELVES] arms and those [arms] of our

[SELVES] allies, through the whole course of this year, and with serious and steady resolution to prosecute the advantages we [SELVES] have gained, till we [SELVES] reap the desired [MEANS] fruit of them [advantages], in an honorable and durable peace. The goodness of God has brought this happy prospect [peace] so much nearer to us [SELVES], that if we be not wanting ourselves [SELVES], we [SELVES] may, upon good grounds, hope [MEANS] to see such a balance of power established in Europe, that it shall no longer be at the pleasure of one prince [POWER AUTHORITATIVE PARTICIPANTS] to disturb the repose, and endanger [MEANS] the liberties, of this part of the world.

The positive tone, concern with peace, and concern with European affairs characteristic of this address exists almost a full cycle later, in the address of 1737. This speech is presented by representatives of the King (commissioners); hence the many references to "His Majesty" rather than first-person pronouns:

We are, by His Majesty's command, in the first place, to observe to you, that His Majesty acquainted you last year, that He [His Majesty] had, in conjunction [POWER COOPERATION] with the States-General [POWER AUTHORITATIVE PARTICIPANTS], given his [Majesty's] approbation of certain preliminary articles [POWER COOPERATION] and agreed upon between the Emperor [POWER AUTHORITATIVE PARTICIPANTS] and France, for restoring the peace of Europe....

We are now commanded by His Majesty to inform you that the respective Acts of Cession being exchanged, and orders [POWER AUTHORITATIVE] given for the evacuation and possession of the several countries and placed by the powers concerned, according to the allotment and disposition of the preliminary articles [POWER COOPERATION], the great work of re-establishing the general tranquillity is far advanced.

The last phase, the Conservative, is marked by a retrenchment in public spending and services and a return to traditional moral values. Rather than the progressive redress of social ills that existed 16 years earlier, in this period the basic themes are fiscal economy together with the protection, defense, and reaffirmation of traditional values. In Mercantilist as in Capitalist speeches, it is the co-occurrence of these elements that signifies the Conservative theme, as illustrated by these portions of the April 1713 address (no replication of this theme could be found in the addresses about the years 1746 and 1778):

Progress has been made in reducing the public expense, as the circumstances of affairs would admit. What forces may be necessary for securing our commerce by sea, and for guards and garrisons, I leave entirely to my parliament. Make yourselves safe [ENDS] and I shall be satisfied. Next to the protection of Divine [RECTITUDE RELIGIOUS] Providence [RECTITUDE RELIGIOUS], I depend upon the affection of my people....

I cannot, however, but expressly mention my displeasure, at the unparalleled licentiousness in publishing seditious and scandalous libels. The impunity such practices have met with, has encouraged the blaspheming everything sacred [RECTITUDE RELIGIOUS], and propagating of opinions tending to the overthrow of all religion [RECTITUDE RELIGIOUS] and government. Prosecutions have been ordered, but it will require some new law, to put a stop to this growing evil (RECTITUDE RELIGIOUS), and discourage it [publishing seditious and scandalous libels].

Following the Conservative phase, thematic content shifts to Parochial concerns, signaling the beginning of another iteration of the cycle.

The preceding excerpts provide substantial textual evidence showing that in the period 1689–1795 there exists a 32-year culture cycle consisting of our themes whose interpretation is Parochial, Progressive, Cosmopolitan, Conservative. As noted earlier, this same sequence was found in American party platforms and in post-1795 British speeches, although the wavelengths there are 48 and 52 years, respectively. The following section examines the relationship between the Mercantilist short thematic cycle and economic fluctuations.

CULTURE AND ECONOMY IN THE MERCANTILIST PERIOD

The relationship between economic performance and the short thematic cycle is of great theoretical and substantive interest. In his study of K-cycles and "great power" wars, Goldstein's (1985, p. 437) periodizes the interval 1689–1790 differently from that suggested by the preceding content-analytic evidence. In this time interval he finds two complete economic cycles,[22] 58 and 43 years long. The first begins in 1689 with an upswing, reaches a peak in 1719, and then declines until 1746. The second begins in 1747 with an upswing, reaches a peak in 1761, and then declines until 1789.

During the period roughly spanning the seventeenth and eighteenth centuries, Goldstein (1985) finds "a repeating pattern or 'signature' of great power war, in which a series of wars of escalating severity culminates in a high-fatality war, then a relatively peaceful period. This pattern repeats four times, the war peaks ending respectively in 1648, 1713, 1763, and 1815" (p. 426). In what is here called the Mercantilist period, the war peaks of 1713 and 1763 match Goldstein's estimates of K-cycle peaks in 1719 and 1761 quite well.

However, the content analysis data suggest an entirely different picture: economic depressions occur at very different points in time, specifically, in 1690, 1722, 1754, and 1786,[23] and peaks in 1706, 1738, and 1770. If Goldstein's dating of the economic cycle in the eighteenth century is mistaken, then this raises serious questions about the relationship between economic fluctuations and great power wars.

[22]Goldstein's methods allow for variation over time in wavelength.

[23]There is a match between the content analysis estimates and Goldstein's at the beginning and end of this time period. Also, the period about 1789 marks the beginning of what most scholars (e.g., van Duijn, 1977, 1983) consider to be the first Kondratieff cycle.

A full investigation of the relationship between Goldstein's data and the 32-year thematic cycle is beyond the scope of the present chapter, and will be pursued in future research. This section presents preliminary results based on graphing Goldstein's economic data and the content analysis data for the Mercantilist period. Two approaches are used: (1) graphically examining the relationship in the Mercantilist period between Goldstein's British Producer's Price Series and the estimated points of maximal concern with each of the four short-cycle phases, and (2) graphing the same price series and selected content categories.[24] Not unambiguously, the results suggest that Goldstein's price data are related both to the short cycle as a whole and to selected content categories, and therefore, that Goldstein's dating of K-cycles in this period is in error.

Short-Cycle Phases and Goldstein's Price Data

Goldstein and I agree that the relationship between price data and economic performance is to be interpreted as follows: Periods of good economic performance will be periods of rising inflation and therefore, of rising prices, while periods of poor economic performance will be periods of declining inflation and therefore, of declining prices.

In the hypothesized relationship between the 32-year thematic cycle and economic fluctuations is true, than the following specific hypotheses will also be true:

- The Parochial theme corresponds to a period of low prices.
- The Progressive theme corresponds to a period of rising prices.
- The Cosmopolitan theme corresponds to a period of high prices.
- The Conservative theme corresponds to a period of declining prices.

Figure 5.2 presents Goldstein's (1986b, B-7) British Producers' Price Index series 1689–1790. These data are the only economic series for this time period analyzed in Goldstein (1985). The graph has been marked to indicate the time points when the content analysis results indicate maximal concern with each of the four short-cycle themes. As shown, these data suggest a strong relationship between prices and the Parochial and Progressive themes, but no relationship between prices and Cosmopolitan and Conservative themes.[25] This interpretation is summarized in Table 5.3,

---

[24]Experiments with ARIMA time-series models (Box and Jenkins, 1976; Gottman, 1981; McCleary and Hay, 1980) generally support the conclusions drawn from the graphs. However, because the content analysis data violate the statistical assumption of equally spaced observations, these data are not presented here. Future research will explore estimating differential (rather than difference) equations, which relax the requirement of equally spaced observations.

[25]Goldstein plotted his data on a log rather than linear scale. Neither this nor a log transformation of the data changed the substantive conclusions.

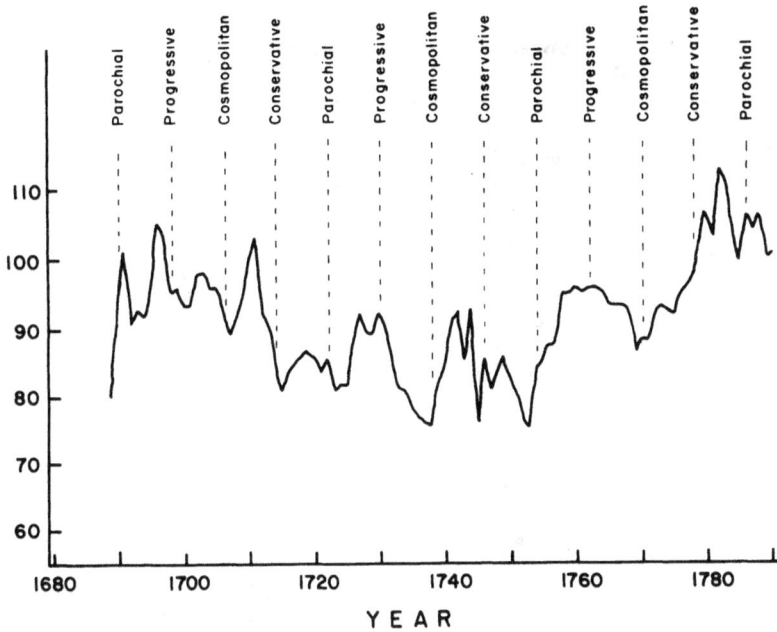

FIGURE 5.2. **British Producer Prices and Short Cycle Phases, 1689–1795.**

which presents the estimated dates of maximal concern with each of the four short-cycle phases during the Mercantilist period together with a "reading" of Figure 5.2. during the same period.

There are several important caveats. First, fitted sine curves and the "wheel" model assume that wavelength is constant over time. To the extent that price swings reflect uneven fluctuations, then there is unlikely to be a match between the model and these price data. Also, the sine wave model assumes that the "up" phase is the same length as the "down" phase, while no such constraint is imposed on the price series (or by Goldstein's methods of periodization).

As shown in Figure 5.2 and Table 5.3, the Parochial and Progressive phases match Goldstein's series pretty well while the Cosmopolitan and Conservative phases do not. These findings are explained in part by the difference mentioned just above between the equal phase lengths of the culture cycle and the unequal (up–down) phase lengths of the economic data.[26] Also, given the vicissitudes of economic performance, irregular

---

[26]Many people have noted that the Capitalist K-cycle tends to have an upswing of 30 years and a downswing of 20 years. I am unaware of any good explanation for this result. It would appear from the results here that the up and down phases of the economy during the Mercantilist period are also asymmetric.

TABLE 5.3.
**Relationship between Culture Cycle and Goldstein
Graphed Data**

Year	Culture cycle phase	Price series	Match?
1690	**Parochial**	bottom	**yes**
1698	**Progressive**	upswing	**yes**
1706	Cosmopolitan	local maximum	maybe not
1714	Conservative	decline	yes
1722	**Parochial**	bottom	**yes**
1730	**Progressive**	upswing	**yes**
1738	Cosmopolitan	bottom	no
1746	Conservative	decline after peak	maybe not
1754	**Parochial**	bottom	**yes**
1762	**Progressive**	upswing	**yes**
1770	Cosmopolitan	slight decline	maybe not
1778	Conservative	upswing	no
1786	**Parochial**	bottom	**maybe***

*1786 is very near the beginning of the first Kondratieff cycle and is thus a depression in terms of what follows it, but is not clearly a depression in terms of what precedes it.

rather than regular fluctuations are more likely. Thus any systematic relationship between the 32-year culture cycle and these economic data is notable.

The preceding data are suggestive, certainly. Note, however, that the four short-cycle themes are an abstraction based on the behavior of many content categories. Thus it is useful to explore the relationships between selected content categories and the British Producer's Price Index data.

Graphing Selected Categories and Price Data

Figure 5.3 and 5.4 present the relationships between two content categories and the price data. One indicator of the Cosmopolitan theme is the category UNDEFINABLE, which contains words such as *due, fill, frontier,* and *resumption* that cannot be classified for one reason or another in terms of the other LVD categories (see Chapter 2). As an indicator of the Cosmopolitan theme, we would expect that the levels of the price series and concern with this category would be related; that is, when prices are high, concern with UNDEFINABLE will be high and when prices are low, concern with this category will also be low. As shown in Figure 5.3, this is generally true with two exceptions. First, in the period between 1730 and 1740 these two series move in opposite directions. Also, after 1765 they move opposite to each other. Yet for two substantial periods, they do move in phase as the model predicts.

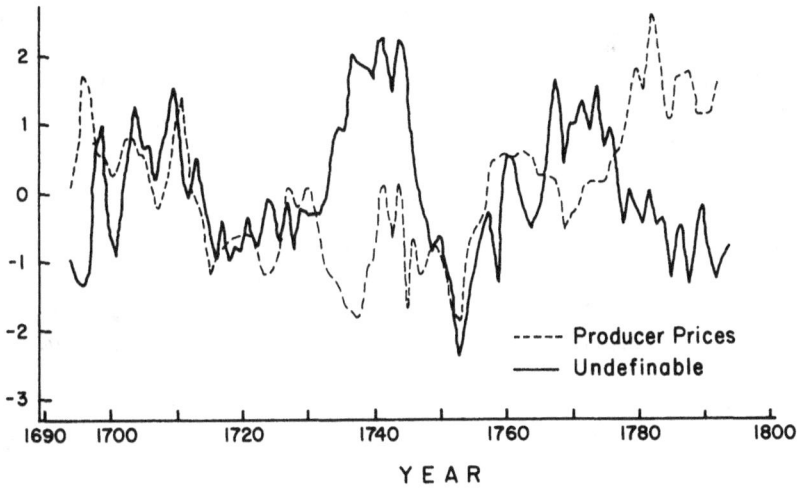

FIGURE 5.3. British Producer Prices and Concern with UNDEFINABLE 1689–1795 (Data transformed to mean of 0 and standard deviation of 1).

Figure 5.4 presents similar results for the category AUDIENCE, which contains references to second-person pronouns. When the economy is good, references to *we* predominate; when the economy is poor, references to *you* predominate. As predicted, this category generally varies in opposition to the price series.

The preceding data suggest that the 32-year culture cycle is correlated with economic fluctuations in the period 1689–1790. This relationship is at

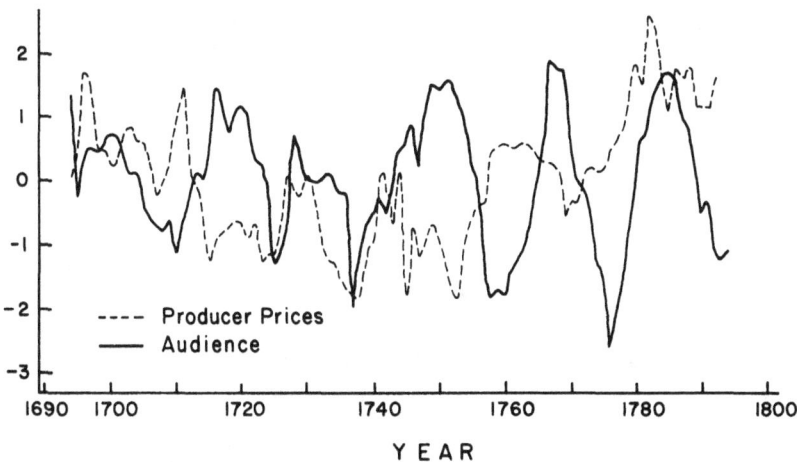

FIGURE 5.4. British Producer Prices and Concern with AUDIENCE 1689–1795 (Data transformed to mean of 0 and standard deviation of 1).

odds with Goldstein's findings and interpretations. What it suggests is that the dynamics of culture and economy under Mercantilist economic rules, assumptions, and behavior are similar to those under Capitalist economic rules, assumptions, and behavior, but that the wavelengths of both the economic and culture cycles differ between these periods and thus between these economic regimes.

Why should the wavelength of the short cycle differ between these periods? Here is a hypothesis. The twin goals of Mercantilist economic thought and practice were "power and plenty" (Viner, 1969). To achieve these ends, the state and Mercantilist enterprise emphasized preindustrial manufacturing, especially processing of raw materials into finished goods. Imports of raw materials were restricted, and exports of finished goods encouraged. Given the slowness and hazards of transportation and communications, it must have been relatively difficult to control the influx and production of raw materials given what finished goods could be and had been recently sold. Thus it is possible that the 32-year economic cycle, if it exists, is analogous to the much shorter, modern inventory cycle [see van Duijn (1983, pp. 8–15) and the sources cited there].

Although the mechanism driving the economic cycle differs between Mercantilist and Capitalist political economy, the consequences of this economic cycle are the same: Changes in the economy produce changes in culture. The reaction of culture to changing economic fortunes may be universal: In times of rising economic performance there is a preoccupation with fixing perceived social ills and a general mood of optimism. In declining times culture becomes more preoccupied with the lessons of the past and with belt-tightening. During periods of poor economic performance culture is preoccupied with this disaster, while at the top of the expansion, attention is focused on the world at large rather than preoccupied with economic difficulties. The following section explores this relationship between culture and economy during the Capitalist period.

THE SHORT CULTURE CYCLE, 1790–1972

After removing a linear trend and/or a long sine curve, a second sine curve was observed in many residuals for the post-1795 period. Consistent results across the two data filters were found for 38 content categories.[27]

Table 5.4 presents the estimated wavelengths, year of maximal concern, standardized peaks, the percent of residual and total variance accounted

---

[27]For a category to be retained in this analysis, the estimated peaks for the data transformed by the moving averages and aggregation filters had to be within a quarter of a cycle, or 13 years of each other.

TABLE 5.4
Curve-Fitting Results for Short Cycle, 1795–1972, 9-Year Moving Average Transformation

Content category	Wavelength in years	Peak year	Standardized peak	Residual variance explained*	Total variance explained*
Power Authoritative Participants	53	1860	1860	20	3
Power Authoritative	33	1839	1840	7	3
Power Conflict	44	1856	1863	24	15
Power Cooperation	54	1864	1863	24	15
Power Losses	72	1875	1865	12	8
Power Other	55	1842	1842	28	18
Power Participants	57	1887	1883	31	9
Rectitude Ends	68	1860	1885	39	22
Rectitude Ethics	40	1848	1851	39	18
Rectitude Gains	66	1863	1858	39	18
Rectitude Religious	42	1838	1838	22	6
Rectitude Total	42	1844	1845	19	7
Respect Gains	35	1850	1856	15	11
Respect Other	50	1866	1867	13	6
Respect Total	48	1867	1869	11	5
Skill Total	54	1851	1851	16	5
Wealth Other	47	1840	1840	8	3
Wealth Participants	63	1891	1882	54	32
Wealth Total	45	1841	1841	11	4
Well-being Losses	58	1887	1883	6	4
Well-being Physical	47	1859	1861	16	4
Well-being Total	27	1853	1867	34	14
Enlightenment Gains	52	1870	1870	31	8
Enlightenment Other	46	1840	1840	29	12
If	49	1842	1842	56	20
Not	56	1883	1880	29	11
Positive Affect	76	1855	1850	17	10
Sure	48	1839	1839	13	4
Undefined	49	1839	1839	26	5
Undefinable	53	1844	1844	36	13
Arenas	39	1874	1886	12	5
Audience	54	1890	1888	16	3
Means	56	1844	1844	22	9
Others	75	1890	1874	31	17
Ends	53	1840	1840	21	4
Time–Space	89	1918	1885	35	19
Transaction Gains	53	1849	1849	19	5
Transaction Losses	41	1863	1870	13	11

*In percent.

for, and the correlation between the estimated curve and the residualized data for the 9-year moving averages.[28]

The fitted sine curves on average account for 24% of the variance after removing a linear trend and a long sine wave (where present), and 10% of the total variance (correlations of .49 and .32, respectively). The best-fitting sine curve (for the category WEALTH PARTICIPANTS) accounts for 54% of the residual and 32% of the total variance; these correspond to correlations of .73 and .57, respectively. The worst-fitting curve that replicated across data filters (WELL-BEING LOSSES) accounts for 7% of the residual and 3% of the total variance (correlations of .26 and .17, respectively). In this period the sine curves do not fit quite as well as those for the British Mercantilist data.

The locations of peak or maximal years of concern with these categories are plotted on the rim of a circle whose circumference represents a 52-year progression of themes (Figure 5.5). At the bottom of the circle (1790, 1842, 1894, 1946), there is maximal concern with WEALTH, certainty and uncertainty (SURE and IF); ambiguous references (with respect to the LVD category scheme) (UNDEFINED), and knowledge (ENLIGHTENMENT). There is also concern with power generally (POWER OTHER) and with legitimate power in particular (POWER AUTHORITATIVE). The speeches of these periods reflect an overriding concern with the poor performance of the economy.

Moving clockwise to the "9 o'clock" position (1803, 1855, 1907, 1969), there is maximal concern with craft and techniques (SKILL), the granting of respect and rectitude (RESPECT and RECTITUDE GAINS), ethics (RECTITUDE ETHICS), and rectitude for its own sake (RECTITUDE ENDS) rather than as a means to an end. The speeches from these periods indicate a preoccupation with social welfare and conflict. There is also concern with programmatic means and justifications to remedy problems and conflicts.

At the top of the circle (1816, 1868, 1920, 1972) there is peak concern with RESPECT and WELL-BEING, conflict and cooperation (POWER CONFLICT and POWER COOPERATION), and the increase of knowledge (ENLIGHTENMENT GAINS). Retrievals from the documents indicate an international orientation.

In the "3 o'clock" position of the circle (1829, 1881, 1933) there is concern with the loss of well-being (WELL-BEING LOSSES), with various actors in contests for wealth and power (WEALTH and POWER PARTICIPANTS), negativity (NOT), and with general arenas of value transactions (e.g., the term *world*) (ARENAS). There is also maximal concern with the TIME-SPACE category, which suggests the reevaluation of past, present, and future policies. This is confirmed by retrievals from the documents of these periods, which also indicate extensive concern with fiscal retrenchment and traditional values.

These clusters of content categories are interpreted as a four-phase

---

[28]Again, in the interest of brevity, the estimates for the 4-year aggregations are omitted here.

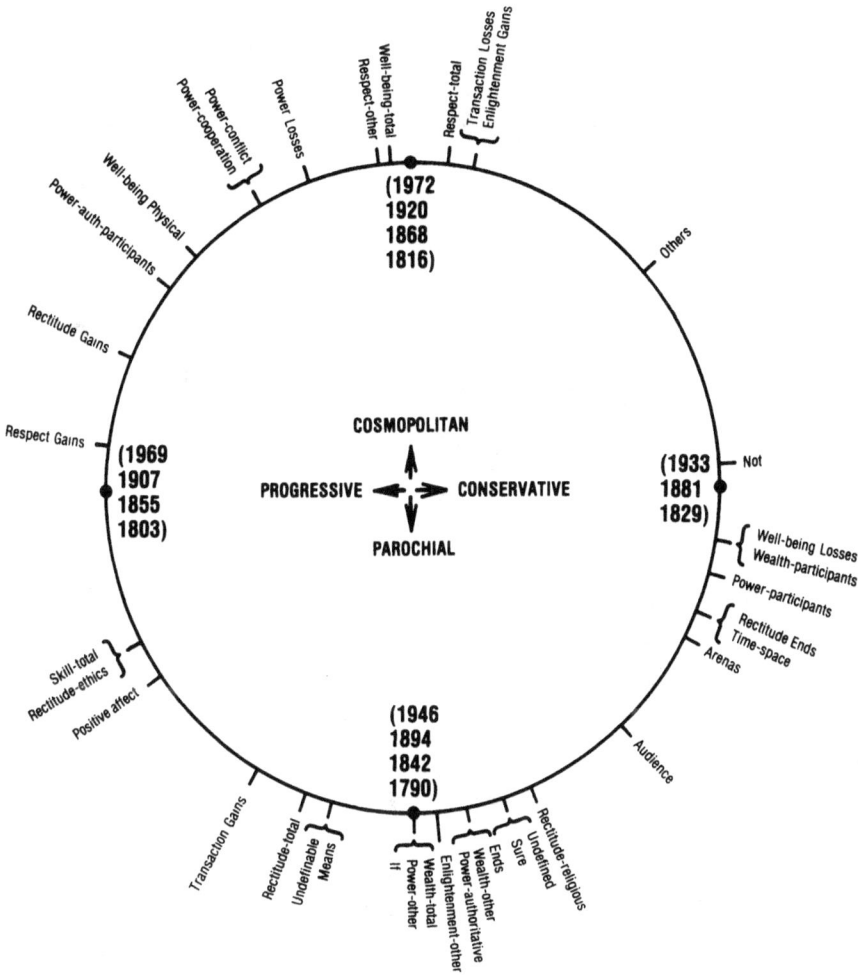

FIGURE 5.5. **Internal Structure of the Short Cycle in Britain from 1795 (Cycle lengths set to 52 years, variable origins).**

thematic progression: Parochial, Progressive, Cosmopolitan, Conservative. This interpretation[29] is summarized in Table 5.5.

As before, examples from the text establish the reality of these themes. During the Parochial phase, the speeches are primarily concerned with

---

[29]Comparing American party platforms (Chapter 3) and British speeches, there are some differences in the relationship between categories and themes. For example, while WEALTH categories indicate the Parochial theme in both sets of documents, POWER CONFLICT and POWER COOPERATION indicate the Progressive theme in American platforms but the Cosmopolitan theme in Speeches from the Throne. These results indicate that there are no fixed relationships between categories and themes. In addition, these results also indicate that different texts discuss the **same** issues in **different** terms. See Chapters 9 and 10 for further consideration of this issue.

TABLE 5.5
Content-analytic Indicators of Short-Cycle Themes in Great Britain, 1795–1972

Parochial (1790, 1842, 1894, 1946, 1978)	Progressive (1803, 1855, 1907, 1969)	Cosmopolitan (1816, 1868, 1920, 1972)	Conservative (1829, 1881, 1933)
Wealth Other	Skill Total	Power Conflict	Well-being Losses
Wealth Total	Rectitude Ethics	Power Cooperation	Wealth Participants
If	Rectitude Gains	Well-being Total	Power Participants
Sure	Well-being Physical	Power Losses	Not
Undefined	Respect Gains	Respect Total	Time–Space
Undefinable	Power Authoritative Participants	Respect Other	Arenas
Power Authoritative	Positive Affect	Enlightenment Gains	Rectitude Ends
Power Other	Transaction Gains	Transaction Losses	Audience
Rectitude Total			
Enlightenment Other			
Rectitude Religious			
Means			
Ends			

economic performance and other wealth-related matters. The entire speech of 1842, for example, is devoted to the state of the economy and inadequate government income, as illustrated by this excerpt:

> You will have seen with regret, that for several years past, the annual income [WEALTH] has been inadequate to bear the public charges [WEALTH], and I feel confident that fully sensible of the evils which must result from a continued deficiency of this nature during peace, you will carefully consider the best means of averting it [a deficiency of revenue [WEALTH]]

This excerpt indicates an awareness that there had been several years of declining economic fortunes, which is consistent with the K-cycle's extended period of falling economic performance.

Similar issues appear one whole cycle later in the address of 1895:

> I regret that agriculture [WEALTH] continues in a seriously depressed condition. This subject [agriculture [WEALTH]] is still under the consideration of the Commission which I appointed in the end of 1893. In the meantime, a proposal will be submitted to you for facilitating the construction of a light railway, a measure which will, I trust, be found beneficial to the rural districts. Bills will also be presented for the promotion of conciliation in trade [WEALTH] disputes, and for the amendment of the Factory [WEALTH] Acts.

During the Progressive phase, a willingness exists to alter existing social arrangements. Reform measures will be considered as long as fundamental capitalist relations are not altered. The Progressive theme is illustrated by this portion of the January 1854 speech.:

> Measures will be submitted to you for the amendment of the laws related to the representation of the Commons [POWER AUTHORITATIVE PARTICIPANT] in Parliament [POWER AUTHORITATIVE PARTICIPANT]. Recent experience has shown that it is necessary to take more effectual [SKILL] precautions against the evil of bribery [RECTITUDE ETHICS] and corrupt [RECTITUDE ETHICS] practices at elections. It will also be your duty [RECTITUDE ETHICS] to consider whether more complete effect might not be given to the principles [RECTITUDE ETHICS] of the Act of the last reign, whereby reforms were made [SKILL] in the representation of the people in Parliament [POWER AUTHORITATIVE PARTICIPANT].

In America, the Progressive period is marked by policy justifications based upon ethical and/or doctrinaire considerations (Namenwirth, 1973, Ch. 3). However, during the British Progressive period, reforms are proposed with little or no justification, as illustrated by this excerpt from the 1907 address, one complete cycle later:

> You will also be invited to consider proposals for the establishment of a Court of Criminal [RECTITUDE ETHICS] Appeal, for regulating the hours of labour [SKILL] in mines; for the amendment to the patent laws; for improving the law related to the valuation of property in England and Wales; for enabling [SKILL] women to serve on local bodies [POWER AUTHORITATIVE PARTICIPANTS]; for amending the law effecting small holdings in England and Wales; and for the better housing of the people.

The Cosmopolitan theme is characterized by international concerns often stated aggressively, as in the address of November 1867:

> The sovereign of Abyssinia, in violation of all international law, continues to hold in captivity several of my subjects, some of whom has been especially accredited to him by myself, and his persistent disregard of friendly representations has left me no alternative but that of making a peremptory demand for the liberation of my subjects, and supporting it, by an adequate force. I have accordingly directed an expedition to be sent for that purpose alone.

The First World War occurs one whole cycle later. Even after the cessation of hostilities, Cosmopolitan concerns continue to preoccupy the speeches, as exemplified by this portion of the February 1921 address:

> Conferences will be held at an early date in London, which will be attended by our allies [POWER COOPERATION] in the late war [POWER CONFLICT], and also by representatives of Germany and Turkey. I earnestly trust that by this means further progress will be made in giving effect to the treaties of peace, in re-establishing concord [POWER CONFLICT] in Europe and in restoring tranquillity in the Near East.

As the economy turns downward, the tone and mood of the addresses becomes increasingly somber. There are calls for fiscal retrenchment; innovation and experimentation are anathema. The critical issue becomes halting the downturn. To allay fears, the present situation is compared with more prosperous times in the past and, it is hoped, ahead. The Conservative theme is illustrated by this excerpt from the February 1830 speech, delivered by commissioners rather than by the monarch in person:

> His Majesty has directed the estimates for the current [TIME-SPACE] year [TIME-SPACE] to be laid before you. They [the estimates] have been framed with every attention to economy, and it will be satisfactory to you to learn that His Majesty will be enabled to propose a considerable reduction in the amount of the public expenditure, without imparing [WELL-BEING LOSSES] the efficiency of our naval or military establishment [POWER PARTICIPANT].

Conservative concerns are also stated one cycle later, in 1880:

> I notice with satisfaction that the imports and exports of the country, as well as other signs, indicate some revival in trade. But the depression, which has lately been perceived in the revenue, continues without abatement. The estimates of income which were laid before the last Parliament were framed with moderation, but the time [TIME-SPACE] which has since [TIME-SPACE] elapsed exhibits no [NOT] promise that they [the estimates] will be exceeded.

These illustrations of Conservative concerns suggest that the downturn has only recently begun. The bottom has not yet been reached, and there is an effort to prevent further decline through fiscal moderation. Nevertheless, the cycle begins again with the next Parochial theme as the economy descends into depression.

Taken together, the preceding excerpts lead to three conclusions: First, the themes identified from the content-analytic and curve-fitting procedures are not artifactual, but real. Second, these themes repeat in essentially the same form, but with certain differences that reflect changing historical circumstances. Third, the speeches' contents are consistent with the argument that varying economic conditions identified with the K-cycle give rise to a 52-year thematic cycle.

THE KONDRATIEFF AND THEMATIC CYCLES

Many economists deny the existence of the K-cycle (e.g., Garvy, 1943; Burns and Mitchell, 1946; Fellner, 1956; Gordon, 1961). The argument against cycles in general and Kondratieff in particular is in part ideological and in part semantic. One critic clearly states the negative case, as follows:

> Although business cycles represent **recurring** alternations of prosperity and depression, virtually all authorities agree that there is nothing periodic about these movements. There is no evidence that business cycles tend to recur over and over again in virtually the same form, with the same duration, and the same amplitude of movement [Gordon, 1961, p. 25, emphasis in original].

Given the complexities of social and economic life, it is not surprising that economic data do not conform to strict requirements of periodicity.[30] This type of argument against periodicity is advanced by the Keynesian-minded who wish to intervene in and direct the economy. They also argue against deterministic economic fluctuations beyond direct, voluntaristic intervention.

Doubts about the K-cycle notwithstanding, the relationships among the Kondratieff cycle and the British and American short culture cycles are explored in Table 5.6, which presents Kondratieff's (1935) and van Duijn's (1979) estimates of the peaks and troughs of the economic cycle for Britain and America 1790–1932,[31] and the estimated points of maximal concern with Cosmopolitan and Parochial themes. These themes are hypothesized to correspond to the economic maxima and minima, respectively. Table 5.6

---

[30]As Gordon indicates, periodicity requires constant wavelength and amplitude. The sine curves fitted to the British and American data assume constant wavelength and amplitude. Additional analysis of these data will attempt to discover if variations in amplitude have systematic causes.

[31]Kondratieff (1935) estimated the long wave for the period 1790–1920, and 1932 is used as a rough estimate for the Great Depression.

TABLE 5.6
Estimated Minima and Maxima of Economic and Culture Cycles in Great Britain and America

	Minimum economic cycle*	Parochial value phase[†]	Maximum introvert phase[‡]	Maximum economic cycle*	Cosmopolitan value phase[†]	Maximum introvert phase[‡]
Britain	1789	1790	—	1819	1816	—
	1849	1842	—	1873	1868	—
	1896	1894	—	1920	1920	—
	1932	1946	—	—	—	—
America	1790	1788	—	1814	1812	1811
	1849	1836	1830	1866	1860	1858
	1896	1884	1881	1920	1908	1905
	1932	1932	1929	—	—	—

	Minimum economic Cycle[§]	Parochial value phase[†]	Maximum introvert phase[‡]	Maximum economic cycle[§]	Cosmopolitan value phase[†]	Maximum introvert phase[‡]
Britain:	1783	1790	—	1815	1816	—
	1837	1842	—	1866	1868	—
	1884	1894	—	1921	1920	—
	1938	1946	—	1967	1972	—
America	1783	1788	—	1815	1812	1811
	1837	1836	1830	1866	1860	1858
	1884	1884	1881	1921	1908	1905
	1938	1932	1929	1967	1956	1954

*From Table 1 in Kondratieff (1935, p. 110). Kondratieff did not estimate the minima corresponding to the Great Depression; 1932 is used as an approximate date.

[†]The estimates for the American short cycle are from Namenwirth (1973, Ch. 3).

[‡]Estimates based on Klingberg (1983, p. 2) and Holmes (1985, p. 21).

[§]Estimates from van Duijn (1977, p. 563). Slightly different estimates are given in van Duijn (1983, p. 143).

also presents Klingberg's (1952, 1983, p. 2) estimates of Introvert and Extrovert phases in American foreign policy concerns. The estimates in the table represent the midpoints of each phase, when the so-called Extrovert and Introvert periods should be at their greatest intensity.[32]

As the data in Table 5.6 indicate, the estimates for the thematic and economic cycles in Britain and America are highly congruent.[33] Also,

[32]The estimate for the American post–World War II Extrovert phase is based on Holmes (1985, p. 21).

[33]Ib Damgaard Peterson observes (personal communication) that there seems to be a lag relationship between the British and American estimates of the Parochial and Cosmopolitan themes, respectively. Whether this difference merely results from the 4-year difference in wavelength between the two estimates or reflects some underlying substantive result is a

Klingberg's estimates of Extrovert and Introvert periods are highly correlated with the Cosmopolitan and Parochial phases of the short thematic cycle and with the maximum and minimum of the K-cycle.[34] These cycles were estimated using very different data bases and different techniques. Specifically, Kondratieff used moving averages and graphic techniques to estimate turning points from price series. Van Duijn made informed judgments on the basis of several different estimates, but used largely production series. Klingberg (1952, 1983) and Holmes (1985) use a wide variety of detailed information concerning American presidents, foreign policy decisions, war and peace, and public opinion to estimate fluctuations in Extrovert and Introvert orientations. Therefore, it is unlikely that the strong relationship between economic and thematic cycles is merely spurious.

A CYBERNETIC EXPLANATION OF K-CYCLES

This section provides a brief description of the several dynamics that cause or result from the K-cycle and the short culture cycle documented above, and a description of the relationships among them. This description also states a cybernetic explanation of the short culture cycle in terms of the **processes** underlying the relationship between culture and economy. There are, moreover, two senses in which the following explanation is a cybernetic one. First, the shorter thematic cycle shows that society monitors the performance of its economic subsystem.[35] Second, the four themes address either the consequences of good economic performance or the restoration of economic growth in a declining or depressed economy. In good economic times, society's attention is devoted to ameliorating social ills or conflicts in the international arena. In poor times, society's attention is devoted to the restoration of economic growth, either through a return to traditional moral values and fiscal restraint or through economic reorganization. Thus the content of the short cycle implies a negative feedback loop that maintains long-run economic growth.

During each of the four short thematic cycle phases, Figure 5.6 indicates

---

difficult question. I treat the difference in wavelengths as not substantively important; hence, I am inclined to view the lag differences between the two countries as more likely the result of chance than substance.

[34]Klingberg (1983) eschews explanation, preferring instead to focus on "the convincing quality of the evidence for the existence of the cycles, rather then upon a speculative analysis of the alleged 'causes' of the cycles" (p. 11).

[35]This monitoring is explicit in the content of the communications analyzed (speeches and party platforms). An analysis of communication channels within the economy would indicate how the economic subsystem monitors its own performance. Such channels would include specialized business publications.

COSMOPOLITAN

Maximum of economic expansion. Beginning of decline
in profits from the cluster of innovations that fueled the
30 year upswing. Process innovations in basic industries
are most likely at the beginning of this phase. Maximum
economic, political, and social influence of the social
groups that benefited from the previous reorganization.
"Great Power" wars are more likely at the beginning of
this phase. Maximum of Klingberg's "Extrovert" phase.
Maximum of self-confident concern with foreign affairs.

PROGRESSIVE

Maximum rate of economic expansion.
Maximum profits from clusters of
innovations that underlie the structural
reorganization of the economy. Product
innovations are the basis of new industries.
Expanding opportunity structure.
High conflict between the "winners"
and "loosers" of the economic reorganization.
Maximum concern with ameliorating
social ills. Transition between Klingberg's
"Introvert" and "Extrovert" phases.

CONSERVATIVE

Maximum rate of economic decline.
Declining profitability of innovations
that fueled the last upswing. Belief
in adjusting rather than reorganizing
the economy. Little innovation in this
period. Contracting opportunity structure.
Maximum concern with traditional
moral values and with fiscal restraint.
Transition between Klingberg's
"Extrovert" and "Introvert" phases.

PAROCHIAL

Bottom of the economic cycle. Recognition that
reorganization of economy is required to restore
profits and capital accumulation. Product
innovations in existing industries. Process
innovations in existing industries. Maximum
concern with economic problems. Maximum of
Klingberg's "Introvert" phase.

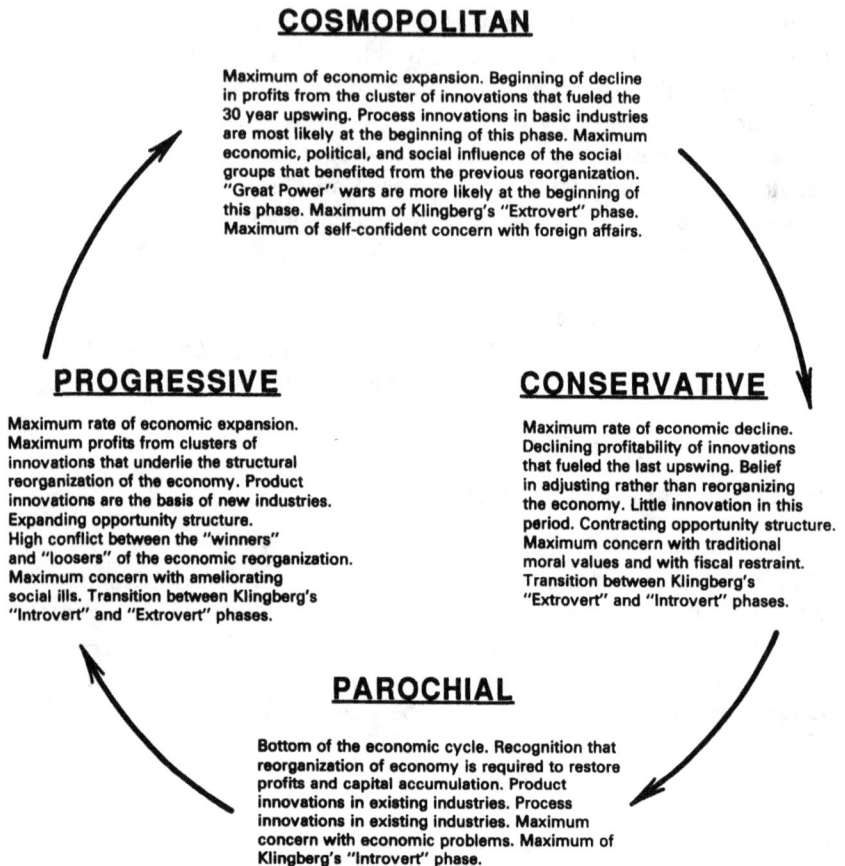

FIGURE 5.6. **Theory of K-Cycles in Capitalist World System.**

the various dynamics that are causes and/or consequences of the K-cycle.[36]
These variables and dynamics include cycles in technological innovations,
changes in the opportunity structure for individual and group mobility,
K-cycles in the economy, Klingberg's Extrovert/Introvert alternations,
great power wars, and the short thematic cycle.[37]

Beginning at the bottom of the figure, during the Depression attention is,
not surprisingly, focused on economic problems, their presumed causes, and

[36]An earlier version of this chapter (Weber, 1981) adopted a largely Marxist interpretation
and explanation of the relationship between the K-cycle and the short culture cycle since the
1790s. Because that class of explanations relies heavily on historically particular explanations, I
have discarded it as a general explanation. The cybernetic explanation developed in the
remainder of this chapter avoids historicist pitfalls while perhaps providing an integrated
explanation of broader scope and greater power.

[37]Although I have not done so here, I believe this model can also explain McClelland's
(1975) "power/affiliation" hypothesis for the cause of wars and periods of social ameliora-

their consequences. The Parochial theme represents this discussion. The mood of the country is what Klingberg refers to as Introvert. The Parochial theme also represents a three-part debate within the nation, if not the world system, on alternative courses of action. First, the realization occurs that the present situation differs from normal business cycles and thus requires strong actions. Second, some set of actions are chosen. Third, the decision must be justified. The justification is couched in terms of the greatest good for the greatest number of people, even if some classes or groups benefit more than others.

At this time, innovations in manufacturing processes in existing industries are more likely as managers attempt to increase efficiency and hence profits (van Duijn, 1983, pp. 129–144). Also, product innovations in existing industries are more likely now than at other times. Both types of innovations try to make the best use of existing capital and resources. More important for the economy is the beginning of the shift of capital from older, less profitable technologies toward newer, more profitable ones.

The economic expansion that corresponds to the Progressive period results from investments in new products and industries that bring higher rates of profits. As the economy begins to expand, part of the additional profits and wealth is redistributed to workers, especially those in the industries leading the upswing. Early in the Progressive period, conflicts may arise between those workers in old, declining industries and those in new, rising ones (cf. Gordon *et al.*, 1982). Also, some social ills are ameliorated. This occurs in such a way that inequities in the distribution of power and wealth are not seriously jeopardized. These actions are discussed in the Progressive theme. The Progressive period also marks the transition from Klingberg's Introvert to Extrovert "moods." The increasing optimism documented in Klingberg's work and above probably reflects the expanding opportunity structure, especially for those in the leading industries (cf. Powers, 1980, 1981; Powers and Hanneman, 1983).

Following two decades of increasing output and real, but limited gains for workers, the economy reaches its maximum point of expansion.[38] As the innovations that fueled the 30-year upswing become diffused both within

---

tion. For example, because of widespread hard times, concern with affiliation predominates concern with power during the Parochial period. However, as the economy improves, concerns shift to social amelioration (Progressive concerns, in our terms), and then to power, especially in the international arena (Cosmopolitan concerns). There is also a great deal of overlap between this model and the Powers/Pareto model of sociocultural dynamics (Powers, 1980, 1981; Powers and Hanneman, 1983). Finally, as Namenwirth (Chapter 3) points out, the Progressive/Conservative alternation in America corresponds to Schlesinger's (1939) Liberal/Conservative oscillation.

[38]Since the 1790s there has been a long-term "secular" economic expansion. The K-cycle represents fluctuations about the long-term trend. Thus the peak is the maximum for the cycle, not the absolute historical maximum.

the country and internationally, their profitability declines. As profits begin to decline, so does the economy. In an attempt to reverse this trend, better means are introduced for producing goods within the leading sectors. These process innovations merely postpone, but cannot prevent, the eventual decline of profits and the leading industries of the period.

At the economic peak, attention shifts to foreign affairs, including relations between the political center and periphery. In Klingberg's terms, the mood of the country becomes Extrovert. There are calls for greater political and economic activity in the international arena, partly justified by the promise of additional benefits to workers and capitalists alike. Also, Goldstein shows that "great power" wars are more likely at the beginning of this phase than at other times.

However, as profits continue their decline, the Conservative theme encompasses a discussion of the restoration of profits and capital accumulation. Believing that the current economic problems can be resolved within the present economic structure, the attention of the country again shifts, this time toward traditional moral values and fiscal austerity. The general feeling is that returning to tradition—church, family, God, and morality—and fiscal conservatism will resolve the current economic difficulties without the necessity of a major reorganization of the economy. Faced with shrinking profits, little technological innovation is applied either to production processes or to new products.

Nevertheless, confronted with a major depression and with ineffectual solutions within the old framework, the country soon realizes that nothing short of structural change will resolve the crisis. Hence the cycle begins again with the next Parochial theme.

CONCLUDING REMARKS

The long-term dynamics discussed above have cross-national implications as well. As noted, the British and American economic and culture cycles are in phase with each other; that is, when there is maximal concern with restructuring the economy in Britain, there is maximal concern with the same problem in America. This finding stands in marked contrast to the phase relationship of the longer thematic cycles discussed at length in the previous chapter. For example, when there is maximal concern with broad goals and the identity of society in America (the Expressive phase)—i.e., during the Civil War—there is maximal concern with worker participation in politics and the franchise in Britain (the Integrative phase).

The phase relationships between the short and long culture cycles provide strong empirical support for Wallerstein's (1974, 1979, 1980) "world system" concept. In his view, nation-states are linked by means of their economies; i.e., although there are many nation-states in the same world system, there is only one economy: the world-system economy.[39] Nevertheless, the internal political dynamics of these nation-states are autonomous.

This conceptualization is powerfully supported by the content-analytic investigation of British and American political texts. Linked economies are reflected by virtually identical thematic sequences, wavelengths, and congruent phase relations for the British and American short cycles, plus the congruence of their Kondratieff cycles. However, the similar-phase sequences and wavelengths but out-of-phase long cycles in Britain and America are consistent with the hypothesis of independent political dynamics.

Although the long and short thematic cycles have different causes, their explanations are related in an important conceptual manner. Each explanation reflects one of two contrasting approaches to the concept of "power" in macrosociology (Parsons, 1969; Lehman, 1977). The first approach primarily addresses the power of the state or system as a whole, over and above the total power of its constituent elements. This view of power is found in structural functionalism and general system theory (e.g., Berrien, 1968; von Bertalanffy, 1968; Buckley, 1968; Deutsch, 1966; Kuhn, 1974; Weinburg, 1975). The contrasting position, usually associated with Marxist theories, views power as zero-sum: if one group within society gains power, it is necessarily at the expense of other groups. The power of the state or of the system is used by the few to oppress the many.

The longer thematic cycle mentioned above is interpreted as a problem-solving sequence related to the adaptation of collective actors to their larger social, cultural, and physical environments. In this view, power is not zero-sum, but a resource for system adaptation and survival. The short thematic cycle, in contrast, is related to competition within the collectivity for the limited supply of goods and services. In this view, power is zero-sum under conditions of scarcity (cf. Thurow, 1980).

Finally, rather than suggesting an analytical synthesis of the predominant theoretical positions in macrosociology (e.g., Lenski, 1966), the two culture cycles and their interpretations suggest that both frames of reference are required to explain social and cultural change. Therefore, macrosociological theories that do not incorporate both the wholistic and zero-sum conceptualizations of power are likely to be deficient.

---

[39]Economies are integrated into the world-system economy to varying degrees. Thus future research must address the extent to which K-cycles affect economies of states in the semiperiphery and periphery in contrast to core states. The present analysis is biased to the extent that it concerns itself with two of the key core states and their economies.

6

Political Issues, Economic Performance, and Presidential Election Outcomes, 1892–1964[1]

In democratic societies, elections provide for the orderly transfer of power and give voice to the body politic. Communications among candidates, party workers, voters, and other political actors are an essential aspect of the electoral process. Analyzing the content of these communications is vital for understanding election outcomes because the dynamics of public opinion formation and candidate strategy are based in large part on these messages. In presidential campaigns, party platforms are a broad statement of the party's position on a variety of issues.[2] Platforms are framed to inform the party faithful and attract less committed voters to the candidates[3] (Johnson, 1978, p. ix; Pomper, 1966). In addition, Monroe (1983) found that party platform "planks" are "related to policy decisions both when public majorities favored those proposals and when majorities opposed them. Thus, there is stronger support for the inference of a causal link between party stands on the issues and their eventual disposition by government" (pp. 38–39).

[1]We thank H. Douglas Price for comments on an earlier draft and Barbara Norman for editorial assistance. A somewhat longer version appeared in Spanish as "La mediacion cultural del functionamiento economico como determinante en las elecciones presidenciales U.S.A., 1892–1964" [The cultural mediation of economic performance as a determinant of presidential elections, 1892–1964] in the *Revista Internacional de Sociologia* (Madrid), 1985, 43(1):59–85.

[2]Party platforms are not mere rhetoric. A substantial number of promises are eventually carried out (David, 1971; Pomper and Lederman, 1980, pp. 156–178).

[3]A concise history of the party conventions that adopted these platforms is provided by Bain and Parris (1973).

Robert Philip Weber and J. Zvi Namenwirth wrote this chapter.

Based on a computerized content analysis of Democratic and Republican platforms, the research described below indicates a considerable relationship between the position of the parties on selected issues and the election-to-election change in the division of the two-party presidential vote. We also find that changes in the unemployment rate have substantial direct effects on these selected issues, but no direct effects on changes in the two-party vote. Finally, these relationships are stable in that they are not highly influenced by any single election of the 19 analyzed here.[4]

Specifically, we find that following increases in unemployment rates the Democrats stress the federal government as the ultimate source of legitimate authority, and the Republicans stress individual leaders, primarily Republican leaders, as those best able to reverse the economic setbacks. For the Democrats, stressing the legitimacy of the federal government is a justification for interventionist economic policies, while for the Republicans, emphasizing the role of individual Republican leaders avoids having to debate alternative policies ("stay the course"). Conversely, in response to declining unemployment, Democrats emphasize the role of the states rather than the role of the federal government. The Republicans emphasize the role of the Republican party and Republican principles as factors in the declining unemployment rates. Thus in prosperous times, both parties adopt more conservative positions, but employ different justifications, **and therefore, different rhetorics**.

In the aggregate, the Democrats increase their share of the two-party vote when they have stressed the legitimacy of the federal government and when Republicans have reiterated the role of individual Republicans rather than employed different legitimations. The Republicans increase their share of the two-party vote when they emphasize the Republican party and Republican, often conservative, principles and when the Democrats underscore the role of the states and adopt a less interventionist position.

In this chapter we support with data and develop the argument that culture plays a crucial mediating role in determining election outcomes. Culture provides the framework within which economic "facts" are interpreted and policies justified in order to appeal to constituencies for support. The electorate, then, chooses not only on the basis of its pocketbook, but on the basis of alternative interpretations of economic "facts." Put another way, the electorate not only chooses between candidates, it chooses between interpretations of reality as well.

After a brief review of earlier findings based on macroeconomic and political data, we present our measures of political issues in party platforms and then consider alternative models of election outcomes and election-to-election changes in the two-party vote.

---

[4]Although platforms from 1844 through 1964 were analyzed, our causal analysis begins in 1892 because there are few reliable economic data prior to that date.

PREVIOUS RESEARCH AND THEORY

Previous analyses of presidential and congressional[5] election outcomes employing time-series designs[6] stress material and utilitarian rather than ideational explanations. For example, Kramer (1971) showed that increases in real income per capita before congressional elections were related to higher votes for the incumbent party, and that decreases in real income were related to higher votes for the party out of office. These results, according to Kramer, indicate that the electorate is in part rational and votes along lines of self-interest. Kramer omitted the elections of 1912 (the Taft–Roosevelt split) and the elections during the world wars on the grounds that these elections were unusual. Stigler (1973) showed that Kramer's results in part depended upon which elections were analyzed,[7] thereby calling into question the stability and generality of Kramer's findings.

Analyzing presidential elections from 1948 through 1976, Tufte (1978) found that support for the candidate of the incumbent party was a function of changes in real disposable income per capita and what he calls the "net presidential candidate advantage" of favorable to unfavorable mentions by voters (Tufte, 1978, pp. 116–123). Drawing on the results of voter surveys conducted by the Survey Research Center at Michigan, Tufte calculated the ratio of (favorable mentions of incumbent minus unfavorable mentions of incumbent) to (favorable mentions of nonincumbent minus unfavorable mentions of nonincumbent). This variable measures the average aggregate disposition of the electorate toward the presidential candidates.[8] Tufte

[5]Congressional elections may not be strictly comparable to presidential campaigns, but models based on time-series designs used to account for congressional voting are similar to those suggested for presidential voting. Hence their consideration here; see, for example, Kramer and Lepper (1972); Li (1976); and Piereson (1975). Bloom and Price (1975) provide evidence indicating that the effects of changes in real income are asymmetric: Voters punish the incumbent party for poor economic performance but fail to reward them for good economic performance. Unfortunately, we lack sufficient cases to test this hypothesis, and symmetric effects are assumed to prevail.

[6]Li (1976) fits stochastic (ARIMA) models (Box and Jenkins, 1976; Hibbs, 1974) to House and presidential election results. Univariate ARIMA models explain variation of a time series only in terms of itself and random variation, thereby leaving external causes undetermined.

[7]Stigler (1973, p. 163) shows that including the election of 1912 plus elections during the war years has some effect on the conclusions, but deleting elections before 1902 and extending the series to 1970 has greater effects on the model. We are now extending our data base through 1980, but because of recent changes in content analysis technology and computer programs, we are forced to perform extensive cross-validation studies of the new and original content analysis systems. These studies are in their initial phase.

[8]As is well known, conclusions based on aggregate data may or may not reflect disaggregated results. Kramer (1983) shows that individual-level data are more biased than aggregate data in studies relating economic conditions to elections. In time-series models, aggregation may lead to spurious conclusions regarding causality, especially regarding feedback loops (McClearly, personal communication). However, as we have not postulated feedback models, we believe the issue to be unimportant here.

shows that the more favorably disposed the voters are toward the candidate
of the incumbent party (relative to the nonincumbent), the more likely that
candidate is to win the election. Furthermore, Tufte (1978, pp. 127–134)
uses other survey data to show that the perceptions of candidates by voters
is moderately related to the voters' perception of changes in their economic
fortunes. Thus, economic performance is the major explanatory variable in
Tufte's model.

Political scientists and economists often stress the theoretical and
empirical significance of changes in real income as opposed to changes in
the unemployment rate as factors in election outcomes. Consider two
examples. First, in explaining the lack of statistically significant effects of
changes in the unemployment rate on the division of House seats when real
income and unemployment are both included in regressions, Kramer (1971,
p. 139) lists three issues:

- Real income and unemployment are highly correlated. As is well
  known, collinearity usually inflates the standard errors of the estimated
  coefficients.
- Unemployment data may be subject to larger measurement errors,
  especially for the pre–World War II period.
- More important is the fact that the unemployed are less likely to vote,
  and thus have little effect on aggregate voting statistics.

Second, in supporting the primacy of real income over unemployment,
Stigler (1973, p. 162) notes that the unemployed, "concentrated in the
young, unmarried, and less educated," constitute a small proportion of the
voting electorate, and except at extreme levels of unemployment denoting
economic mismanagement, the unemployed are not likely to have a sizable
effect on election outcomes.

This type of argument assumes a rational electorate in which individuals
vote by their "pocketbooks" and totally ignores the symbolic meaning of
unemployment rates. While it is obviously true that changes in real income
directly affect a far larger group than do changes in unemployment, the
latter may nevertheless threaten or comfort the working majority. We
suggest that changes in the unemployment rate are **interpreted** as an
indicator of effective economic management and subsequent collective
well-being. As our data indicate, Democrats and Republicans respond to
changing unemployment rates **differently**. The electorate is then asked to
choose between competing parties based on competing interpretations of
economic reality. In short, we argue against a radical empiricism in which
the economic facts "speaks for themselves" and against the vision of a
rational electorate that votes its economic self-interest. We argue for a
theory in which culture plays a critical role in interpreting "facts" and in
shaping and constraining understandings about the "real" interests of

voters. In the following section, we elaborate and operationalize the idea of interpretion in terms of the position of the parties on broad political controversies.

ISSUES IN PARTY PLATFORMS

For each presidential campaign, the platform presents the party's stand on political controversies. These controversies divide the engaged electorate, the parties, and contending factions within each of the parties. Therefore, parties frequently change their positions depending upon

- which faction happens to be in power,
- what position the contending party embraces,
- the country's political and economic fortunes, and
- the interaction of the preceding factors.

Undoubtedly, some controversies arise only in particular elections. Other controversies entail generic issues that are deeply embedded in American political culture. For example, one generic issue is the controversy over the conditions of national survival (Chapters 1 and 9). Platforms will suggest, perhaps falsely, that the survival of the nation is imperiled unless the suggested analysis, remedies, policies, and positions are accepted and acted upon. It is always assumed that the nation's survival is at stake; that is never the controversy. Instead, the source and resolution of the peril are at issue, and platforms stress one or another counterview or position. Accordingly, some platforms stress that the state of the domestic economy (wealth) threatens survival while others concentrate on foreign adversaries (war). It is a rare instance when both positions are balanced and neither platform suggests that the vicissitudes of the national economy and foreign hostilities are intertwined.

It is important to note that the terms *controversy*, *issue*, and *position* wrongly imply an explicitness of formulation that in fact never occurs. Party platforms do not literally state "the survival of the country is at stake; there are two alternative courses of action; we recommend this course for these reasons." Instead, these general disputes are implicit in particular positions taken by parties (cf. Chapters 1 and 9).

Content analysis is a set of strategies for making inferences from text (Stone *et al.*, 1966; Gerbner *et al.*, 1969; Holsti, 1969; Krippendorff, 1980; Weber, 1985a; Chapter 8). Applied to party platforms, content analysis produces quantitative indicators of changing symbol attention (or political concerns). These concerns vary between parties and over time. Using General Inquirer procedures (Stone *et al.*, 1966), the text of Democratic and Republican[9] party platforms from 1844 through 1964 was classified into content categories defined by the Lasswell Value Dictionary (Lasswell and Namenwirth, 1968; Chapter 2). The content analysis produces a great many time series, each indicating changing attention to a particular content category. These time series were detrended as required for subsequent analysis.[10] The detrended data (or residuals) were then factor-analyzed.[11] Of the 42 residual content variables, 10 produced two factors **identical** across parties, which accounted for over 50% of their total variances.[12] Based on separate analyses of Democratic and Republican platforms, the remaining 32 variables produced **equivalent** (rather than identical) factor structures of five factors each, explaining 58% of the variance in Democratic and 59% of the variance in Republican platforms.[13]

Each factor represents a divisive issue consisting of two counterviews or positions. Variation in this unmeasured issue is inferred from covariation among detrended content categories. If the parties use the same language to talk about the same issues, then we deal with **identical** issues. If, however, the parties discuss the same issues using different sets of symbols, then we define them as **equivalent** issues[14] (Table 6.1). The majority parties will often articulate the same issues in quite distinct language when arguing for the same or similar positions. In this manner they maintain their separate identities by linguistic means only. No doubt, the opposition of actual policies is far too costly. Thus defined and measured, these identical and equivalent issues constitute the underlying dimensions of political controversies in American society. Having clarified our conceptual and measurement framework, we can now address the two equivalent issues utilized in our models of election outcomes.

[9]Whig platforms were used for the elections of 1844–1852.

[10]The trends proved to be a compounding of two sine curves that were interpreted as 152- and 48-year cycles (Namenwirth, 1973; Chapter 3; Namenwirth and Bibbee, 1976; Namenwirth and Weber, 1979). The longer cycle constitutes a problem-solving sequence related to cohort succession and critical realignments (Burnham, 1976; Weber, 1982; Chapter 4). The shorter cycle is related to the economic fluctuation known as "the Kondratieff cycle" (Namenwirth, 1973; Chapter 3; Weber, 1981, 1983b; Chapter 5).

[11]The method used was principal components analysis, which differs from classical factor analysis in that it reproduces the variance of the original variables rather than their communalities. However, we will use the terms interchangeably. Other types of factor analysis were tried, but these did not produce substantively different results. We have not explored whether the structure of the factor solutions is constant or variable over time; this constancy was assumed.

[12]This similarity was indicated by a procedure of factor correlation and comparison developed by Ahmavaara (1954a, 1954b; Rummel, 1970, pp. 463–471).

[13]If issues are general, then they should exist independently in both sets of data.

[14]Chapters 9 and 10 address problems related to different content categories indicating the same themes. In the present case, the equivalence of themes across parties was established by comparing retrievals from the text (cf. note 16).

TABLE 6.1.
Identical and Equivalent Issues in Democratic and Republican Campaign Platforms*

IDENTICAL ISSUES
    Factor 1. Survival: wealth vs. war
    Factor 2. Solidarity: unity vs. inequality

EQUIVALENT ISSUES
    Democratic issues
        Factor 1. Legitimate authority: federal government vs. states
        Factor 2. Justification: ideological vs. quasifactual
        Factor 3. Effective government: people vs. laws
        Factor 4. Domestic responsibilities: rights vs. welfare
        Factor 5. Protagonists: individuals vs. collectivities
    Republican issues
        Factor 1. Legitimate authority: federal government vs. individuals
        Factor 2. Justification: ideological vs. quasifactual
        Factor 3. Effective government: persuasion vs. laws
        Factor 4. Domestic responsibilities: rights vs. welfare
        Factor 5. Protagonists: individuals vs. collectivities

*All factors number in order of variance explained.

Democrats 1. Legitimate Authority: Federal Government versus States

The opposed positions of federal government vs. states is suggested by the factor structure presented in Table 6.2. On the one hand, there is an association of concerns with the federal government (POWER AUTHORITATIVE PARTICIPANT) and the republic and territories (POWER ARENAS). Related to this concern is a preoccupation with helping, aiding and supporting (TRANS-ACTION GAINS). On the other hand, there is an association of concern with the states and the destruction of authority (POWER CONFLICT) by evil design, calculation, and intellectual tricks (ENLIGHTENMENT TOTAL). In this context, therefore, the concern with ENLIGHTENMENT is negative and philistine; intellect and intellectual values are feared and denigrated. Furthermore, where authority is perceived as vested in the states (or local governments), the federal power is perceived as abusing the welfare (AFFECTION TOTAL) of the people (ARENAS), their WELL-BEING, and their rights (RECTITUDE ETHICS).

A fundamental question in political philosophy is the source of legitimate authority (we refer to this variable as LEGIT). Many answers have been given, including the divinity (Bodin), the common will (Rousseau), and the party (Lenin). In America the debate has centered on two sources—the federal government and the states. Whether final legal authority should be invested in the federal government or in the states is a dispute that is further complicated by two related questions: First, which matters will be decided on either the federal or the state level, and second, who will decide the

TABLE 6.2
Indicators of Selected Democratic and Republican Issues

Category	Loading*
Democrats 1. Legitimate authority: Federal government versus States	
Power Authoritative Participant	.54
Transaction Gains	.52
Power Arenas	.48
Rectitude Ethics	−.48
Well-being Physical	−.51
Arenas	−.60
Affection Total	−.70
Power Conflict	−.75
Enlightenment Total	−.84
Republican 5. Protagonists: Individuals versus Collectivities[§]	
Respect Gains	.77
Undefined	.46
Rectitude Ethics	−.59
Selves	−.68

*Factor loadings <|.30| omitted.
[†]Variance explained: 16.7%.
[§]Variance explained: 10.1%.

former question? On both scores, Democratic platforms have often vacil-
lated.[15]

The federal government position is clearly indicated by this portion of
the 1936 Democratic platform (which attacks a Republican "states rights"
plank):[16]

> The Republican platform proposes to meet many pressing national problems
> solely by action of the separate States. We know that drought, dust storms,
> floods, minimum wages, maximum hours, child labor, and working conditions in
> industry, monopolistic and unfair business practices cannot be adequately
> handled exclusively by 48 separate State legislatures, 48 separate State ad-
> ministrations, and 48 separate State courts. Transactions and activities which
> inevitably overflow State boundaries call for both State and Federal treatment.
> [Johnson, 1978, p. 362]

[15]Upon further inspection of the platforms, it appears that the philosophical dispute is in
part a ruse masking the effort to support or sustain privileges of political collectivities—for
example, the farmers, urban labor, or immigrants.

[16]These retrievals were selected from platforms with the highest positive and negative factor scores for the period under investigation. Documents with high factor scores are those that
show an excess of attention to the cluster of categories that could have been expected on the
basis of trend levels. As noted, the latter were already removed from the data. It is therefore
comforting to find textual evidence for interpretations based on such intricate statistical
transformations.

The states' side of the issue is illustrated by this section of the 1944 Democratic platform:

> We favor Federal aid to education administered by the states without interference by the Federal Government. . . . We favor enactment of legislation granting the fullest measure of self-government for Alaska, Hawaii and Puerto Rico, and eventual statehood for Alaska and Hawaii. [Johnson, 1978, p. 403]

Republicans 5. Protagonists: Individuals versus Collectivities

In distinguishing events and formulating and justifying policies, Republican party platforms also distinguish implicitly between two classes of protagonists. These protagonists are seen as creating or being responsible for such events. The two classes are individuals, usually presidents or other men in high office, and collectivities, especially the Republican party itself. (We refer to this variable as PROTAGS.)

The positive end of this factor (Table 6.2) defines the individual value theme, and is mainly a concern with words such as *admire*, *appreciate*, *honor*, and *respect* (RESPECT GAINS). The negative pole is defined by references to the Republican party (SELVES) and to such words as *duty*, *ethics*, *responsible*, and *justice* (RECTITUDE ETHICS).

The individual theme is biographical in its approach to an understanding of history, often attributing political fortunes and tragedies to the doings of great men. The collective theme, in contrast, attributes the state of the nation and changes therein to the principles and actions of the Republican party, as indicated by the frequent use of the pronoun *we* (SELVES).

Individual protagonists are illustrated by this portion of the 1932 Republican platform, which lauds Hoover (and which sounds exceedingly familiar,[17] given the state of the economy in the 1980s):

> For nearly three years the world has endured an economic depression of unparalleled extent and severity. . . . When victory comes, as it will, this generation will hand on to the next a great heritage unimpaired. This will be due in large measure to the quality of the leadership that this country has had during this crisis. We have had in the White House a leader—wise, courageous, patient, understanding, resourceful, ever present in his post of duty, tireless in his efforts and unswerving faithful to American principles and ideals. [Johnson, 1978, p. 340]

In Republican platforms, collective protagonists are illustrated by this excerpt from the 1952 campaign:

---

[17]The similarity between the Reagan and Hoover Administrations may not be entirely fortuitous, but may result from long-term economic fluctuations that affect culture (Chapters 3 and 5; cf. Weber, 1983a).

> We shall eliminate from the State Department and from every Federal office,
> all . . . who share responsibility for the needless predicaments and perils in which
> we find ourselves. We shall also sever from the public payroll the hordes of
> loafers, incompetents and unnecessary employees who clutter the administration
> of our foreign affairs. . . . We shall substitute a compact and efficient organization
> where men of proven loyalty and ability shall have responsibility for reaching our
> objectives. [Johnson, 1978, p. 498]

To summarize, our two issue variables are (1) legitimate authority:
federal government vs. states (LEGIT); and (2) protagonists: individuals vs.
collectivities (PROTAGS). Having defined our thematic variables, we turn
to our economic and political variables and models of outcomes in presidential campaigns.

MODELS OF PRESIDENTIAL VOTING

Data for unemployment and for the political variables "incumbency,"
"share of two-party vote Democratic"[18] (DEMVOTE), and the change in
the Democratic vote (ΔVOTE) were obtained from the *Historical Statistics
of the United States* (U.S. Bureau of the Census, 1975). Our indicators of
voter reward or punishment of economic management by the incumbent are
based on changes in real income per capita.[19] Changes in real income per
capita[20] during the year of the election and one year prior were multiplied
by 1 or -1 indicating a Democratic or Republican incumbent, respectively.
This variable for changes during the election year and one year prior will be
referred to as ECONMAN and ECONMAN(-1), respectively.[21]

---

[18]Four distinct dependent variables can be constructed from presidential voting data. We
chose (1) the share of the two-party vote received by the Democratic candidate. This variable
excludes third-party protest votes, and our models assume that they do not exist. This variable
and our models also exclude nonvoters, who may or may not be protest nonvoters. An
alternative variable is (2) a binary variable indicating which party won the election. This
variable does not indicate the extent to which a party won and we therefore did not use it here
(but see Namenwirth and Weber, 1979). Another possible variable is (3) the share of the total
vote won by the victorious party. This variable would implicitly account for protest voting, but
because the dynamics of third- and minor-party voting may well be different from majority-
party voting, we elected not to use this variable. Finally, one could analyze (4) the percent of
the eligible vote garnered by the victorious party, but this variable makes it hard to
differentiate the dynamics of voting or not voting from the dynamics of winning the election.

[19]Our measure of "real income per capita" was constructed following Bloom and Price
(1975).

[20]To avoid awkward phrasing when discussing real income, "per capita" will be omitted
from the text.

[21]Some possible confusion might arise regarding the description of the difference terms. We
refer to changes from one year before the election year to the election year as "changes during
the year of the election." In addition, we refer to changes from two years to one year before
the election as "changes one year prior to the election," and use the symbol (-1) to represent
this change.

A positive relationship between ECONMAN [or ECONMAN(−1)] and the share of the two-party vote Democratic indicates that voters reward the incumbent party for economic growth and punish it for economic decline. For example, with a Democratic incumbent an increase in real income is related to a higher share of votes for the Democratic candidate, and a decrease in real income is related to a lower share.

Finally, changes in percent of the labor force unemployed the year of the election and one year prior (not multiplied by incumbency) will be referred to as ΔUNEMP and ΔUNEMP(−1), respectively.

The work of Kramer, Tufte, and others cited above indicates that voters reward the incumbent party for economic growth and punish it for economic decline. In other words, economic management has direct effects on the percentage of the two-party vote won by the Democratic candidate. We replicated this result and then found that models including thematic variables that predicted the **level** of the Democratic vote were substantively uninteresting, and so we briefly summarize these results: (1) There is little difference between ECONMAN and ECONMAN(−1) as predictors of the Democratic vote. (2) Two selected issue variables[22] have statistically significant effects on DEMVOTE. However, various "influence statistics" (Belsley *et al.*, 1980) indicate that the results for one issue variable are unstable, depending largely on the election of 1912. (3) Economic Management has no direct effects on the thematic variables. Consequently, these results lead to a simple prediction equation for DEMVOTE rather than a more satisfying model of the structure among these variables.

A more dynamic analysis would explain the election-to-election **change** in the Democratic vote rather than the **level** of the Democratic vote. Thus, our primary dependent variable is the change in the percentage of the two-party vote won by the Democrats, that is,

$$\Delta VOTE = DEMVOTE - DEMVOTE(-1)$$

where DEMVOTE is the current campaign and DEMVOTE(−1) is the previous campaign.

Table 6.3 presents the zero-order correlations and covariances among ΔVOTE and four predictor variables: ΔUNEMP and ΔUNEMP(−1), the change in the percentage of the labor force unemployed the year of the election and one year prior, respectively; LEGIT, the Democratic legitimacy issue; and PROTAGS, and Republican protagonist issue described above. Note that ΔUNEMP(−1) has a greater correlation with ΔVOTE and the issue variables than does ΔUNEMP.

---

[22]We chose issue variables that were highly correlated either with the split of the two-party vote or with the election-to-election change in the two-party vote. Other dependent variables could have been specified that would have had different issues as predictors. See note 18 above.

TABLE 6.3
Zero-Order Correlations and Covariances among ΔVOTE and Predictor Variables*

	ΔUNEMP	ΔUNEMP(−1)	LEGIT	PROTAGS	ΔVOTE
ΔUNEMP	8.417	3.677	0.684	1.008	5.705
ΔUNEMP(−1)	.445	8.114	0.878	1.120	11.718
	(.06)				
LEGIT	.382	.500	0.381	0.056	3.126
	(.11)	(.03)			
PROTAGS	.445	.503	.117	0.610	3.633
	(.06)	(.03)	(.63)		
ΔVOTE	.212	.443	.547	.502	85.880
	(.38)	(.06)	(.02)	(.03)	

*Variances/covariances on and above diagonal; correlation coefficients/significance, two-tailed, below diagonal, $N = 19$.

Analysis of the autocorrelation (ACF) and partial autocorrelation functions (PACF) (Box and Jenkins, 1976; Hibbs, 1974; McCleary and Hay, 1980) for the residuals from some equations estimated below indicate that the residual series are not completely white noise. Specifically, the ACFs and PACFs for the residuals suggest an autoregressive process with a two-election lag; that is, a relationship of the form

$$R_t = b * R_{t-1} + \epsilon$$

where R_t is the value of the residual for the current election, b is a regression coefficient, R_{t-1} is the value of the residual two campaigns earlier, and ϵ is a random (white-noise) sequence.

After subtracting the mean from each variable, we hypothesize the following set of structural equations:

$$\text{LEGIT}_t = b1 * \Delta\text{UNEMP} + b2 * R1_{t-1} + \epsilon_1$$

$$\text{PROTAGS}_t = b3 * \Delta\text{UNEMP} + \epsilon_2$$

$$\Delta\text{VOTE}_t = b4 * \text{LEGIT}_t + b5 * \text{PROTAGS}_t + b6 * \Delta\text{UNEMP} \\ + b7 * R3_{t-1} + \epsilon_3$$

The structural model defined by this set of equations is not identified. Consequently, we are unable to simultaneously estimate the unknown coefficients. Estimating each equation separately, Tables 6.4 and 6.5 present exact maximum likelihood estimates[23] of the unknown coefficients, their standard errors, t statistics, and standardized coefficients when ΔUNEMP and ΔUNEMP(−1), respectively, are included in the equations. Because of collinearity between the two unemployment variables, neither

[23]These equations were estimated with SAS796's PROC TARIMA.

TABLE 6.4
Estimated Parameters: ΔVOTE, LEGIT, PROTAGS, and ΔUNEMP, 19 Elections, 1892–1964

	Unstandardized coefficient	Standard error	t	Standardized coefficient
$b1$	0.074	0.043	1.72	0.346
$b2$	−0.461	0.212	2.18	—
$b3$	0.120	0.057	2.11	0.447
$b4$	7.831	2.848	2.75	0.521
$b5$	4.550	1.918	2.37	0.384
$b6$	−0.279	0.532	0.52	0.087
$b7$	−0.563	0.248	2.27	—

$R^2(\Delta\text{VOTE}) = 0.406$

has significant effects on the issue variables or ΔVOTE when both are included in the equation (data not presented here). Inspection of the ACF and PACF for the residuals when ΔUNEMP(−1) predicts LEGIT indicates that the series is white noise, and hence no autoregressive parameter was estimated.

As Tables 6.4 and 6.5 indicate, changes in aggregate unemployment rates have direct effects on LEGIT and PROTAGS but no direct effects on the election-to-election change in the Democratic presidential vote.[24] Table 6.6 reports the estimation of the equation for ΔVOTE omitting the unemployment variables, as they have no direct effects. Similar results were obtained when the dependent variable was the growth rate in the Democratic vote, that is [DEMVOTE − DEMVOTE(−1)]/DEMVOTE(−1). However, we report first differences rather than growth rates to avoid difficulties in interpretation.[25]

Ignoring the autoregressive parameters, examination of influence statistics indicates that the results do not reflect the extreme influence of any particular election. Thus, our general conclusions are not dependent either

[24]Inspection of the loglikelihood surface near the various parameter estimates suggests that collinearity is a problem when the unemployment variables are included in the equation predicting ΔVOTE. However, we conclude that unemployment has no direct effects because (1) the parameter estimates for the unemployment variables are so far from being statistically significant, (2) similar conclusions are reached using growth rates rather than first differences as the dependent variable, and (3) there is only a 2% difference in variance accounted for with unemployment in or out of the prediction equation. This last point indicates that there is little information in unemployment not already accounted for by the issue variables. Consequently, the time-ordering of the variables requires an intervening variable model.

[25]One problem in interpreting growth rates is that the growth rates for the Democrats and Republicans are not symmetrical, producing slightly different results when correlated with other variables. In considering the split of the two-party vote, our results are the same whether one considers first differences for the Democratic or for the Republican share of the vote.

TABLE 6.5
Estimated Parameters: ΔVOTE, LEGIT, PROTAGS, and ΔUNEMP(−1), 19 Elections, 1892–1964

	Unstandardized coefficient	Standard error	t	Standardized coefficient
$b1$	0.108	0.044	2.45	0.496
$b2$	----------------	not estimated	----	------------
$b3$	0.138	0.056	2.47	0.503
$b4$	6.898	2.904	2.38	0.459
$b5$	3.925	1.975	1.99	0.331
$b6$	0.263	0.630	0.42	0.081
$b7$	−0.594	0.237	2.50	—

$$R^2(\Delta\text{VOTE}) = 0.406$$

upon the particular form of changes in the two-party vote analyzed, or upon any particular election of the 19 analyzed.

Note that the effect of ΔUNEMP on LEGIT is less than that of ΔUNEMP(−1), and may be zero. This may indicate that the Democrats respond earlier than the Republicans to changes in the unemployment rate; that is, the Democratic response to the economy may be determined closer to the midterm congressional election than to the presidential election.

To summarize, our results clearly indicate that changes in the unemployment rate have substantial direct effects on the Democratic concern with legitimacy and Republican concern with protagonists. Furthermore, there is no direct effect of changes in the unemployment rate on the proportional change in the Democratic vote; unemployment has indirect effects only through political issues.

Finally, preliminary analysis of the effects of a binary variable reflecting

TABLE 6.6
Estimated Parameters: ΔVOTE, LEGIT, and PROTAGS, 19 Elections, 1892–1964

	Unstandardized coefficient	Standard error	t	Standardized coefficient
$b4$	7.340	2.615	2.81	0.489
$b5$	4.253	1.792	2.37	0.360
$b6$	----------------	not estimated	----	------------
$b7$	0.580	0.232	2.50	—

$$R^2(\Delta\text{VOTE}) = 0.385$$

$$\Delta\text{VOTE}_t = b4 * \text{LEGIT}_t + b5 * \text{PROTAGS}_t + b7 * R3_{t-1} + \epsilon_3$$

incumbency indicates (data not presented here) that incumbency has direct effects only on PROTAGS, and that the rest of the model holds controlling for incumbency. Specifically, Republican candidates tend to stress individual protagonists, usually the incumbent, with a Republican president, and tend to stress the Republican party and principles with a Democratic presidential incumbent.

CONCLUDING REMARKS

Two of the central questions of social inquiry are usually stated this way: What is the role of ideas in history? Are ideas causes or consequences of structural arrangements? Our research suggests, however, that these questions may be wrongly put. First, our research shows that prevailing cultural themes are largely determined by long-term trends of one kind or another. Second, the deviations from such trends have altogether different causes because fluctuations in the national economy determine them. Third, trend deviations in ideas mediate between election and economic fluctuations (and their various positive and negative accelerations). Ideas, therefore, are intervening variables. To the extent that economics and politics affect structural arrangements, producing transformation or maintenance, neither a materialist nor an idealist conception of history proved right, thus requiring a more complex approach than that presumed by the two original questions.

7

Values in American Science: Culture Dynamics in Three Professional Societies since 1900[1]

THE PROBLEM

Until recently, in the sociology of science, social-structural questions predominated.[2] Accordingly, there are a growing number of studies concerning the changing size, differentiation, stratification, and resource allocation of, or in, various disciplines (Barber, 1952; D. K. Price, 1962; D. Price, 1963; Hagstrom, 1965; Storer, 1966; Crane, 1969; Ben-David, 1971; Cole and Cole, 1971; Mullins, 1973; Blume, 1974; Collins, 1975). Of course, ideational considerations are rarely absent. But as with most intellectual history, their description and analysis rely heavily on traditional historiographic methods (Hughes, 1958; Brinton, 1963). Implicitly, the latter orientation remains antithetical to quantitative or sociological inquiry.

[1]The research for this study was supported by NSF Grant BMS 75-17988. Robert Philip Weber was in charge of computer operations, programming, analysis, and dictionary construction. Nancy Carter-Menéndez, Marilyn Rankin, and Charlene Bartnicki assisted him. He also provided critical editorial assistance. Without the generous assistance of David Baron and Kevin Kearny of the University of Connecticut Computer Center, this study would not have succeeded. William N. Singleton and Randi L. Miller helped to document otherwise unfounded assertions; they clarified many of the issues. Albert K. Cohen read an earlier version of the manuscript, rectifying important errors of judgment. Susan Spiggle did the same with a later version. I am greatly indebted to all. The responsibility for any remaining errors, however, is mine alone.

[2]Collins (1983) and other British scholars have shifted this focus to what is now called "the sociology of scientific knowledge."

J. Zvi Namenwirth wrote this chapter.

Admittedly, survey methods have been used sparingly (Blume, 1974, p. 12) but there, as elsewhere, they have some inherent weaknesses: They seem more suited for the description of popular opinions than for the interpretation of intellectual ideas. More importantly, however, fundamental ideas, values, and paradigmatic orientations (Barber, 1961; Kuhn, 1961, 1962; Friedrichs, 1970; Feuer, 1974; Collins, 1975) are not likely to change precipitously. Consequently, their description requires the examination of data over long periods of time, for which survey information simply does not exist. The researcher must therefore depend on documentary evidence and appropriate methodologies. Certainly, content analysis is such a methodology, and automated versions are useful for this purpose (Stone *et al.*, 1966; Kelly and Stone, 1975; Weber, 1985a). Hence, the following research questions arise:

- What is the nature of value changes in various scientific disciples?
- Are these changes the same in all sciences or are they discipline specific?
- What are the social causes and consequences of these ideational changes?

Questions concerning the role of ideas in social change have a venerable tradition (Hegel, 1967; Marx, 1970; Weber, 1958; Mannheim, 1936; Lukacs, 1971; Meinecke, 1970; Troeltsch, 1931; Miller, 1953, Brinton, 1963; Parsons, 1971). Concerning science and its changes, the role of ideas seems hard to deny because the productions of science are ideas to begin with (Parsons, 1951; Popper, 1961, 1968; Ben-David, 1971). Traditionally, therefore, the question is not about the global role of universal ideas, but about the role of extrascientific ideas in social structural dynamics for the formation of scientific knowledge (Gaston, 1970; Weingart, 1974; Whitley, 1974; Collins, 1975). In sum, this chapter will examine the relationship between on the one hand, changing social ideas and values concerning the good society, including communities of scientists, and on the other, structural features of the same.

The various disciplines change their culture orientations in a uniform manner. For instance, economists, chemists, and other scientists become equally less Metatheoretical[3] and more Methodological in their orientations. Hence, this and other changes seem less a response to changing structural features of (and unique to) each of the disciplines: They are more likely consequences of changing features of all of society and its culture. Conversely, existing differences between the disciplines—for example, the Applied orientations of the economists and the Pure Theoretical orientations

[3]The names of themes, orientations, and dilemmas are treated as proper names, and hence the initial letter is capitalized throughout. These themes are defined in detail below.

of the natural scientists, or the Libertarian orientations of economists and biologists and the Regulatory orientations of the chemists—remain fairly constant over time. This constancy suggests disciplinary autonomy both in each discipline's specific structural relations with society and in its intellectual heritage. Therefore, we shall argue that competition, if not conflict (i.e., the Libertarian orientation) remains a central explanatory principle for both economists and biologists, while principles of ordering, interdependence, and (mutual) attraction of various elements (i.e., the Regulatory orientation) play far more important explanatory roles in the natural sciences.

The relationships between social and economic changes, exigencies, or structural transformations, on the one hand, and cultural dynamics, on the other, are not simple. In fact, our investigations prove them highly complex. For instance, Parochial and Cosmopolitan themes frequently contrast in many of our investigations (Chapter 9). Usually, when the economy expands, the national culture[4] turns more Cosmopolitan; it turns in a Parochial direction when the economy contracts. However, there is a strong suggestion that the articulations of the scientific disciplines do not follow this "law." When the economy contracts, the presidential addresses of scientific associations do not turn more Parochial; instead, they turn more Cosmopolitan. Does this finding invalidate the law?

On further inspection and reflection, we concluded that the observed contradiction did not refute the often-observed regularities. This seeming contradiction derives from a misperception of actual social relativity and incommensurate points of reference: While society is external to the scientific enterprise, this enterprise is largely internal to society. Therefore, when society turns inward and Parochial during economic contraction, the sciences turn outward or Cosmopolitan. Or, what is "inward" for society is "outward" for the sciences and perhaps all other specialized institutions.[5] It is in this manner that this study answers some outstanding or recurrent questions while further specifying or elaborating on others.

The next section explains the design of the study, the specific research questions of this study, and its content-analytic methodology. Because factor analysis and its interpretations play such an important role, a separate section discusses these matters. Changes over time and contrasts among scientific organizations discriminate among five factors. Five sections, factor by factor, document the factorial findings and the manner in which they change over time or differ among the studied disciplines. A final section summarizes these results and discusses their implications.

[4] Actually, Chapters 3 and 5 indicate that it is the culture of the capitalist world system that alternates between Parochial and Cosmopolitan.

[5] In this scheme, what is inward to science and what is outward to society have no common reference.

METHODOLOGY

To detect changes (and differences), the study analyzes documents, in this case, the yearly presidential addresses to three scientific organizations—the American Chemical Society (ACS), the American Association for the Advancement of Sciences (AAAS), and the American Economic Association (AEA). To describe and classify changes in these documents, the investigators used automated content analysis. The latter's central feature is a dictionary, here the Lasswell Value Dictionary (Lasswell and Namenwirth, 1968; Chapter 2), which classifies most words in the English language in a restricted number of categories.

In each document, the basic datum of the inquiry is a frequency count of words belonging to one or another category, thus providing a frequency profile for all documents. Rather than investigating each content category (or variable) separately, the analysis uses scaling procedures—here, factor analysis. Therefore, it describes changes (and differences) among documents for combinations of categories. These combinations constitute issues or dilemmas (and issue themes or orientations) whose meanings are further illustrated by selected excerpts from the presidential speeches.[6] The analysis produced 5 issues (or 10 contrasting orientations) that demonstrated change over time or contrasts among the three scientific organizations. At this point, the selection of scientific organizations, presidential addresses, time periods, and mode of analysis requires some justification.

The three organizations were chosen for several reasons. The inclusion of both natural and social sciences was meant to maximize thematic contrasts. Besides, value change is a slow process, so that to be selected, the organizations must have existed for an extended period. It is quite surprising to find how few American scientific organizations existed before the turn of the century. Also, among the latter, even fewer published the addresses of their presidents.

Why presidential addresses? To be attractive to a large audience—the scientific organization's entire membership—presidential addresses must be of general rather than arcane interest. Therefore, they differ markedly from the usual papers read at yearly meetings. Furthermore, these addresses are written by departing (or incoming) presidents who usually represent various currents of thought existing at the center of the discipline's concerns, so these speeches are likely to address fundamental issues of the day. In fact, the discussion of outstanding intellectual or professional issues has been the central objective of such addresses since their inception, and hence, shifting

---

[6]The meaning of the factor interpretations is illustrated if not validated by excerpts from the speeches with high factor scores. Such speeches are very much characterized by opposing themes, and the strategy provides textual evidence rather than statistical proof (cf. Chapters 8, 9, and 10).

concerns cannot be attributed to a change of objective. Instead, they must reflect alterations in the intellectual or social life of the organization. Also, these speeches are published regularly, at yearly intervals, which greatly helps longitudinal research and comparisons. Finally, the ceremony of yearly addresses has become a feature of many different types of organizations, including the state, and this will allow for future interinstitutional comparisons.

For comparisons over time, three periods were chosen: 1900–1910, 1930–1940, and, 1960–1970. This choice was largely based on practical considerations. Before 1900, the required information was not available for all three organizations. At the time of the research, 1960–1970 was the last full decennium. The decade 1930–1940 consisted of the middle period. It was an extra bonus that it happened to be of special interest because of critical changes in American society itself at the time.

The design of the study is quite obvious. The plan was to investigate 10 presidential addresses from three scientific organizations for each of three time periods, or 90 speeches in all. In this manner, it would be possible to answer the research questions concerning changes over time, contrasts among scientific organizations, and their structural causes or consequences. A balanced ANOVA design would reveal whether the content-analytic findings differed significantly among time periods and organizations, and whether the observed changes and differences could be interpreted by delineating an underlying structure. Unfortunately, this comprehensive design was seriously unbalanced because of missing data.[7] Table 7.1 presents the distribution of the analyzed speeches. While seriously unbalanced, the actual design, it was judged, would still allow an estimation of the various ANOVA effects.

What about the final research question concerning the structural causes of consequences of the measured ideational changes? The research design (two-way analyses of variance) estimates three distinct sources of ideational changes and contrasts. One source is time itself, its passing, and the

TABLE 7.1
Frequency Distribution of Speeches by Organization and Time Period

	AEA	AAAS	ACS
1900–1910	9	7	7
1930–1940	8	7	1
1960–1970	8	9	8

[7]Belatedly, it was discovered that the ACS stopped publishing its presidential addresses during the depression years. Furthermore, the transcription costs far exceeded anticipations. Consequently, only 64 of the planned 90 speeches were studied, as detailed in Table 7.1.

structural changes within science and society associated with the transition. Another source is the structural differences among the three organizations and the disciplines they represent. Finally, there is a third source (statistical interaction) that leads to discipline-specific changes over time, causing convergence, divergence, or reversal in articulations among the three organizations. Nevertheless, because the design does not include direct measurements of the relevant structures, the search for structural causes and consequences remains speculative. Also, an extended design would require formal time-series analyses of dependent and independent variables rather than a mere contrast of three selected time periods. At this point, only a more restricted design was feasible, which seemed prudent considering the state of the art.

FACTOR-ANALYTIC DESIGN AND FINDINGS

As noted, the computer compiled profiles of frequency counts for each content category[8] in each presidential address.[9] Because it is more enlightening and parsimonious to describe the findings in themes (or clusters of covarying categories), factor analysis was used to detect such themes.[10]

The 44 categories retained for further analysis produced 12 factors with eigenvalues greater than or equal to 1. Of these 12 factors, only 5 showed significant changes from the early to the late period or significant differences among the scientific organizations (at the 5% level or better).[11] Since possible causes of variation in the other 7 factors are not included in the research design, these original factors (4 through 10) were omitted from

[8]Chapter 2 describes the dictionary in detail. It consists of over 7,000 words and 10,000 word senses that proved important for this mode of investigation. Besides these basic words (or entries), the dictionary was augmented by some additional entries to accommodate the special language of scientific addresses. Also, the dictionary was expanded for the present study by the addition of an ad hoc category, COLLECTIVE PARTICIPANT, which includes the names of the scientific organizations.

[9]To control for the variable length of the addresses (between 1,724 and 10,802 words), each category count was expressed as a percentage of the total number of words in each speech. These percentages are the basic data for later statistical analysis (after arc-sine square root transformation to stabilize variances across the units of comparison).

[10]Principal component analysis with varimax rotation. Of the original 71 categories, 27 were eliminated because they had either frequent zero occurrences, low variances, low means, or a combination thereof. Also, in Lasswell's dictionary, the eight major categories are further divided into subcategories. To prevent double classifications, and therefore the use of part–whole correlations, either major categories **or** subcagories were included. Distributional characteristics determined the choice.

[11]Multivariate hypotheses (MANOVA) of no overall time effect and no overall organization effect were rejected at the .001 level. The details are omitted in the interest of brevity.

further consideration. The remaining 5 factors were renamed 1 through 5 in order of variance explained (explaining 37% of the total variance). Anticipating a more extensive discussion, they are named as follows:

Factor 1. Value orientation: Value Laden vs. Value Neutral
Factor 2. Scientific orientation: Applied vs. Theoretical
Factor 3. Organizational scope: Cosmopolitan vs. Parochial
Factor 4. Order orientation: Liberty vs. Regulation
Factor 5. Scientific progress: Metatheory vs. Methods

Before we deal with the specifics of each factor, let us first consider the more general question: What is a factor in this mode of content analysis?[12] During their yearly congresses, the newly elected (or retiring) presidents of the organizations present their views on current issues and elaborate on their positions, which are inherently, but frequently implicitly, contrasted to opposing positions. Therefore, the issues are potentially controversial and can be characterized by opposing-issue themes. In this project[13] the issues are varied—for instance, concerning matters of epistemology, metatheoretical style, or disciplinary politics. It is well to remember, however, that we deal here with latent issues, positions, orientations, oppositions, and controversies: They are explicated by the analysis but may well remain hidden from both speaker and audience. For instance, the speaker never stated: "These are the controversial issues at hand on which I take the following positions." Rather, it is in a much more indirect manner that each factor represents potentially divisive issues, consisting of two counterviews or issue themes. Instead, variation in these dilemmas is inferred from the covariation among measured content categories. The following example illustrates these points.

One dilemma is the question of value orientation: Will a speech support (or not support) a value orientation of any kind? In their responses to the issue, the speeches range between two issue themes, from Value Laden to Value Neutral. Thus, some speeches are very Value Neutral, some are very Value Laden, and the remainder fall in between.

To summarize thus far, there are five dilemmas that are independent (or orthogonal); in other words, knowing how a speech responds to one of the issues does not foretell how it will respond to any of the others. The five issues, their contrasting thematic responses, and the ways in which those change or contrast are all dealt with next.

[12]Categories that are highly loaded on the positive end of the factor covary. So, if a speech is highly concerned with one content category, it is concerned with other categories in that cluster. The cluster's interpretation is the problem here addressed.

[13]Chapter 6 provides a similar treatment of factor interpretation in a very different context. Chapter 9 addresses the description and explanation of dilemmas and issues identified through factor analysis and other techniques.

Factor 1. Value Orientation: Value Laden versus Value Neutral

Factor 1 raises the question: Does a particular speech commit itself to values, or does it not? However, if an address commits itself to a value position, it does not choose just any value position from a wider theoretical spectrum. Instead, the Value Laden theme is one of a particular type: It stresses traditional moral values with a distinctly Victorian flavor. Thus, the theme often concerns philanthropy, honor, honesty, and industry. These virtues are thought to reside in the individual while, in contrast, sin dwells among the collective actors or anonymous processes and masses of con-temporary society. It follows that the speeches that celebrate the Value Laden theme make frequent references both to persons named and revered (AUTHORITATIVE PARTICIPANT)[14] and to persons of more lowly origins (PARTICIPANTS, OTHERS).[15] Frequent use of the last category indicates a concern with status differentiation, making distinctions between higher and lower orders. Here, the distinctions are based on the moral virtues of AFFECTION, RESPECT, RECTITUDE, and PSYCHOLOGICAL WELL-BEING that are presented in an aura of good feeling (POSITIVE AFFECT). Table 7.2 contains the statistical specifics. An excerpt from Jenks's (1907) speech to the AEA, "The Modern Standards of Business Honor," further clarifies the Value Laden theme:

TABLE 7.2
Loadings on Factor 1. Value Orientation*

Category	Loading
VALUE LADEN	
Participants	0.88
Affection Total	0.77
Respect Total	0.77
Rectitude Total	0.62
Power Authoritative Participant	0.49
Positive Affect	0.47
Others	0.47
Collective Participant	0.43
Well-being Psychological	0.32
VALUE NEUTRAL	
Undefinable	−0.66
Undefined	−0.63
Time–Space	−0.44
Leftovers	−0.40

*Loadings < |.30| not reported; variance explained = 11.6%.
†Or "Analytic."

[14]Category names are capitalized throughout.
[15]The category OTHERS includes all third-person pronouns, singular and plural.

> The fact that within the last few years so many influential businessmen, not only in the United States, but also in other countries, have engaged in operations that have shocked the sense of justice and honor and fair-dealing, seems out of harmony with the general trend of social events. It was certainly not to be expected that men who seem entirely conscientious in all their dealings, public and private, men who apparently in all private relations lead exemplary lives, men who have won universal respect, should suddenly in their business be found engaged in acts illegal and dishonorable. [p. 1]

In good sociological fashion (Comte, 1875; Weber, 1947; Nisbet, 1953; Toennies, 1931; Ellul, 1964; Marcuse, 1964), the speaker bewails the threatening loss of community and its standards that would result from the increasing scale of both business and society. Additionally, the prevailing standards are never questioned; they are proclaimed to be of a universal nature.

The factor analysis also well identifies the opposite issue theme: Value Neutrality. Previous research shows that the categories UNDEFINED and UNDEFINABLE are often highly correlated, usually indicating an absence of value concerns and the presence of descriptive or analytic prose (Namenwirth and Bibbee, 1975). This inference is supported by the prevalence of words in the TIME-SPACE category, connoting a preoccupation with specifics rather than universals, with facts rather than principles. The presence of the category LEFTOVERS[16] in this cluster does not come as a surprise. The prevalence of low-frequency words that are excluded from the Value Dictionary simply reflects a characteristic of technical scientific language, namely, that it has many unusual words. The Value Neutral theme thus pervades the discussion of purely scientific speeches; they are likely to be couched in specialized technical language. An excerpt from Eyring's (1967) address to the AAAS, "Untangling Biological Reactions," expresses the Value Neutral theme most pronouncedly; this is the speech that contrasts most clearly with the one preceding.

> Newton Harvey introduced me to Frank Johnson, with a brief summary of the peculiar effects of pressure of luminescence that Johnson, Brown and Marksland had just observed. Below the temperature maximum hydrostatic pressure decreases the light intensity of luminescent bacteria in solution, and above this temperature maximum pressure increases the light intensity. Harvey emphasized the seeming paradox in these observations. Pressure should either increase the brightness of luminescence or decrease it but not both. [p. 1609]

Table 7.3 describes the average change in value orientation. There is a drastic change from Value Laden to Value Neutral. Among all the documents, about 15% of the variation in this issue must be attributed to

---

[16]This category contains words not classified in the dictionary. It primarily consists of words that appear quite infrequently.

TABLE 7.3
**Temporal Changes in Factor 1. Value
Orientation: Value Laden vs. Value Neutral***

Time	Average factor score
1900	.575
1930	−.148
1960	−.440

*$F = 7.92$; $df = 2, 63$; $p = .0009$; and $\omega^2 = .1492$.

changes associated with the passing of time from 1900 to 1970.[17] The average change is not much larger during the first 30 years, so that for now a constant rate of change seems probable. While it is impossible for any rate of change to remain constant for an infinite period, the time series are too short to settle the issue here.

The average differences among the three organizations are not statistically significant and neither are organization-specific changes over time (i.e., interaction). In conclusion, we note an important historical change in the value issue, from Value Laden to Value Neutral, which occurs similarly among organizations of economists, chemists, and the AAAS. In the beginning of this century, the various disciplines proved more concerned with moral and social issues, and this concern has declined since, in favor of analytic and nonvalue questions.

Factor 2. Scientific Orientation: Applied versus Theoretical

This issue raises the question: What is scientific inquiry for, and therefore, what shall we study or what type of inquiry will occupy our time and minds? In the addresses the answers to this question range between two limiting cases: Applied vs. Theoretical. Perhaps the term *Applied* is not completely adequate, because the Applied theme is not atheoretical; at times, it is very theoretical indeed. What distinguishes the Applied theme is the belief that scientific problems are not, or ought not be, generated by the purely internal development of the discipline, but rather by external social circumstance. In Applied approaches, questions of utility predominate, in Theoretical ones, questions of truth (Campbell, 1952; Popper, 1963).

In the speeches, the externally generated problems are largely economic in nature.[18] Hence, a cluster of WEALTH subcategories defines the Applied

---

[17] As indicated by the measure, $\omega^2 = .1492$ (Hays, 1963, p. 407). Its square root, .39, estimates the correlation between the passing of time and the issue theme.

[18] This may be fortuitous, resulting from the choice of economics as a social science discipline, but more likely it is inherent in the theme and its utilitarian perspective.

theme (Table 7.4).[19] It is further characterized by words such as *leadership*, *policy*, and *politics* (POWER ENDS); verbs such as *distort*, *exaggerate*, and *misunderstand* (ENLIGHTENMENT LOSSES), and *afflict*, *deprive*, and *exclude* (TRANS-ACTION LOSSES).[20] The concern with these categories implies a discussion of policy options that, according to economic theory, will alleviate its dismal problems. An excerpt from Friedman's (1967) address to the AEA, "The Role of Monetary Policy," illustrates the theme and point:

> The past two years, to come closer to home, would have been steadier and more productive of economic wellbeing if the Federal Reserve had avoided drastic and erratic changes of direction, first expanding the money supply at an unduly rapid pace, then, in early 1965, stepping on the brake too hard, then, at the end of 1966, reversing itself and resuming expansion until at least November, 1967, at a more rapid pace than can long be maintained without appreciable inflation. [p. 12]

The factor-analytic findings only poorly define the contrasting Theoretical Value theme. There are just two categories, and they have low loadings. Addresses that are preoccupied with these categories tend to use more specialized words (LEFTOVERS)[21] in conjunction with ENLIGHTENMENT OTHER[22]

TABLE 7.4
Loadings on Factor 2. Scientific Orientation*

Category	Loading
APPLIED	
Wealth Other	.83
Wealth Transaction	.74
Wealth Participant	.73
Power Ends	.58
Enlightenment Losses	.54
Transaction Losses	.40
Transaction Gains	.33
THEORETICAL	
Enlightenment Other	−.48
Leftovers	−.34

*Loadings < |.30| not reported; variance explained = 9.5%.

[19]These categories include WEALTH OTHER, a residual category; WEALTH TRANSACTION, a category of verbs and verb forms, e.g., *buying*, *selling*, *lending*, WEALTH PARTICIPANT, a category of trades and occupations.

[20]The category TRANSACTION LOSSES contains words indicating deprivation, but the particular values involved are not consistently indicated. In this particular case, however, these losses all concern the travails of the economy.

[21]As noted earlier, this is a residual category containing words not otherwise defined anywhere in the Lasswell Value Dictionary.

[22]As all OTHER categories, this is a long list of residual ENLIGHTENMENT word senses that are not defined in the remaining ENLIGHTENMENT subcategories.

words—for instance, *characteristic*, *scholarship*, and *debatable*. This suggests a preoccupation with abstract and theoretical matters, as a perusal of speeches with high negative factor scores further confirms. An excerpt from Boas's (1932) address to the AAAS, "The Aims of Anthropological Research," illustrates the interpretation:

> We have sufficient evidence to show that morphological form is subject to environmental influences that sometimes will have similar effects on unrelated forms. Even the most skeptical would admit this for size of the body. [p. 607]

On the average, the three organizations do not change significantly over time (see Table 7.5). Instead, the changes over time demonstrate a statistical interaction: They are discipline (or organization) specific. As Figure 7.1 indicates, the economists (AEA) become increasingly more Applied in their concerns. Conversely, in the 1900s and 1960s the ACS and the AAAS are not very different from one another, but during the same period they diverge, moving in opposite directions, with the ACS becoming more Applied and the AAAS becoming more Theoretical. Finally, from 1900 to the 1960s the two organizations exchange places (another statistical interaction): The ACS is the most theoretical in the first period and the AAAS in the last. During the years of the Depression, the AEA becomes more Applied and the AAAS more Theoretical, while in the prosperous 1900s and 1960s the two organizations are far more alike in scientific orientation. In contrast, the presidents of the ACS have become more and more Applied in their concerns. Clearly, the various disciplines respond differently to the changing times when the issue is one of scientific orientation. These interactions explain about 12% of the variance in this issue, for a qualitative correlation of .35.

Nevertheless, there is also a consistent and stronger difference among the three organizations, irrespective of time, with a contrast that explains a little less than 37% of the variance ($\omega = .60$). The economists (AEA) are by far the most Applied in their orientation, the AAAS is the most Theoretical, and the chemists (ACS) take, on the average, an intermediate position.

TABLE 7.5
Organizational Differences on Factor 2.
Theoretical Orientation: Applied
vs. Theoretical*

Organization	Average factor scores
ACS	−.326
AEA	.782
AAAS	−.622

*$F = 26.33$; $df = 2, 55$; $p < .0001$; and $\omega^2 = .3682$.

APPLIED

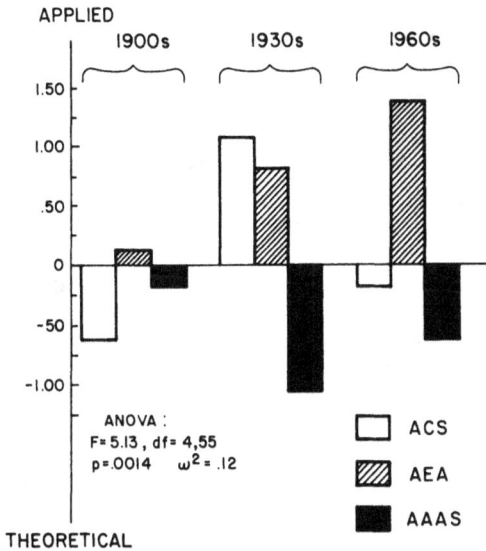

FIGURE 7.1. **Concern with Scientific Orientation. Applied vs. Theoretical, by Time and Organization.**

Factor 3. Organizational Scope: Cosmopolitan versus Parochial

The issue organizational scope addresses the question: Shall the organization deal with the internal affairs of the organization or with problems external to the discipline? Cosmopolitan orientations are complexly related to the actual factor-analytic findings, and this relationship requires some careful elaboration.

Previous research (Namenwirth and Bibbee, 1975) revealed frequent clustering of the categories IF, NOT, and SURE, and the appearance of this cluster always indicates a large measure of defensiveness by writers or speakers. The defensiveness reflects a careful presentation of facts and counterfacts, arguments and counterarguments with many *buts*, *ifs*, and *howevers* suggesting patient appraisal and objectivity. In fact, the defensiveness seems part of a strategem to convince the audience of a hidden partisan view. Here (Table 7.6), the defensiveness is associated with the use of verbs such as *conquer, constrain,* and *threaten* (POWER LOSSES), and *afflict, deprive,* and *exclude* (TRANSACTION LOSSES); and with the expression of other negative feelings (NEGATIVE AFFECT). The essential feature of the Cosmopolitan theme is that it locates issues at the border of the discipline with the world at large, while the Parochial theme, in contrast, locates these problems at the center. An excerpt from Millis's (1934) address to the AEA, "The Union in Industry: Some Observations on the Theory of Collective Bargaining," further illustrates the Cosmopolitan theme:

TABLE 7.6
Loading on Factor 3. Organizational Scope*

Category	Loading
COSMOPOLITAN	
If	.74
Not	.64
Power Losses	.58
Negative Affect	.54
Transaction Losses	.50
PAROCHIAL	
Collective Participant	−.64
Enlightenment Other	−.57
Transaction Gains	−.33

*Loading < |.30| not reported; variance explained = 7.3%.

I hope you will pardon me if I seem to talk shop. I disclaim talking of the shop of that branch of the Federal Service with which I am at present connected. Yet I cannot avoid the appearance of talking shop for my views are quite as much the result of experience and observation in industry as of reading and reflection in my study. [p. 1]

The opposing theme is well indicated by only one category, COLLECTIVE PARTICIPANT, containing the names of the three organizations. Clearly, speeches that strongly express this theme concern themselves with the life and fate of the scientific organization rather than with the problems of the surrounding world. In contrast to the Cosmopolitan theme, which is so defensive in tone, the prose of the Parochial theme is upbeat and optimistic, with a Chamber of Commerce flavor of boosterism. Arveson's (1964) address to the ACS catches this flavor very well indeed:

My title is your "New" Society, with the word "New" in quotation marks. Another title I thought of was "Your President's Eye View." Still another was "1944 to 1964: A Good Score." The period 1944 to 1964 has been a very exciting one for your Society, and to be exposed to, or be involved in, a large number of the exciting events of this period has been my good fortune.... Your Society is a vital force in this world. With its virtual 100,000 members representing the largest of the sciences, it is an awsome force in a science-minded era. [p. 126]

On the average, all three organizations are more Parochial in the 1960s than ever before (Table 7.7). This change, however, is cyclical rather than linear. All three organizations are most Cosmopolitan during the Depression years and far less so in the early 1900s. About 11% of the variance in the issue is explained by the observed changes over time. Also, about this issue, the differences among the three organization are negligible (statistically insignificant), and so are the organization-specific changes.

TABLE 7.7
Temporal Changes in Factor 3.
Cosmopolitan vs. Parochial*

Time	Average factor score
1900	.156
1930	.548
1960	−.489

*$F = 5.92$; $df = 2$, 55; $p = .0047$; and $\omega^2 = .1060$.

Factor 4. Order Orientation. Liberty versus Regulation

This factor represents a long-standing issue in social theory. The question is: As now constituted, is social order the product of liberty or of regulation and planning? In the Liberty view, conflict and strife, including competition, are necessary and desirable because they will lead to improved social conditions, favoring the realization of all human potentialities. For the coordination of freely chosen individual activities, society must rely on the workings of competition on markets, or biological selection mechanisms, and their unintended yet always beneficial social consequences. This is really the competitive utilitarian theory of social order (Dowse and Hughes, 1972, p. 31). Contrarily, the Regulation view holds that conflict will destroy the social order and therefore, the very basis of anything of value. Hence, the coordination of competitive impulses will require authoritative planning, social organization, and other forms of intervention, regulation, or legislation, depending on the field of activity.

The positive end of the factor is well defined (Table 7.8). Four POWER

TABLE 7.8
Loadings on Factor 4. Order Orientation*

Category	Loading
LIBERTY	
Power Conflict	.79
Power Other	.68
Power Losses	.54
Power Doctrine	.50
Enlightenment Losses	.40
Negative Affect	.32
Anomie	.32
REGULATION	
(None)	

*Loadings $< |.30|$ omitted; variance explained = 5.0%.

subcategories explain its meaning. The POWER CONFLICT category contains nouns such as *conflict, competition,* and *strife*; POWER DOCTRINE contains the names of ideologies such as democracy; POWER OTHER is a residual POWER category; while POWER LOSSES speaks for itself. Clearly, yearly addresses that score high on this factor express a concern with questions of social order and disorder (or anomie) and with institutionalized conflict (or power) as a means to contain them. Matthew Hammond's (1930) speech to the AEA, "Economic Conflict as a Regulatory Force in International Affairs," further illustrates this interpretation:

> Economic conflict is neither a new nor a strange phenomenon. If today we have ceased to accept the naive argument that competition is wholly a stimulating, never a destroying force in our economic life, it is not because we do not believe that competition can be made to serve it in the stimulating way in which Smith and his followers contended that it would act. When it fails, it is because the competitors do not possess equal strength and foresight and the stronger and more foresighted are likely to insist that their individual interests are those of the group. The weaker members are then obliged to combine in order to restrain competition and prevent it from both destroying itself and them. [p. 1]

The factor analysis does not define the negative pole of this issue. In these documents no combination of categories were found that are unambiguously associated with the theme. However, by inference, it follows that the theme must be characterized by a concern with either of two different themes—an absence of conflict; or with the opposite of conflict, peace and accommodation as the consequence of some form of Regulation. Since the latter theme is a well-known alternative to utilitarianism in social theory, this interpretation was chosen.[23] Farlow's (1905) speech to the AAAS, "The People's Conception of the Scientific Man at the Present Day," justifies this choice:

> We have seen that the public are[24] more interested than they were in the welfare of scientific men, and the better they understand existing conditions, the better for us. If they know that organization and concentration are necessary in science as in business, they should also understand that organization has its dangers as well.... The organization in science does not consist in having scientific work placed under the control of purely business men but of scientific men who have a capacity for administration.... Science should be a republic. [p. 14]

---

[23]The absence of a positive definition of the Regulation theme may well result from either of two causes: (1) The category system of the Lasswell Value Dictionary is insufficient for the identification of the theme usually or as expressed in the language of these addresses; (2) this theme is uniquely defined in each of the characteristic speeches because the suggested mode of regulation will vary with the topic at hand. In either case, such speeches have in common only the absence of categories defining the opposite theme on the issue.

[24]Throughout, the author treated the word *public* as a plural noun.

TABLE 7.9
Organizational Differences on Factor 4.
Order Orientation: Liberty vs. Regulation*

Organization	Average factor scores
AEA	.486
AAAS	−.205
ACS	−.464

*$F = 5.52$; $df = 2, 55$; $p = .0066$; and $\omega^2 = .1169$.

Table 7.9 demonstrates a statistical difference among the three organizations that explains nearly 12% of the variance in this issue: The AEA is most Libertarian, the ACS is most regulation oriented, and the AAAS takes an intermediate position on the average. Within the AAAS there is a suggestion of a further division. Usually, the biologists are more Libertarian; the natural scientists more Regulation oriented. Why would this be? A plausible explanation requires further discussion.

For both economists and biologists, competition, rather than cooperation and design, has become a central ordering principle of ecospheres and biospheres. Contrary doctrines, such as those of command and institutional economics or those of Prince Kropotkin (n.d.) never found much favor in American economics or biology. Even in agricultural economics, optimal ordering is sought in the workings of competition and free markets rather than domestication. At any rate, in these disciplines there is an interesting spillover from disciplinary to social doctrine and vice versa. At this point, we note an interchange between theoretical and extratheoretical ideas. The relationships between these two idea systems and the social order is an altogether different question. Barring the life sciences, whether a similar spillover would exist in the natural sciences between theoretical and extratheoretical idea systems is an open question. At any rate, in these speeches the leaders of the physical science disciplines put their trust in Regulation and Organization for the acquisition and transmission of scientific knowledge, that is, for research and education.

The observed differences between the physical sciences on the one hand, and the life sciences and economics on the other must be rather stable. About these opposing conceptions of the mechanisms of order, the contrasting orientations (or themes) have remained constant since 1900. There were neither significant changes over time nor statistical interactions in the content-analytic findings.

Factor 5. Scientific Progress: Metatheory versus Methods

Factor 5 is a residual factor explaining only 4.1% of the variance (Table 7.10). Even so, it represents an interesting issue, having a plausible inter-

TABLE 7.10
Loadings on Factor 5.
Scientific Progress*

Category	Loading
METATHEORY	
Rectitude Total	.38
Skill Aesthetic	.32
METHODS	
Means	−.86
Ends	−.43

*Loadings < |.03| not reported; variance
explained = 4.1%.

pretation. True, the defining categories are few and have low loadings. The exception is the category MEANS, and this category first suggested the interpretation of this pole.

The issue raises the following question: What produces scientific progress? The speeches provide two contrasting answers. Some of the speeches argue that speculation, ontological elaboration, and consequently, the development of metatheory precondition scientific progress. Other addresses insist that the development of science depends on the development of methods of all kinds and of instrumentation in particular. This position is indicated by a frequent use of words such as *device, equipment,* and *method* (MEANS). Excerpts from the two most typical addresses further show the interpretation. The 1930 address to the AAAS, "Present Status of Theory and Experiment as to Atomic Disintegration and Atomic Synthesis," exemplifies the Metatheory theme. Its author, Millikan (1930) puts the matter thus:

> Prior to the middle of the nineteenth century little experimental evidence of any sort had appeared, so that the problem was wholly in the hands of the philosopher and the theologian. Then came, first, the discovery of the equivalence of heat and work and the consequent formulation of the principle of the conservation of energy, probably the most far-reaching physical principle ever developed.
>
> Following this ... came, second, the discovery ... of the second law of thermodynamics as necessitating the ultimate "heat-death" of the universe and the final extinction of activity of all sorts. ... This is classically ... stated in the Humpty-Dumpty rhyme.
>
> As a natural if not a necessary corollary to this was put forward by some, in entire accord with the demands of medieval theology, a *deux ex machina* to initially wind up or start off this running-down universe. [pp. 1–2]

The Methods theme sharply contrasts with the former, as is best revealed in Klopsteg's address (1961) to the AAAS. It is called: "The Indispensable Tools of Science."

TABLE 7.11
Temporal Changes on Factor 5.
Scientific Progress: Metatheory
vs. Methods

Time	Average factor score
1900	.236
1930	.337
1960	−.433

*$F = 4.01$; $df = 2$, 55; $p = .02$; and $\omega^2 = .0863$.

During these interesting years it has been my good fortune to have been intellectually and physically concerned with the instruments of science—the indispensable tools of science. Gladly do I avail myself of the traditional prerogative to draw together some facts and ideas regarding the role of instruments, whether in the exploration of the unknown or the elucidation of the known. . . .

To say that instruments with their associated apparatus occupy a place of the utmost significance to research, both in advancing basic knowledge and in applying it for human betterment [is to say the obvious]. [p. 1,913]

The differences among the three organizations are negligible and statistically insignificant. But, as Table 7.11 indicates, over time there are significant overall changes from Metatheoretical to Methodological. However, here the change looks cyclical as well, rather than simply linear, increasing the Metatheoretical concerns slightly from the 1900s to the 1930s, followed by a far more drastic decline since then. At any rate, the change over time explains nearly 9% of the variance in this issue.

SUMMARY OF FINDINGS AND DISCUSSION

Three issues changed significantly over time and two contrasted significantly among the three scientific organizations. Table 7.12 recapitulates the specifics.

Even though the number of significant findings is about the same, the amount of variance explained is considerably less than in previous studies (Namenwirth, 1969a, 1969b, 1973; Namenwirth and Bibbee, 1975; Namenwirth and Brewer, 1966). There are several probable explanations: First, the language of presidential speeches to scientific gatherings contains far more esoteric language (and words) than newspaper editorials or party platforms. This must increase noise and error variance in the content analysis. Second, these presidential addresses, even grouped by discipline and time period, are far less homogeneous sources of articulations than either newspaper editorials or party platforms. In other words, presidential

TABLE 7.12
Summary of Significant Find ings in Five Issues

Factor	Issues	Changes
ISSUES THAT CHANGE OVER TIME		
1	Value orientation	From Value Laden to Value Neutral
3	Organizational scope	From Parochial to Cosmopolitan and back
5	Scientific progress	From Metatheoretical to Methodological
ISSUES THAT VARY BY ORGANIZATION		
2	Scientific orientation	AEA most Applied, AAAS most Theoretical
4	Order orientation	AEA most Libertarian, ACS most Regulatory

addresses of this kind are to a greater extent unique expressions of the personalities of the speakers than is the case with the other sources. This fact must further increase error variance. Third, missing data caused the absence of some replications in the ANOVA design, and this further complicated the estimation of various variance sources.

At the outset, this chapter raised three questions. So far it has answered the first: What is the nature of changes and contrasts in various disciplines? Thus, there remain two questions: (1) Are such changes the same in all sciences or are they discipline specific? and (2) What are the social causes and consequences of these ideational changes?

Concerning the first question, the analysis of five issues found but one significant statistical interaction. Mainly, therefore, the observed changes are the same in the three disciplines; they are **not** discipline specific. Orientational changes of this kind and over a long period do not differ from discipline to discipline. This has also strong implications for the answer to the next question.

If the issue orientations change in a same manner, then the cause or causes of these changes must be the same as well. Even though the data of this study are insufficient to settle the classical controversy between materialist and idealist theories of social causation, some of the findings are very suggestive. For instance, the increasing Value Neutrality and growing stress on Methodological concerns, at the expense of Value Laden and Metatheoretical issue themes, fits the changing requirements of the increasing interactions between society and its economy, on the one hand, and academia on the other. To deserve increasing material and ideational support, the sciences may well have had to change their stances. If this was in fact the case, then the changing orientations of the sciences had certainly material rather than ideational causes—namely, the changing requirements of the national economy. However, orientational changes, which were studied here, are not the same as action changes (Chapters 3–6) and this point requires further elaboration.

The two types of changes are not the same because of the autonomy of societal and cultural dynamics. The common expectation that value changes have invariably predictable behavioral consequences is hardly justified by the facts. Indeed, the opposition between values and social action is characteristic of all prophetic values. In contrast, it is not inconceivable that under certain conditions, orientational change might prove an adequate and cheaper substitute for action changes, and this is here suspected. Facing new societal demands, the sciences changed their rhetoric and orientations rather than their actions. In truth, however, we know but little of these conditions and their dynamics.

Thus far, there is an implicit suggestion that the observed changes in issues are linear, and nothing could be further from the truth. About the organizational scope issue, there is good evidence of cyclical changes and it is more than likely that the same is true for the other two issues. At least, long-term orientational changes in national politics are cyclical (Namenwirth, 1973; Namenwirth and Weber, 1979; Weber, 1981, 1982; Chapters 3-5). Why would this be different in other institutional arenas?

The last paragraph suggests a similarity between, or even identity of, orientations (and orientational changes) in various sources, such as American party platforms and the yearly addresses to scientific organizations. Questions concerning the similarity or identity of issues and their orientations across sources pose baffling methodological problem (Chapters 2, 6, 8, and 9) that comparative content analysis cannot avoid. For instance, the issue themes Cosmopolitan vs. Parochial appear time and again in a great variety of content analyses using different methodologies (Namenwirth and Bibbee, 1975; Chapters 3, 5, and 8). Usually, Parochial themes prevail when the economy is seriously depressed. In contrast, Cosmopolitan themes appear preponderant when economic growth is at a long-term peak. However, the present study strongly suggests that this "law" does not here pertain and therefore, it refutes the law. This is so because the law is either general, or not a law at all because at the outset it did not specify any limiting conditions. The closing paragraphs to the opening section of this chapter first addressed the issue (p. 169): "When the economy contracts, the presidential addresses to scientific associations do not turn more Parochial; instead, they turn more Cosmopolitan. Does this finding invalidate the law?" At first sight, there appear two clear-cut answers to the question. (1) Orientations have the same meaning across different sources of documents. Parochial is Parochial wherever it appears and always has the same causes. Therefore, economic contraction must produce an increase in Parochial orientations in any or all types of documents for a causal law relating economic activity and variations in the survival dilemma to be true. Hence, this particular causal law is proven false. (2) Orientations may have the same label, yet vary in "intrinsic" meaning across different sources of documents. Here, the Parochial orientation or theme means one thing in, say, party platforms but quite something else when applied to presidential science speeches. Therefore, one should not expect that a national, or international, contraction of the economy has the same or similar consequences for otherwise similarly labeled orientations in different kinds of documents. Whatever else the reader may think about this answer, it largely obviates the possibility of comparative research using content analysis and therefore, the very purpose of our various studies.

On further reflection, we have come to believe that the two more obvious answers to the question are mistaken because they overlook the fact of hierarchical relativity. To explain the point, the Parochial orientation is one answer to the survival dilemma (Chapter 9). It argues that threats to the survival of the system **at hand** originate and reside at its center, for instance, in its economy. The threats derive from the inside. Conversely, the Cosmopolitan orientation argues that they derive from the outside. Now, when the economy contracts, society-wide documents will increasingly argue that economic threats, or internal ones, are increasing; these documents will turn Parochial. Presidential science addresses will argue the same and turn to economic and associated problems. Only from the standpoint of the sciences, these problems are not internal but external, part of the external world of nature and society. Hence, their documents become increasingly Cosmopolitan (or society-oriented). It is in this sense that what is Parochial to society is Cosmopolitan to the institution of science—thus, the concept of hierarchical relativity. However, the opposite does in no way obtain, for what is Cosmopolitan to society is not Parochial to the sciences. These two orientations have no reference in common. Societal Cosmopolitan orientations concern themselves with other societies and cultural worlds, while scientific Parochial orientations address troubles and accomplishments of either the discipline itself, often of a practical nature, or its membership. Therefore, the relativity is not just orientational, it has a hierarchical component.

Among peers, I am I and you are you from the orientation of ego. Of course, the situation is reversed from alter's point of view. This is a matter of orientational relativity. In hierarchical relations, the situation is more complicated. If the inferior is I, then the superior is Thou, but if the superior is I (or We) then the inferior is merely You. Similar complications arise among hierarchically ordered collective actors, or society and its institutions. And it is immaterial whether the division of labor produces such hierarchies or functionally spurious processes of stratification. Once a hierarchy becomes established, downward interactions are upward for the lower order, while upward interactions of the superordinate party and downward interactions of the subordinate party have no target in common. This condition we call therefore *hierarchical relativity*. Such hierarchical relativity explains the anomalous finding that economic contractions produce Cosmopolitan orientations in presidential scientific addresses. We expect that a similar hierarchical relativity pertains to all interrelationships between a society and its institutions. Thus, it is our hypothesis that the relationship between the national economy and the rhetoric of specialized institutions will mirror the one found in the speeches this chapter studied.

Content analysis of presidential science addresses produced culture indicators that proved instrumental in answering some classic questions of cultural and social dynamics. It also helped discover some anomalous findings that furthered a discussion of orientational and hierarchical relativity in intrasocietal differentiation. It described and attempted to explain some suspected and unexpected culture changes of the American sciences since the beginning of this century. In addressing, answering, or elaborating questions of culture change in three scientific disciplines, we may approach the font of culture dynamics in contemporary society.

3

Theoretical and Methodological Issues

8

Measurement Models for Content Analysis[1]

Making inferences from a symbolic medium—usually text—is the essence of content analysis. The rules of this inferential process have not yet been rigorously formalized; however, the fundamental procedure is to make inferences about some characteristic of a message, its source, and/or its audience from the content of that communication (Stone *et al.*, 1966; Holsti, 1969; Markoff *et al.*, 1974; Krippendorff, 1980, Weber, 1984b, 1985a).[2] This chapter addresses fundamental methodological problems in the analysis of text by computer-aided content analysis based on word counts.[3] Operationally, word-count content analysis entails the mapping of

[1] I am indebted to J. Z. Namenwirth, who suggested that the problems of content analysis might be investigated with modern statistical tools. Although he is not responsible for the way in which I have developed that idea, this chapter is the outgrowth of a long dialogue with Namenwirth and others, including Philip J. Stone, Peter Philip Mohler, and Hans-Dieter Klingemann. Carol Z. Lawton and Barbara Norman provided editorial assistance. An earlier version was published as Weber (1983a)

[2] For other definitions see Krippendorff (1980), Holsti (1969), and Gerbner *et al.*, (1969).

[3] Other computer-based approaches to content analysis include artificial intelligence models of human cognition. See, for example, Abelson (1963, 1973, 1975), Boden (1977), Lehnert and Ringle (1982), Schank and Colby (1973), Schank and Abelson (1977), Schank *et al.* (1980), Winograd (1972, 1983), and Winston (1984). Dreyfus (1979), Searle (1984), Weizenbaum (1976), and Winograd and Flores (1986) give negative assessments of computer understanding and/or artificial intelligence. At this writing, developments in "Computational Hermeneutics" hold great promise for natural language understanding and social science applications. See Alker *et al.* (1985), Duffy (1986), Duffy and Mallery, (1984, 1986a, 1986b), Hurwitz *et al.* (1986), Mallery (1985, 1986), Mallery and Duffy (1986), Mallery, Hurwitz, Alker, and Duffy (1986), and Mallery, Hurwitz, and Alker (1986).

Robert Philip Weber wrote this chapter.

the many words in documents or other texts into many fewer content categories. Scores representing the relative frequency[4] of these categories in each document are usually the basic variables in subsequent analyses. Each variable indicates the strength[5] or level of concern with a particular content category. Thus these variables are ratio scale (having a true zero point) intensity measures.

Sometimes the categories are analyzed separately, but more often their covariance is used to identify meaning structures in texts, such as themes, issues, and dilemmas (Chapters 2, 9, and 10). This chapter addresses several important technical issues in the identification and analysis of meaning structures based on category covariance.

The coding rules for mapping words are frequently contained in a thesaurus-like dictionary that can be read by the computer. General-purpose dictionaries, such as the Harvard IV (Kelly and Stone, 1975; Dunphy et al., 1974) and the Lasswell Value Dictionary (Lasswell and Namenwirth, 1968; Chapter 2), consist of a list of several thousand words and the categories to which they have been assigned. Details and problems of dictionary construction are discussed later in this chapter.

An important use of content analysis is the generation of reliable and valid cultural indicators (Rosengren, 1981; Namenwirth, 1969a, 1969b, 1970, 1973; Namenwirth and Bibbee, 1975, 1976; Namenwirth and Lasswell, 1970; Namenwirth and Weber, 1979; Weber, 1981, 1982, 1984a; Mohler, 1978; Klingemann et al., 1982). In literate societies, a large portion of culture is represented in texts such as newspapers, political documents, books, and scripts from radio, television, and film. Cultural indicators generated from such texts constitute an essential set of variables for the study of cultural dynamics such as changes in ideology or political agendas. Furthermore, generating cultural indicators from large amounts of text has been made significantly easier and less costly because of recent innovations in optical character reading[6] and in capturing text from electronic media such as newswires, newspaper editing systems (De Weese,

---

[4]Proportions or percentages are often used to standardize for the length of document. Because the mean and variance of proportions are related, these should be transformed by the arcsine square root transformation (e.g., see Schuessler, 1970, pp. 411–416; Freeman and Tukey, 1950) in analysis of variance and perhaps other designs.

[5]An important unresolved question is whether the relationship between the strength or level of concern and relative word or category frequency is linear or not. As Weber (1985b) notes, holding length of text constant, the fiftieth mention of some category may require much more effort than say the third. This is so because in principle attention is zero-sum (Chapter 1): more attention to one category requires less attention to others. Also, there may be stylistic constraints on continued attention to one category.

[6]Kurzweil Computer Products, 185 Albany Street, Cambridge, MA 02139, USA, makes and markets an omnifont optical character reader. In pilot tests conducted at Kurzweil, this machine read the platforms of the Democratic and Republican parties, 1968–1980, quite easily and with few errors.

1977), word processing systems, and text-format cable and television broadcasting (teletext) systems. Content-analytic cultural indicators are discussed at length elsewhere in this volume, and will not be addressed in detail here.

Compared with social indicators (Bauer, 1966; Sheldon and Moore, 1968; Land and Spillerman, 1975; Wilcox, 1972; Carley, 1981), research has lagged not only in cultural indicators, but in computer-aided content analysis as well. After a promising start in the 1960s (e.g., Stone *et al.*, 1966; Gerbner *et al.*, 1969), computer-based content analysis—indeed, almost all content analysis—was virtually abandoned by American social science. Many factors contributed to this decline.[7] One was the conclusion in the late 1960s that artificial intelligence[8] would quickly render obsolete the General Inquirer (Stone *et al.*, 1966; Kelly and Stone, 1975) and other word-count approaches (Iker and Harway, 1969; Cleveland *et al.*, 1974; McTavish and Pirro, 1984). Only now is natural language processing beginning to achieve some of the early expectations. Even so, few if any implemented systems easily handle a wide variety of texts for social science purposes.[9]

A second problem was that the General Inquirer and similar strategies were often applied to substantive questions for which, in my opinion, they were not well suited (and for which artificial intelligence approaches may well represent the preferred strategy). These questions involve psychological and social psychological problems in which the investigator wishes to make inferences concerning the subjective emotional and cognitive states of individuals (cf. Ogilvie, 1966).[10] Consequently, there developed no large body of content-analytic results integrated with both theory and results from other methods. As a result, researchers abandoned content analysis for more productive grounds.

[7]In addition to the reasons cited in the text, content analysis has not become a widely used methodology because no institutional apparatus evolved to support its development. The contrast with survey research is especially revealing, because at one time there were a number of "big names," such as Harold Lasswell, who were active in content analytic research. For reasons that are not at all clear, the money went to support survey research. Janowitz's (1969) appraisal of content analysis is typical of the negative views current in the 1960s. Other reasons for the lack of interest in computer-aided content analysis are the difficulties in using existing computer software, the relatively high costs of computing during the 1960s and early 1970s, and the great expense of encoding the text in machine-readable format. The last problem has been largely resolved by omnifont optical character readers and the ability to capture text from other electronic media, such as newswire services or newspaper editing and composition systems.

[8]See the references in note 3.

[9]See in this regard the work of Mallery and Duffy cited in note 3.

[10]On the other hand, the extensive work by Gottschalk and others (Gottschalk, 1979) demonstrates that content-analytic variables representing the emotional states of individuals are related to a wide range of physiological measures.

One of the most important problems, however, was the failure to approach disputes concerning rival techniques or strategies for content analysis within an integrated framework. For example, questions were debated involving the analysis of word counts rather than category counts, the use of dictionaries with assumed category schemes rather than categories inferred through factor analysis from the covariation of high-frequency words, and the classification of words into single rather than multiple categories. These and other disputes were seldom resolved. Without a methodological framework, the ad hoc intellectual arguments that were proposed were often viewed as arcan by nonspecialists, who left the debate and the field to the experts.

An equally serious difficulty was the failure to empirically investigate methodological problems of content analysis. Unlike well-known efforts in survey research, for example, to study the problems of alternative question wordings, scale construction, sampling techniques, or telephone interviews, there was little or no systematic attempt to study the consequences of alternative operational procedures for content classification and analysis. It was never ascertained, for example, whether analyzing inferred or assumed content categories led to different or similar interpretations. Similarly, there was no systematic effort to determine whether different assumed content classification schemes led to similar or conflicting results.[11] Consequently, there was little empirical evidence to support the rival claims made by various factions.

This essay reconceptualizes methodological problems of word-count content analysis in terms of structural equation models, and suggests a framework for future research based on measurement models for content analysis. To achieve these ends, several neglected problems in word-count content analysis are redefined, including

- category reliability and validity,
- single vs. multiple classification dictionaries,
- assumed vs. inferred categories,
- measurement models and levels of aggregation, and
- the consequences of different dictionaries on substantive results.

These problems are discussed in detail below.

As the principal frame of reference, I shall use the analysis of covariance structures as developed by Jöreskog and embodied in the LISREL computer program. I use the LISREL model as a metalanguage or framework in

[11]The Dutch content analysis group formerly at the Free University of Amsterdam, lead by Irmtraud Gallhofer and Willem Saris (see, for example, Gallhofer, 1978, Gallhofer and Saris, 1980, 1979a, 1979b) have made extensive use of contemporary statistical methods to analyze data generated by hand-coded content analysis (see esp. Saris-Gallhofer et al., 1978; Saris and Gallhofer, 1981).

whose terms these issues will be defined and investigated. The LISREL approach to the analysis of covariance structures is employed because it is quite general and can handle a variety of models. In addition, the LISREL model is becoming increasingly known within the social science community, thus making it easier to communicate these models and the issues at stake. A brief overview of the LISREL model is presented next.

MEASUREMENT MODELS FOR CONTENT ANALYSIS

The general LISREL model (Jöreskog and Sörbom, 1979, 1980, 1981, 1984) consists of two parts: the measurement model and the structural equation model. The primary emphasis here is on the measurement model, which indicates how latent or unobserved variables are related to observed variables. The measurement model specifies the measurement properties of the observed and latent variables. The structural equation model specifies the causal relationships among latent variables and indicates the causal effects and unexplained variance. The structural equation aspect of the LISREL model will be used later in this chapter to define second order confirmatory factor analysis models. In the models defined below, the observed variables are usually words or word senses,[12] while the latent variables are content categories and/or themes in texts. The covariance matrices to be analyzed with the number of observations equal to the number of documents or other unit of text (e.g., paragraphs), and with each variable in the matrix representing the relative frequency of a word for each document.

The measurement model for the endogenous (dependent) variables is given in matrix notation by:

$$Y = \Lambda_y \eta + \epsilon$$

where Y is a vector of observed variables, Λ_y are the factor loadings of the observed variables on the latent variables η, and ϵ the measurement errors. Figure 8.1 illustrates a simple measurement model of this type. In a similar fashion, the measurement model for the Xs, or exogenous (independent) variables is given by:

$$X = \Lambda_x \xi + \delta$$

where X is a vector of observed variables, Λ_x are the factor loadings of the observed variables on the latent independent variables ξ, and δ the measurement errors for the X variables.

---

[12]As discussed below, some content analysis systems can distinguish among words with more than one sense. In this case, the unit of analysis is the word sense.

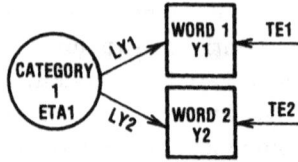

FIGURE 8.1. **Measurement Model for Two Words and One Category.**

The structural model is given by:

$$\beta\eta = \Gamma\xi + \zeta$$

where β is the matrix of causal coefficients among the Y or dependent variables, Γ the causal coefficients linking the independent and dependent variables, ζ a matrix of residuals of the dependent variables, and ξ and η are as noted before. Figure 8.2 illustrates a simple structural equation-measurement model with two measured X variables, two measured Y variables, and one latent independent and dependent variable.

Let S be the covariance matrix among all the Xs and Ys—that is, among all observed variables. The LISREL program estimates a predicted covariance matrix Σ as a (complicated) function of eight parameter matrices that may contain both fixed or predetermined elements and unknown coefficients to be estimated. LISREL produces maximum-likelihood estimates of these parameters under the assumption of multivariate normality:[13]

1. Lambda Y (LY): factor loadings of the observed Ys on the unobserved dependent variables;

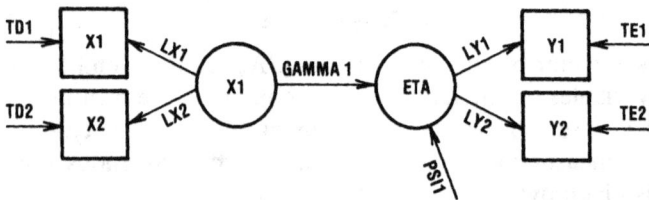

FIGURE 8.2. **Elementary Causal Model with Two Latent Variables and Four Observed Variables.**

[13]If one wishes not to make distributional and other strong assumptions, most of the models here can be estimated using Wold's (1975, 1985) partial least squares procedures instead of LISREL. However, PLS estimation minimizes the errors in predicting the data. PLS parameter estimates are not maximum likelihood. Also, the latest versions of LISREL implement generalized least squares as an alternative to maximum likelihood estimates.

2. Lambda X (LX): factor loadings of the observed Xs on the un-observed independent variables;
3. Theta Delta (TD): covariance matrix of δ, the residuals or error term for the measurement model of the latent independent variables;
4. Theta Epsilon (TE): covariance matrix of ϵ the residuals or error term for the measurement model of the latent dependent variables;
5. Beta (BE): causal coefficients among the dependent variables;
6. Gamma (GA): causal coefficients linking dependent and independent variables;
7. Phi (PH): covariance matrix of the latent independent variables; and
8. Psi (PS): covariance matrix of the residuals in the structural model.

In addition to estimating the measurement and structural equation models simultaneously, another important aspect of the LISREL model is that it indicates how well the predicted covariance matrix Σ reproduces or fits the observed covariance (or correlation) matrix S. This indicator is an approximation to χ^2 with appropriate degrees of freedom for the number of free and constrained parameters. The lower the χ^2, the better the fit of the model to the data. Contrasted with ordinary regression techniques, which assess only the parameter estimates and their significance, the ability to test the overall fit of a model with LISREL represents a significant advance in model testing and estimation. Furthermore, two models may be compared by subtracting the χ^2 values and degrees of freedom. The difference in χ^2s is itself a χ^2 whose significance indicates whether the models are, in a statistical sense, significantly different.[14] Thus LISREL provides a powerful method of model estimation, comparison, and revision.

Finally, not all models that can be stated in terms of LISREL can be estimated using real data. Some models have too many unknown parameters or have parameters that cannot be uniquely determined (i.e., the model is underidentified).[15] However, restricted models can be estimated by imposing reasonable constraints on the model.

CATEGORY RELIABILITY AND VALIDITY PROBLEMS

Two of the most important problems in content analysis are the reliability and validity of content analysis dictionaries.

[14]Based on the work of Tucker and Lewis (1973), Bentler and Bonett (1980) have proposed a goodness-of-fit measure for maximum likelihood estimates ρ, that is independent of the degrees of freedom. Their approach also yields a similar statistic for comparing the differences in fit of two models. Sobel and Bohrnstedt (1985) critique and extend this approach.

[15]Based on the information matrix, LISREL provides a convenient but not infallible check on the identifiability of the model.

Reliability

Reliability in its broadest sense refers to the consistency of measurements. We will be concerned with the reliability of the assignment of entries to dictionary categories and with the reliability of the classification of the words in texts into these dictionary categories.

Prior to computer-aided content analysis, the principal reliability problems stemmed from the consistency with which human coders applied rules for classifying words in text. Coder reliability problems were solved by the computer, which required as a first step the formalization of the coding rules. Once formalized, a valid computer program would consistently apply the rules.

Some of the remaining sources of error in computer-aided content analysis involve the formalization of the rules to be applied by the computer. There are two major difficulties: First, category definitions may be ambiguous so that some words are erroneously assigned to categories. Second, words themselves are often ambiguous. Let us first consider the limitation of category definitions.

The usual procedure when coders disagree is to estimate the extent of their agreement (reliability) and to accept or reject the coding on the basis of some level thereof. This procedure was not followed in the construction of the Lasswell Value Dictionary (Lasswell and Namenwirth, 1968; Namenwirth and Weber, 1974; Chapter 2) and the latest Harvard dictionary (Dunphy *et al.*, 1974). In both instances, it was felt that there should be substantial agreement once the rules of classification were known. Consequently, whenever disagreement occurred, the classifiers—that is, those who grouped isolated words and word senses into predefined categories—were asked to resolve their dispute in terms of commonly accepted standards.[16] Although disputes were resolved in all cases, the decision rules frequently remained implicit or ad hoc. Consequently, the rules of classification are contained explicitly only in the actual assignments of words to categories and are represented only partially in the definitions of these groupings.

The ambiguity in the meaning of words needs but little illustration. Take the word *face*. It might refer to the part of the body, to a surface, to appearance, or to a face-to-face conversation, if not flight in the face of violence. Similarly, consider the word *eye*, which might refer to the organ of sight, a glance or regard, anything shaped like an eye (e.g., a hook and eye), keeping an eye on something, fixing eyes on something else, or being pleased to set eyes on an old friend. How are these riddles resolved?

---

[16] As noted in Chapter 2, this procedure was not optimal. I agree with Krippendorff (1980, p. 132) that researchers should calculate the reliability **before** disagreements are adjudicated so that the minimal reliability is known.

As part of the General Inquirer (Kelly and Stone, 1975), the latest versions of the Harvard (Dunphy *et al.*, 1974) and Lasswell (Chapter 2) dictionaries incorporate rules for distinguishing among the various senses of homographs, that is, words with more than one sense or meaning. These disambiguation routines were validated using broad samples of text (Kelly and Stone, 1975), and they can be easily modified as necessary.

Another source of error stems from the common practice of single classification—that is, assigning each word sense to only one basic category and then weighting equally all words assigned to the same category. But do all words in a category reflect that category to the same extent? For example, in their economic senses, do the words *bank, interest, buy,* and *investment* equally indicate concern with wealth or economic matters? And if not, what are the consequences on reliability and validity?

Even though there has been substantial progress in error reduction, the amount of error remaining and its sources have yet to be empirically investigated. The use of general-purpose dictionaries would rest on firmer ground if we had empirical evidence regarding the measurement properties of content categories.

If we view category construction as a problem in scale or test construction, then according to classical test theory (e.g., Lord and Novick, 1968; Jöreskog, 1974) there are three possible measurement models for test or category construction: (1) parallel measures, (2) τ-equivalent measures, and (3) congeneric measures. Figure 8.1 represents one scale with two measures. Each of the classical test measurement models imposes a different set of restrictions. Specifically, the parallel test model is given in equation form by

$$y_1 = \Lambda_{11}\eta_{11} + \epsilon_1$$
$$y_2 = \Lambda_{21}\eta_1 + \epsilon_2$$
$$\Lambda_{11} = \Lambda_{21}$$
$$\sigma^2(\epsilon) = 1$$
$$\sigma^2(\epsilon_1) = \sigma^2(\epsilon_2)$$

where the ys are observed variables, the Λs are factor loadings, the ηs are latent variables, and the ϵs are errors.

The parallel test model states that each item measures the scale to the same extent ($\Lambda_{11} = \Lambda_{21}$), that the variance of scale is unity, and that both items are fallible to the same extent [$\sigma^2(\epsilon_1) = \sigma^2(\epsilon_2)$].

The τ-equivalent measurement model is similar, but without the requirement of equal error variances; that is, $\sigma^2(\epsilon_1)$ does not have to equal $\sigma^2(\epsilon_2)$. The congeneric measurement model places no restrictions on either the factor loadings (the Λs), the variance of the scale (η_1), or the error structure. For the model in Figure 8.1, the congeneric measurement model is:

$$y_1 = \Lambda_{11}\eta_1 + \epsilon_1$$
$$y_2 = \Lambda_{21}\eta_1 + \epsilon_2$$

To the best of my knowledge, these measurement models have never been estimated using computer-aided content analysis data. These models can be estimated through LISREL with appropriate parameter constraints. The observed variables would be medium- and high-frequency word senses,[17] and the latent variables would be content categories. The measurement model in Figure 8.1 will be substantially elaborated below in the context of validity.

Using the best-fitting model, the reliability of each category can be calculated by summing the squared factor loadings Λ. However, another procedure is required to get an estimate of reliability for the entire set of categories included in the model. Given that the LISREL measurement model is the same as a first order common factor analysis model but with added constraints, the Ω (Heise and Bohrnstedt, 1970) reliability coefficient can be calculated from the LISREL results.

Another powerful feature of LISREL is that the same model may be estimated simultaneously for more than one group or set of documents. Furthermore, some or all of the parameters to be estimated may be constrained to be equal across sets of documents, or they may be permitted to vary completely across sets. One tests for the equality of coefficients across groups by comparing the goodness-of-fit χ^2 when parameters are constrained to be equal, with the χ^2 when they are permitted to vary across groups. This provides a powerful facility for determining which parameters are most sensitive to the particular set of documents analyzed, thereby giving an indication of reliability across sets of documents.

Validity

In addition to questions concerning reliability, content analysis has always faced difficult validity problems. *Validity* refers to the extent to which one measures the theoretical concept one intends to measure. It is useful to distinguish four major types of validity: (1) criterion validity, (2) hypothesis validity, (3) construct validity, and (4) face or content validity (cf. Brinberg and McGrath, 1982). The first two are forms of external validity because they entail some aspects of the research design external to the content analysis itself. The last two are forms of internal validity because they entail only aspects of the research design internal to the content analysis.

A measure has criterion validity to the extent that it predicts some

---

[17]High- and medium-frequency word senses are those appearing in the text at the rate of 10 or more per 1,000 words.

behavior. For example, if one wanted to create a test that predicted academic performance in college, then that measure would have criterion validity to the extent that it was in fact correlated with a variable such as grade point average. But content categories reflect meaning or shared understandings of language, and what variables can be used as external criteria for content categories? It would seem that there are no external criterion variables for content categories, bur the issue is not clear-cut. For example, in pilot research designed to cross-validate some of the categories of the Lasswell Value Dictionary for German language text, Weber[18] (1984a) found a strong relationship between economic fluctuations and concern with WEALTH categories in the speeches of the Kaiser, 1870–1914. This finding is consistent with earlier results based on American political documents and economic performance (Namenwirth, 1969b). Is this criterion validity, and if so, what criterion variables exist for categories such as LOVE or UNCERTAINTY? Even if some categories can be criterion validated, most cannot. Therefore, content analysis will have to rest on a different sort of validation.

Until now, content analysis has relied heavily on face or content validity. A measure is content valid to the extent that the content of the items or the meanings of the words in a scale or category appear to measure what one intends to measure. Although great care was taken in the construction of the Harvard and Lasswell dictionaries, some remain unconvinced of the validity of these instruments. Part of this skepticism stems from the ambiguities of category definitions and word senses noted above, especially in borderline cases, of which there are many.

A measure of a theoretical variable has hypothesis validity (Brinberg and Kidder, 1982) if it "behaves" as the concept it measures should. With respect to content analysis, *hypothesis validity* means that content variables are related to other phenomena in accordance with a theory or model. In a number of studies involving cultural indicators based on long series of documents, the results have been consistent with pertinent interpretations of social, political, and economic change in America (Namenwirth, 1969b, 1973; Namenwirth and Lasswell, 1970), Great Britain (Weber, 1981, 1982), Sweden (Rosengren, 1981), and Germany (Mohler, 1978).

In addition to such external validity as that represented by hypothesis validity, measures may have internal construct validity. For example, if one has various measures of alienation, and the data are consistent with a measurement model that presumes nine subscales, then judged on internal criteria, these measures have internal validity. A content analysis dictionary has internal construct validity if data based on several sets of texts are consistent with a measurement model for that dictionary. Such a measure-

---

[18]This work was done in collaboration with Hans-Dieter Klingemann and Peter Philip Mohler.

ment model is proposed just below. Indeed, a main objective of the research suggested in this chapter is the assessment of the internal validity of content analysis dictionaries.

In the discussion of category reliability above, the measurement model illustrated in Figure 8.1 decomposes variation in relative word frequency into two components: variance in common with other word senses that constitute a content category, and random measurement error. This measurement model is an oversimplification in two respects. First, it fails to take into account systematic sources of error—that is, variance that can be reliably measured but is not the result of the construct one intends to measure. Second, the model ignores the causes of category variation. Failure to account for these sources of variance constitutes misspecification of the measurement model.

Krippendorff (1980, pp. 121ff.) and others argue that such procedures as the General Inquirer are flawed because they ignore the larger semantic context of the words analyzed. This assertion is in error in at least three ways. First, the disambiguation rules for homographs discussed above are based on the usage of words within sentences. In addition to syntactical information, the Inquirer uses information about the other words in the sentence to distinguish the various senses of homographs. Furthermore, a group of words that constitute a semantic unit can be counted as a single occurrence—for example, phrases such as *United Nations* or *Office of Management and Budget* and idioms such as *point of view, broken heart,* or *have in common.*

Second, the usage of words in text often indicates concern with a particular issue, theme, or message; sometimes word usage reflects stylistic considerations or syntactical necessity. In a given set or type of document, this stylistic and syntactical usage may be reflected in systematic rather than random variance. To the extent that this variance is systematic, it will adversely affect the estimation of content-analytic measurement and causal models. Word-count techniques do not directly model stylistic or syntactical sources of variance. Hence this systematic source of variance is a method artifact. Figure 8.3 presents a measurement model for two categories with the addition of a method artifact that causes variation in some but not all word senses. The existence of this method artifact is a hypothesis that remains to be tested. The model in Figure 8.3 may be estimated with LISREL if appropriate constraints are imposed to permit identification of the model.[19]

---

[19]Weeks (1980) estimated a similar model by actually modifying the LISREL program. But as Judd and Krosnick (1982) illustrate, this model can easily be estimated with the "plain vanilla" LISREL program.

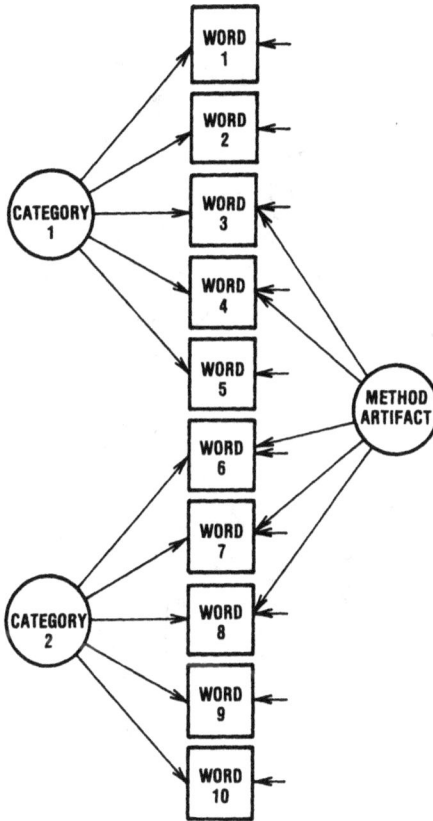

FIGURE 8.3. **Measurement Model for Words and Categories with Method Artifact.**

Finally, Krippendorff is in error in one other respect. It is crucial not to lose sight of the fact that the words analyzed were written or spoken to communicate some message about some issue or set of issues. The models above imply that word usage occurs in the abstract, that is, independent of concern with particular issues or themes. Consider Figure 8.4, which represents a measurement-causal model of word sense variation for a particular set of texts. This model includes the method factor noted just above, but also includes one latent variable representing a theme.

This model is a confirmatory second order factor analysis model and incorporates several hypotheses, including these:

- Observed variation in word senses can be decomposed into reliable and valid category variance, random measurement error, and reliable method variance;

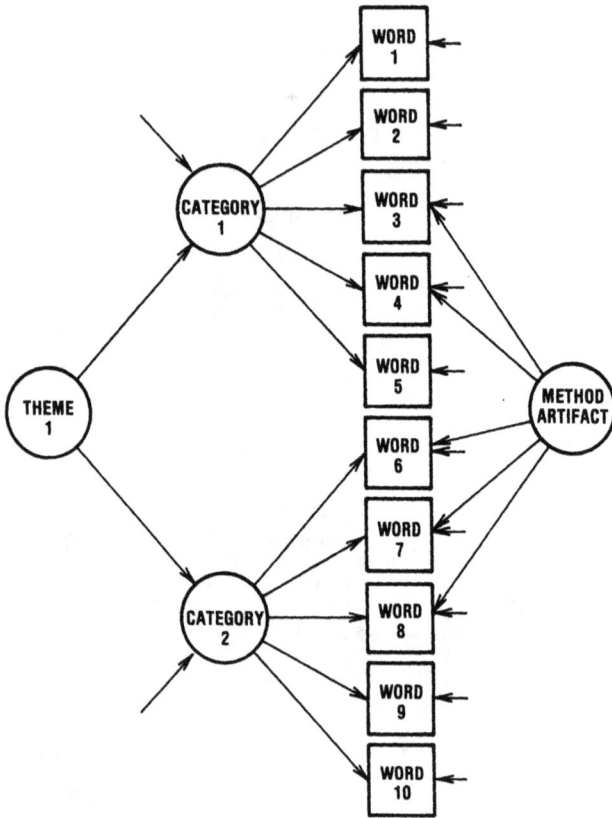

FIGURE 8.4. **Measurement Model for Words and Categories with Method Artifact and Theme.**

- Variation in the latent category variables is caused by concern with (latent) themes and random error;
- Variation in latent themes is measured without error; and
- Taking into account measurement error and the effects of themes, the categories are uncorrelated.[20]

The causes of concern with themes are not included in this model. To the extent that this measurement model fits the data for several sets of texts, then the Lasswell and Harvard dictionaries (or other dictionaries) have both reliability and internal validity.

---

[20]This hypothesis argues that categories that are conceptually distinct will be empirically unrelated. With suitable constraints, models with some empirical correlation among the categories can be dealt with while maintaining the identification of the measurement model.

SINGLE VERSUS MULTIPLE WORD CLASSIFICATION

As noted in Chapter 2, in classifying a word into a particular dictionary category, one really answers the question: does the entry generally have a certain attribute (or set of interrelated attributes)? There are two answers to this question: Yes, the entry does, and it is therefore thus classified; or, the answer is no, and therefore the entry is not classified under this heading. This formulation points at two complications. In the first place, having one attribute does not logically preclude having another. Second, not all entries need have the same attribute to the same extent. The qualities in terms of which words are classified may be continuous rather than dichotomous, thus leading to variation in intensity. In the model represented by Figure 8.4, intensity is indicated by magnitude of the factor loadings. Double or multiple classification of entries resolves the first problem, but creates others. For the Lasswell Dictionary it was decided that the gain in semantic precision would not outweigh the loss of logical distinctiveness and exclusiveness (Lasswell and Namenwirth, 1968; Chapter 2). Above all, logical exclusiveness is required for subsequent statistical analysis.[21] Therefore, when the Lasswell Dictionary was constructed, if an entry could be classified under more than one category it was classified in the category that seemed most appropriate, most of the time, for most texts. As for intensity, although it is true that not all category entries will have the same pertinence to the category, a dichotomous rather than a weighted classification scheme was chosen nonetheless.

The category scheme of the current Harvard Dictionary was constructed on a somewhat different strategy. It has a set of elementary or "first order" categories in which entries are assigned on a mutually exclusive basis. These basic categories are then combined into higher-order categories.

A second major methodological question focuses on multiple classification. A strategy for investigating this problem follows naturally from the second order factor analysis model described just above. As depicted in Figure 8.4, each word sense loads only on one category. Although the procedure for dictionary construction and the measurement model posit the independence of categories, some categories are close conceptually. For example, consider the WEALTH subcategories of the Lasswell Dictionary: WEALTH PARTICIPANTS, WEALTH TRANSACTIONS, and WEALTH OTHER. The first category contains the names of those persons or positions

---

[21]Most multivariate procedures assume that the variables are not logically confounded. Including both subcategory and total category variables in, say, a factor analysis would produce a spurious factor merely because the total category counts include subcategory counts. For this reason, we usually analyze **either** the subcategories **or** the total category, but not both.

involved in the creation, maintenance, and transfer of wealth, such as *banker*. The TRANSACTION category contains references to exchanges of wealth, such as *buying*, *selling*, and *borrowing*. The WEALTH OTHER category contains wealth-related words not classified in the other two categories. Perhaps references to *banker* indicate a concern with both PARTICIPANTS and TRANSACTIONS. After all, bankers do execute transactions.

Given LISREL estimates for the measurement model in Figure 8.4, it is possible to use certain diagnostic information produced by the LISREL program to determine whether a better-fitting model might result from the double or multiple classification of some word senses.[22] These diagnostic indicators may suggest that a double or multiple classification scheme is more appropriate than the single classification approach used thus far in the Harvard and Lasswell dictionaries. Should the data indicate the need for multiple or double classification, then within the limits imposed by identification problems, the consequences of double or multiple classification can be explored in conjunction with the three problems discussed in the remainder of this chapter.

ASSUMED VERSUS INFERRED CATEGORIES

Compared with hand-coding, one advantage of computer-based content analysis is that one set of texts can be classified by different dictionaries. However, this leads to multiple descriptions of the same textual reality. Consequently, there arose an important debate over whose dictionary should be used. Some (Stone *et al.*, 1966; Dunphy *et al.*, 1974; Namenwirth and Weber, 1974; Chapters 1 and 2) held that the category scheme should be theoretically justified, and therefore, that the investigator's categories should be used. For example, the earliest Harvard Psychosocial dictionaries were based in part on Parsonian and Freudian concepts (Stone *et al.*, 1966), while the Lasswell Value Dictionary (Lasswell and Namenwirth, 1968; Namenwirth and Weber, 1974; Chapter 2) is based on Lasswell and Kaplan's (1950) conceptual scheme for political analysis.[23]

Others (Iker and Harway, 1969; Cleveland *et al.*, 1974; Krippendorff, 1980, p. 126; McTavish and Pirro, 1984) argued that assumed[24] category

---

[22]The details are given in (Jöreskog and Sörbom, 1981, 1984).

[23]I would like to call attention to what I immodestly refer to as "Weber's Paradox": Results using the Lasswell Dictionary have not been interpreted and explained using Lasswell's theory, and results using the Harvard Dictionary have not been interpreted and explained using Freudian or Parsonian theory.

[24]In Weber (1983a) these were called "a priori" category schemes; "Assumed" is more accurate.

schemes impose the reality of the investigator on the text. The better course of action, they argued, is to use the categories of those who produced the text. These categories are inferred from covariation among high-frequency words using factor analysis or similar techniques. As a result, different category schemes were inferred from different sets of texts, which then required a theory of categories in order to explain variation in category schemes (Namenwirth and Weber, 1974).

This dispute stems from both difficult methodological problems and conceptual confusion. Let the term *category* be reserved for groups of words that have **similar** meanings and/or connotations (Stone *et al.*, 1966; Dunphy *et al.*, 1974). For example, the words *banker*, *money*, and *mortgage* might be classified in a WEALTH or ECONOMIC category. Now let the term *theme* refer to clusters of words with **different** meanings or connotations that taken together refer to some theme or issue. For instance, the sentence "New York bankers invest money in many industries both at home and abroad" in part reflects concern with economic issues or themes. This disagreement over categories is largely a dispute between those who define categories as words with different meanings that covary (inferred categories) and those who define categories as words with similar meanings that may or may not covary[25] with words in other categories, say POWER, UNCERTAINTY, or WELL-BEING, rather than with other ECONOMIC words.

Moreover, each approach entails a different measurement model. Specifically, first order exploratory factor analysis is the statistical model that corresponds to inferring themes from word covariation. In Joreskog's (Jöreskog and Sörbom, 1979) notation, the model for first order exploratory factor analysis is given by

$$\Sigma = \Lambda \Phi \Lambda' + \Xi$$

where Σ is the covariance matrix among the observed variables, Λ is the matrix of factor loadings, Φ is an identity matrix if the factors are orthogonal or a matrix of correlations among the factors if the solution is oblique, and Ξ is a matrix whose diagonal elements are error variances and whose off-diagonal elements are zero. When used to derive inferred content categories, the variables are words and the cases are documents or some other unit of text such as paragraphs or themes. As is well known, without imposing constraints on this model there is no unique solution, although the factor loadings may be substantively more interesting after certain rotations than after others. As discussed extensively above, the measurement model

---

[25]For example, pronouns and other anaphors are often substituted for a word or phrase for stylistic reasons. Hence unless anaphoric references are identified—a capability beyond many computer systems for natural language processing—covariation among semantic units will go undetected.

for single classification assumed dictionaries corresponds to a restricted second order confirmatory factor analysis.

I am unaware of any attempt to analyze the same texts using both measurement models. Therefore, it is uncertain whether these different approaches yield similar or different substantive findings. To investigate consequences of very different measurement models on the substantive results, both models should be applied to various sets of documents and the results compared. In addition, it would be worthwhile to determine whether themes inferred from word covariation are more or less strongly related to noncontent variables, such as type of newspaper (mass/elite) or economic fluctuations. This same strategy of inquiry can be applied to a variety of text data sets and the generality of the findings assessed.

UNITS OF AGGREGATION PROBLEMS

The choice of "document" as the logical unit of analysis is only one of several possibilities. For example, one might use sentences, paragraphs, or themes. There is some evidence (Saris-Gallhofer et al., 1978; cf. Grey et al., 1965) indicating that the reliability of content categories varies by the level of aggregation: when comparing hand- and computer-coded content analysis of the same texts, sentences and documents had the highest reliabilities, while the reliability for paragraphs was slightly lower. In addition, the reliability at all levels of aggregation was substantially less than the reliabilities for specific words or phrases.

These findings call into question long-standing practices regarding aggregation of words into larger units in both hand-coded and computer-aided content analysis. Future research should examine the consequences of different levels of aggregation. To evaluate systematically the consequences of aggregation, the second order factor model developed above can be estimated using data aggregated at both the paragraph and document level. The null hypothesis is that aggregation makes no difference; that is, the coefficients do not differ by level of aggregation. This is unlikely to be the case, if only because the variances of words, categories, and themes are likely to be a function of aggregation.

One of the reasons for the likelihood of reliabilities varying with the level of aggregation stems from the fact that if a word (sense) is used, it is unlikely to be used again immediately.[26] For a given document, the longer the length of text considered, the more likely it is that word usage will fall into a stable pattern. Perhaps there is a threshold number of words below which word usage is unstable and reliability is lower, and above which word

[26]Philip Stone pointed this out to me in a personal communication.

usage is stable and reliability is higher. It is unknown whether this threshold, if it exists, is close to the length of the average paragraph. Thus, for each set of documents the investigator can simulate units of text with varying lengths by aggregating over every *n* sentences. The parameters of the second order factor model can be estimated several times, each time based on a constructed unit of text (pseudoparagraph?) aggregated over a different number of sentences. In this way, the relationship between reliability and units of aggregation can be systematically assessed over a wide range of text lengths.

The results of this analysis should indicate whether the reliability and internal validity of dictionaries based on assumed category schemes vary with the level of aggregation. If not, then future investigations can proceed, using the level of aggregation most relevant to the substantive problem at hand. In addition, greater confidence can be placed in previous research irrespective of the level of aggregation employed. If reliability and internal validity do vary by level of aggregation, then investigators must be more cautious in selecting units of analysis. Moreover, if, as Saris-Gallhofer (Saris-Gallhofer *et al.*, 1978) found, greater reliability is associated with smaller units, then it will be necessary to reevaluate past results based on the document as the unit of analysis.

THE IMPACT OF ALTERNATIVE DICTIONARIES

The choice of dictionaries is in part predicated on theoretical considerations. For example, if one wishes to study extensively a particular construct, such as McClelland's "Need Achievement" *N*ach), then one might construct a dictionary that scores only that variable (Stone *et al.*, 1966, pp. 191ff.). General dictionaries such as the Harvard IV follow a different strategy. The category schemes of general-purpose dictionaries consist of many "commonsense" categories of meaning. These categories are chosen to reflect the wide range of human experience and understanding encoded in language.

It is my contention, however, that for general-purpose dictionaries the content classification scheme has little or no effect on the substantive results. That is, if the same text is classified using different general dictionaries and analogous measurement models, then one will arrive at the same substantive conclusions.

There is already some empirical evidence on this score (Namenwirth and Bibbee, 1975, n. 12). In their analysis of newspaper editorials, Namenwirth and Bibbee classified the text using two different dictionaries and then factor analyzed separately the two sets of scores. Comparing the results across dictionaries, Namenwirth and Bibbee found that the factors had similar interpretations. Furthermore, irrespective of which dictionary was used, Namenwirth and Bibbee arrived at similar substantive conclusions.[27]

Holding the general measurement model constant, future research should investigate the relationship between the dictionary used to classify text and the substantive conclusions. Investigators can classify texts using several dictionaries and compare the results. If the substantive conclusions do not depend on the particular category scheme, then this would suggest that standardized, general-purpose category schemes can be adopted by a variety of researchers with varying substantive problems. A practical benefit of this finding would be that where general dictionaries exist, researchers who have been reluctant to use one or another existing dictionary that did not operationalize their conceptual scheme might now be persuaded to do so. In addition, those who might create dictionaries in languages other than English might be persuaded to utilize existing category schemes to maintain cross-language comparability of results.

In the event that the results only partially replicate across dictionaries, additional research should ascertain the circumstances under which the results are similar and variant. Last, if the results indicate that Namenwirth and Bibbee's findings are unique, then this would provide empirical evidence that Berelson (1952) was right and that investigators must pay close attention to category schemes regardless of whether specific or general dictionaries are used.

CONCLUDING REMARKS

Over the last decade there has been some cultural indicator research using both hand-coded and computer-aided content analysis. These studies have analyzed American (Namenwirth, 1969b, 1973), British (Weber, 1978, 1981, 1982), Dutch (Gallhofer, 1978; Gallhofer and Saris, 1979a, 1979b, 1980; Saris and Gallhofer, 1981), Swedish (Rosengren, 1981), and German (Mohler, 1978; Weber, 1984a) text. Taken as a whole, these studies point out that content analysis may be the preferred—indeed, in some cases the only—way to generate valid and reliable quantitative indicators spanning long periods of time. Substantively, the results of these studies complement and extend other findings regarding long-term social, political, and economic change. For example, analyzing German college entrance examinations from 1917 to 1971, Mohler (1978) found that the values of

---

[27]It should be noted that both the Harvard and Lasswell dictionaries emphasize institutional aspects of social life. In addition, Zvi Namenwirth played a large role in the creation of the Lasswell and early Harvard dictionaries. Therefore, some will not be surprised if his results do replicate across dictionaries.

German students remained stable through the 1920s and 1930s, but that there was a profound change in 1945 with the loss of the war and the Allied occupation.

In part, these cultural indicator studies have not received wide attention because content analysis methodology is suspect. The research suggested above should put content analysis on a sound methodological base. Consequently, content-analytic results may more easily find their way into the mainstream of European and American social science.

Although the immediate focus is methodological, the research proposed above may eventually have its greatest impact on theory. Social scientists will be able to utilize computer-aided content analysis with greater confidence to address a wide variety of theoretical problems involving the relationships among cultural, social, economic, and political change. Indeed, given the virtual revolution over the last 10 or so years in the statistical analysis of time series (Box and Jenkins, 1976; McCleary and Hay, 1980; Hibbs, 1974, 1977; Bloomfield, 1976; Jenkins and Watts, 1968), this may be an especially good time to address empirically the relationships between cultural and other indicators.

Finally, rather than an end point, the reconceptualization and research proposed here represent first steps toward the eventual reconciliation of word-count content analysis with approaches based on artificial intelligence. The next stage will be to explore both modes of content analysis as complementary strategies for resolving problems of interpretation and the representation of meaning.

9

Ideography:
The Description of Documents
on Selected Ideational Dilemmas

This book includes several empirical studies that have one goal in common: they all describe how a variety of documents vary in meaning and especially in their expressed or implied ideas.[1] But what are ideas? Even more important, how are these ideas differentiated, classified, and measured (or indicated)? At this point, let us not get lost in an ever-regressive discussion of the idea of ideas. Instead, let us merely agree that documents differ because their prose expresses distinct ideas. Therefore, the problem is how to characterize each document by its idea (or ideas). To accomplish this, we used content (or text) analysis.

Content analysis results in many quantitative indices requiring further analysis and interpretation to make much sense. *Ideography* is a set of interpretative procedures that describes the differences among various sets of documents in terms of very similar ideational dilemmas that seem common to all documents. In this interpretation, each document provides a more or less different answer to the same or similar dilemmas. These answers constitute the documents' orientations.[2] This study therefore raises

[1]In these studies, there are other similarities. For instance, nearly all independent variables are either time or types of document from a particular geographical place. These similarities are of lesser consequence here.

[2]These orientations are therefore properties of the documents and not necessarily of their collective writers or readers. Thus, we speak below of "the most Parochial document" or "the least Conservative document" in a sample of documents. Finally, such characteristics of documents constitute the factual basis for inferences about the characteristics of national or specialized cultures.

J. Zvi Namenwirth wrote this chapter.

questions about the logic and meaning of past investigative practices and reformulates the role of interpretation in the process. In so doing, it provides an extensive discussion of the variety of dilemmas and orientations discovered in the descriptive efforts, and discusses the various uses of the resulting ideography.

CONTENT ANALYSIS

Content analysis produces quantitative indicators of symbol usage (Stone *et al.*, 1966; Holsti, 1969; Krippendorff, 1980; Weber, 1985a). These indicators summarize various ideas or ideational positions so that observers can describe documents in several thematic or culture dimensions. These procedures are discussed elsewhere in this volume; here we review only a few major points.

- The text-analytic procedures first classify all words in the text in about 70 categories and produce counts for each category in all documents. In every study, the counts for each content category are the variables.[3]
- Variables, therefore, display profiles of documents.
- For validation, structural specification, or data reduction, investigators usually subject these profiles to one or more multivariate analyses, including time-series analysis, cluster analysis, or factor analysis.
- The quantitative procedures result in the description of each and all documents by several unrelated (or orthogonal) axes.
- These axes, in turn, define a multidimensional conceptual space that provides the terms describing differences and similarities among documents.
- Finally, it is my contention that each axis (or dimension) of this conceptual space represents an ideational dilemma that is the subject of the present inquiry.

The reader may have noted that the above formulations borrow from the logic and terminology of factor analysis. However, many of the actual studies do not use factor-analytic procedures even though they use their conceptual logic. According to this logic, each document is located at a point in the resulting conceptual space. Therefore, measurements on the space's coordinates identify the document's location. It follows that documents similarly located in the space express similar ideas, while differently located documents express different ideas. Also, the analysis of serial documents allows for the analysis of movement (or change over time) in the

---

[3]We usually convert these counts to percentages to control for document length.

same ideational space. This identifies a change in the expressed ideas of the same source (or type of documents)—for example, party platforms or British Speeches from the Throne (Chapters 3–6).

Problems of interpretation are central to the content-analytic enterprise. But what is interpretation? When content-analyzing a document, the investigator really translates the everyday language of the protocol into a more specialized description of a social science language (Winch, 1970; Turner, 1980; Edelson, 1975; Macdonald and Pettit, 1981). Therefore, interpretation inherent in content analysis is a linguistic process. Freud's (1950a) dream interpretation is an excellent example.[4] In psychoanalytic interpretation the everyday language description of a patient's dream is translated in the specialized language of psychoanalysis. As discussed in the last chapter, content analysis translates the everyday language of editorials, speeches, and other documents into the specialized language of various dictionaries and their abstracting classifications.

The computer-assisted procedures of content analysis produce quantitative indices.[5] Without further interpretation, however, these indices must remain mere numbers. There exist two distinct procedures of further interpretation: First, the physical retrieval of sentences that contain certain categories (or combinations of categories) of words (or word senses), and second, the statistical analysis of the patterning of categories.[6] Ideography uses the latter mode of analysis and provides interpretations for the factually determined patterns of themes.

The procedures of content analysis and ideography—in fact, of all interpretation—are largely inductive because by necessity, all translation and abstraction is *a posteriori*. The process of abstraction applied to different everyday language protocols translates them into specialized language accounts. The latter summarize the former. However, the specificity of the originals is forever lost: One cannot deduce the original texts from the more abstract language protocols that result from interpretation. After the fact, however, the researchers may attempt to reconstruct their own logics in use. Chapter 2 attempts to do so for the procedures of computer automation of content analysis. This chapter attempts to do so for the interpretation of the resulting content-analytic data. In either case, it makes a radical distinction between interpretation and explanation that other social scientists rarely maintain.

It is my view that interpretation always asks questions of linguistic

---

[4] In clinical dream interpretation, the process is interactive. Whether the dialectical nature of this process better validates the interpretation is a matter of great controversy.

[5] Admittedly, these procedures can also retrieve sentences for further purposes of interpretation. However, these interpretations most often assist in the explication of the quantitative profiles.

[6] As noted in Chapter 2, the latest version of the content analysis system can distinguish among the various senses of homographs, i.e., words with more than one sense or meaning.

meaning—for example, about the meaning of a document or of the results of its content analysis.[7] However, the explication of mean is not a form of explanation at all. Explanation always answers questions of cause and effect. It requires the demonstration that the relationship between a particular effect (say, the relative prevalence of a certain theme) and a certain social condition (say, the varying rate of unemployment) is a particular instance of a general or conditional law. Without laws of this sort, there are no explanations either.[8] At any rate, ideography[9] raises descriptive questions about the meaning of content-analytic findings. These ideographic findings, in turn, are subject to further causal explanations.

IDEOGRAPHY: THE DESCRIPTION OF DOCUMENTS IN DILEMMA SPACE

In previous analyses, investigators recurrently found the same three types of dilemmas, namely the Survival, the Authority, and the Just Order dilemmas. This replication, so rare in content analysis research, prompts the next two questions:

- What does the dilemma concept mean?
- What are the recurrent dilemmas?

The dilemma concept derives from both empirical findings and a particular conception of the content of documents. This conception asserts that each document is a response to a finite (but probably large) set of possible questions. The dilemmas, then, are those that the researched documents factually[10] discuss. Favorite questions[11] of theoretical social science and

[7]The hard sciences often do not recognize the importance of interpretation since in experimental description and theoretical analysis, mathematics is the language in use, and the meaning of this linguistic description is taken for granted.

[8]These laws are subject to further interpretation, since one can always question their linguistic meaning.

[9]The term *ideography* is an ironic comment and wordplay on Rickert's (1926) historicist claim that ideigraphic, or descriptive, sciences cannot use generalizing methods. The present studies take an opposite position.

[10]As noted in Chapter 1, the poles of the dilemmas are ideal types, seldom if ever observed in their extreme form.

[11]The following are examples of such questions: "Does the document argue for the primacy of ideas or matter?" "Does the document oppose or support its current national government?" "Does it oppose or support current cultural premises?" In fact, attitudinal questions such as the latter two are very infrequent in most types of documents.

moral or political philosophy usually proved conspicuous in their absence,[12] and the analysis probes only actual questions and their answers.

So the studied documents provide disputed answers to a limited set of questions. These questions are called dilemmas because they have no agreed-upon answers. In fact, no one discusses procedures to prove or disprove potential answers because these dilemmas all deal with metaphysical issues. The producers of documents merely posit the answers, and observers can merely note that the collectivities that produce these documents believe in their answers to a smaller or greater extent.

In **principle**, each dilemma has only two limiting answers: the document believes a to be true, and therefore b is false; or it believes a is false, and therefore b is true. In **fact**, most if not all documents take more or less intermediate positions and the limiting cases are solely theoretical markers (or ideal types). These markers define the underlying dilemma on which the documents[13] (or sources) take empirical positions that constitute their orientations. In other words, the poles of the dilemma define a range of locations in culture space. Any document can be located on the axes defined by the extreme values.[14] Consequently, all documents can be quantitatively described and differentiated. Finally, in discussing various dilemmas, it suffices to discuss only the theoretical markers, or poles.

Of the three dilemmas, the Survival dilemma asks: Who are our possible enemies, where are they located, and what is the range of possible answers?[15] Study after study found two polar responses. The Parochial orientation argues that threats to the system reside at its center, while the Cosmopolitan orientation locates these threats at the boundaries with other systems, including nature. Either reply helps mobilize the collectivity for an adequate defense of its resources, aspirations, or very existence. Yet is also raises further questions that the next dilemma addresses.

The Authority dilemma asks: Who or what is in charge? Who will lead us? Who is responsible for an adequate response to the Survival dilemma? Or, what caused the last dilemma to begin with? To this question, documents vary between two opposing answers. Either the documents assert that the people are responsible (the Democratic orientation) or some ruling elite is responsible (the Aristocratic orientation). However, the resolution of

---

[12]The reasons for this absence are various. First, no document may ever raise such questions. Second, it may raise such questions, yet all provide the same answers. Obviously, empirical procedures will recognize only questions producing answers that vary from document to document. Finally, current text-analytic procedures may fail to recognize or differentiate the documents' answers to some questions.

[13]As noted in Chapter 2, documents are collective products rather than individual ones.

[14]If a document does not concern itself with a particular dilemma, then the analysis places it at the zero, or midpoint of the axis.

[15]Even if insiders and outsiders combine at the same time, there is still the question of which of the two camps is in charge.

these two dilemmas is rarely purely instrumental. The choice among contrasting orientations requires a prior conception of the good society addressed by the third and final dilemma.

The Just Society dilemma raises the question: Among possible strategies, which one will guarantee not only the survival of the collectivity at hand but the maintenance or attainment of a just one? In answering the last dilemma, documents recognize a variety of opposing orientations that are easily but simplistically summarized as Conservative vs. Progressive. The Conservative orientation usually maintains that the status quo is the best of all possible worlds, while the Progressive orientations argues the opposite: It is the worst.

In this manner, the three dilemmas constitute necessary elements of (or questions for) collective maintenance or attainment of social existence. Before discussing the dilemmas in greater detail, let us first stress or reiterate some conceptual distinctions and observations.

- Each document, or bounded piece of prose, consists of the implicit answers to a limited set of dilemmas.
- The investigator infers the dilemmas from the text of the documents. Therefore, the dilemmas often remain consciously unknown to its producer or consumer.
- The exact number of dilemmas remains unknown because the examined data constitute only a select sample of documents.
- Each dilemma has two opposing and limiting answers that typify the dilemma but that rarely occur in this extreme form in the actual prose of the documents. These idealized responses ideography calls *orientations*, *poles*, or *themes*.
- The dilemmas appear with far greater specificity and concreteness in the actual prose of the documents than is the case in the more abstract formulations of interpretation.

Of course, many of the above observations are inherent in the interpretative process. Consequently, different documents will express the same polar orientations in very different semantic formulations. Hence, very different combinations of words or dictionary categories can and do suggest an otherwise similar Survival dilemma (cf. Chapter 10). With this in mind, let us now explore some actual dilemmas.

THE SURVIVAL DILEMMA

As already noted, the Survival dilemma poses questions about the likely location of threats to the survival of the collectivity at hand. Obviously, those locations and threats will vary from collectivity to collectivity and over time. Yet some features remain invariant, and it is those that we examine here. Particularly widespread is the idea that the locations of these threats are of two kinds: They exist at the center or at the periphery. Nevertheless, the question of thematic equivalence across sources raises difficult issues, as the following illustration demonstrates.

When editorials in American newspapers (Namenwirth, 1969a; Namenwirth and Bibbee, 1975) are Parochial, they express this orientation with references to American personalities and especially to the president, his close advisors, and so forth.[16] The Parochial theme "stresses a fortress America stance: nationalism and isolationism best serve American interests and world peace" (Namenwirth and Bibbee, 1975, p. 53), as illustrated by this excerpt from the *Boston Daily Record*, May 4, 1951, titled "Now Let Us Have Facts":

More than 10,500 Americans are dead in Korea because these three men [Truman, Acheson, and Marshall[17]] had a vested interest in their own mistakes.... Our concern is our sons in Korea. We frankly do not want any more Americans to die on that Asian peninsula seven thousand miles away from our shores, to protect the synthetic reputations of Acheson and Truman. Our sole concern is America and Americans. And that, we truly believe, is the concern of 99 percent of the American people. [Quoted in Namenwirth and Bibbee, 1975, p. 53]

British editorials express Parochial orientations in quite a different manner. Apart from the obvious difference that when Parochial editorials speak of things American, and British editorials of things British, there is also a difference between the **things**. For instance, British editorials express great concern with London rather than with British personalities.[18] While in both cases the concern is with the center rather than the periphery, it is voiced quite differently. Perhaps this difference results from the ambivalence of the word *Washington*. When referring to the father of the American nation the word is revered, but as the name of its capital the word has very different connotations. Then, it stands for a nest of corruption filled with sleazy politicians, and it in no way represents the heart of the nation. This is not so with the word *London*. Another possibility however, seems of greater interest.

As Table 9.1 also suggests, when Parochial, British documents may well invoke institutional or collective actors because they are thought to provide

---

[16]This investigation used the Harvard III General Inquirer Dictionary (Stone *et al.*, 1966), and the content categories were HIGHER STATUS, JOB ROLE, and MALE ROLE. Chapter 2 discusses at length the concept of dictionary in computer-aided content analysis.

[17]The computer cannot identify the referent of ambiguous phrases or pronouns. These referents were therefore added to the text between brackets.

[18]In the Harvard III dictionary, the pertinent categories are BRITISH and SOCIAL PLACE.

TABLE 9.1

Survival Dilemma: Parochial vs. Cosmopolitan. One Dilemma and Two Contrasting Orientations in Three Separate Investigations Using Two Different Dictionaries*

Parochial		Cosmopolitan	
Category	*Loading*	*Category*	*Loading*
AMERICAN NEWSPAPERS[†]		AMERICAN NEWSPAPERS[†]	
American	85	International Institutions	−53
Higher Status	80	Approach	−44
Job Role	79	Sign Accept	−42
Male Role	68	Danger Theme	−34
Selves	43	Static	−32
Sign Authority	35	BRITISH NEWSPAPERS[§]	
BRITISH NEWSPAPERS[§]		Understate	−60
British	60	Overstate	−60
Social Place	43	Time Reference	−58
Selves	35	Academic	−48
American	31	Attempt	−45
Technological	30	Thought Form	−44
Political	30	Artistic	−40
PRESIDENTIAL ADDRESSES[‡]		Sign Accept	−34
Collective Participant	64	Approach	−33
Enlightenment Other	57	Sensory Reference	−32
Transaction Gains	33	PRESIDENTIAL ADDRESSES[‡]	
		If	−74
		Not	−64
		Power Losses	−58
		Negative Affect	−54
		Transaction Losses	−45

*Factor loadings × 100. Loadings < |0.30| omitted.

[†]Namenwirth and Bibbee (1975, p. 53).

[§]Namenwirth (1969a, p. 347).

[‡]Chapter 7, Table 7.6 (180° rotation). This table and Chapter 2 explain the categories of the column.

the last line of defense against disturbances from the center. In contrast, American documents, when they feel that the nation is threatened, invoke great individuals or, failing that, high-status individuals. Thus, when confronted with a threat to its survival, the British Parochial orientation thinks of the center of the social world as venerable institutions and actors. In one particular case, a British Parochial editorial has also a nationalistic flavor, identifying Britain as an actor in the preservation of the world order and expressing a "persistent fear of American political encroachments on the freedom of British action," as illustrated by this short editorial from the *Daily Express*, April 25, 1963:

The visit of the British and American ambassadors to Mr. Krushchev may lead to a summit meeting on nuclear disarmament. How is Britain able to take this initiative along with America? Because she is strong. Because like Russia and the U.S. she is armed with H-bomb. But if Britain alone abandons her nuclear defences she will no longer be able to work effectively for peace between East and West. Those who urge Britain to keep the bomb and her independence are not only realists, they are true pacifists. [Quoted in Namenwirth, 1969, p. 347]

Last, when Parochial, presidential addresses to scientific organizations (Chapters 7, Table 7.6) dwell on the name of the scientific organization at hand (COLLECTIVE ACTOR) and resemble in this regard British editorials. In that case, American scientific organizations also think of collective actors, but these are the memberships themselves rather than venerable institutions.[19] Arveson's (1964) Parochial address to the American Chemical Society catches these points very well indeed:

My title is your "New" Society, with the word "New" in quotation marks. Another title I thought of was "Your President's Eye View." Still another was "1944 to 1964: A Good Score." The period 1944 to 1964 has been a very exciting one for your Society, and to be exposed to, or be involved in, a large number of the exciting events of this period has been my good fortune.... Your Society is a vital force in this world. With its virtual 100,000 members representing the largest of the sciences, it is an awesome force in a science-minded era. [p. 126]

Similarities and differences in Parochial orientations are therefore quite complex. Different expressions of the Cosmopolitan orientation are even more so. When Cosmopolitan, American editorials are preoccupied with the United Nations and other international organizations, as shown by this editorial "Unity in the UN" (Christian Science Monitor, December 3, 1952):

To the anti-communists, the [communist] rejection of the Indian Truce Plan should suggest the possibility of a considerable strain between Moscow and Peking on this matter, a strain which free world diplomacy may exploit to advantage in the future.... It would be a great mistake for the anti-communist world to ignore the possibility [of future Chinese independence from Moscow], as it would be unrealistic for the neutral world to expect too much from it too soon.... Meanwhile the precarious unity of the non-communist countries, as shown in the UN vote, can be best maintained as the United States demonstrates how far it is from seeking to dominate its friends and allies in the iron-fisted Moscow manner. [Quoted in Namenwirth and Bibbee, 1975, p. 54]

British editorials, in contrast, express the Cosmopolitan orientation using

[19]Using very different statistical techniques, the Survival dilemma and its Parochial orientation were also found in quite different sources (Chapters 5 and 6).

academic and defensive language[20] as shown by the following excerpt from an editorial titled "Two Within Six" that appeared in the *Manchester Guardian* of January 23, 1963:

> An end to centuries' old rivalry, such as the Franco-German treaty signed yesterday, ought to be welcomed without restraint. . . . It is a noble achievement. A shadow, however, falls across the scene. . . . It must now be asked whether the Franco-German alliance is meant to be something beyond a warm and friendly burying of old hatreds. Is it meant to become the dominating force within the whole of Western Europe? . . . The anxiety is lest this [French-led] Europe is to be a closed community, looking in on itself and its own interests alone.
>
> In such a Europe lies the seeds of a future war. Not only will the West as a whole be wrecked by the division and withering of the Atlantic Alliance but at the same time Western Europe's exclusiveness may bring it into conflict instead of cooperation with groups in Africa, Asia, and perhaps Eastern Europe. [Quoted in Namenwirth, 1969a, p. 348]

For yearly addresses to scientific organizations, a typical example of the Cosmopolitan theme[21] is equally defensive even though a very different dictionary formed the basis of its content analysis[22] (Chapter 7). Here, the address is Cosmopolitan because it does not deal with the internal affairs of the organization but with external affairs that relate both to the association and its discipline. Also, the language is defensive as the result of a careful weighing of the evidence for or against the speaker's various observations. An excerpt from Millis's (1934) address to the American Economic Association, "The Union in Industry: Some Observations on the Theory of Collective Bargaining," further illustrates the orientation and its equivalence to the two previous ones:

> I hope you will pardon me if I seem to talk shop. I disclaim talking the shop of that branch of the Federal Service with which I am at present connected. Yet I cannot avoid the appearance of talking shop for my views are quite as much the result of experience and observation in industry as of reading and reflection in my study. . . .
>
> Before proceeding to the economic phases, permit me to remark that the interests of workers in collective bargaining may not be limited to details of the

[20]Documents do not either overstate or understate their case as common sense would have it. Instead, they tend to do both together, showing a defensive orientation that is part of the Cosmopolitan theme in the English language (Dunphy, 1966, p. 311; Namenwirth and Brewer, 1966; Namenwirth, 1969a, 1970; Namenwirth and Bibbee, 1975). The same, however, appeared in French and German editorials that were translated into English for the content analysis.

[21]At this pole, the use of negative categories (POWER LOSSES, TRANSACTION LOSSES, and NEGATIVE AFFECT) is descriptive of the sorry state of society's economy that concerns that Cosmopolitan orientation.

[22]Comparative analyses of texts using different dictionaries create further complications and require extensive knowledge of these dictionaries. Without such knowledge, nominal differences are easily confused with substantial ones.

labor contract. To unionists generally, collective bargaining means something in addition to wages, hours, tenure, and working conditions. For it establishes a new "government in industry," "industrial democracy," "representative government," "citizenship in industry," to employ a few of the more frequently used terms. If citizens have a voice and vote in political affairs, why should they not have voice and vote in industry? [pp. 1–2]

The above examples show how very different combinations of words or dictionary categories can and do suggest an otherwise similar Survival dilemma. For instance, the word *London* in British editorials indicates Parochial orientations, but the same word in American editorials may not. Yet, in American editorials, references to *President Eisenhower* are equivalent to references to *London* in British papers. Only human interpretation determines this kind of similarity; at the present state of the art, computer computations (or purely mechanical operations) are inadequate for this purpose. Now, our computer procedures simply lack the ability to represent the theoretical, real-world, and substantive knowledge that is required to validate our observations (Weber, 1985a, Ch. 4). For the time being, a more clinical approach remains necessary.

THE AUTHORITY DILEMMA

When confronted with the Survival dilemma, a next question arises: Who and what is responsible? Or what caused the problem to begin with and therefore, what kind of response is required to reestablish the status quo or to establish a new form of social order? Philosophical analysis has recognized a great variety of answers, such as divine will, the absolute power of the prince, or the consent of the people. Empirical research (Namenwirth, 1969a; Namenwirth and Brewer, 1966; Namenwirth and Lasswell, 1970; Namenwirth and Bibbee, 1975), however, found prose that suggests very different sources and types of authority.[23] In earlier studies, the opposing polar themes or solutions to the underlying Authority dilemma are often Economic vs. Military. In other words, the **final** cause[24] and therefore,

[23]Social scientists prize conceptual distinctions among the actual, the possible, the probable, and the obligatory; documents rarely make such distinctions. In conservative quarters, it is often felt that what is, must be, and that it is possible, probable, valuable, and necessary. On the left, there exists an equally pervasive but inverted set of beliefs.

[24]Dilemmas and their themes concern essences or essential (rather than apparent) properties of various worlds and their final (rather than proximate) causes and consequences. They are therefore properties of cultures that are part of a largely metaphysical discourse. The analysis merely attempts to describe the discourse and to discover its internal affinities and external causes and consequences. It does not judge the logical consistency or philosophical adequacy of the discourse.

resolution of disruptions are seen as either Economic or Military.[25] There-fore, discussions of the economics of military exploits, or the coercive features of economics and economic actions rarely occur. The question is, What do these contrasting orientations signify?

From the outset of human existence, the utilization and domination of a hostile natural environment took two opposing modalities related to a sexual division of labor: hunting vs. gathering. In the cultural evolution of social forms, hunting was transformed into, or became associated with, warfare and its institutions, while gathering evolved into early agriculture and subsequently into domestic, tribal, and other modes of economics (Montague, 1962, 1974).

Because of societal evolution, the culture of Economic control (over nature and persons) in all likelihood reveals orientations toward things and values that contrast utterly and universally with the orientations of the culture of Military control. For instance, the former values nurturance, toil, prudence, industry, and cunning; the latter prizes subjugation, exploitation, exploits, excitement, trickery, and heroics. Some might think that these contrasting orientations toward the dilemma represent opposing world views of subject and ruling classes, but a different conclusion is certainly possible. It seems more likely that these contrasting orientations stem from a division within the ruling class itself.[26]

Certainly, the Military orientation is close to an Aristocratic cast of mind, while the Economic orientation characterizes the Democratic ethos of the bourgeoisie.[27] Let us therefore now rename the polar themes of the Authority dilemma as Aristocratic vs. Democratic.[28]

The opposing Aristocratic and Democratic orientations appeared in Namenwirth and Brewer's (1966, pp. 401–427) first investigation of prestige newspaper editorials from France, West Germany, England, and America. The factor-analytic results (Table 9.2) support the interpretation of a Military vs. Economic contrast, but the most typical editorials confirm the present understanding. Thus, the most Aristocratic editorial[29] states

[25]Namenwirth and Brewer (1966, p. 413) offer a variant of these same themes.

[26]In the latter vein, Pareto (1935, IV, Ch. 12), citing Machiavelli (1952), spoke of foxes and lions; Veblen (1921) of engineers and financiers. The factual distinction remains an ancient one.

[27]The social basis of this status distinction is quite fundamental, yet is often overlooked. Warriors and military officers are in many societies recruited from a landed aristocracy that occupy their time with the administration of large-scale agricultural holdings and rent; the city patriciate, in contrast, engages in capital-based enterprises—commerce and shipping, industry, banking, and the administration of interest.

[28]The Aristocratic orientation always presents itself as immoral or at least amoral, while the Democratic orientation, in final analysis, often bases its claims on moral authority.

[29]I.e., the editorial with highest positive factor score.

TABLE 9.2
**Authority Dilemma. Military vs.
Economic/Aristocratic vs.
Democratic Orientations**

Category*	Loadings†
Aristocratic orientation	
Atlantic	70
Military	69
Danger Theme	57
Male Role	56
Soviet	55
Job Role	54
American	46
Large Group	43
Reject	42
Tool	36
Democratic orientation	
Economic	−75
European	−65
International Institution	−51
Food	−48
Work	−44

*Adapted from Namenwirth and Brewer (1966, p. 413). These categories are part of the Namenwirth Political Dictionary, which is a modification of the Harvard III General Inquirer Dictionary.
†Factor loadings × 100; loadings < |.35| omitted.

The Nuclear-Test Ban Treaty is a promising beginning of a new epoch in East-West relations. More extensive agreements will depend on Khrushchev who has indicated that, although he will not use nuclear weapons, he intends to continue his drive toward Communist world domination. As for France, Kennedy may persuade her to adhere to the treaty if the United States treats her like Britain and supplies her with the same information now given to the British. If France adheres to the treaty now, she may later join in building the NATO nuclear force and thereby restore Western solidarity. [Quoted in Namenwirth and Brewer 1966, p. 416]

In this excerpt from a *New York Times* editorial of July 28, 1963, titled "After the Treaty," the actors are nations and great leaders who move history and rule the world. In this regard the reference to France as *she* seems quite revealing of an Aristocratic cast of mind that contrasts rather sharply with the editorial most expressive of the Democratic orientation.[30] It appeared in the Frankfurter *Allgemeine Zeitung* of February 22, 1963, under the title "EEC-Quality":

[30]On this dimension, it had the highest negative factor score.

The term "EEC-Quality," which was used frequently by entrepreneurs at the Frankfurt-Fair, refers to goods which in price and quality can compete against Common Market goods in spite of Common Market tariffs. Its frequent usage implies that the Common Market is already an accepted concept in the minds of such entrepreneurs. [Quoted in Namenwirth and Brewer, 1966, p. 416]

In brief, the Democratic orientation recognizes common usage in the marketplace (rather than elite articulation) as the determinant of social reality and the preferred solution to the Authority dilemma: The merchants are in charge.

An investigation of presidential addresses to scientific organizations (Chapter 7) discovered a similar Authority dilemma. This chapter named the polar themes Value Neutral and Value Laden, but now it seems quite likely that the Value Neutral theme is the same as the Aristocratic orientation, and the Value Laden theme strikingly resembles the Democratic orientation. This argument requires some elaboration.

Proponents of the value-free position argue that **true** scientific inquiry is and must be value free because its practitioners must avoid pollution by the political strife of the hoi polloi. In this view, scientists are servants of the common and nonutilitarian good, i.e., truth, welfare, and universal well-being. Collegial control will suffice to protect all practitioners to stay clear from the corruptions necessarily associated with the worlds of money, commerce, lowly labor, or practical politics. The singular pursuit of scientific truth untrammeled by extrascientific considerations—political, practical, and other sentimental concerns—is not just a scientific but a universal interest. This Aristocratic orientation asserts reason and fact, while dismissing public opinion as mere fashion and prejudice.[31]

To proponents of the Democratic orientation, the pursuit of truth for truth's sake is certainly not value free, but elitist. Therefore, it represents a particularly pernicious set of values. Because the elitist program tramples on the interests and worth of the common man, those of a Democratic orientation consider it immoral rather than amoral. Worse, it is impractical and therefore constitutes a waste of valuable resources, and all waste is sinful. Also, they believe that all aristocrats must think as they do because their interests are neither disinterested nor universal, as claimed. In fact, proponents of the Democratic orientation are seen as partisans of the wrong cause because all aristocrats are considered as wasteful scoundrels, exploiting the productive forces in society. Thus, the true democrat knows that a science[32] that does not engage in common practice creates only falsehoods. Hence, in the Democratic view, value-free science is a contradiction in

[31]In contemporary societies, this Aristocratic cast of mind is not just found in the high academy, but also in the high church, in the higher civil service, among flag officers, and within other contemporary nobilities (Etzioni 1964).

[32]For *science*, one can also read *civil service, church,* or *general staff.*

terms. Any so-called value-free activity is by necessity exploitative and value-alien. In contrast, a science in pursuit of truth, or for that matter in pursuit of any **true** value, must be value-laden, committed, and democratic.

The Aristocratic orientation to the Authority dilemma sides with what has also been called *professionalism* (Greenwood, 1957; Goode, 1969). Professional performance can be judged only by professional standards. In this view, therefore, popular demands and opinions are irrelevant. Rather, authority must and does derive from location in the social structure and nobility of birth or merit. The Democratic orientation inverts these beliefs; it distrusts professional standards as the mere reflection of unwarranted privilege. Popular consent of all productive citizens, rather than professional judgment, is and must be the basis of all **true** authority.

THE JUST ORDER DILEMMA

In different types of documents, several additional dilemmas and their contrasting orientations appear that seem thematically related: Progressive vs. Conservative; Conflict vs. Consensus; Liberty vs. Regulation. What do they have in common? Chapter 7 documents the last variant with statistical and textual materials. Among the three, it is probably the most fundamental one and represents a long-standing issue in social theory. The question has a strong normative component because it asks: "How is the best and most just social order constituted?" The two contrasting responses to the dilemma are the Liberty and the Regulation orientations.

Liberty versus Regulation

As noted in Chapter 7, the Liberty view holds that strife and competition are necessary and desirable because they will produce improved social conditions favoring the realization of all, most, or average human potentialities. For the optimum coordination of freely chosen individual activities, societies must rely on the workings of competition on markets, or even biological selection mechanisms in other arenas. These mechanisms of coordination are optimum because they have solely unintended yet always beneficient social consequences. This is, in fact, the competitive utilitarian theory of social order (Dowse and Hughes, 1972, p. 31).

Contrarily, the Regulation view holds that unbridled conflict will destroy even a modicum of social order and therefore, the very basis of any value. Without regulation, persons and institutions that survive or flourish are not necessarily the best, but often the worst. Hence, the coordination of free humans will require persuasion, tolerance, and democratic yet authoritative planning, social organization, and other forms of intervention, regulation, or legislation. The instrument of regulation must depend on the field of activity to guarantee the rights of all as much as the common good.

Progressive versus Conservative

How do Conservative and Progressive views (Namenwirth and Lasswell, 1970, p. 54) relate to the Liberty and Regulation orientations? This depends on historical circumstances. Progressives oppose the status quo, conservatives favor it. The content of the status quo, both its values and practices, are not given once and for all. If the Regulation orientation is in the ascendency, progressives will oppose it; if Liberty views are the ruling ideas, conservatives will favor those and progressives will oppose them for that reason alone. This is related to other ingrained notions. Thus, conservatives often argue that what is, must be, and that this constitutes the best of all possible worlds. Otherwise, it would never have come about to begin with. In this view, the mere demonstration of factual existence has positive normative implications. Certainly, progressives would deny this out of hand or even argue the opposite.

A brief review of previous research (Namenwirth and Lasswell, 1970, pp. 53–56) confirms this interpretation. In a selection of American party platforms, factor analysis produced the following Just Order dilemma, with its Conservative and Progressive poles.

Specifically, the Conservative orientation concerns itself with power as a societal resource (POWER OTHER, POWER AUTHORITATIVE PARTICIPANT), as is often the case, while Progressive orientation stresses power as a distributive good (POWER CONFLICT, POWER GAINS).[33] Also, the more Progressive platforms discuss the psychological needs and happiness (WELL BEING TOTAL, WELL-BEING PSYCHOLOGICAL, WELL-BEING LOSSES) of the common man (PARTICIPANT) in the whole nation rather than the interests of states or privileged circles (POWER AUTHORITATIVE PARTICIPANT). Furthermore, Conservative documents seem affect-neutral and perhaps celebratory, while Progressive ones are affect-laden[34] and critical (ANOMIE; POSITIVE AFFECT; NEGATIVE AFFECT). Finally, there is a difference in justifications: Conservative documents appeal to religious grounds (RECTITUDE RELIGIOUS) and the Progressive orientation to secular ones (RECTITUDE ETHICS).

---

[33]As Chapters 2, 4, and 10 discuss, these two types of power are often negatively correlated.

[34]Common sense suggests that documents are either positive or negative in tone but this is rarely the case and the categories POSITIVE and NEGATIVE AFFECT are usually positively correlated (across documents). Therefore the contrast is otherwise and documents are either more or less affect-laden.

TABLE 9.3
**Just Order Dilemma: Conservative vs.
Progressive Orientations**

Category*	Loading[†]
Conservative orientation	
Power Other	58
Rectitude Religious	55
Rectitude Ends	50
Power Authoritative Participant	50
Selves	43
Power Arena	35
Progressive orientation	
Anomie	−67
Rectitude Ethics	−35
Enlightenment Ends	−79
Participant	−70
Well-being Psychological	−73
Well-being Total	−62
Well-being Gains	−40
Negative Affect	−57
Positive Affect	−53
Power Conflict	−55
Power Gains	−47
Means	−38
Affection Total	−35

*Adapted from Namenwirth and Lasswell (1970), Table 21, column IV). Categories from the Lasswell Value Dictionary (Chapter 2).
[†]Factor loadings × 100; Loadings < |.35| omitted.

Excerpts from the Whig Platform of 1852 (Porter and Johnson 1961, p. 20) shows the Conservative orientation to the Just Order dilemma in great detail:

The Government of the United States is of a limited character, and it is confined to the exercise of powers expressly granted by the Constitution, and such as may be necessary and proper for carrying the granted powers into full execution.

Since the word *conservative* is not part of the identifying characteristics of this orientation, the first sentence of the same platform confirms the interpretation surprisingly well:

The Whigs of the United States in convention assembled, firmly adhering to the great conservative principles by which they are controlled and governed.

Finally, the psychological foundations of the Conservative orientation are perhaps unwittingly revealed by this excerpt:

> That while struggling freedom everywhere enlists the warmest sympathy by the Whig party, we still adhere to the doctrines of the Father of his Country, as announced in his Farewell Address.

The second most Progressive platform, the Democratic platform of 1864 (Porter and Johnson 1961, p. 34), echoes many features of the contrasting Progressive orientation:

> *Resolved.* That in the future, as in the past we will adhere with unswerving fidelity to the Union under the Constitution as the only solid foundation of our strength, security, and happiness as a people, and as a framework of government equally conducive to the welfare and prosperity of all States, both Northern and Southern.

Conflict versus Consensus

The correspondence between Conflict and Consensus views of social order and those discussed before is equally troublesome. Conflict theoreticians are often nominalists and deny the objective existence of society and a commonwealth. Society is merely a place or arena wherein conflicting parties—either persons or such social divisions as classes, races, ethnic groups, religious communities, generations, sexes, and other conflict groups—struggle for superordination. These parties are the real agents in and of history, while society is not. Indeed, the very conception of society is merely a ruse of exploitive parties to suggest that their exploitation benefits the exploited as much as the exploiters. In contrast, consensus theoreticians are usually realists who postulate society and its institutions as the sole moral entity and authority. Therefore, all good derives from society and were it not for society, humans would be monsters. Those conclusions are embedded in other central characteristics that differentiate these polar themes.

In the Conflict view, both abundance and scarcity are socially produced and not inherent parts of nature. Resources are scarce because of prevailing social arrangements. Through struggles, however, the exploited will come to prevail over the exploiters in bringing about a new dispensation. The new order will eliminate all existing and inherently **artificial** scarcities and thereby also eliminate most sources of human misery. The Consensus view or theme contrasts with this sharply in holding that both abundance and scarcity are part of the natural order and that they are therefore not subject to change through human intervention. Therein lies another distinction.

The Conflict theme asserts that humans are fundamentally robust and good but easily corrupted by the evils of the status quo. Contrarily, the consensus view maintains that most men and women are essentially fragile, if not evil, and require restrictive social control to keep them on the straight and narrow. For this purpose, social institutions are **the** sources of creativity, and of all social good, if not of redemption. Therefore, woe will befall those who tamper with their constitution: The institutions' society is necessarily doomed.

So the opposing themes of the ends and the necessity of either Conflict or Consensus also constitute internally rather consistent world views that are really fundamental disputes in social philosophy and theoretical sociology (Dahrendorf, 1958a, 1958b; Horowitz, 1962; Horton, 1964, 1966; Adams, 1966; Williams, 1966; Bottomore, 1974; Collins, 1975; Berbard, 1983).

The question as to whether Conflict and Consensus views are always Progressive or Conservative depends again on their current ranking in the status quo. In contrast, the affinities among the Regulation, Consensus, Conflict, and Liberty themes remain very much disputed in both theory and factual analysis. In America, for instance, those who currently favor economic Liberty also stress the importance of ideational Consensus and even moral Regulation, while those who favor economic Regulation also wish to expand civil Liberties and seem most uneasy with the dictates of some moral majorities. In the Soviet Union and its satellites, by contrast, those affinities seem reversed. In brief, these relationships remain very much disputed in contemporary social theory and analysis: They go to the heart of unsolved controversies concerning social and just orders.

SOME DESCRIPTIVE USES OF IDEOGRAPHY

Thus far this study has recognized and extensively discussed several dilemmas and their contrasting orientations that regularly surfaced in various investigations. These dilemmas constitute some of the dimensions for the numerical description and classification of documents and their idea systems.[35] As noted before, these dimensions do not exhaust the universe of pertinent dimensions because they are not derived from a random sample of documents, possible content-analytic categories, or instruments. Even so, the results of these selective samples allow us to discuss ideography, its principles, and heuristics.

---

[35]The classificatory system is nonhierarchic and is based on orthogonal coordinates in contrast to, for instance, a logical tree format (Hunt *et al.*, 1966; Stone *et al.*, 1966). The latter type of classification is particularizing; the former is generalizing and parsimonious. Since generalizability and parsimony are of greater concern than even particular factuality, our ideographic procedures use this type of classificatory system.

First, many features of ideography, such as the description and classification of documents according to their ideational contents, are central to the humanist enterprise. On this score, ideographic studies are part of this enterprise. Second, the humanist enterprise prefers categoric description. For instance, a document or idea system is, or is not, Parochial. In contrast, the present studies have self-consciously opted for continuous or quantitative categorization (or measurement) and description, allowing us to assess the **extent** to which a document is of one or another kind—say, Parochial or Cosmopolitan. On that score, ideography is part of a scientific rather than a humanist endeavor.[36] This is equally true for the final point. While accurate description, which requires a weighty concern with the coding, decipherment, and therefore interpretation of meaning, is an important concern and step in the various research projects, it is rarely the end in view. Before explaining the more scientific purposes of ideography, let us first discuss its descriptive uses and their complications.

Depending on the number of dilemmas, each document is classified in an n-dimensional space, providing a profile on each of these n dimensions. Even such a descriptive profile is found by implicit comparisons, because the dimensions themselves, if they prove of any utility, must be founded on qualitative inspection or quantitative analyses of a larger sample of documents. Most descriptive analyses involve more explicit comparisons.

Text analysts frequently wish to compare the contents of different sources, such as editorials in mass and prestige newspapers (Namenwirth, 1969a; Namenwirth and Brewer, 1966; Namenwirth and Bibbee, 1975), or Republican and Democratic party platforms.[37] In the absence of a quantitative theory and measurement of sources, these comparisons must remain qualitative. Specifically, the independent variable or source is classified by attributes rather than measured. Each document, such as an editorial or platform, is located in an n-dimensional space and the research question is whether there are grouped differences among the sources on any or all of the dilemmas. This mode of research remains descriptive because the theoretical distinctions among sources remain impressionistic and poorly articulated.

In text analysis, comparisons over time seem quite obvious. True time-series analyses, however, are quite complicated.[38] Therefore, many re-

---

[36]We opt for what Lewin (1935, pp. 1–42) calls the *Galilean* rather than the *Aristotelian* scientific world view.

[37]The contributions in Part 2 of this book provide many examples of such descriptive comparisons.

[38]Chapters 6–8 use a form of time trend analysis procedures that are not very advanced to assess the main frequencies in these content-analytic data. Spectral analysis (Bloomfield, 1976; Jenkins and Watts, 1968), however, requires data several times the longest frequency, which for party platforms would require more than 1,000 years of data.

searchers try to simplify their designs by treating time as an attribute rather than a true variable.[39] Thus, they group their documents in some fashion, such as "before" and "after" documents or "early," "middle," and "late" ones. Subsequently, the investigator traces grouped changes over time. This mode of analysis remains also quite descriptive since the passing of time is at best a surrogate for the yet unknown or unspecified causes of change.[40]

Infrequently, differences among sources interact with changes in time. There are three types of such interactive changes. convergence, divergence, and reversal. In the first case, sources become more similar in their responses to one or more dilemmas. In the second case, they become more dissimilar. In the last case, the sources remain in the end equally dissimilar, but during the process they have exchanged places. Such rare interactive results are of importance for the description and analysis of integrative and distintegrative cultural dynamics.[41]

THE EXPLANATION OF IDEATIONAL LOCATION

Ideography is largely an interpretative and descriptive effort to locate documents in ideational conceptual space so that the investigators can more precisely identify content differences among sets of documents and track their changes of content over time. But these efforts are all preliminary to causal investigations, raising questions about why sets of documents are differently located in the discussed ideational space, or about the conditions of their locational changes.

When confronted with the question of why a document is located at its particular place in dilemma space, the single best predictor of a document's position in the cultural dilemma space is its previous position. This is just another way of saying that repeated documents will constitute a time series in the dilemma space. Many of the chapters in this collection raise questions about the form of these time series, whether they are linear or nonlinear. They demonstrate that nonlinear and, in fact, cyclical successions often predominate. This raises questions concerning the true form of the time

[39]Chapter 9 offers an example of this approach.

[40]Development resulting from biological aging is a metaphor rather than an explanatory variable in social processes or cultural dynamics (Namenwirth and Lasswell, 1970).

[41]For example, concern with wealth matters manifested in Democratic and Republican party platforms 1844–1980, respectively, are first negatively correlated, then positively correlated, and then negatively correlated again. These transformations correspond to realignments of the party system (Weber, 1982, 1985a, Chapter 3; Chapter 4).

series and the particular form of mathematical functions that best summarize such series.[42]

Thus far, extrapolation equals prediction. Certainly, that kind of prediction does not constitute explanation. Who would value the observation that in a series of documents, the previous location of a document is the best explanation of its present one? Instead, the observed sequence can be described by a general mathematical function that is theoretically interpreted as the outcome, for instance, of a developmental or cyclical sequence. This sequence and process, in turn, explain the observed movement of documents through the dilemma space.

Each of the induced mathematical functions is in fact a law, and specifically a historical law because the functions may vary from one historical epoch to the next. Also, such functions are often compound ones that are readily decomposed in more elementary functions or laws of movement, change, or even evolution in the discussed dilemma space.[43] Once these movements are accounted for, there remain only nonhistorical differences, which are therefore subject to explanation by timeless or nonhistorical regularities or universal laws.[44] Admittedly, the latter laws remain now only very partial, inconclusive, and statistical rather than deterministic.[45] Nevertheless, ideography strives for a systematization in its descriptions of cultural dynamics that allows for lawlike explanation.

CULTURE PARTICIPANTS VERSUS OBSERVERS

Self-consciously, ideography provides only the observer's interpretation of participants' meanings. Therefore, it represents the outsiders' (rather than the insiders') views (Merton, 1972). The former are most often agnostic; the latter, partisan. The uses of ideography, therefore, pertain to the uses by observers in their various inquiries. These interpretations may only very partially overlap with those of the participants. In ideographic

[42]Nonlinear functions are inherently of greater interest than linear progressions. Also linear and exponential progressions can include only a limited span of observations, since otherwise the phenomena studied would become infinitely large (Sorokin, 1937–1941; Namenwirth and Weber, 1979).

[43]Chapters 5–7 clearly show these contentions concerning historical laws.

[44]Universal (or covering) laws are also contingent: They take the general form, if A then B. Contingent laws will never specify whether and when A and therefore B will be present. In contrast, historical laws always specify the origins of their sequence in real time. In the social sciences, the logical and factual relationships between historical and universal laws are poorly understood.

[45]Chapter 8 offers a good example of these contentions.

studies, the interpretations by culture participants are part of the textual data and of importance[46] in that manner and that manner only.

There remains the question: Why do investigators find recurrently the same three types of dilemmas—namely, the Survival, the Authority, and the Just Order dilemmas? As noted before, it may be merely a methodological artifact produced by a systematic bias in the samples of documents. At this point we don't have the evidence to dismiss this possibility. In principle, it is certainly possible to test a hypothesis of universality by examining documents from different institutional realms, from different societies with differing structures. Such research would certainly result in further refinement, reformulation, and greater specification.

Regarding the universality of culture dilemmas, why not ask the culture participants? Don't they know best? Might they not know? My answer to these questions is in the negative and confirms a collectivist position. Native speakers are not familiar with properties of other cultures. In fact, they are unfamiliar with many fundamental properties of their own culture and prove unable to specify its structural rules. Consider the rules of speech and its grammar. Most native speakers cannot tell these rules apart, yet use them accurately more often than not. Even grammarians have a hard time in completely formulating such rules. Now, orientational dilemmas that speech reveals operate on speech in a manner that is rather similar to that of grammar. They are both rule systems that prescribe the proper ordering of elements of speech and thought, such as syntax, sequence, words, sentences, and arguments. Therefore, while both help organize sound into speech, they remain nevertheless unconscious properties of the speaker's culture and its deep structure. This explains why, to recover culture's properties and rules, we cannot ask culture's participants to answer these questions. Instead, we must rely on outsiders as investigators and use their methods, however unreliable these may prove to be. In the absence of evidence to the contrary, we shall trust our accumulated knowledge that points in the direction of a minimally three-dimensional structure of cultures' dilemmas.

CONCLUDING REMARKS

To the observers who are outsiders, the insiders' understandings constitute protocols that are subject to further translation, description, and explanation useful to ideography's purposes. One of these is the description of a collectivity's options. We make the fundamental presumption that neither collectivities nor their documents choose their possible options. It is

---

[46]As have many before them, Wuthnow *et al.* (1984) reject this position out of hand. Chapter 1 discusses the arguments in great detail.

not the existence of a particular physical or social reality that determines the collectivity's perceptions of, and orientations to, the discussed dilemmas. Instead, it is its culture, however historically determined, that will determine the nature it perceives and the reality it knows (Chapter 4).

Ideography, therefore, reveals the dimensions of community options. Once we understand the collectivity's orientations on these dilemmas, we can predict and perhaps understand its view of nature and its knowledge of social reality. With such a universal grasp of the community's diverse conceptualizations, the enumeration of particular collective actions can proceed.

The search for uniformities that characterizes ideography is at odds with the recent stress, in much communication research, on uniqueness and the unique meaning of both language and speech in different places, times, and among individuals. Yet the concept of unique language is a contradiction in terms, since language, meaning, and understanding are inherently collective phenomena. Meaning that is not shared is not meaning at all. The same is true for any language. In this conception, the unique is at best an unusual and limiting variant of the general case and thus of great theoretical but no practical concern. This is not to deny that cultural articulations vary from place to place and change over time. In fact, the description and explanation of these variations is one of the prime objectives of ideographic studies. This description, however, presumes the existence of higher-order constancies, and the elucidation of such constancies is an important theoretical task for any ideography.

4

A Concluding
Assessment

10

Evolutionary Curves and Revolutionary Corners in the Progression of Culture and Its Explanations

This final chapter presents selected findings and explanations previously discussed and qualified. Because some of these generalizations go well beyond their factual bases, they require further amplification. Toward this goal, the chapter answers these questions:

- Is culture progression or succession curved (continuous) or cornered (discontinuous)?
- What interpretations and explanations exist for longer- and shorter-term culture cycles?
- What is the evidence for discontinuity in culture change, and what are its nature and implications?
- Is materialism or idealism a better doctrine for the explanation of culture dynamics?
- Why rely on quantitative culture indicators?
- What is interpretation, and what role does it play in our findings and explanations?

Before answering these questions, allow us first to raise one more: Why do we select these questions and their simplifying and generalizing answers? The reasons are mnemonic and methodological. Descriptions, interpretations, and explanations that are as complex as the reality they address are of little use: They are inelegant and not parsimonious. Besides, since the facts are gone forever, detailed qualifications restricting findings to a

J. Zvi Namenwirth and Robert Philip Weber jointly wrote this chapter.

particular place that existed only in the past cannot be easily invalidated. Popper (1968, 1983) is correct: invalidation rather than confirmation is a contribution. The latter only repeats what is already known, while the former must lead to revisions of original, yet incomplete or even faulty understandings. To aid the inevitable revisions of our results and explanations, modesty and extensive qualifications are of little use; indeed, over-statements are a service. Thus, we draw three conclusions: First, as is well known, generalized findings and models cannot be validated using the data from which the models were developed; additional data bases must be examined. Second, the strategy of pushing models far beyond the available data yields social science generalizations that are easy to falsify, and therefore, these generalizations are always provisional. Third, the process of developing, testing, modifying, and retesting models is limited only by the time and energy available to our enterprise; the process is virtually endless.

CURVED FINDINGS AND THEORIES

Continuous descriptions and theories of social and culture change have been very popular in the social sciences since their inception. Enlightenment thinkers argued for continued and continuous progress or evolution that would take a linear[1] or even exponential form, producing ever-bigger and -better human conditions because of substantive reason, increasing freedom, liberty, equality, prosperity, and brotherhood. The horrors of the French Revolution produced a temporary Romantic reaction that placed the Golden Age not in the future, but in the medieval past or beyond. At any rate, Romantic thinkers did not foresee progress, only continuous decay. However, once the promises of industrialization and capitalism proved more general and enduring, evolutionary ideas again took a firm hold in the Christian world, only to be abruptly dashed by the alarming forebodings and large-scale inhumanity of the First World War (Nisbet, 1969). This latter trend was further reinforced by the ensuing Great Depression, Second World War, and the atomic age. Thus, in recent times we find a new flourishing of decay theories and more ancient ideas of Greek and Roman skeptics and their followers, such as the cyclical theories of Spengler (1932), Toynbee (1947–1957), and Sorokin (1937–1941).

While it is true that we arrive at similar descriptions and explanations of culture dynamics, this is hardly the result of our original inclinations. In fact, we expected culture and its ideas about the good society to change in continuous fashion, but in one analogous to the maturation of organisms, and therefore best described by the logistic or "S" curve. Following diffusion theory (e.g., Hamblin *et al.*, 1973; Rogers, 1983; Mahajan and

---

[1]Linear progressions are a limiting case of the family of curved successions.

Peterson, 1985), we thought that new ideas would first slowly spread, starting from a minimum level, growing faster in acceptance, then reaching a turning point, after which the rate of growth would decline as the new ideas became widely diffused throughout the culture.

However, our analyses of culture indicators based on long series of public documents proved otherwise. These data suggested recurring sequences or cycles of culture issues or problems. In fact, these cyclical progressions proved more complex than earlier theories suggested, because our data and methods revealed several independent cycles, both within and across particular culture indicators (content categories), requiring separate explanations for each observed culture dynamic. We elaborate.

In the analysis of party platforms (Chapter 3), change in each of many variables representing concern with the various categories of our dictionary (Chapter 2) seems best described not by one, but by two cycles. The first is a long cycle of about 150 years in length, and the second is a shorter cycle superimposed on the first, of about 50 years' length. Figure 3.2 in Chapter 3 illustrates this point. In short, we have decomposed the variation in each of our variables into three parts, namely, a long-term cyclical trend, a shorter-term cyclical trend, and a residual variable from which longer-term trends have been largely eliminated.[2] Each of these parts constitutes a different set of observed dynamics, and each dynamic requires a potentially different set of interpretations and explanations.

The observed trends are multicyclical in another sense because they repeat themselves across content categories, often in a leading or lagging fashion: The rise (or fall) in one indicator precedes this change in another indicator. Therefore, the rise and fall across indicators are systematically interrelated. For each variable, we plotted the year when a curve peaks along the rim of a circle whose circumference represents cycle length (Chapters 3–5). We refer to these circles as "wheels of time" since they represent the sequence and therefore the time structure[3] of the variables plotted along the rim. Thus the two "wheels" presented in Chapter 3, for example, represent systemic relationships among observed cyclical changes in culture indicators.

The long wheel of time represents the longer-term cyclical changes across indicators; the short wheel of time, the shorter-term cyclical changes.

[2]The accounts given herein are simplifications. Weber (1978) found and statistically removed linear trends before estimating sine curves. Changes in slope between Mercantilist and Capitalist Britain reflect the change from community to society, or any of the related similar distinctions. Also, the rate of secularization was higher during the Capitalist than the Mercantilist period.

[3]In other words, we transform historical time into cycle time. Ideally, one would like to be able to establish what might be called "process time"—that is, time whose reference is the process one is trying to analyze (cf. Goldstein, 1985, p. 439). For example, we are unsure whether our assumption of equal phase lengths is factually true or not. (See note 6 below and Chapters 4 and 5 for further discussion.) Thus we would like to employ techniques that allow this parameter to vary.

An interpretation and explanation of each wheel of time produces two dynamic theories explaining the interdependencies within both forms of continuous culture successions. Finally, these same observations and interdependencies occur in two altogether different data sets, namely, American party platforms since 1844 (Chapter 3) and British Speeches from the Throne (Chapters 4 and 5).

Before discussing the interpretations and explanations of the replicated dynamics, let us first address this section's question: Is culture progression or succession curved (continuous) or cornered (discontinuous)? What do these terms mean, and, what is the answer? A *curved* explanation asserts that the same explanation or process explains culture change over the entire time interval under consideration. A *cornered* explanation asserts that different explanations hold at different points over the time interval under consideration. Thus defined, the answer cannot be simple, because culture change is both continuous **and** discontinuous, and in more than one way. Factual and theoretical reasons strongly suggest a large measure of continuous change in the dynamics of culture. For example, the outcomes of extensive curve-fitting procedures (reported in Chapters 3–5) constitute the factual reasons for this observation. Not only did these sine curves represent long-term continuous culture change in many of our content categories, but examination of selected texts showed that textual content varied accordingly. Parsimony provides one major theoretical reason because one mathematical function describes each curve, providing or requiring the same interpretation and explanation throughout and at each successive point. However, discontinuous progressions require a distinct explanation for each corner or junction.

Another theoretical reason is that the explanations we employ for the long and short thematic cycles are themselves continuous. The dynamic tension model that underlies the Bales–Parsons problem-resolution (AGIL) cycle asserts that the process is continuous over time. Similarly, the innovation-market saturation theory that underlies the explanation of the 50-year thematic cycle is also largely continuous.[4]

We elaborate and qualify these assertions below.

THE LONG WHEEL OF TIME: INTERPRETATIONS AND EXPLANATIONS

As noted, the long wheel of time summarizes the sequential relationships among a great many 150-year cycles observed in many content categories

[4]During the recovery from each depression there is a structural reorganization of the economy; however, this reorganization takes place within the constraints imposed by capitalist political economy.

in both American and Capitalist British documents.[5] We interpreted the sequence of peaks in concern with various content categories as indicating a sequence of broad collective issues; that is, clusters of content categories that were located near each other along the rim of the circle were interpreted as manifest indicators of an underlying theme or issue. These issues were themselves interpreted using the Bales–Parsons four-function (AGIL) scheme (Bales, 1950; 1953; Bales and Strodtbeck, 1953; Parsons et al., 1953; Parsons and Bales, 1953; Parsons and Smelser, 1956). This interpretation holds that there are four sequential thematic issues that address the following:

1. questions of collective identity or expressive orientations,
2. questions of goal attainment or issues concerning the proper governmental structures to realize the fundamental goals,
3. questions of adaptation or issues of economic organization raised by previous discussions and actions, and
4. questions of integration raised by increasing differentiation and inequalities produced in attempts to solve the earlier three issues.

Once questions of integrated are settled in one way or another, questions of identity are raised anew, to reaffirm now-established answers or to modify the nation's founding ideas. In the 150-year sequence, each of these four issues predominates in a 37- to 38-year period.[6]

How does one explain this sequential alteration in preoccupation with these political issues? We speculate that a similar set of problems confronts all societies. Namenwirth (Chapter 3; Namenwirth and Bibbee, 1976) holds that there exists a logic of problem solving that requires this order of sequential phases. Chapter 4 described a different sequence of issues in preindustrial Great Britain, thus falsifying the assertion that other sequences are impossible (Namenwirth and Bibbee, 1976). Nevertheless, we are now unable to systematically explain all possible logics or sequences.

In addition, parties specialize in the solution of problems that predominate in certain phases rather than others, so that the changing emphasis on these themes is related to a party realignments in both America (Burnham, 1976) and Great Britain (Chapter 4). Finally, the succession of citizen cohorts (cf. Beck, 1974), each with its own enduring political preoccupation, explains the various phases of changing concerns, party realignments, and their timing and duration.

---

[5]Chapter 3 reports on these findings in both Democratic and Republican party platforms in America; Chapter 4 reports on further replication in British documents since 1795.

[6]A discussion follows about Weber's finding of discontinuity in the dynamics of the long-term thematic concerns in Great Britain before and after 1795. Also, Chapter 4 shows that the phases of the long cycle in Capitalist Britain may be of unequal lengths. Thus, the hypothesis of equal-length phases is partly imposed on our data by our detrending methods.

SHORT WHEEL OF TIME: INTERPRETATIONS
AND EXPLANATIONS

The short wheel of time also summarizes a temporal sequence of peaks in concern with many content variables. The average wavelength is about 50 years in America (Chapter 3) and Capitalist Britain and 32 years in Mercantilist Britain (Chapter 5). As before, clusters of categories that have similar wavelengths and that peak about the same time (i.e., are located near each other on the rim of the wheel) are interpreted as a theme or issue. Specifically, at one point in this ongoing thematic sequence, culture is very Parochial, representing one pole of the Survival dilemma (Chapter 9), which suggests that threats to society are seen as internal and largely economic. These concerns then change and become more and more Progressive, representing one pole of the family of Just Order dilemmas, which argues about drastic alterations in the status quo as expressed in a frequent concern with both POWER CONFLICT and POWER COOPERATION. Subsequently, these concerns change anew and become Cosmopolitan, representing the opposite pole of the Survival dilemma. At this point in the sequence, threats to society are thought to exist at the boundaries with other nation-states—that is, from without rather than within. Finally, culture becomes Conservative, representing the opposite pole of the Just Society dilemma, when documents argue that only the maintenance and safeguarding of existing dispensations will secure justice and order. Finally, with the passing of this Conservative phase and its cultural preoccupations, the Parochial phase returns. Each of the four sequential phases, therefore, lasts 12 to 13 years or so.[7] The same cycles were found in both Democratic and Republican party platforms since 1844 (Chapter 3) and in British Speeches from the Throne since 1795 (Chapter 5). Namenwirth also found similar contrasting themes and their underlying bipolar orientational dilemmas in many other sources (Chapter 9).

What is the explanation of this cyclical phase movement? Wallerstein (1980), Gordon et al. (1982), and many others have noted a long-term contraction and growth of the economy, the so-called Kondratieff (1926) or K-cycle.[8] The relationship between the K-cycle and the 50-year thematic cycle is as follows (Chapters 3 and 5; Weber, 1983b): When the economy is at a 50-year trough, the culture of society at large becomes very Parochial; during the upturn, it grows Progressive; at a sustained plateau of prosperity, it becomes Cosmopolitan; and during the following downturn, it grows more and more Conservative.

---

[7]As noted in Chapter 5 and below, the K-cycle, which explains the short-term thematic cycle reported in Chapters 3 and 5, is often thought to have an upswing of 30 years and a downswing of 20 years. Our current methods cannot directly capture this asymmetry.

[8]Weber (Chapter 5; cf. Weber, 1983b) reviews recent explanations of the K-cycle.

In contrast, evidence exists (Chapter 7) that the relationship between the culture of societal subsystems and the K-cycle is inverted. While a sustained 12-year depression causes Parochial preoccupations in the larger culture, it causes Cosmopolitan concerns in specialized institutional cultures. Locational relativism may well explain the difference: The institutions, including the sciences, are internal to society, but society is external to its institutions. When economic hardships strike, the institutions become more concerned with the encompassing society: They become more Cosmopolitan. At the same time and under similar economic conditions, the larger culture becomes more Parochial.[9]

Weber (Chapter 5; 1983b) argues that the short-term thematic cycle found in the larger culture since the 1790s reflects a debate within the Western capitalist world system about economic performance generally, and specifically about the need to restructure the economy whenever its performance declines in several successive years. Concern with restructuring the national and international economy reflects efforts by elites and economic institutions to adapt the capitalist world system to changing internal and external conditions. This periodic restructuring contributes to the long-term vigor and viability of capitalism. However, various conflict groups and institutions continuously dispute proffered modes of adaptation, and the shift in dilemmas and their orientations do reflect the sequentially changing balance.

DISCONTINUITIES IN CULTURE CHANGE

Discontinuous descriptions, interpretations, and explanations of historical change are certainly as common as continuous ones. "One-corner," or "before and after," are especially popular. The corner represents an extraordinary critical moment that signifies a qualitative modification. In fact, the corner is so critical that historic time is counted from then on, while previous years are counted in negative numbers. Different one-corner theories are marked by the following selected turning points: God's presentation of the Ten Commandments on Mount Sinai; the birth of Christ, the Savior; the flight of Muhammed from Medina; and the French and later revolutions.

Within particular theoretical traditions, the one-corner explanation

---

[9]Scientific rhetoric (Chapter 7) did not reveal changes over time or interdisciplinary differentiation in the Progressive vs. Conservative polarity of the Just Order dilemma. The Freedom vs. Regulation polarity did differentiate among disciplines, but did not change over time. In the articulations of scientists, perhaps the ideas concerning a just dispensation in society are personal rather than discipline-wide.

seems insufficient to characterize all striking transformations. Therefore, two- or multiple-corner delineations are suggested. Each corner represents an unique event, requiring event descriptions and explanations. But because unique events require unique interpretations and explanations,[10] this very mode of description cannot produce comprehensive theories. Instead, each corner requires a distinct interpretation and explanation.

Our own findings suggest at least four distinct types of discontinuity in dynamics of culture.

First, since all observations over time are necessarily finite, they can in principle always be described in either a continuous or discontinuous manner. Therefore, the preference for continuous or discontinuous descriptions, interpretations, and explanations is largely theoretical and perhaps ideological (hence the title of this chapter).

Second, the deviations (residuals) from a continuous description[11] such as a long sine curve can be described either continuously, as was reported in Chapters 3 and 5, using a shorter sine curve, or discontinuously. In the former case, the residuals from the second sine curve are themselves discontinuous deviations. However, the latter cornered sequences are most often of a fundamentally different order. They represent very short-term changes whose explanations are generally not constant (continuous) over time.

Third, Weber and Namenwirth (Chapter 6) analyzed such short-term (high-frequency) deviations from their trend cycles and found them meaningfully interrelated. Factor analyses of these residuals identified various culture themes that we were able to interpret. Some of these themes were identical in both Democratic and Republican party platforms, and the remainder were rather similar. Also, we found that selected themes constituted intervening variables between short-term economic fluctuations and the division of the two-party vote for presidential candidates. Controlling for these themes, changes in economic performance had no direct effect on the two-party vote. This means that **cultural interpretations** of changes in the economy determine presidential elections and not these economic changes in and by themselves. However, these economic fluctuations also partially determine the variation in their cultural interpretations[12] (or themes).

[10]Some would argue that the concepts of unique interpretations and unique explanations constitute contradictions in terms.

[11]Because of random errors and systematic disturbances, it is only within the limiting case that observations will perfectly fit a continuous description.

[12]The fact that these deviations from our trends are systematically interrelated and predictably mediate between economic fluctuations and election outcomes in a significant manner, further confirms the adequacy of trend estimations. It is most unlikely that systematically wrong trend estimates could produce the noted systemic results based on the residuals.

The relationships among detrended data are generally atemporal or ahistorical. Therefore, they represent either universal or conditional laws under which the conditions are variable but not time-specific. This is in sharp contrast with time-specific curved or cornered progressions. The latter constitute historical laws that are conditional on, or operate within, specific periods. The next point discusses this altogether different order of discontinuity.

Fourth, Weber (Chapter 4) discovered such a discontinuity in the dynamics of thematic concerns in Great Britain. Specifically, there appears a corner of discontinuity between the periods before and after 1795 that affects the length of the long cycle and the sequence (rather than nature) of themes within each cycle.[13] Hence, the discontinuity marks the end of one era and the beginning of another. In each era, different historical laws order the observed sequences of culture themes and issues. Thus, in the period 1689–1795 (the Mercantilist era) there is a long cycle of themes whose length is half the length of the long cycle after 1795 (the Capitalist era). Weber argues that cycle lengths and thematic sequences differ because of transformations of the political economy—in particular, the replacement of state control by free-market control over the economic factors of land, labor, and capital (Polanyi, 1957). This replacement produces the noted corner or discontinuity between these eras or epochs.

Weber concludes that there exists continuity within epochs and discontinuity between two epochs. The observed period of time[14] revealed but two epochs. It is therefore not possible to argue that these two epochs are part of one or another sequence of stages[15] or other higher-order regularities in the sequencing of epochs. In fact, the observed discontinuity supports a vision of culture change that Namenwirth finds difficult to comprehend, because he doubts that the fundamental organization of culture can change overnight. As noted, this dispute is not just one of facts but also reflects beliefs concerning the relative adequacy of evolutionary and revolutionary thought and action.

Weber argues that the preceding argument is flawed on two grounds. First, there is, in principle, no necessary relationship between discontinuous change and historically specific explanations. While **some** discontinuities may result from unique events, the extent to which an event is unique is not intrinsic to the event itself, but is determined by the level of abstraction at which a particular theory used to explain the event operates. The transformation from a more centralized, state-controlled system of political

---

[13]Chapter 5 discusses analogous transformations in shorter-term cycles.

[14]Obviously, there exists a relationship among the frequency of observations, cycles, and discontinuities. For instance, it is not possible to observe monthly cycles within yearly observations.

[15]Tilly (1985) provides an incisive and critical discussion of stage theories.

economy to a more free-market system is in fact a transformation—whether discontinuous or not—that certainly characterizes the history of many nation-states. Thus, state-controlled or mercantilist and free-market capitalist political economies are useful theoretical constructs that Weber uses to interpret and explain aspects of his data.

Equally important is the fact that Weber's analysis concentrates obviously on the content within one channel of communications over a long period. With the "great transformation" that Polanyi (1957) describes comes a change in the content within that channel. Nothing in Weber's argument addresses the extent to which the two culture systems (mercantilist and capitalist) existed simultaneously—one growing and becoming more diffuse, and the other declining. Content-analytic data from one channel cannot be used to decide whether the observed transformation is a "channel artifact" or a more general discontinuous phenomenon.

However, the relationship between the observed transformation in culture dynamics and Polanyi's (1957) "great transformation" in the 1790s is unlikely to be mere chance. The significance of the 1790s is that in this decade, changes that had already taken place in the social and cultural fabric of Britain were institutionalized and legitimated by law. This legitimation had two consequences. First, it officially changed some of the basic assumptions on which later perceptions and actions were predicated. Second, the terms of debate changed, and it is these changes that Weber detected. For example, while the same abstract themes were detected in both the Mercantilist and Capitalist periods, the specific content differed between periods. For example, in the earlier period one of the central conflicts was between the king (or queen) and his (or her) subjects, while in the later period the conflict was between the government and the then-enfranchised citizens on one side, and the disenfranchised on the other.

In short, Namenwirth holds a too narrow view of discontinuous system transformations. He fails to acknowledge the possibility of general theories of discontinuous state changes.

DOCTRINE OR EMPIRICAL THEORY IN EXPLAINING CULTURE CHANGE

In the explanation of culture change, materialism and idealism are the major doctrines. Our investigations prove both inadequate: Ideational processes as much as material circumstances are agents or even efficient causes. This is not too surprising: it is a rare case wherein only one of the arguments in ancient disputes is right. Usually, the question in debate requires modifications before more adequate answers emerge. Until then, the question persists, because opposing answers seem reasonable and command contrary illustrations. To settle the question at hand, we must first distinguish among different aspects of culture and social change because these different aspects show trends of different lengths, amplitudes, and origins—or no trend at all. Finally, different dynamics operate on the various components of culture and social change.

We attribute the dynamics of the longer cycle to a sequence of societal problem solving. But is societal problem solving a mental or material process, and therefore, is our explanation part of an idealist or materialist doctrine? The solving part of the process requires mental activity, but the determination of problems, the sequencing of their relative priority, and the weighting of proposed resolutions require at some point the introduction of material evidence. The reality of the problem-solving sequence is not given by mind or culture alone, but must in part result from interaction with the world(s) in which the problem-solver lives. The extent of that part we don't know yet, but it seems that societal problem-solving theory is dialectical rather than either idealistic or materialistic, and so is the proposed explanation of 150-year cyclical culture change.

The explanation of the 50-year thematic cycle in America and Capitalist Britain is certainly a materialist one—namely, the K-cycle of a 50-year growth and contraction of the capitalist world economy. But what about the explanation of the K-cycle itself? Economists prefer endogenous explanations; that is, they prefer theories in terms inherent to the workings of national or international economies. The lack of convincing economic explanations makes them doubt the very existence of the K-cycle. More convincing explanations, such as innovation cycles (e.g., Mensch, 1979; van Duijn, 1979, 1983), are neither purely endogenous nor exogenous, but involve an interaction among social, economic, political, and cultural domains. Other explanations include a war cycle that would cause the ensuing economic expansion and contraction Goldstein (1985, 1986a, 1986b), but this argument may well mistake causes for effects and vice versa. In any event, K-cycle theories are dialectical rather than either materialistic or idealistic. So, while our own explanation of the 50-year[16] thematic cycles appears purely materialistic, it may require a wider theoretical context that is not.

As noted above, we found that short-term variation in selected themes intervened between short-term economic fluctuations and the outcome of presidential elections (Chapter 6). Controlling for these selected themes, changes in economic performance had no direct effect on the two-party vote. This means that cultural interpretations of changes in the economy determine presidential elections, and not these economic changes in and by

[16]Since the cause of the 32-year thematic cycle in Mercantilist Britain is less well developed in Chapter 5, we do not address it at this point.

themselves. We also found that economic fluctuations partially determine the variation in preoccupation with these themes.

Now, Marx and Engels may define elections, politics, and all state functions as part of the superstructure (Marx, 1960), but even contemporary Marxists of different stripes disagree on this score (von Beyme, 1973; Grezijbowski, 1973; Evans *et al.*, 1985; Alford and Friedland, 1985). Certainly, within academic (or bourgeois) social science, elections are part of a system of social interactions with real social consequences rather than just ideological maneuvers of the capitalist class. In this view, both economics and politics are social subsystems of specialized interactions. Also, each of these social, or material, subsystems has its own culture, ideology, or superstructure. Our analyses (Chapter 6) of some trendless changes in culture indicators strongly suggest that the latter neither cause nor simply follow from material changes in one or another social system. Rather, such party-specific culture changes mediate between economic and political change, in part by providing autonomous interpretations of economic existence. It is not the economy in and by itself that produces changes in election outcomes, but rather it is culture that constrains the available interpretations that intervene between economic change and election outcomes. In effect, the electorate is being asked in part to choose between competing interpretations of the same "reality." This is neither a materialist nor a mentalist theory, but its exact status still escapes a proper name or definition.

THE DIALECTIC AMONG THEORY, FINDINGS, AND METHOD

Findings are inevitably theory- and method-bound, while the choices of either theory or method have implications for one another. Nevertheless, factual worlds have a certain autonomy and do not yield equally to all possible theoretical suppositions or methodological inclinations. Even so, extratheoretical reasons play a role in social science choices, and these reasons may vary from discipline-wide conventions to frankly ideological predilections. In our methods, we have self-consciously opted for quantitative descriptions of culture dynamics, which inevitably affected our findings and explanations. What motivated our choice in these matters?

What is the difference between quantitative and qualitative descriptions? This question is much more difficult to answer than critics of quantification in the social sciences have assumed. At first blush we might argue that the contrast is between different modes of interpretation of the same "reality"—that is, numerical versus literary descriptions. But this is a false contrast because there exist no numerical descriptions without literary distinctions, as an examination of any of the tables or figures in this book will readily reveal. Their titles and the names of vertical or horizontal distinctions as yet have no simple numerical expression. Besides, the quantification of such distinctions would necessarily require new qualifications and literary circumlocutions at a higher level of abstraction. If the contrast is not a simple one of numerical versus literary description, neither is it one of mathematical versus literary approaches. Not all systems of mathematics are numerical, and their "logics" are quite distinct. In fact, the same holds for existing systems of qualitative or literary interpretations. A disadvantage of the latter systems is that their logics are less easily explicated, if they can be explicated at all.

This opposition and conflict probably result from contrasting and deeply held "gut" feelings about the nature of human beings and desirable social relations. Critics of quantification claim that to reveal the fundamental nature of social interaction, quantifiers must smash the system to count its parts. To smash human relations will not yield understanding, but only exploitation and administrative reason and domination. In this view, quantification represents the intrusion of a money economy into meaningful human relations, an intrusion that must destroy its very nature. This scheme is even more valid in the interpretation of human communications, the exchange of ideas, and, usually, in the analysis of culture. Quantification may have its uses for the analysis of very simple systems but it violates the complexity of human realities, which require wholistic approaches for emancipatory understandings.

The arguments of the critical view are inverted in part. Simple systems require simple methods. It is the very complexity of social and culture systems that makes quantitative approaches unavoidable. The description of monocausal models does not require mathematics for interpretation and analysis, even though mathematics will probably yield more precise analytic results. The description of multicausal models and their analysis, especially if the various causes interact (a hallmark of many literary multicausal theories) quickly exceeds the capabilities of nonmathematical inquiry. In our particular case, the determination of multiple trends in the change of culture indicators and the investigation of the dynamics of these trends and their residuals could not even be approached without the introduction of quantifying procedures.

The opposition between qualitative and quantitative procedures probably raises false issues and hides important questions concerning the superiority of various more or less integrated systems of inquiry, all of which make qualitative and quantitative assumptions about "things" social and cultural. Thus, we meet again that troublesome question about the validity of possible modes of interpretation.

INTERPRETATION IN TEXT ANALYSIS, IDEOGRAPHY, AND
ITS EXPLANATIONS

Some have argued that the only acceptable interpretation of a subject's actions and thoughts is the subject's own. This may be so, if one wishes to examine how individuals or groups describe and interpret their own actions, or, to be more sophisticated, how they attempt to explain their thus perceived and interpreted actions. In the latter case the investigator studies and describes prevailing folk theories of various actors in a society. This was not our purpose. We did not study the explicit interpretations and ideologies of collective actors but rather phenomena that are implicit in a people's culture. Clearly, the writers of our documents cannot know what part of their writing expresses long-term, short-term, or residual change, nor do they have any conscious control over these matter. They cannot possibly provide explanations for facts that must remain unknown to them. It is for these reasons that our interpretations are interpretations by out-siders and not insiders (Merton, 1972). Therefore, our projects require that, by providing and examining our own interpretations and explanations, we study aspects of our subjects' documents that they produced in a largely unwitting fashion.

However crude our methods of interpretation may appear, they con-sistently yield results explained by preexisting theories; this is so for a variety of texts. As Figure 10.1 schematically illustrates,[17] interpretation enters critically at three distinct points in the process of content analysis. Before recapitulating a discussion of methods used at each point, let us first restate what we mean by *interpretation*: It consists of the translation of one set of linguistic or linguistically expressed elements into another (Chapters 2 and 9). We use the term *mapping* as a synonym for "translation."

The process of interpretation constitutes mapping from one language to another. Each language consists of a set of rules that define what con-stitutes a valid sentence in the language. Using these rules, speakers of the language can generate a virtually infinite number of sentences (Chomsky, 1965). Given a text in one language, translation consists in large part of mapping the syntactic and semantic structures that constitute the text in the first language into structures that are valid for the second and that convey the meaning of the first text. As is well known, even translation from one into another everyday language is a difficult process.[18] But for everyday language translation, a procedure for checking its validity exists—namely, back-translation. What is back-translation? The text in the target language is translated back into the original language. Subsequently,

[17]As a convenience to the reader, we reproduce Figure 2.1 here as Figure 10.1.
[18]Steiner (1975) presents a comprehensive discussion of the difficulties in such inter-language translation.

the investigator compares the original text with the back-translated one. When original and back-translated texts are the same, then and only then is the process of translation or interpretation valid.

The translation of one everyday language into another is reversible; that is, an adequate translation can reconstruct the translated text into its original. However, this reversibility does not exist within the theoretical and abstracting translation or interpretation that exclusively concerns our procedures. Because abstraction entails a many-to-one (i.e., reductive) mapping, some information is forever lost during this process. Consequently, there cannot exist a direct test for the validity of these procedures of interpretation. In fact, the original text is translated several times in subsequently more abstract, more esoteric, and more specialized languages. Figure 10.1 specifies three distinct moments when interpretation enters the process of inquiry. First, content analysis translates the text of documents into the specialized language of category counts (Chapter 2). Second, using multivariate statistical procedures, ideographic analysis and description translate covariation of category counts into the more abstract language of orientational dilemmas and their polar themes. Finally, causal analysis of one kind or another relates changes in the ideographic position of sets of documents, or changing cultural orientations, to changes in the social and/or economic environment. In an attempt to elucidate and interpret these connections in some theoretical language, these causal connections

PROCEDURES

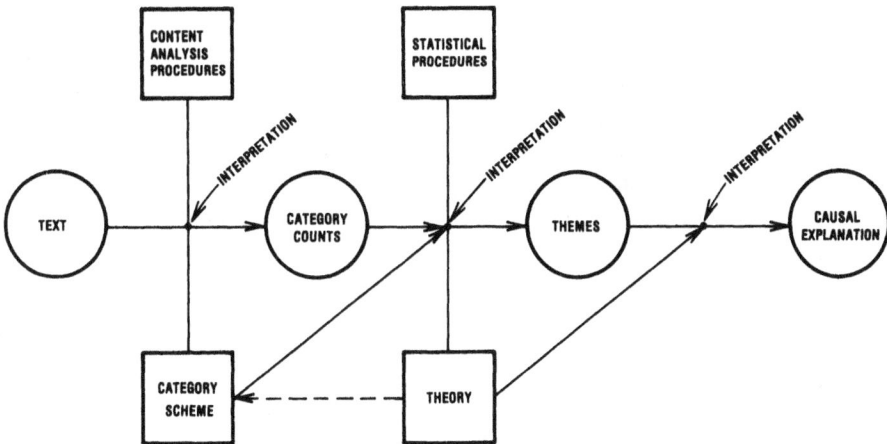

CONCEPTS AND THEORY

FIGURE 10.1. **The Process of Content Analysis.**

are described in ever more abstract languages. Let us examine these three interpretative moments in somewhat greater detail.

Text-Analytic Interpretation

Our content-analytic procedures classify each word and word sense[19] in the text. A preexisting classification scheme and assignments of words to categories, the Lasswell Value Dictionary (LVD), described in Chapter 2, determines the outcome. As a result, text content is described by a quantitative profile of the frequency of occurrence for each category. This quantitative description constitutes an abstracting translation of the original text into the language of the Lasswellian category system. This represents one form of translation and interpretation, but certainly not the only possible one. Is it the best one? This is an elliptical question since it does not specify the purpose of the endeavor nor the available practical alternatives. Our claims for these procedures are more modest. The procedures have some advantages. They are public, so that others can use the same procedures. Reapplied to the same texts, they will generate the same quantitative description. In text analysis, this is not a trivial gain. Applied to new or additional texts, these procedures generate quantitative descriptions formally equivalent to earlier ones of different documents. Also, these descriptions allow for comparisons over time and across similar or dissimilar sets of documents, which provide facts and insights not otherwise available. Finally, the resulting quantitative descriptions ease the analysis of nontextual causes and consequences of textual content that must otherwise remain purely anecdotal.

Of course, all through these endeavors the question at issue greatly concerned us. It is a question about the relative validity of one or another translation or interpretation. Thus put, the question unfortunately conflates two separate issues. The first question asks, For translation, is one language better than another? In ordinary language translation, we would ask, Is it better to translate this text into Japanese or Hungarian? Without further specifying the purpose of the translation, this question seems quite silly. It is perhaps equally silly to compare the worth of various theoretical (rather than everyday) languages unless we specify their particular ends. The second question is quite different. Here we ask, Given that we wish, for one reason or another, to translate an English text into Japanese, is the result correct, more or less adequate, and so on? If we wish to translate an English text into a more or less specific theoretical language—say, Lasswell's classification system of symbolic actions and speech—the same question pertains: How adequate was this translation or interpretation? Regarding

---

[19]Chapter 2 discusses the distinction between words and words senses.

both questions, usefulness rather than validity is an important consideration; or, the proof is in the pudding.

Content-analytic translation produces numerical profiles that by themselves remain mere numbers. However precise and publicly derived, these numbers communicate little about the original text. However, if we compare these profiles across documents, across categories, and over time, the investigators introduce a new and further mode of interpretation that greatly simplifies communication about the original texts and causal analyses.

Ideographic Interpretation

Because the preceding chapter discussed in detail ideographic procedures and outcomes, our conclusions here are quite brief. Multivariate analyses of category profiles across documents such as factor analysis produce mathematical descriptions that require substantive interpretation or translation into one or another theoretical language. In our case, we arrived at a still provisional model of interpretation dialectically. Inductively, we found recurrent patterns of clusters of categories, such as the frequent association between the POWER CONFLICT and POWER COOPERATION categories. Testing our interpretations against newer textual materials, we refined our interpretations in an effort to establish a comprehensive language and articulation that could account for a great variety of textual patterns. It seems that category profiles factually cluster because they are the overt expressions of an underlying latent set of orientational concerns. In the preceding chapter Namenwirth noted three sets of such concerns: the Survival, the Authority, and the Just Order dilemmas. In this interpretation, all documents express a greater or lesser concern with these issues, and favor to greater or lesser extent one or the other side of each dilemma. For instance, about the Survival dilemma, documents assert that threats arise from the inside or from outside of the sociocultural system at hand: They have a Parochial or a Cosmopolitan orientation, respectively. Accordingly, we can determine the orientation of each document on these three dilemmas and see how they may change over time or differ from one class of documents to the next.

The orientations to each dilemma constitute opposing themes, or clusters of categories. It would be fortunate if exactly the same cluster of categories always suggested the same theme. As Chapter 9 explicitly shows, and other factual chapters demonstrate more implicitly, this is rarely the case. Consequently, from one study to the next, orientations to each of the three dilemmas and other recurring dimensions are similar, rather than the same or exact replications. This point requires further elaboration.

In the relationships among words, categories, and themes or orientations,

Themes Indicated By: **Same words,** **Same Categories** **(Cell 1: + +)**	Themes Indicated By: **Different Words,** **Same Categories** **(Cell 2: + −)**
(Cell 3: − +) Themes Indicated By: **Same Words,** **Different Categories**	**(Cell 4: − −)** Themes Indicated By: **Different Words,** **Different Categories**

FIGURE 10.2. **The Relationship Between Words, Categories, and Themes.**

there are two possible variations.[20] First, the relationship between words and categories is either constant or variable. Second, the relationship between categories and themes is also either constant or variable.

Figure 10.2 presents these relationships in a four fold table. Cell 1 (+, +) represents the most parsimonious state of affairs. Here the same words are assigned to the same categories, and covariation among the same categories indicates the same themes in all documents across all document sources. However, this is but a theoretically limiting case at odds with the results of our factual studies.

Cell 2 (+, −) represents the instance wherein categories indicate the same themes, but words are assigned to categories differently across document sources,[21] that is, different sets of documents. Here, different documents discuss the same issues using categories with the same name and meaning, but the words assigned to categories vary across types (sources) of documents. These circumstances imply that word meanings vary from source to source. Since in practice, words or word senses were mainly assigned to the same category, this case need not concern us here. Cell 3 (−, +) represents the instance wherein words are assigned to the same categories, but the same categories cluster differently from one set of documents to the next. Here, different document sources discuss the same issues using different categories containing the same words and word senses. In other words, different clusters of similarly defined categories may

[20]This discussion presumes a measurement model whereby latent themes are inferred from category covariation, and each word or word sense is assigned to only one category. See Chapter 8 for an extended discussion of measurement models for content analysis.

[21]In some studies words (or word senses) were added to existing LVD categories on an ad hoc basis because they seemed of particular relevance. Never were words (or word senses) deleted or reassigned.

express the same theme or orientation. As noted, this is the prevalent case in our factual studies.

Finally, Cell 4 $(-, -)$ suggests global instability; that is, the relationships between words and categories and between categories and themes vary across sets of documents. Here different documents discuss the same issues using different categories containing different words and word senses. We believe this to be another theoretically limiting case that has never been empirically observed.

How does one recognize instances of the Cell 3 case? First, previous studies have sensitized us to recurrent themes and dilemmas. Hence, we ask ourselves whether newly observed contrasting clusters of categories resemble previously found dilemmas. If they do, we always try to validate this provisional interpretation by matching the actual prose of documents considered to be extreme instances[22] with our expectations. Despite the high level of abstraction in the interpretation of themes and dilemmas, the actual prose seldom forces us to substantially revise our preliminary interpretations.

Ideography is a set of procedures for the interpretation and description of particular kinds of content-analytic findings. These findings are selective and are not the only possible ones, because ideography does not provide the only possible set of procedures. It stresses and selects the ideational content and contrasts in the documents, and neglects, for instance, attitudinal matters. We have little to say about attitudes toward various actors and objects. Attitudinal research based on documents probably requires quite different modes of content analysis, but that is another story. Our claim is that ideography provides information about interesting aspects of texts that are quite significant yet not immediately obvious. Besides, these interpretations are quantitative, and therefore facilitate subsequent analysis of causes and consequences of textual variations.

Causal Modeling

The interpretations of content and ideographic analyses have a descriptive purpose: They reveal the extent to which various documents concern themselves with recurrent ideational dilemmas. Description, however, is not the end all of our investigations. Instead, we wish to explain by establishing

---

[22]These extreme cases constitute either documents with extreme positive or negative factor scores, or documents that correspond to points in time when maximal concerns with a particular theme was expected. While extreme instances may meet the expectations, does this guarantee the validity of the interpretation for intermediate case? It does so only if our assumptions of linearity are correct, and these assumptions require further examination. Also, the inspection of actual prose guarantees more valid results when the document is short (as happens in editorials) rather than very long. With very long documents, one might find evidence for any interpretation and selectively show the results. This issue, so prevalent in recent party platforms, also requires further examination.

causal and lawlike relationships between textual characteristics and non-textual social, economic, and political circumstances. Thus, we implicitly or explicitly introduce causal models. For explanation's sake, we do not introduce one cause or just one causal theory. In fact, our efforts are self-consciously multicausal and multifarious. For instance, in the category counts of American party platforms (Chapters 3 and 6) and British Speeches from the Throne (Chapters 4 and 5), we first distinguish between trend data and trendless data, and then decompose the former into longer and shorter cyclical trends. Ideographic procedures delineate and interpret clusters of longer and shorter trends and of detrended data. After interpreting these various sets of clusters as parts of different sets of orientational dilemmas, we attempt to explain the waxing and waning concern with sets of interrelated and contrasting orientations or themes, by introducing various causal models. This procedure requires some illustration.

Ideographic interpretation of shorter-term cycles in both American party platforms and British Speeches from the Throne recognizes the two now-familiar orientational dilemmas of Survival and Just Order, with their contrasting themes of Parochial vs. Cosmopolitan and Conservative vs. Progressive, respectively. The documents display over time a waxing and waning concern with each of these themes that rather precisely matches the growth and decline of the economy as described by the K-cycle, at least in America and Capitalist Britain. In Mercantilist Britain, a 32-year thematic cycle with the same phase sequence seems related to economic fluctuations of about the same wavelength. Hence, economic fluctuations cause the various shorter-term cycles in culture indicators. This causal model may require further elaboration by a specification of intervening mechanisms.

In the long-term wheel of time (Adaptive, Instrumental, Integrative, and Expressive),[23] there are also two dilemmas, each with two contrasting themes. The Instrumental vs. Integrative contrast seems part of the familiar Authority dilemma, wherein one pole stresses the need of efficient, effective, and authoritative if not authoritarian government, while the opposite Integrative pole stresses egalitarian requirements of an often populist bent. The Expressive vs. Adaptive dilemma seems less familiar, because at this level of analyses and articulation economic problems[24] of adaptation to the requirements of the external world indicate a Cosmopolitan orientation, while the opposing social-emotional concerns with questions of identity and core values signify a Parochial orientation. Hence,

---

[23]In Chapters 3 and 4, the phases are labeled *Adaptive, Instrumental* (rather than the Parsonian term *Goal attainment*), *Integrative*, and *Expressive* (rather than *Latency*), but they are fundamentally the same as the classic Parsonian AGIL scheme.

[24]Therefore, frequent references to Wealth categories in the long cycle indicate a Cosmopolitan orientation, while similar references in the short cycle indicate the opposite, namely, a Parochial orientation. This is an excellent yet most worrisome example of the Cell 3 case in Figure 10.2, as discussed before.

the Adaptive vs. Expressive debate in this view concerns the Survival dilemma. The Survival and Authority dilemmas are themselves part of a four-phase problem-solving sequence posited by Bales (1950, 1953; Bales and Strodtbeck, 1953) and Parsons (Parsons and Bales, 1953; Parsons *et al.*, 1953; cf. Parsons and Smelser, 1956). The purpose of this problem-solving sequence and mechanism is the pursuit of **system** goals, rather than the pursuit of goals of subgroups such as classes, races, or other social divisions. In Namenwirth's view, it is the logic of group problem solving that **causes** the observed sequence of peaking and waning orientations, because to solve a problem, we must first define the solvers' ends, then debate the required authority structure, then organize and assign the required material and social resources, and finally turn to considerations concerning the unequal distribution of rewards that problem solving may require or produce.

In Weber's view, the results presented in Chapter 4 falsify a single logic of problem solving. While the number of different four-phase sequences is limited, the cause or causes of any particular phase sequences remains undetermined. To solve this puzzle, we need either more empirical cases or better theoretical analyses. Also, we have analyzed two Western societies that at different times counted among the "great powers"; we have yet to determine whether similar cycles can be observed in other Western countries such as Germany or Italy, or in non-Western societies such as Japan or China.

The causal model of problem solving is postulated and cannot be directly observed, not even in short-term interactions of small groups and certainly not in the 150-year actions of complex and collective actors. What we observed are some of its consequences—namely, the shifting articulations of party platforms and Speeches from the Throne. Particularly, this thematic sequence was observed in America by Namenwirth (1973; Chapter 3; Namenwirth and Bibbee, 1976), elaborated by Burnham (1976), and ob-observed in Britain also (Weber, 1982; Chapter 4). Some may question the factuality of the observed consequences and therefore dismiss the theoretical and causal explanation. We opted for a different strategy. To examine the theory, we analyzed changing culture indicators in different times, societies, and societal subsystems to discover whether the same or similar problem-solving mechanisms pertain and thus confirm, revise, or dismiss the theory. Once the theory is fully formalized, we might further examine other possible deductions and consequences, or investigate the consistency of the theory's internal logic. In either case, the mathematization of the theory would greatly ease the present project. Whatever its outcome, in the process we formulated a possible theoretical explanation for observed dynamics of culture. This theory is couched in a specialized language of small-group problem-solving, and the application of this yet imperfect language to observed facts and relationships constitutes a translation or interpretation.

Chapter 6 presents several causal models as mathematical equations to describe relationships among indicators of various kinds. These mathematical equations describe the observed or inferred relationships in a most precise manner, devoid of any substantive information. The variables, parameters, and various mathematical symbols do not tell the reader what worlds and times they pertain to. To convey such information requires translation into one or another theoretical language that has some bearing on the world at hand; it requires theoretical interpretation that can both illuminate and distort the mathematical formulations.

CONCLUDING REMARKS: EVOLUTION OR REVOLUTION

In the social worlds of actions and reactions, violent change of established order is the rule, because few rulers yield their privileges willingly, irenically, and without a bitter fight. Therefore, rulers of the realm resist drastic transformations of the status quo, and those others who oppose the violent removal of said rulers implicitly support the existing dispensation of privilege and inequality. True, the forces of revolution are themselves socially produced, and these forces may precede the bloody onslaught. Conservatives will implicitly ask whether all this murder was really necessary (Tocqueville, 1955), or what Americans really gained that Canadians or Australians now lack. So, while the necessity of revolution for desirable social transformation may be disputed, our question addresses cultural and not social orders. It is about the transformation of rules, not rulers, and not about the renewal of explicit rules or laws of state, but about the implicit rules of culture. The latter are rarely or only complexly subject to legislative intervention. The question thus is, does the structure of rules and of other features of culture change gradually or abruptly? Is the change curved or cornered, evolutionary or revolutionary?

Our various studies of culture dynamics demonstrate that, at least since the French Revolution and the onset of the industrial revolution, culture change, in contrast to social change, is for the better part gradual and evolutionary, rather than revolutionary. *Evolutionary* may be the wrong term because this change is not forever upward, better, bigger, or richer (Nisbet, 1980), but seems cyclical instead. In this gradual change, Weber (Chapters 4 and 5) discovered an important discontinuity that separates the structure and its features of longer- and shorter-term trends, and he thus recognized in the cultural realm an abrupt and perhaps revolutionary transition during the last decade of the eighteenth century. It is most tempting to attribute this transformation of culture dynamics to concurrent transformations in the social order, but further proof remains necessary.[25] Certainly, however pleasing its elegance and theoretical power for understanding troubled times, the sine curve (or system of sine curves), with its fixed periodicity and amplitudes, will prove too restricted and inflexible a model. Thus remains our question: To better fit known indicators and presumed realities, shall we yield to discontinuous descriptions or to continuous modification and understanding? Shall we resort to revolutionary interventions or seek for evolutionary mechanisms? While research on dynamics of culture did not originate these troublesome questions, our procedures and facts have presented them time and again. These procedures provide for greater precision and explanatory power in the study of culture and its dynamics. One day they will also provide more enduring answers.

[25]Kuhn (1970) discerns revolutionary changes in one specialized area of culture, namely, science. Kuhn (1970), Althusser (1969), and Bachelard [as discussed in Lecourt (1975)] share this unusual cornered conception in the philosophy of science. While Kuhn explicitly excludes the social sciences from his account because they lack well-rounded paradigms, social scientists have found much merit in his theory. Philosophers and historians of science remain skeptical because of his sociogenic understanding of scientific development and the observed vagaries of the paradigm concept (Masterman, 1970). His critics, however, rarely address the continuity vs. discontinuity issues. Singleton (1985) discusses these matters at length.

References

Abelson, R. P. 1963. "Computer Simulation of 'Hot' Cognition." In S. S. Tomkins and S. Messick (eds.), *The Computer Simulation of Personality: Frontier of Psychological Research*. New York: John Wiley.

Abelson, R. P. 1973. "The Structure of Belief Systems." In R. C. Schank and K. M. Colby (eds.), *Computer Models of Thought and Language*. San Francisco: W. H. Freeman.

Abelson, R. P. 1975. "Concepts for Representing Mundane Reality in Plans." In D. B. Bobrow and A. Collins (eds.), *Representation and Understanding: Studies in Cognitive Science*. New York: Academic Press.

Ackoff, R. L. 1953. *The Design of Social Research*. Chicago: University of Chicago Press.

Adams, Bert N. 1966. "Coercion and Consensus Theories: Some Unresolved Issues." *American Journal of Sociology*, **71**:712–717.

Ahmavaara, Y. 1954a. "The Mathematical Theory of Factor Invariance Under Selection." *Psychometrika*, **19**:27–38.

Ahmavaara, Y. 1954b. "Transformation Analysis of Factorial Data." *Annales Academiae Scientiarum Fennicae*, **88**:1–150.

Alford, R. R. and R. Friedland. 1985. *Powers of Theory, Capitalism, the State, and Democracy*. Cambridge and New York: Cambridge University Press.

Alker, H. R., Jr., J. E. Bennett, and D. Mefford. 1980. "Generalized Precedent Logics for Resolving Insecurity Dilemmas." *International Interactions*, **7**:165–206.

Alker, H. R., Jr., G. Duffy, and J. C. Mallery. 1985. "From Quantity to Quality: A New Research Program in Sequential Prisoner's Dilemmas." Paper presented to the American Political Science Association, New Orleans, August 1985.

Allport, F. H. 1924. *Social Psychology*. Boston: Houghton Mifflin.

Althauser, R. P. 1974. "Inferring Validity from the Multitrait–Multimethod Matrix: Another Assessment." In H. L. Costner (ed.), *Sociological Methodology 1973–1974*. San Francisco: Jossey-Bass.

Althusser, L. 1969. *For Marx*. New York: Random House.

Alwin, D. F. 1974. "Approaches to the Interpretation of Relationships in the Multitrait–Multimethod Matrix." In H. L. Costner (ed.), *Sociological Methodology 1973–1974*. San Francisco: Jossey-Bass.

Archer, M. 1985. "The Myth of Cultural Integration." *British Journal of Sociology*, **34**:333–353.

Arveson, M. H. 1964. "Your 'New' Society." *Chemical and Engineering News*, **42**:126–130.

Bain, R. C., and J. H. Parris. 1973. *Convention Decisions and Voting Records* (2nd ed.). Washington, D.C.: The Brookings Institution.

Bales, R. F. 1950. *Interaction Process Analysis: A Method for the Study of Small Groups*. Reading, MA: Addison-Wesley.

Bales, R. F. 1953. "The Equilibrium Problem in Small Groups." In T. Parsons, R. F. Bales, and E. Shils (eds.), *Working Papers in the Theory of Action*. New York: Free Press.

Bales, R. F., and F. L. Strodtbeck. 1953. "Phases in Group Problem Solving." *Journal of Abnormal and Social Psychology*, **46**:485–495.

Barber, B. 1952. *Science and the Social Order*. New York: Free Press.

Barber, B. 1961. "Resistance by Scientists to Scientific Discovery." *Science*, **134**:596–602.

Barraclough, G. 1974. "The End of an Era." *New York Review of Books*, **21**(11):14–21.

Bateson, G. 1972. *Steps to an Ecology of Mind*, New York: Ballantine Books.

Bateson, G. 1979. *Mind and Nature: A Necessary Unity*. New York: E. P. Dutton.

Bauer, R. A. 1966. *Social Indicators*. Cambridge: MIT Press.

Beck, P. A. 1974. "A Socialization Theory of Partisan Realignment." In R. G. Neimi (ed.), *The Politics of Future Citizens*. San Francisco: Jossey-Bass.

Becker, L. W. 1967. "Neo-Kantianism." In P. Edwards (ed.), *The Encyclopedia of Philosophy*, Vol. V, pp. 468–473. New York: Macmillan (Free Press).

Bell, D. 1978. *The Cultural Contradictions of Capitalism*. New York: Basic Books/Harper Torchbooks.

Belsley, D. A., E. Kuh, and R. E. Welsch. 1980. *Regression Diagnostics*. New York: Wiley (Interscience).

Ben-David, J. 1971. *The Scientist's Role in Society*. Englewood Cliffs, NJ: Prentice-Hall.

Bendix, R. 1964. *Nation-Building and Citizenship*. New York: John Wiley.

Benedict, R. 1961. *Patterns of Culture*. Boston: Houghton Mifflin.

Benson, L. 1961. *The Concept of Jacksonian Democracy: New York as a Test Case*. Princeton: Princeton University Press.

Bentler, P. M., and D. G. Bonett. 1980. "Significance Tests and Goodness of Fit in the Analysis of Covariance Structures." *Psychological Bulletin*, **88**:588–606.

Berbard, T. J. 1983. *The Consensus Conflict Debate*. New York: Columbia University Press.

Berelson, B. 1952. *Content Analysis in Communications Research*. New York: Free Press.

Berger, P. L., and T. Luckman. 1966. *The Social Construction of Reality: A Treatise in the Sociology of Knowledge*. Garden City, NY: Doubleday.

Berrien, F. K. 1968. *General and Social Systems*. New Brunswick, NJ: Rutgers University Press.

Bertalanffy, L. von 1968. *General Systems Theory*. New York: George Braziller.

Bettelheim, B. 1976. *The Uses of Enchantment: The Meaning and Importance of Fairy Tales*. New York: Alfred A. Knopf.

Bloom, H. S., and H. D. Price. 1975. "Voter Response to Short-Run Economic Conditions: The Asymmetric Effect of Prosperity and Recession." *American Political Science Review*, **69**:1240–1254.

Bloomfield, P. 1976. *Fourier Analysis of Time Series: An Introduction*. New York: John Wiley.

Blume, S. S. 1974. *Toward a Political Sociology of Science*. New York: Free Press.

Boas, F. 1932. "The Aim of Anthropological Research." *Science*, **76**:605–615.

Boden, M. 1977. *Artificial Intelligence and Natural Man*. New York: Basic Books.

Bottomore, T. B. 1974. *Sociology and Social Criticism*. New York: Pantheon Books.

Box, G. E. P., and G. M. Jenkins. 1976. *Time Series Analysis: Forecasting and Control* (2nd ed.). San Francisco: Holden-Day.

Brinberg, D., and J. E. McGrath. 1982. "A Network of Validity Concepts Within the Research Process." In D. Brinberg and L. H. Kidder (eds.), *Forms of Validity in Research*. San Francisco: Jossey-Bass.

Brinton, C. 1963. *The Shaping of Modern Thought.* Englewood-Cliffs, NJ: Prentice-Hall.

Bryant, C. G. A. 1985. *Positivism in Social Theory and Research.* London: Macmillan.

Buckley, W. 1968. *Sociology and Modern Systems Theory.* Englewood Cliffs, NJ: Prentice-Hall.

Bunce, V. 1981. *Do New Leaders Make A Difference?* Princeton: Princeton University Press.

Burnham, W. D. 1970. *Critical Elections and the Mainsprings of American Politics,* New York: Norton.

Burnham, W. D. 1976. "Revitalization and Decay: Looking Toward the Third Century of American Electorial Politics." *Journal of Politics,* **38**:146–172.

Burns, A. F., and W. C. Mitchell. 1946. *Measuring Business Cycles.* New York: National Bureau of Economic Research.

Butler, D., and Stokes D. 1974. *Political Change in Great Britain* (2nd. ed.). London: Macmillan.

Campbell, D. T., and D. W. Fiske. 1959. "Convergent and Discriminant Validation by the Multitrait–Multimethod Matrix." *Psychological Bulletin,* **56**:81–105.

Campbell, D. T., and E. J. O'Connell. 1982. "Methods as Diluting Trait Relationships Rather Than Adding Irrelevant Systematic Variance." In D. Brinberg and L. H. Kidder (eds.), *Forms of Validity in Research.* San Francisco: Jossey-Bass.

Campbell, N. 1952. *What Is Science?* New York: Dover.

Carley, M. 1981. *Social Measurement and Social Indicators: Issues of Policy and Theory.* London: Allen & Unwin.

Catton, W. R. 1966. *From Animistic to Naturalistic Sociology.* New York: McGraw-Hill.

Chomsky, N. 1965. *Aspects of the Theory of Syntax.* Cambridge: MIT Press.

Chubb, J. E. 1978. "Systems Analysis and Partisan Realignment." *Social Science History,* **2**:144–171.

Clarke, H. 1847. "Physical Economy." *Railway Register.*

Cleveland, C., D. G. McTavish, and E. B. Pirro. 1974. "Quester-Contextual Content Analysis Methodology." Paper presented at 1974 Pisa Conference on Content Analysis.

Chubb, J. M., W. H. Flanigan, and N. H. Zingale. 1980. *Partisan Realignment: Voters, Parties, and Government in American History.* Beverly Hills, CA: Sage.

Cohen, A. K. 1974. *The Elasticity of Evil: Changes in the Social Definition of Deviance.* Oxford: Basil Blackwell.

Cole, J. R., and S. Cole. 1971. *Social Stratification in Science.* Chicago: University of Chicago Press.

Collins, H. M. 1983. "The Sociology of Scientific Knowledge." In R. H. Turner and J. F. Short, Jr. (eds.). *Annual Review of Sociology,* Vol. 9, pp. 265–285. Palo Alto, CA: Annual Reviews.

Collins, R. 1975. *Conflict Sociology.* New York: Academic Press.

Comte, A. 1875. *System of Positive Polity.* London: Longman, Green, and Co.

Comte, A. 1976. *Auguste Comte and Positivism,* ed. G. Lenzer, New York: Harper and Row.

Cornford, J. 1963. "The Transformation of Conservatism in the Late Nineteenth Century." *Victorian Studies,* **7**:35–66.

Cornford, J. 1970. "Aggregate Election Data and British Party Realignments, 1885–1910." In E. Allardt and S. Rokkan (eds.), *Mass Politics: Studies in Political Sociology.* New York: Free Press.

Crane, D. 1969. "Social Structure in a Group of Scientists: A Test of the 'Invisible College' Hypothesis." *American Sociological Review,* **34**:335–352.

Crewe, I., B. Sarlvik, and J. Alt. 1977. "Partisan Dealignment in Britain 1964–1974." *British Journal of Political Science,* **7**:129–190.

Csikszentmihalyi, M., and E. Rochberg-Halton. 1981. *The Meaning of Things: Domestic Symbols and the Self.* Cambridge: Cambridge University Press.

Dahrendorf, R. 1958a. "Out of Utopia." *American Journal of Sociology,* **64**:115–127.

Dahrendorf, R. 1958b. "Toward a Theory of Social Conflict." *Journal of Conflict Resolution*, 2:170–183.

Dallmayr, F. R. 1984. *Language and Politics*. Notre Dame, IN: University of Notre Dame Press.

David, P. T. 1971. "Party Platforms as National Plans." *Public Administration Review*, 31:301–315.

Deal, T. E., and A. A. Kennedy. 1982. *Corporate Cultures: The Rites and Rituals of Corporate Life*. Reading, MA: Addison-Wesley.

Dean, J. 1950. "Pricing Policies for New Products." *Harvard Business Review*, 28:45–53.

Deutsch, Karl W. 1966. *The Nerves of Government*. New York: Free Press.

De Weese, L. C., III. 1977. "Computer Content Analysis of 'Day-Old' Newspapers: A Feasibility Study." *Public Opinion Quarterly*, 41:91–94.

Dowse, R. E., and J. A. Hughes. 1972. *Political Sociology*. London: John Wiley.

Dreyfus, H. L. 1979. *What Computers Can't Do: The Limits of Artificial Intelligence* (rev. ed.). New York: Harper Colophon Books.

Duffy, G. 1986. "Categorial Disambiguation." In AAAI-86: *Proceedings of the American Association for Artificial Intelligence*, Philadelphia, August 1986 (pp. 1057–1061).

Duffy, G., and J. C. Mallery, 1984. "Referential Determinism and Computational Efficiency: Posting Constraints from Deep Structure." In AAAI-84: *Proceedings of the American Association for Artificial Intelligence*, Austin, TX, August 1984 (pp. 101–105).

Duffy, G., and J. C. Mallery. "The Relatus Natural Language System: An Overview." MIT Artificial Intelligence Laboratory Memo No. 847.

Duffy, G., and J. C. Mallery. 1986b. "Relatus: An Artificial Intelligence Tool for Natural Language Modeling." Paper presented to International Studies Association, Anaheim, CA, March 1986.

Dunbabin, J. P. D. 1966. "Parliamentary Elections in Great Britain, 1868–1900: A Psephological Note." *The English Historical Review*, 81:82–99.

Dunphy, D. C. 1966. "Social Change in Self-analytic Groups." In P. J. Stone. D. G. Dunphy, M. S. Smith, and D. M. Ogilvie (eds.), *The General Inquirer: A Computer Approach to Content Analysis*. Cambridge: MIT Press.

Dunphy, D. C., C. G. Bullard, and E. E. M. Crossing. 1974. "Validation of the General Inquirer Harvard IV Dictionary." Paper presented at 1974 Pisa Conference on Content Analysis.

Durkheim, E. 1954 (1915). *The Elementary Forms of the Religious Life*. New York: Free Press.

Durkheim, E. 1974. *Sociology and Philosophy*. New York: Free Press.

Edelson, M. 1975. *Language and Interpretation in Psychoanalysis*. Chicago: University of Chicago Press.

Ellul, J. 1964. *The Technological Society*. New York: Vintage.

Eyring, H. 1967. "Untangling Biological Reactions." *Science*, 154:1609–1613.

Etzioni, A. 1964. *Modern Organizations*. Englewood Cliffs, NJ: Prentice-Hall.

Evans, P. B., D. Rueschemeyer, and T. Skocpol (eds.) 1985. *Bringing the State Back In*. Cambridge and New York: Cambridge University Press.

Farlow, W. G. 1905. "The Popular Conception of the Scientific Man at the Present Day." *Science*, 23:1–14.

Fellner, W. J. 1956. *Trends and Cycles in Economic Activity*. New York: Holt.

Feuer, L. S. 1974. *Einstein and the Generation of Science*. New York: Basic Books.

Firestone, J. M. 1972. "The Development of Social Indicators from Content Analysis of Social Documents." *Policy Sciences*, 3:249–263.

Forrester, J. W. 1976. "Business Structure, Economic Cycles, and National Policy." *Futures* (June):165–214.

Forrester, J. W. 1977. "Growth Cycles." *De Economist* (Netherlands) 125(4):525–543.

Freeman, C. (ed.) 1983. *Long Waves in the World Economy*. London: Butterworths.

Freeman, M. F., and J. W. Tukey. 1950. "Transformations Related to the Angular and the Square Root." *Annals of Mathematical Statistics*, 21:607–611.

Freud, S. 1950a. *The Interpretation of Dreams*. Trans. A. A. Brill. New York: Modern Library.

Freud, S. 1950b. *Totum and Taboo: Some Points of Agreement Between the Lives of Savages and Neurotics*. New York: Norton.

Freud, S., and D. E. Oppenheim. 1958. *Dreams in Folklore*. Trans. A. M. O. Richards. New York: International Universities Press.

Friedman, M. 1967. "The Role of Monetary Policy." *The American Economic Review*, 58:1–17.

Friedrichs, R. W. 1970. *A Sociology of Sociology*. New York: Free Press.

Furniss, E. S. 1957. *The Position of Labor in a System of Nationalism*. New York: Kelly & Millman.

Gallhofer, I. N. 1978. "Coder's Reliability in the Study of Decision Making Concepts, Replications in Time and Across Topics." *Methoden en Data Nieuwsbrief*, 3:58–74.

Gallhofer, I. N., and W. Saris. 1979a. "The Decision of the Dutch Council of Ministers and the Military Commander in Chief Relating to the Reduction of Armed Forces in Autumn 1916." *Acta Politica*, 14:95–105.

Gallhofer, I. N., and W. Saris. 1979b. "An Analysis of the Argumentation of Decision Makers Using Decision Trees." *Quality and Quantity*, 13:411–430.

Gallhofer, I. N., and W. Saris. "Decision Theory Applied to Foreign Policy Decisions." Paper presented to International Society of Political Psychology, Boston, 1980.

Garvy, G. 1943. "Kondratieff's Theory of Long Cycles." *The Review of Economic Statistics*, 25:203–220.

Gaston, J. 1970. *Originality and Competition in Science*. Chicago: University of Chicago Press.

Gay, P. 1966–69. *The Enlightenment, An Interpretation*. New York: Alfred A. Knopf.

Gay, P. 1973. *The Enlightenment: A Comprehensive Anthology*. New York: Simon and Schuster.

Gerbner, G. 1969. "Toward Cultural Indicators: The Analysis of Mass Mediated Public Message Systems." *Communication Review*, 17(2):137–148.

Gerbner, G., O. R. Holsti, K. Krippendorff, W. Paisley, and P. J. Stone (eds.) 1969. *The Analysis of Communication Content*. New York: John Wiley.

Geyer, F., and J. van der Zouwen (eds.). 1986. *Sociocybernetic Paradoxes*. London: Sage.

Goldstein, J. S. 1985. "Kondratieff Waves and War Cycles." *International Studies Quarterly*, 29:411–444.

Goldstein, J. S. 1986a. "Long Waves in Production, War, and Inflation: New Empirical Evidence." Paper presented at the International Studies Association, Anaheim, CA, March 26, 1986.

Goldstein, J. S. 1986b. *Long Cycles in War and Economic Growth*. Ph.D. thesis, MIT.

Goode, W. J. 1969. "The Theoretical Limits of Professionalization." In A. Etzioni (ed.), *The Semi-Professions and their Organization*. New York: Free Press.

Gordon, D. M. 1978. "Up and Down the Long Roller Coaster." In Crisis Reader Editorial Collective (eds.), *U.S. Capitalism in Crisis*, New York: Union for Radical Political Economics.

Gordon, D. M., R. Edwards, and M. Reich. 1982. *Segmented Work, Divided Workers: The Historical Transformation of Labor in the United States*. Cambridge: Cambridge University Press.

Gordon. R. A. 1952. *Business Fluctuations*. New York: Harper.

Gordon, R. A. 1961. *Business Fluctuations* (2nd. ed.). New York: John Wiley.

Gottman, J. M. 1981. *Time-Series Analysis: A Comprehensive Introduction for Social Scientists*. Cambridge: Cambridge University Press.

Gottschalk, L. A. 1979. *The Content Analysis of Verbal Behavior: Further Studies*. New York: SP Michael & Scientific Books.

Gouldner, A. W. 1970. *The Coming Crisis of Sociology*. New York: Basic Books.

Granger, C. W. J. 1964. *The Spectral Analysis of Economic Time Series*. Princeton: Princeton University Press.

Greenwood, Ernest. 1957. "Attributes of a Profession." *Social Work*, 2:45–55.

Grey, A., D. Kaplan, and H. D. Lasswell. 1965. "Recording and Context Units—Four Ways of Coding Editorial Content." In H. D. Lasswell, N. Leites, and Associates (eds.), *Language of Politics*. Cambridge: MIT Press.

Grezijbowski, K. 1973. "State." In C. D. Kenig (ed.), *Marxism, Communism, and Western Society: A Comparative Encyclopedia*, Vol. 8, pp. 94–106. New York: Herder and Herder.

Hagstrom, W. O. 1965. *The Scientific Community*. New York: Basic Books.

Hamblin, R. L., R. B. Jacobsen, and J. L. L. Miller. 1973. *A Mathematical Theory of Social Change*. New York: John Wiley.

Hammond, Matthew B. 1930. "Economic Conflict As a Regulating Force in International Affairs." *American Economic Review*, 21:1–9.

Hanham, H. J. 1968. *The Reformed Electoral System in Great Britain, 1832–1914*. London: Historical Association.

Hansard. 1804–. *Parliamentary Debates*, 5 series. London: Hansard.

Hansard. 1812. *Parliamentary History of England (Corbett's Parliamentary History): 1066–1803*. London: Hansard.

Hayes, A. C. 1980. "A Semi-formal Explication of Talcott Parsons's [sic] Theory of Action." *Sociological Inquiry*, 50:39–56.

Hays, William L. 1963. *Statistics*. New York: Holt, Rinehart and Winston.

Hegel, G. W. F. 1967. *The Phenomenology of Mind*. New York: Harper and Row.

Heise, D. R., and G. W. Bohrnstedt. 1970. "Validity, Invalidity, and Reliability." In E. F. Borgatta and G. W. Borhnstedt (eds.), *Sociological Methodology 1970*. San Francisco: Jossey-Bass.

Herbst, J. 1965. *The German Historical School in American Scholarship: A Study in the Transfer of Culture*. Ithaca: Cornell University Press.

Herman, V. 1974. "What Governments Say and What Governments Do: An Analysis of Post-War Queen's Speeches." *Parliamentary Affairs*, 28:22–30.

Hernes, G. 1976. "Structural Change in Social Processes." *American Journal of Sociology*, 82:513–547.

Heyck, T. W. 1974. *The Dimensions of British Radicalism: The Case of Ireland, 1875–97*. Urbana: University of Illinois Press.

Hibbs, D. A., Jr. 1974. "Problems of Statistical Estimation and Causal Inference in Time Series Regression Models." In H. L. Costner (ed.), *Sociological Methodology 1973–1974*. San Francisco: Jossey-Bass.

Hibbs, D. A., Jr. 1977. "On Analyzing the Effects of Policy Interventions: Box-Tiao vs. Structural Equations Models." In H. L. Costner (ed.), *Sociological Methodology 1977*. San Francisco: Jossey-Bass.

Holmes, J. E. 1985. *The Mood/Interest Theory of American Foreign Policy*. Lexington: University Press of Kentucky.

Holsti, O. R. 1969. *Content Analysis for the Social Sciences and Humanities*. Reading, MA.: Addison-Wesley.

Holzhey, H. 1984. "Neukantianismus." In J. Ritter and K. Gruender (eds.), *Historisches Woerterbuch der Philosphie*, Vol. VI, pp. 749–754. Basel: Schwabe & Co.

Horowtiz, H. 1981. "The UNESCO Framework for Cultural Statistics and a Cultural Data Bank for Europe." *Journal of Cultural Economics* 5:1–18.

Horowitz, I. L. 1962. "Consensus, Conflict, and Cooperation: A Sociological Inventory." *Social Forces*, 41:177–188.

Horton, J. 1964. "The Dehumanization of Anomie and Alienation." *British Journal of Sociology*, 15:283–300.

Horton, J. 1966. "Order and Conflict Theories of Social Problems as Competing Ideologies." *American Journal of Sociology*, 71:701–713.

Hughes, E. C. 1958. *Men and Their Work*. Glencoe: Free Press.

Hunt, E. B., J. Marin, and P. J. Stone. 1966. *Experiments in Induction*. New York: Academic Press.

Huntington, S. P. 1966. "Political Modernization: America vs. Europe." *World Politics*, **18**:378–414.

Hurwitz, R., J. C. Mallery, and G. Duffy. 1986. "Hermeneutics: From Textual Explication to Computer Understanding," MIT Artificial Intelligence Laboratory Memo No. 871. [Also forthcoming in the Encyclopedia of Artificial Intelligence.]

Iker, H. P. 1974. "An Historical Note on the Use of Word-Frequency Contiguities in Content Analysis." *Computers and the Humanities*, **8**:93–98.

Iker, H. P., and N. I. Harway. 1969. "A Computer Systems Approach to the Recognition and Analysis of Content." In G. Gerbner, O. R. Holsti, K. Krippendorff, W. Paisley, and P. J. Stone (eds.), *The Analysts of Communication Content*. New York: John Wiley.

Inglehart, R. 1977. *The Silent Revolution: Changing Values and Political Styles Among Western Publics*. Princeton: Princeton University Press.

Inglehart, R. 1984. "Measuring Cultural Change in Japan, Western Europe and the United States." In G. Melischek, K. E. Rosengren, and J. Stappers (eds.), *Cultural Indicators: An International Symposium*. Vienna: Austrian Academy of Sciences.

Janowitz, M. 1969. "Content Analysis and the Study of the 'Symbolic Environment.'" In A. A. Rogow (ed.), *Politics, Personality, and Social Science in the Twentieth Century: Essays in Honor of Harold D. Lasswell*. Chicago: University of Chicago Press.

Jenkins, G. M., and D. G. Watts. 1968. *Spectral Analysis and Its Applications*. San Francisco: Holden-Day.

Jenks, J. W. 1907. "The Modern Standard of Business Honor." *Publications of the American Economic Association*, **8**:1–22.

Johnson, Donald B. 1978. *National Party Platforms, 1840–1976*. Urbana: University of Illinois Press.

Jöreskog, K. G. 1974. "Analyzing Psychological Data by Structural Analysis of Covariance Matrices." In D. H. Krantz, R. C. Atkinson, R. D. Luce, and P. Suppes (eds.), *Contemporary Developments in Mathematical Psychology*, Vol. 2. San Francisco: W. H. Freeman.

Jöreskog, K. G., and D. Sörbom. 1979. *Advances in Factor Analysis and Structural Equation Models*. Cambridge: Abt Books.

Jöreskog, K. G., and D. Sörbom. 1980. *LISREL IV (Analysis of Linear Structural Relationships by the Method of Maximum Likelihood) Users Guide*. Chicago: National Educational Resources.

Jöreskog, K. G., and D. Sörbom. 1981. *LISREL V (Analysis of Linear Structural Relationships by Maximum Likelihood and Least Squares Methods) Users Guide*. Chicago: National Educational Resources.

Jöreskog, K. G., and D. Sörbom. 1984. *LISREL VI (Analysis of Linear Structural Relationships by Maximum Likelihood and Least Squares Methods) Users Guide*. Mooresville, IN: Scientific Software.

Judd, C. M., and J. A. Krosnick. 1982. "Attitude Centrality. Organization, and Measurement." *Journal of Personality Social Psychology* **42**:436–447.

Jung, C. G. 1969. *The Archetypes and the Collective Unconscious*. Trans. R. F. C. Hull. Princeton: Princeton University Press.

Kandel, A. 1982. *Fuzzy Techniques in Pattern Recognition*. New York: John Wiley.

Kant, I. 1952. *The Critique of Judgment*. Chicago: Encyclopedia Brittanica Press.

Kaplan, A. 1964. *The Conduct of Inquiry*. San Francisco: Chandler.

Kaufmann, F. 1958. *Methodology of the Social Sciences*. New York: Humanities Press.

Kelly, E. F., and P. J. Stone. 1975. *Computer Recognition of English Word Senses*. Amsterdam: North Holland.

Key, V. O. 1955. "A Theory of Critical Elections." *Journal of Politics*, **17**:3–18.

Kleinknecht, A. 1981. "Innovation, Accumulation, and Crisis: Long Waves in Economic Development." *Review*, **4**:683–711.

Klingberg, F. L. 1952. "The Historical Alternation of Moods in American Foreign Policy." *World Politics*, **4**:239–273.

Klingberg, F. L. 1983. *Cyclical Trends in American Foreign Policy Moods: The Unfolding of America's World Role*. Lanham, MD: University Press of America.

Klingemann, H. D., P. P. Mohler, and R. P. Weber. 1982. "Cultural Indicators Based on Content Analysis." *Quality and Quantity*, **16**:1–18.

Klopsteg, P. E. 1961. "The Indispensable Tools of Science." *Science*, **132**:1913–1922.

Kluckhohn, C. 1951. "The Concept of Culture" In D. Lerner and H. D. Lasswell (eds.), *The Policy Sciences*. Palo Alto: Stanford University Press.

Kluckhohn, C., and W. H. Kelly. 1945. "The Concept of Culture." In R. Linton (ed.), *The Science of Man in the World of Crisis*. New York: Columbia University Press.

Kondratieff, N. D. 1926. "Die Langen Wellen der Konjunktur." *Archiv fur Sozialwissenschaft und Sozialpoltik*, **56**:573–609. [Trans. as "The Long Waves in Economic Life." 1979. *Review*, **2**(4):519–562.]

Kondratieff, N. D. 1935. "The Long Waves in Economic Life." *The Review of Economic Statistics*, **17**:105–115. (Partial translation of Kondratieff, 1926.)

Kramer, G. H. 1971. "Short-Term Fluctuations in U.S. Voting Behavior, 1896–1964." *America Political Science Review*, **65**:131–143.

Kramer, G. H. 1983. "The Ecological Fallacy Revisited: Aggregate- versus Individual-level Findings on Economics and Elections, and Sociotropic Voting." *America Political Science Review*, **77**:92–111.

Kramer, G. H., and S. J. Lepper, 1972. "Congressional Elections." In W. O. Aydelotte, A. G. Bogue, and R. W. Fogel (eds.), *The Dimensions of Quantitative Research in History*. Princeton: Princeton University Press.

Krippendorff, K. 1980. *Content Analysis: An Introduction to Its Methodology*. Beverly Hills, CA: Sage.

Kroeber, A. L., and C. Kluckhohn. 1952. "Culture: A Critical Review of Concepts and Definitions." *Harvard University Peabody Museum of American Archeology and Ethnology Papers*, **47**:1.

Kroeber, A. L., and T. Parsons. 1958. "The Concept of Cultures and of Social System." *American Sociological Review*, **23**:582–593.

Kropotkin, P. n.d. *Mutual Aid: A Factor of Evolution*. Boston: Extending Horizons Books.

Kuhn, A. 1974. *The Logic of Social Systems*. San Francisco: Jossey-Bass.

Kuhn, T. S. 1961. "The Function of Dogma in Scientific Research." In A. C. Crombie (ed.), *Scientific Change*. New York: Basic Books.

Kuhn, T. S. 1970. *The Structure of Scientific Revolution*, 2nd Enlarged Edition. Chicago: University of Chicago Press.

Lakoff, G., and M. Johnson. 1980. *Metaphors We Live By*. Chicago: University of Chicago Press.

Land, K. C., and S. Spillerman. 1975. *Social Indicator Models*. New York: Russell Sage.

Lasswell, H. D. 1941. "The World Attention Survey." *Public Opinion Quarterly*, **5**(3):456–462.

Lasswell, H. D., and A. Kaplan. 1963 (1950). *Power and Society: A Framework for Political Inquiry*. New Haven: Yale University Press.

Lasswell, H. D., and J. Z. Namenwirth. 1968. *The Lasswell Value Dictionary* (3 vols.). New Haven: Yale University, mimeo.

Leach, E. 1976. *Culture and Communication: The Logic by Which Symbols Are Connected*. Cambridge: Cambridge University Press.

Lecourt, D. 1975. *Marxism and Epistemology: Bachelard, Canguilhem and Foucault*. London: New Left Books.

Lehman, E. W. 1977. *Political Society: A Macrosociology of Politics*, New York: Columbia University Press.

Lehnert, W. G., and M. H. Ringle (eds.). 1982. *Strategies for Natural Language Processing*. Hillsdale, NJ: Lawrence Erlbaum.

Lenski, G. E. 1966. *Power and Privilege: A Theory of Social Stratification*. New York: McGraw-Hill.

Lenski, G. E., and J. Lenski. 1982. *Human Societies: An Introduction to Macro-Sociology*. New York: Oxford University Press.

Levi-Strauss, C. 1966. *The Savage Mind*. Chicago: University of Chicago Press.

Levi-Strauss, C. 1969. *The Raw and the Cooked*. Trans. J. and D. Weightman. New York: Harper and Row.

Levi-Strauss, C. 1979. *Myth and Meaning*. New York: Schocken Books.

Levitt, T. 1965. "Exploit the Product Life Cycle." *Harvard Business Review*, **43**:81–94.

Lewin, K. 1935. *A Dynamic Theory of Personality: Selected Papers of Kurt Lewin*. New York: McGraw-Hill.

Li, Richard P. Y. 1976. "A Dynamic Comparative Analysis of Presidential and House Elections." *American Journal of Political Science*, **20**:671–669.

Lipset, S. M., and S. Rokkan. (ed.). 1967. *Party Systems and Voter Alignments: Cross-National Perspectives*. New York: Free Press.

Lord, F. M., and M. R. Novick, 1968. *Statistical Theories of Mental Test Scores*. Reading, MA.: Addison-Wesley.

Lorenz, K. 1966. *On Aggression*. New York: Harcourt, Brace & World.

Lukacs, G. 1971. *History and Class Consciousness*. Cambridge: MIT Press.

Lukes, S. 1968. "Methodological Individualism Reconsidered." *British Journal of Sociology*, **19**:119–129.

Macdonald, G., and P. Pettit. 1981. *Semantics and Social Science*. London: Routledge and Kegan Paul.

Machiavelli, N. 1952. *The Prince*. New York: Mentor Books.

MacIver, R. M. 1942. *Social Causation*. New York: Ginn.

MacIver, R. M., and C. H. Page. 1949. *Society, An Introductory Analysis*. New York: Rinehart.

Mahajan, V., and R. A. Peterson. 1985. *Models for Innovation Diffusion*. Beverly Hills and London: Sage. [Sage University Series Paper on Quantitative Applications in the Social Sciences, series no. 07-048.]

Mallery, J. C. 1985. "Universality and Individuality: The Interaction of Noun Phrase Determiners in Copular Clauses." In *23rd Annual Meeting of the Association for Computational Linguistics: Proceedings of the Conference*, Chicago, July 1985 (pp. 35–42).

Mallery, J. C. 1986. "Constraint-Interpreting Reference." MIT Artificial Intelligence Laboratory, AI Memo No. 827.

Mallery, J. C. and G. Duffy. 1986. "A Computational Model of Semantic Perception." MIT Artificial Intelligence Laboratory, AI Memo No. 799.

Mallery, J. C., Hurwitz, R., and H. R. Alker, Jr. 1986. "Anarchy or Community?: A Comparative Study Of Developmental Patterns in SPD Games." Paper presented to International Studies Association, March 1986.

Mallery, J. C., R. Hurwitz, H. R. Alker, Jr., and G. Duffy. 1986. "Analyzing Natural Language Protocols of Sequential PD Games." Paper presented to the American Political Science Association, Washington, August 1986.

Mandel, E. 1975. *Late Capitalism*. London: Verso.

Mandel, E. 1980. *Long Waves of Capitalist Development: The Marxist Interpretation*. Cambridge: Cambridge University Press.

Mandelbaum, M. 1955. "Societal Facts." *British Journal of Sociology*, **6**:305–317.

Mannheim, K. 1936. [1929]. *Ideology and Utopia*. New York: Harcourt, Brace & World.

Mannheim, K. 1952. "The Problem of Generations." In P. Kecskemeti (ed.), *Essays on the Sociology of Knowledge*. London: Routledge and Kegan Paul.

Marcuse, H. 1964. *One-Dimensional Man*. Boston: Beacon Press.

Marias, J., and M. Rintala. 1968. Generations. In D. L. Sills (ed.), *International Encyclopeadia of Social Science*, Vol. 6, pp. 88–96. New York: Mcmillan and The Free Press.

Markoff, J., G. Shapiro, and S. Weitman. 1974. "Toward the Integration of Content Analysis and General Methodology." In D. R. Heise (ed.), *Sociological Methodology 1975*. San Francisco: Jossey-Bass.

Markus, G. B. 1983. "Dynamic Modelling of Cohort Change: The Case of Political Partisanship." *American Journal of Political Science*, **27**(4):717–739.

Martin, E. 1984. "Cultural Indicators and the Analysis of Public Opinion." In C. E. Turner and E. Martin (eds.), *Surveying Subjective Phenomena*, Vol. 2. New York: Russell Sage.

Marx, K. 1960. *Politische Schriften* (2 vols.). Ed. K. Lieber. Stuttgart: Cotta.

Marx, K. 1964. *Selected Writings in Sociology and Social Philosophy*. Ed. and trans. T. B. Bottomore. London: McGraw-Hill.

Marx, K. 1970. *A Contribution to the Critique of Political Economy*. New York: International Publishers.

Marx, K., and F. Engels. 1930. *The German Ideology*. New York: International Publishers.

Masterman, M. 1970. "The Nature of a Paradigm." In I. Lakatos and A. Musgrave (eds.), *Criticism and the Growth of Knowledge*. Cambridge: Cambridge University Press.

Mayer, T. F., and W. R. Arney. 1974. "Spectral Analysis and the Study of Social Change." In H. L. Costner (ed.), *Sociological Methodology, 1973–1974*. San Francisco: Jossey-Bass.

McCawley, J. D. 1981. *Everything That Linguists Have Always Wanted to Know About Logic: But Were Ashamed to Ask*. Chicago: University of Chicago Press.

McCleary, R., and R. A. Hay, Jr. 1980. *Applied Time Series Analysis for the Social Sciences*. Beverly Hills, CA: Sage.

McClelland, D. 1975. "Love and Power: The Psychological Signals of War." *Psychology Today*, **8**:44–48.

McTavish, D. G., and E. B. Pirro, 1984. "Contextual Content Analysis." Paper presented at the Pacific Sociological Association Meetings, Seattle, April 12, 1984.

Meinecke, F. 1970. *Cosmopolitanism and the National State*. Princeton: Princeton University Press.

Melischek, G., K. E. Rosengren, and J. Stappers (eds.). 1984. *Cultural Indicators: An International Symposium*. Vienna: Austrian Academy of Science.

Menger, C. 1963 (1883). *Problems of Economics and Sociology*. Urbana: University of Illinois Press.

Mensch, G. 1979. *Stalemate in Technology: Innovations Overcome the Depressions*. Cambridge, MA: Ballinger. [Translation of *Das technologische Patt*. 1975. Frankfurt: Umschau Verlag.]

Merton, R. K. 1972. "Insiders and Outsiders." *American Journal of Sociology*, **78**:9–47.

Metz, R. 1984. "Long Waves in Coinage and Grain Price-Series from the Fifteenth to the Eighteenth Century: Some Theoretical and Methodological Aspects." *Review*, **7**:599–647.

Miller, P. 1953. *The New England Mind*. Cambridge: Harvard University Press.

Miller, W. 1971. "Cross-voting and the Dimensionality of Party Conflict in Britain During the Period of Realignment: 1918–31." *Political Studies*, **19**:455–461.

Millikan, R. A. 1930. "Present Status of Theory and Experiment as to Atomic Disintegration and Atomic Synthesis." *Science* **73**:1–5.

Millis, H. A. 1934. "The Union of Industry: Some Observations on the Theory of Collective Bargaining." *American Economic Review*, **25**:1–13.

Mitchell, C. W. 1927. *Business Cycles*, Vol. 1. New York: National Bureau of Economic Research.

Mohler, P. P. 1978. *Abitur 1917–1971: Reflektionen des Verhaltnisses zwischen Individuum und kollektiver Macht in Abituraufsatzen*. Frankfurt: Peter Lang.

Monroe, A. D. 1983. "American Party Platforms and Public Opinion." *American Journal of Political Science*, **27**(1):27–42.

Montague, A. (ed.). 1962. *Culture and the Evolution of Man*. New York: Oxford University Press.

Montague, A. 1974. *Culture: Man's Adaptive Dimension*. London: Oxford University Press.

Montesquieu, C. L. de S. 1949. *The Spirit of the Laws*. Trans. T. Nugent. New York: Hafner.

Mullins, N. C. 1973. *Theories and Theory Groups in Contemporary American Sociology.* New York: Harper and Row.

Namenwirth, J. Z. 1969a. "Marks of Distinction: A Content Analysis of British Mass and Prestige Newspaper Editorials." *American Journal of Sociology,* **74**:343–360.

Namenwirth, J. Z. 1969b. "Some Long and Short Trends in One American Political Value." In G. Gerbner, O. R. Holsti, K. Krippendorff, W. Paisley, and P. J. Stone (eds.). *The Analysis of Communication Content.* New York: John Wiley.

Namenwirth, J. Z. 1970. "Prestige Newspapers and the Assessment of Elite Opinions." *Journalism Quarterly,* **47**:318–323.

Namenwirth, J. Z. 1973. "The Wheels of Time and the Interdependence of Value Change." *Journal of Interdisciplinary History,* 3:649–683.

Namenwirth, J. Z. 1984. "Why Cultural Indicators?" In G. Melischek, K. E. Rosengren, and J. Stappers (eds.), *Cultural Indicators: An International Symposium.* Vienna: Austrian Academy of Science.

Namenwirth, J. Z., and R. Bibbee. 1975. "Speech Codes in the Press." *Journal of Communication,* **25**:50–63.

Namenwirth, J. Z., and R. Bibbee. 1976. "Change Within or of the System: An Example From the History of American Values." *Quantity and Quality,* **10**:145–164.

Namenwirth, J. Z. and T. L. Brewer. 1966. "Elite Editorial Comment on European and Atlantic Communities in Four Countries." In P. J. Stone *et al.* (eds.), *The General Inquirer: A Computer Approach to Content Analysis.* Cambridge: MIT Press.

Namenwirth, J. Z., and H. D. Lasswell. 1970. *The Changing Language of American Values: A Computer Study of Selected Party Platforms.* Beverly Hills, CA: Sage.

Namenwirth, J. Z., R. L. Miller, and R. P. Weber. 1981. "Organizations Have Opinions: Towards a Redefinition of Publics." *Public Opinion Quarterly,* **45**:463–476.

Namenwirth, J. Z., and R. P. Weber. 1974. "The Lasswell Value Dictionary." Paper presented at 1974 Pisa Conference on Content Analysis.

Namenwirth, J. Z. and R. P. Weber, 1979, "Directed and Contingent Value Changes in American and British Political Documents." *Methoden en Data Nieuwsbrief,* **5**:3–44.

Negoita, C. V. 1985. *Expert Systems and Fuzzy Systems.* Menlo Park, CA: Benjamin/Cummings Publishing.

Nietsche, F. W. 1968. *Basic Writings of Nietsche.* Ed. and trans. W. Kaufman. New York: Modern Library.

Nisbet, R. A. 1953. *The Quest for Community.* New York: Oxford University Press.

Nisbet, R. A. 1969. *Social Change and History.* New York: Oxford University Press.

Nisbet, R. A. 1980. *History of the Idea of Progress.* New York: Basic Books.

Ogilvie, D. M. 1966. "Procedures for Improving the Interpretation of Tag Scores: The Case of Windle." In P. Stone, D. D. Dunphy, M. S. Smith, and D. M. Ogilvie (eds.), *The General Inquirer: A Computer Approach to Content Analysis.* Cambridge: MIT Press.

Ogilvie, D. M., P. J. Stone, and E. F. Kelly. 1980. "Computer-Aided Content Analysis." In R. B. Smith and P. K. Manning (eds.), *Handbook of Social Science Research Methods.* New York: Irvington.

Osgood, C. E., W. H. May, and M. S. Miron. 1975. *Cross-Cultural Universals of Affective Meaning.* Urbana: University of Illinois Press.

Osgood, C. E., G. J. Suci, and P. H. Tannenbaum. 1957. *The Measurement of Meaning.* Urbana: University of Illinois Press.

Pareto, V. 1935. *The Mind and Society.* Trans. A. Livingstone. New York: Harcourt Brace Jovanovich.

Parsons, T. 1951. *The Social System.* Glencoe, IL: Free Press.

Parsons, T. 1969. "On the Concept of Political Power," In T. Parsons, *Politics and Social Structure.* New York: Free Press.

Parsons, T. 1971. *The System of Modern Societies.* Englewood Cliffs, NJ: Prentice-Hall.

Parsons, T., and R. F. Bales. 1953. "The Dimensions of Action-space." In T. Parsons, R. F.

Bales, and E. A. Shills (eds.), *Working Papers in the Theory of Action*. New York: Free Press.

Parsons, T., R. F. Bales, and E. A. Shills. 1953. "Phase Movement in Relation to Motivation, Symbol Formation, and Role Structure." In T. Parsons, R. F. Bales, and E. A. Shills (eds.), *Working Papers in the Theory of Action*. New York: Free Press.

Parsons, T., and E. Shills (eds.). 1951. *Towards a General Theory of Social Action*. Cambridge: Harvard University Press.

Parsons, T., and N. Smelser. 1956. *Economy and Society*. New York: Free Press.

Peterson, R. A. 1979. "Revitalizing the Culture Concept." *Annual Review of Sociology*, **5**:137–166.

Peterson, R. A., and M. Hughes. 1984. "Isolating Patterns of Cultural Choice to Facilitate the Formation of Cultural Indicators." In G. Melischek, K. E. Rosengren, and J. Stappers (eds.), *Cultural Indicators: An International Symposium*. Vienna: Austrian Academy of Science.

Piaget, J. 1970. *Structuralism*. Ed. and trans. C. Maschler. New York: Basic Books.

Piereson, J. E. 1975. "Presidential Popularity and Midterm Voting at Different Electoral Levels." *American Journal of Political Science*, **19**:683–693.

Plumb, J. H. 1963. *England in the Eighteenth Century*. London: Penguin.

Polanyi, K. 1957. *The Great Transformation*. Boston: Beacon Press.

Pomper, G. M. 1966. *Nominating the President: The Politics of Convention Choice*. New York: Norton.

Pomper, G. M., and Susan Lederman. 1980. *Elections in America* (2nd. ed.). New York: Longman.

Popper, K. R. 1961. *The Poverty of Historicism*. New York: Harper and Row.

Popper, K. R. 1963. *Conjectures and Refutations*. New York: Harper and Row.

Popper, K. R. 1968. *The Logic of Scientific Discovery*. New York: Harper and Row.

Popper, K. R. 1983. *Realism and the Aim of Science*. Tolowa, NJ: Rowman and Littlefield.

Porter, K. H. and D. B. Johnson. 1961. *National Party Platforms, 1840–1960*. Urbana: University of Illinois Press.

Powers, C. H. 1980. "Fulfilling Pareto's Mission: A Formal Theory of Social Systems." Paper presented at the American Sociological Association meetings, New York, August 27.

Powers, C. H. 1981. "Pareto's Theory of Society." *Revue Europeene des Sciences Sociales et Cahiers Vilfredo Pareto* (Switzerland), **19**(59):99–119.

Powers, C. H., and R. A. Hanneman. 1983. "Pareto's Theory of Social and Economic Cycles: A Formal Model and Simulation." In R. Collins (ed.), *Sociological Theory 1983*. San Francisco: Jossey-Bass.

Price, D. K. 1962. *Government and Science*. New York: Oxford University Press.

Price, D. 1963. *Little Science. Big Science*. New York: Columbia University Press.

Radcliffe-Brown, A. R. 1952. "On Social Structure." In A. R. Radcliffe-Brown (ed.), *Structure and Function in Primitive Society*. New York: Free Press.

Rickert, H. 1926. *Kulturwissenschaften und Naturwissenschaften*. Tuebingen: Mohr.

Roeder, P. G. 1985. "Do New Soviet Leaders Really Make a Difference? Rethinking the 'Succession Connection.'" *American Political Science Review*, **79**:958–976.

Rogers, E. M. 1983. *Diffusion of Innovations*. New York: Free Press.

Rokeach, M. 1973. *The Nature of Human Values*. New York: Free Press.

Rokeach, M. 1974. "Change and Stability in American Value Systems, 1968–1971." *Public Opinion Quarterly*, **38**:222–238.

Rokeach, M. 1979. *Understanding Human Values*. New York: Free Press.

Rokkan, S., with A. Campbell, P. Torsvik, and H. Valen. 1969. *Citizens, Elections, Parties: Approaches to the Comparative Study of the Processes of Development*. New York: David McKay.

Rosengren, K. E. (ed.). 1981. *Advances in Content Analysis*. Beverly Hills, CA: Sage.

Rosengren, K. E. 1984. "Cultural Indicators for the Comparative Study of Culture." In G.

Melischek, K. E. Rosengren, and J. Stappers (eds.), *Cultural Indicators: An International Symposium*. Vienna: Austrian Academy of Science.

Rosengren, K. E. 1985. "Media Linkages Between Culture and Other Societal Systems." In Margaret L. McLaughlin (ed.), *Communication Yearbook 9*. Beverly Hills, CA: Sage.

Rummel, R. J. 1970. *Applied Factor Analysis*. Evanston: Northwestern University Press.

Saris, W. E., and I. N. Gallhofer. 1981. "A Coding Instrument for Empirical Research on Political Decision Making." Manuscript, Free University of Amsterdam.

Saris-Gallhofer, I. N., W. E. Saris, and E. L. Morton. 1978. "A Validation Study of Holsti's Content Analysis Procedure." *Quality and Quantity*, 12:131–145.

Schank, R. C. 1982. *Dynamic Memory*. Cambridge: Cambridge University Press.

Schank, R. C., and R. P. Abelson (eds.). 1977. *Scripts, Plans, Goals, and Understanding*. Hillsdale, NJ: Lawrence Erlbaum.

Schank, R. C., and K. Colby (eds.). 1973. *Computer Models of Thought and Language*. San Francisco: W. H. Freeman.

Schank, R. C., M. Lebowitz, and L. Birnbaum. 1980. "An Integrated Understander." *American Journal of Computational Linguistics*, 6:13–30.

Schein, E. H. 1985. *Organizational Culture and Leadership*. San Francisco: Jossey-Bass.

Schlesinger, A. M., Sr. 1939. *Tides of American Politics*. Yale Review, 29:217–246.

Schneider, L. (Ed.) 1967. *The Scottish Moralists on Human Nature and Society*. Chicago: University of Chicago Press.

Schneider, L., and C. Bonjean (eds.). 1973. *The Idea of Culture in the Social Sciences*. Cambridge: Cambridge University Press.

Schuessler, K. 1970. *Analyzing Social Data: A Statistical Orientation*. Boston: Houghton Mifflin.

Schumpeter, J. A. 1939. *Business Cycles* (2 vols.). New York: McGraw-Hill.

Searle, J. R. 1969. *Speech Acts: An Essay in the Philosophy of Language*. Cambridge: Cambridge University Press.

Searle, J. R. 1984. *Minds, Brains, and Science*. Cambridge: Harvard University Press.

Sheldon, E. B., and W. E. Moore. 1968. *Indicators of Social Change*. New York: Russell Sage.

Simmel, G. 1950. *The Sociology of Georg Simmel*. Trans. and ed. Kurt H. Wolff. New York: Free Press.

Singleton, W. 1985. *Talcott Parsons' Scientific Development and Talcott Parsons' Theoretical Productions*. Unpublished Ph.D. Thesis, University of Connecticut, Storrs.

Skinner, B. F. 1971. *Beyond Freedom and Dignity*. New York: Vintage.

Slater, P. 1966. *Microcosm*. New York: John Wiley.

Slutzky, E. 1937. "The Summation of Random Causes as the Source of Cyclic Processes," *Econometrica*, 5:105–146.

Smith, A. D. 1981. *The Ethnic Revival in the Modern World*. Cambridge: Cambridge University Press.

Sobel, M. E. and G. W. Bohrnstedt. 1985. "The Use of Null Models to Evaluate the Fit of Covariance Structure Models." In N. B. Tuma (ed.), *Sociological Methodology 1985*. San Francisco: Jossey-Bass.

Sorokin, P. 1937–41. *Social and Cultural Dynamics*. (4 vols.). New York: American Book Company.

Spengler, O. 1932. *The Decline of the West*. New York: Alfred A. Knopf.

Sproule-Jones, M. 1984. "Methodological Individualism." *American Behavioral Scientist*, 28(2):167–183.

Steiner, G. 1975. *After Babel: Aspects of Language and Translation*. Oxford: Oxford University Press.

Stigler, G. J. 1973. "General Economic Conditions and National Elections." *American Economic Review Papers and Proceedings*, 64:160–165.

Stone, P. J. 1972. "Social Indicators Based on Communications Content." Proceedings of the Fall Joint Computer Conference.

Stone, P. J., D. D. Dunphy, M. S. Smith, and D. M. Ogilvie (eds.). 1966. *The General Inquirer: A Computer Approach to Content Analysis*. Cambridge: MIT Press.

Storer, N. 1966. *The Social System of Science*. New York: Holt, Rinehart & Winston.

Sundquist, J. L. 1983. *Dynamics of the Party System: Alignment and Realignment of Political Parties in the United States* (rev. ed.). Washington, D.C.: The Brookings Institution.

Sylvan, D. and B. Glassner. 1985. *A Rationalist Methodology for the Social Sciences*. Oxford and New York: Basil Blackwell.

Thompson, W. R., and L. G. Zuk. 1982. "War, Inflation, and the Kondratieff Long Wave." *Journal of Conflict Resolution*, **26**:621–644.

Thurow, L. 1980. *The Zero-Sum Society*. New York: Basic Books.

Tilly, C. 1985. *Big Structures, Large Processes, Large Comparisons*. New York: Russell Sage.

Tinbergen, J. 1983. "Kondratiev Cycles and So-called Long Waves" in C. Freeman (ed.), *Long Waves in the World Economy*. London: Butterworth.

Tinbergen, N. 1951. *The Study of Instinct*. Oxford: Clarendon Press.

Tocqueville, A. de. 1955. *The Old Regime and the French Revolution*. Garden City, NY: Doubleday.

Toennies, E. 1931. *Community and Society*. East Lansing: Michigan State University Press.

Torsvik, P. (ed). 1981. *Mobilization, Center-Periphery Structures, and Nation Building: A Volume in Commeration of Stein Rokkan*. Bergen, Norway: Universitetsforlaget.

Toynbee, A. J. 1947–57. *A Study of History*, Ed. D. C. Somervill. London: Oxford University Press. [Abridgment of volumes I–X.]

Troeltsch, E. 1931. *The Social Teaching of the Christian Churches*. New York: Macmillan.

Tucker, L. R., and C. Lewis. 1973. "A Reliability Coefficient for Maximum Likelihood Factor Analysis." *Psychometrika*, **38**:1–10.

Tufte, E. R. 1978. *Political Control of the Economy*. Princeton: Princeton University Press.

Turner, S. P. 1980. *Sociological Explanation as Translation*. Cambridge: Cambridge University Press.

Tylor, E. B. 1924 (1871). *Primitive Culture*. Gloucester, MA: Smith.

U.S. Bureau of the Census, 1975. *Historical Statistics of the United States, Colonial Times to 1970* (bicentennial ed., Part 2. Washington: U.S. Bureau of the Census.

van Duijn, J. J. 1977. "The Long Wave in Economic Life." *De Economist* (Netherlands), **125**(4):544–576.

van Duijn, J. J. 1979. *De Lange Golf in de Economie*. Assen, Netherlands: van Gorcum.

van Duijn, J. J. 1983. *The Long Wave in Economic Life*. London: Allen & Unwin.

Van Doorn, J. A. A. 1962. "Sociology and the Problem of Power." *Sociologia Neerlandica*, **1**:3–47.

Väyrynen, R. 1983. "Economic Cycles, Power Transitions, Political Management and Wars Between Major Powers." *International Studies Quarterly*, **27**:389–418.

Veblen, T. 1921. *The Engineers and the Price System*. New York: B. W. Huebsch.

Vernon, R. 1966. "International Investment and International Trade in the Product Life Cycle." *Quarterly Journal of Economics*, **80**:190–207.

Vico, G. 1968 (1744). *The New Science of Giambattista Vico*. Trans. T. G. Bergin and M. Harold. Ithaca, NY: Cornell University Press.

Viner, J. 1969. "Power versus Plenty as Objectives of Foreign Policy in the Seventeenth and Eighteenth Centuries." In D. C. Coleman (ed.). Revisions in Mercantilism. London: Methuen & Co. [Originally published in *World Politics*, Vol. 1, 1948.]

von Beyme, K. 1973. "Parliamentary System." In C. D. Kenig (ed.), *Marxism, Communism, and Western Society: A Comparative Encyclopedia*, Vol. 6, pp. 187–203. New York: Herder and Herder. [Extensive bibliography.]

Wallerstein, I. 1974. *The Modern World System*. New York: Academic Press.

Wallerstein, I. 1979. *Capitalist World Economy*. Cambridge: Cambridge University Press.

Wallerstein, I. 1980. *The Modern World System II: The Consolidation of the European World-Economy 1600-1750*. New York: Academic Press.

Watson, J. B. 1925. *Behaviorism*. New York: People's Institute.

Weber, A. 1951. *Kulturgeschichte als Kultursoziologie*. Muenchen: R. Piper.

Weber, M. 1946. "Science as a Vocation." In H. H. Gerth and C. Wright Mills (eds.), *From Max Weber: Essays in Sociology*. New York: Oxford University Press.

Weber, M. 1947. *The Theory of Social and Economic Organization*. New York: Free Press.

Weber, M. 1951. 1951. "Der Sinn der 'Wertfreiheit' der Soziologischen und Oekonomischen Wissenschaften." In J. Winkelmann (ed.), *Gesammelte Aufsaetze zur Wissenschaftslehre*. Tuebingen: J. C. B. Mohr.

Weber, M. 1958. *The Protestant Ethic and the Spirit of Capitalism*. New York: Scribner's.

Weber, M. 1963. *The Sociology of Religion*. Trans. E. Fischoff. Boston: Beacon Press.

Weber, M. 1977. *Critique of Stammler*. Trans. Guy Oakes. New York: Free Press.

Weber, R. P. 1978. *The Dynamics of Value Change, Transformations and Cycles: British Speeches From the Throne, 1689-1972*. Ph.D. dissertation, University of Connecticut.

Weber, R. P. 1981. "Society and Economy in the Western World System." *Social Forces*, **59**:1130-1148.

Weber, R. P. 1982. "The Long-Term Problem-solving Dynamics of Social Systems." *European Journal of Political Research*, **10**:387-405.

Weber, R. P. 1983a. "Measurement Models for Content Analysis." *Quality and Quantity*, **17**:127-149.

Weber, R. P. 1983b. "Cyclical Theories of Crises in the World System." In Albert Bergesen (ed.), *Crises in the World System*. Beverly Hills, CA: Sage.

Weber, R. P. 1984a. "Content Analytic Cultural Indicators." In G. Melischek, K. E. Rosengren, and J. Stappers (eds.), *Cultural Indicators: An International Symposium*. Vienna: Austrian Academy of Science.

Weber, R. P. 1984b. "Computer-Aided Content Analysis: A Short Primer." *Qualitative Sociology*, **7**(1/2):126-147.

Weber, R. P. 1985a. *Basic Content Analysis*. Beverly Hills, CA: Sage.

Weber, R. P. 1985b. "Content Analysis: Problems and Prospects." Paper presented at ZUMA, Mannheim, FRG, June 1985.

Weber, R. P. In press. "Cycles of The Third Kind." *European Journal of Political Research*.

Weber, R. P., and J. Z. Namenwirth. 1985. "La mediacion cultural del functionamiento economico como determinante en las elecciones presidenciales U.S.A., 1892-1964" [The Cultural Mediation of Economic Performance as a Determinant of Presidential Elections, 1892-1964]. *Revista Internacional de Sociologia*, **43**:59-85.

Weeks, D. G. 1980. "A Second-Order Longitudinal Model of Ability Structure." *Multivariate Behavioral Research*, **15**: 353-365.

Weinburg, G. M. 1975. *An Introduction to General Systems Thinking*. New York: Wiley Interscience.

Weingart, P. 1974. "On a Sociological Theory of Scientific Change." In R. Whitley (ed.), *Social Processes of Scientific Development*. Boston: Routledge and Kegan Paul.

Weizenbaum, J. 1976. *Computer Power and Human Reason*. San Francisco: W. H. Freeman.

Whitehead, A. N., and B. Russell. 1910-1913. *Principia Mathematica* (2nd ed.). Cambridge: Cambridge University Press.

Whitley, R. 1974. "Cognition and Social Institutionalization of Scientific Specialities and Research Areas." In R. Whitley (ed.), *Social Processes of Scientific Development*. Boston: Routledge and Kegan Paul.

Whorf, B. L. 1956. *Language, Thought, and Reality: Selected Writings of Benjamin Lee Whorf*. Cambridge: MIT Press.

Wilcox, L. D. 1972. *Social Indicators and Societal Monitoring: An Annotated Bibliography*. Amsterdam: Elsevier.

Williams, B. 1962. *The Whig Supremacy, 1714–1760* (2nd rev. ed.). Oxford: Clarendon Press.

Williams, R. M. Jr. 1966. "Some Further Comments on Chronic Controversies." *American Journal of Sociology*, **71**:717–721.

Winch, P. 1970. "Understanding a Primitive Society." In B. Wilson (ed.), *Rationality*. Oxford: Basil Blackwell. [Originally appeared in *American Philosophical Quarterly*, Vol. 1, 1964].

Winograd, T. 1972. *Understanding Natural Language*. New York: Academic Press.

Winograd, T. 1983. *Language as a Cognitive Process*, Vol. 1: *Syntax*. Reading, MA: Addison-Wesley.

Winograd, T. and F. Flores. 1986. *Understanding Computers and Cognition: A New Foundation for Design*. Norwood, NJ: Ablex.

Winston, P. H. 1984. *Artificial Intelligence* (2nd. ed.). Reading, MA: Addison-Wesley.

Wold, H. 1975. "Soft Modelling by Latent Variables: The Non-linear Iterative Partial Least Squares (NIPALS) Approach." In J. Gani (ed.), *Perspectives in Probability and Statistics, Papers in Honour of M. S. Bartlett*. London: Academic Press.

Wold, H. 1981. "Model Construction and Evaluation when Theoretical Knowledge Is Scarce: On the Theory and Application of Partial Least Squares." In J. Kmenta and J. Ramsey (eds.), *Evaluation of Econometric Models*. New York: Academic Press.

Wright, E. O. 1978. *Class, Crisis and the State*. London: New Left Books.

Wrong, D. H. 1976. *Skeptical Sociology*. New York: Columbia University Press.

Wuthnow, R., J. D. Hunter, A. Bergesen, and E. Kurzweil. 1984. *Cultural Analysis: The Work of Peter L. Berger, Mary Douglas, Michel Foucault and Juergen Habermas*. Boston: Routledge and Kegan Paul.

Yankelovich, D. 1981. *New Rules*. New York: Random House.

Zadeh, L. A. 1965. "Fuzzy Sets." *Information and Control*, **8**:338–353.

Zadeh, L. A. 1971. "Similarity Relations and Fuzzy Orderings." *Information Sciences*, **3**:117–200.

Zadeh, L. A. 1972. "A Fuzzy-Set-Theoretic Interpretation of Linguistic Hedges." *Journal of Cybernetics*, **2**:4–34.

Category Index

Author Index

Subject Index

For Product Safety Concerns and Information please contact our EU
representative GPSR@taylorandfrancis.com
Taylor & Francis Verlag GmbH, Kaufingerstraße 24, 80331 München, Germany